Arata
THE LEGEND

24

We are Man, born of Heaven and Earth,
Moon and Sun and everything under them.

Eyes, Ears, Nose, Tongue, Body, Mind...

Purity will pierce evil and
open up the world of darkness.

All life will be reborn and invigorated.

Appear now.

STORY & ART BY
Yuu Watase

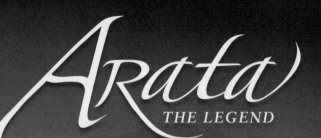

Arata THE LEGEND

CHARACTERS

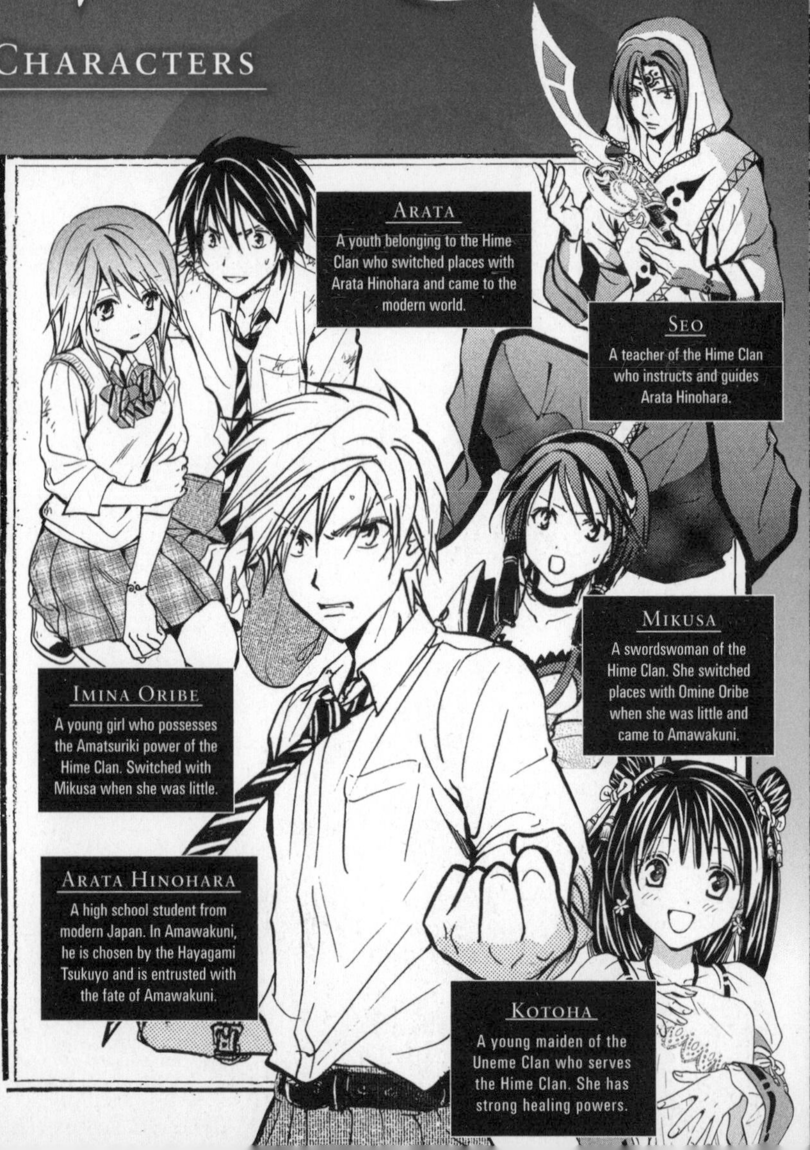

ARATA
A youth belonging to the Hime Clan who switched places with Arata Hinohara and came to the modern world.
SEO
A teacher of the Hime Clan who instructs and guides Arata Hinohara.
MIKUSA
A swordswoman of the Hime Clan. She switched places with Omine Oribe when she was little and came to Amawakuni.
IMINA ORIBE
A young girl who possesses the Amatsuriki power of the Hime Clan. Switched with Mikusa when she was little.
ARATA HINOHARA
A high school student from modern Japan. In Amawakuni, he is chosen by the Hayagami Tsukuyo and is entrusted with the fate of Amawakuni.
KOTOHA
A young maiden of the Uneme Clan who serves the Hime Clan. She has strong healing powers.

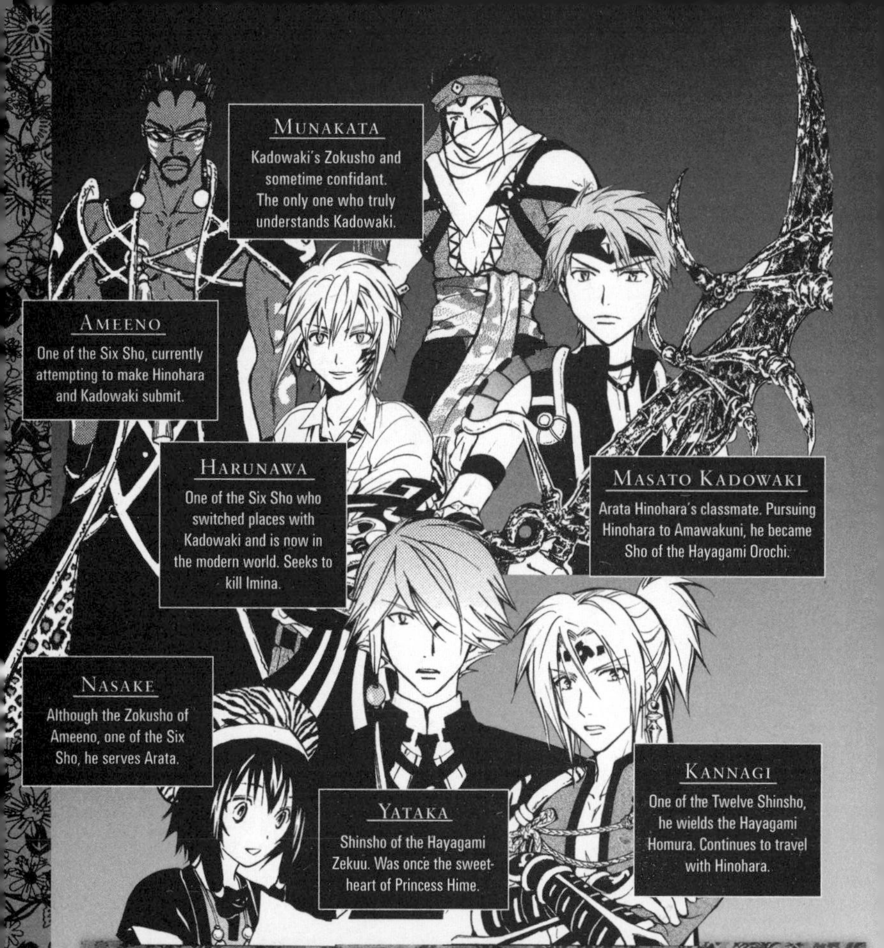
MUNAKATA
Kadowaki's Zokusho and sometime confidant. The only one who truly understands Kadowaki.
AMEENO
One of the Six Sho, currently attempting to make Hinohara and Kadowaki submit.
HARUNAWA
One of the Six Sho who switched places with Kadowaki and is now in the modern world. Seeks to kill Imina.
MASATO KADOWAKI
Arata Hinohara's classmate. Pursuing Hinohara to Amawakuni, he became Sho of the Hayagami Orochi.
NASAKE
Although the Zokusho of Ameeno, one of the Six Sho, he serves Arata.
KANNAGI
One of the Twelve Shinsho, he wields the Hayagami Homura. Continues to travel with Hinohara.
YATAKA
Shinsho of the Hayagami Zekuu. Was once the sweetheart of Princess Hime.

THE STORY THUS FAR

Arata Hinohara, finding himself in Amawakuni, a land in another dimension, is chosen as the successor to the legendary Hayagami Tsukuyo. In order to stop the fighting that ensued after Princess Kikuri's collapse, he continues his journey to make all the Sho submit and unify the Hayagami.

Hinohara is captured by the Sho Ameeno and imprisoned in his palace. The others rush to his rescue, but they are caught in Ameeno's kamui and lose their sense of sight. Only Kadowaki, who possesses the eye of the Sho Akachi, can still see. He manages to reach Hinohara, who is suspended by shackles, but Ameeno is there to confront him. Kadowaki puts up a fierce fight, but Ameeno's attack is too powerful and Kadowaki loses his left arm. In the process Hinohara is freed and summons Tsukuyo...

24
Arata
THE LEGEND

CONTENTS

Chapter 228
FATHER AND SON

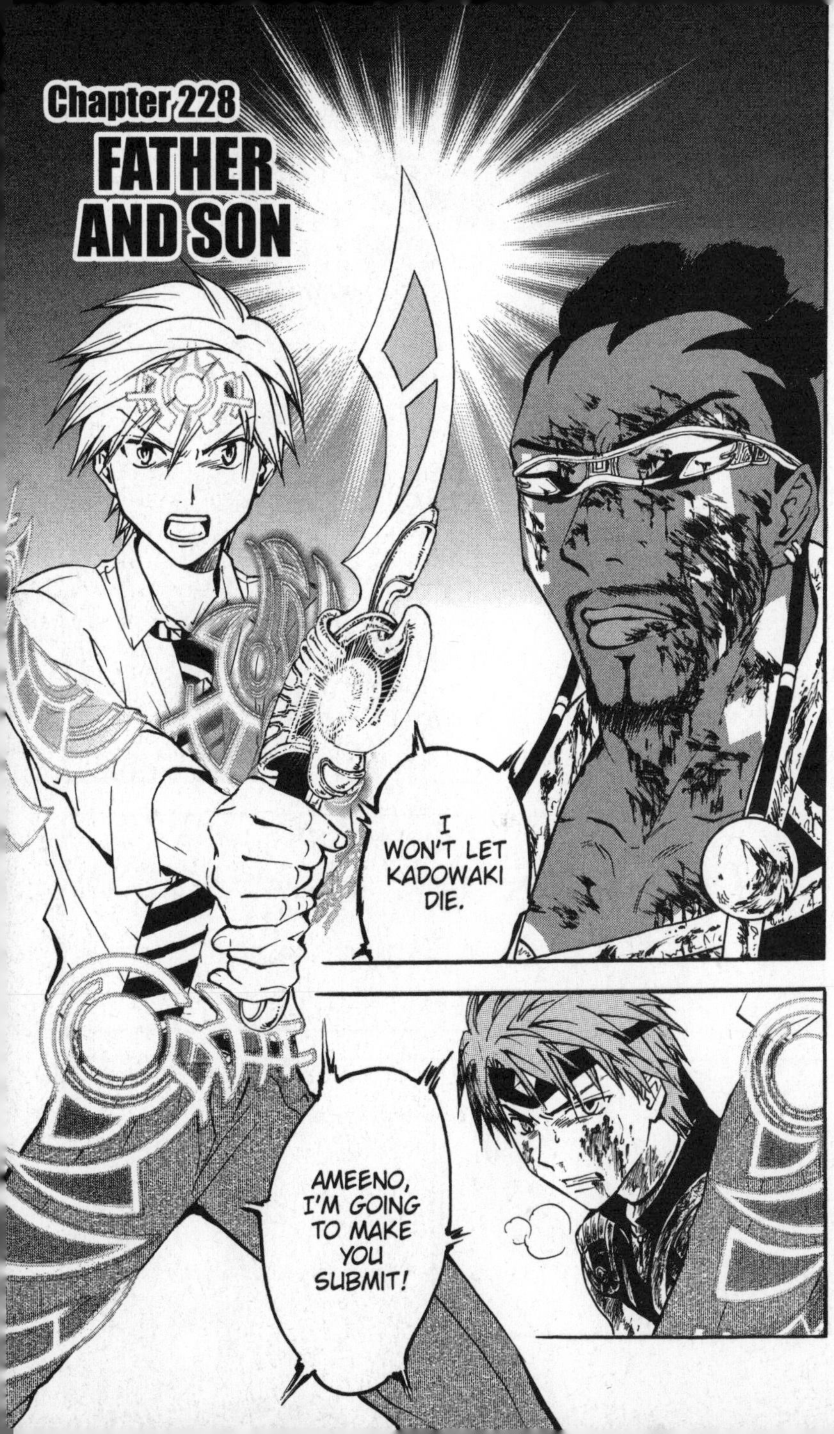
I WON'T LET KADOWAKI DIE.
AMEENO, I'M GOING TO MAKE YOU SUBMIT!

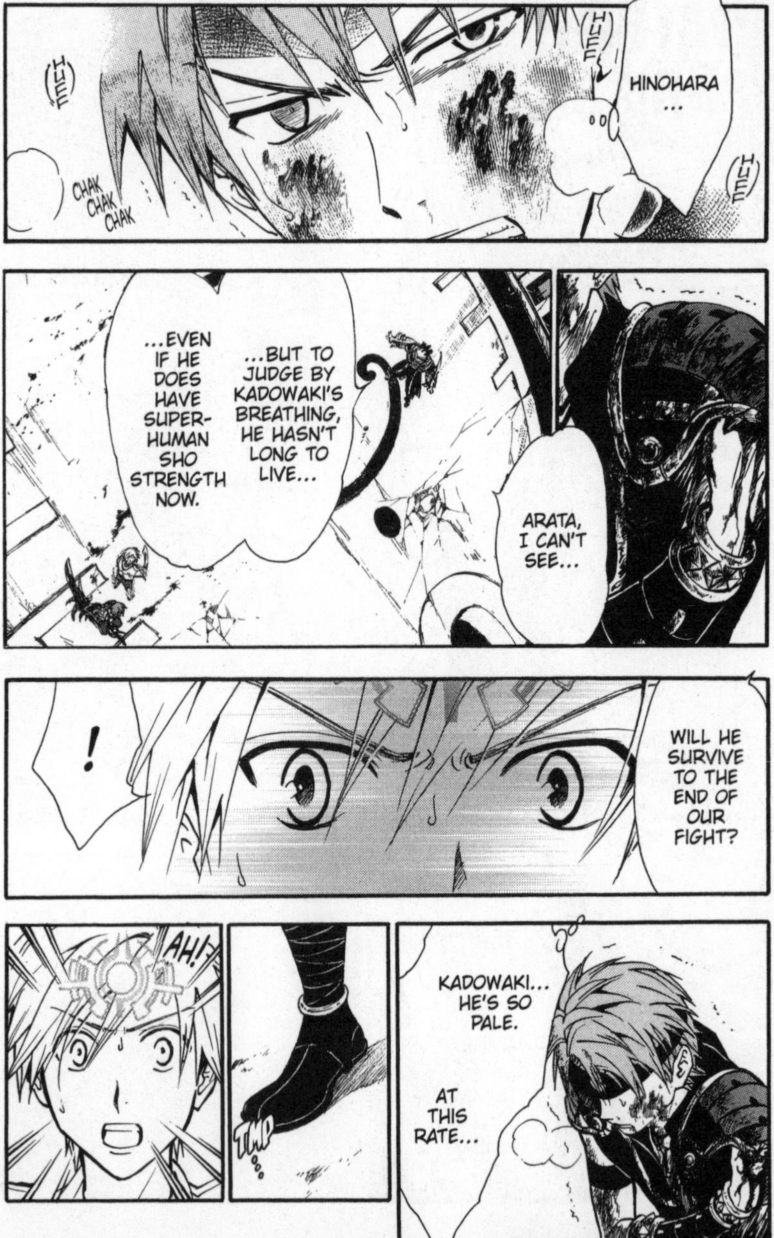
HUFF
HINOHARA ...
HUFF
HUFF
CHAK CHAK CHAK
ARATA, I CAN'T SEE...
...BUT TO JUDGE BY KADOWAKI'S BREATHING, HE HASN'T LONG TO LIVE...
...EVEN IF HE DOES HAVE SUPER-HUMAN SHO STRENGTH NOW.
WILL HE SURVIVE TO THE END OF OUR FIGHT?
!
KADOWAKI... HE'S SO PALE.
AT THIS RATE...
AH!

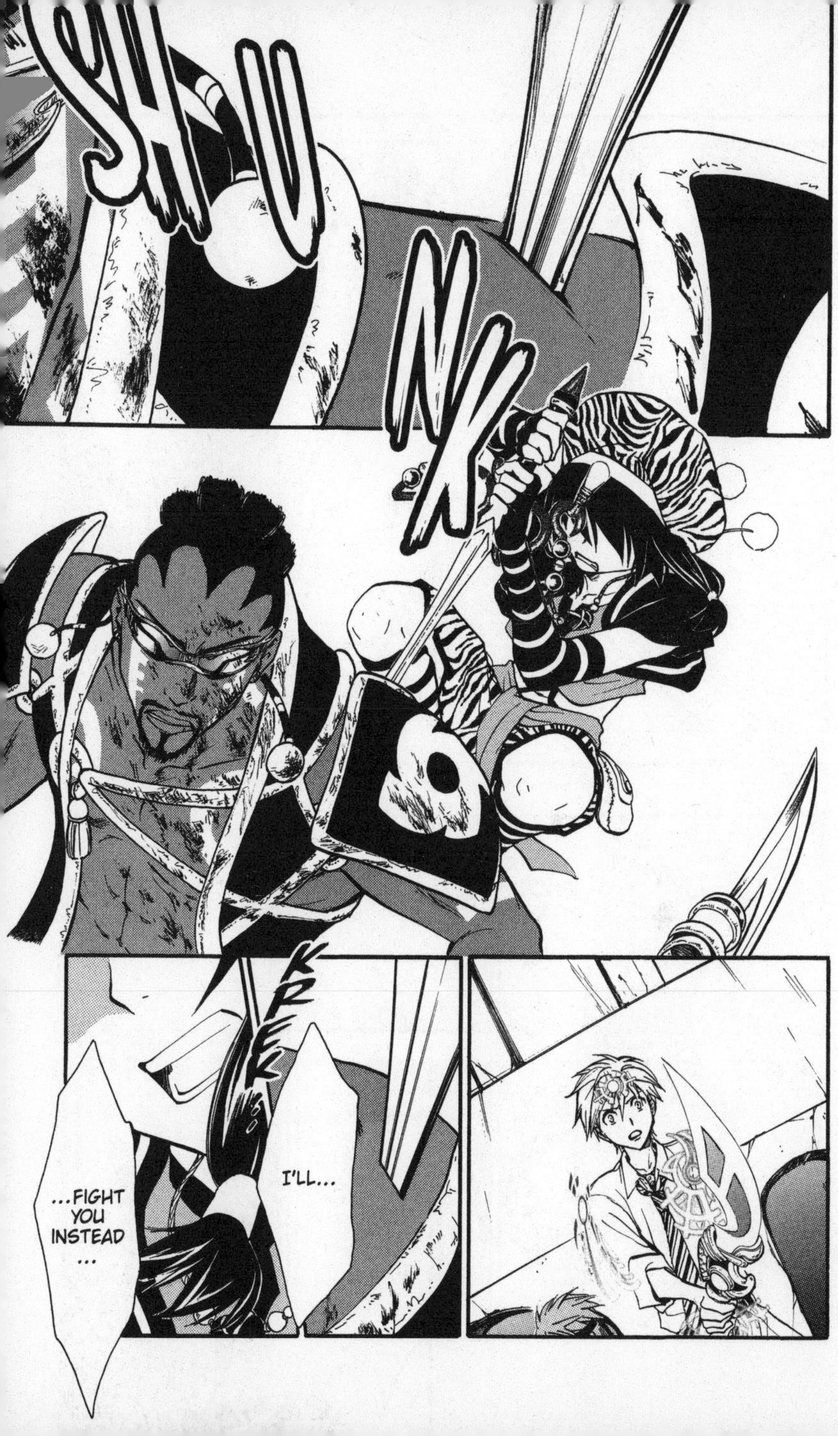
SHUNK
KREEK
I'LL...
...FIGHT YOU INSTEAD ...

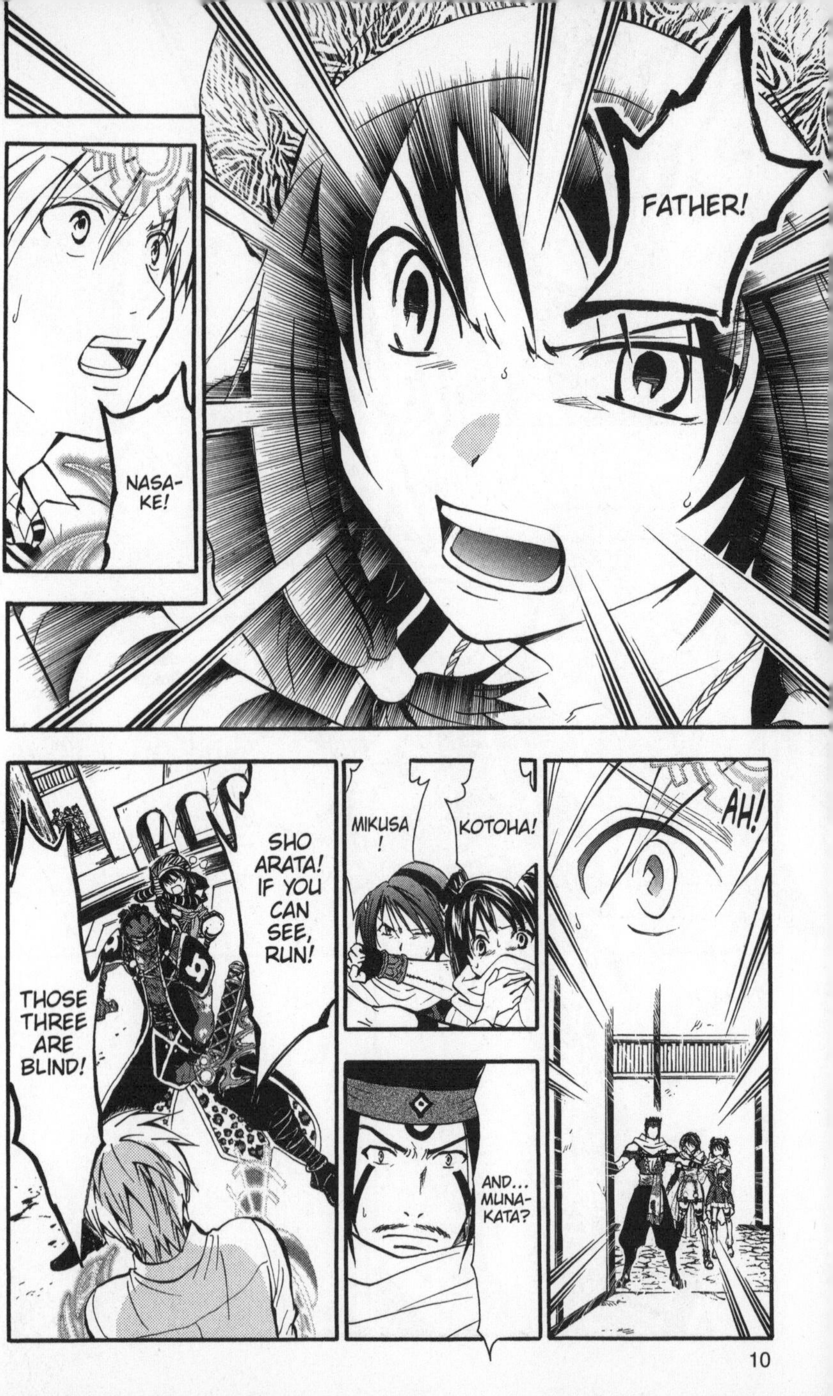
FATHER!
NASA-KE!
AH!
KOTOHA!
MIKUSA!
AND... MUNA-KATA?
SHO ARATA! IF YOU CAN SEE, RUN!
THOSE THREE ARE BLIND!

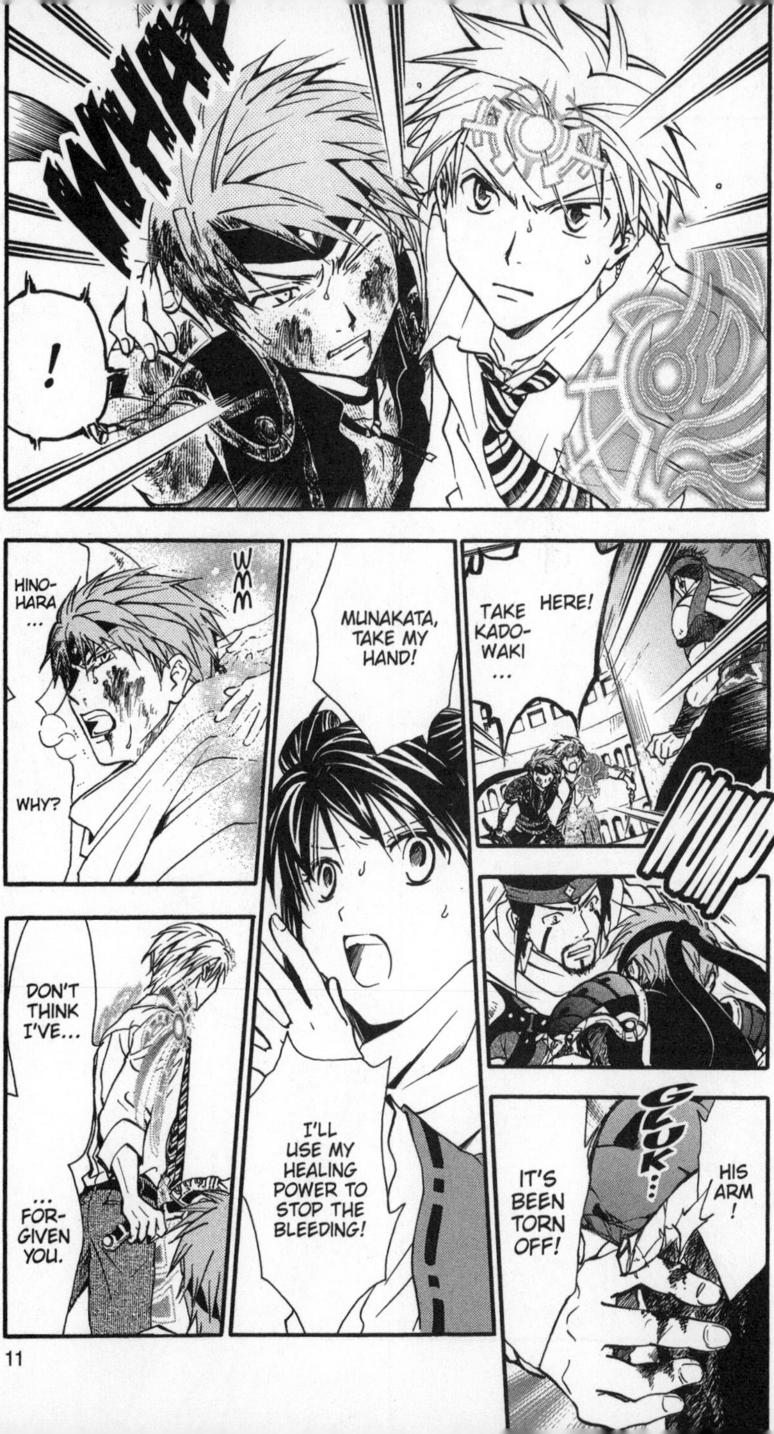
WHAP
!
HERE!
TAKE KADOWAKI...
WHUMP
GLUK...
HIS ARM!
IT'S BEEN TORN OFF!
MUNAKATA, TAKE MY HAND!
I'LL USE MY HEALING POWER TO STOP THE BLEEDING!
WMM
HINO-HARA...
WHY?
DON'T THINK I'VE...
...FOR-GIVEN YOU.

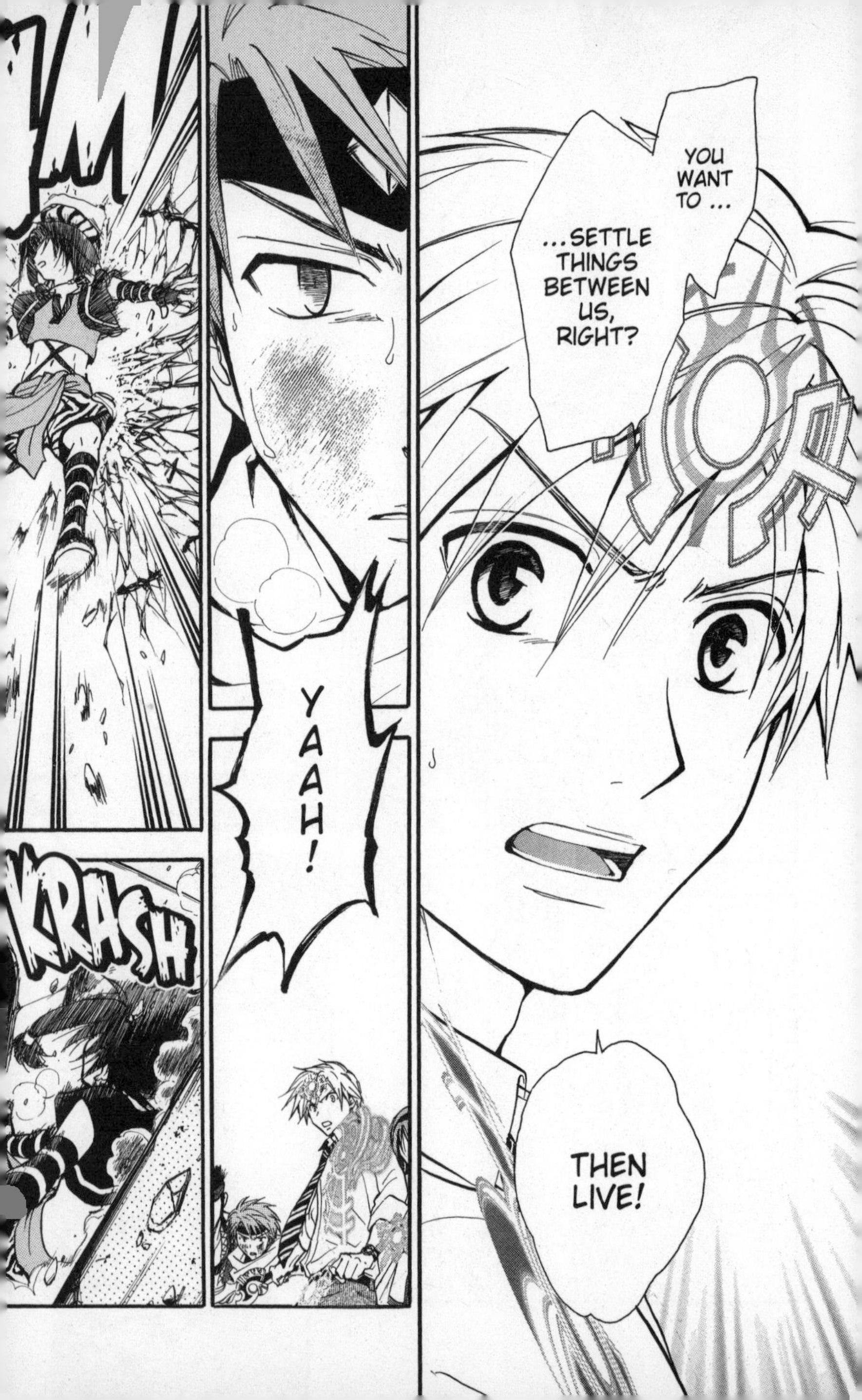
YOU WANT TO ...
...SETTLE THINGS BETWEEN US, RIGHT?
THEN LIVE!
YAAH!
KRASH

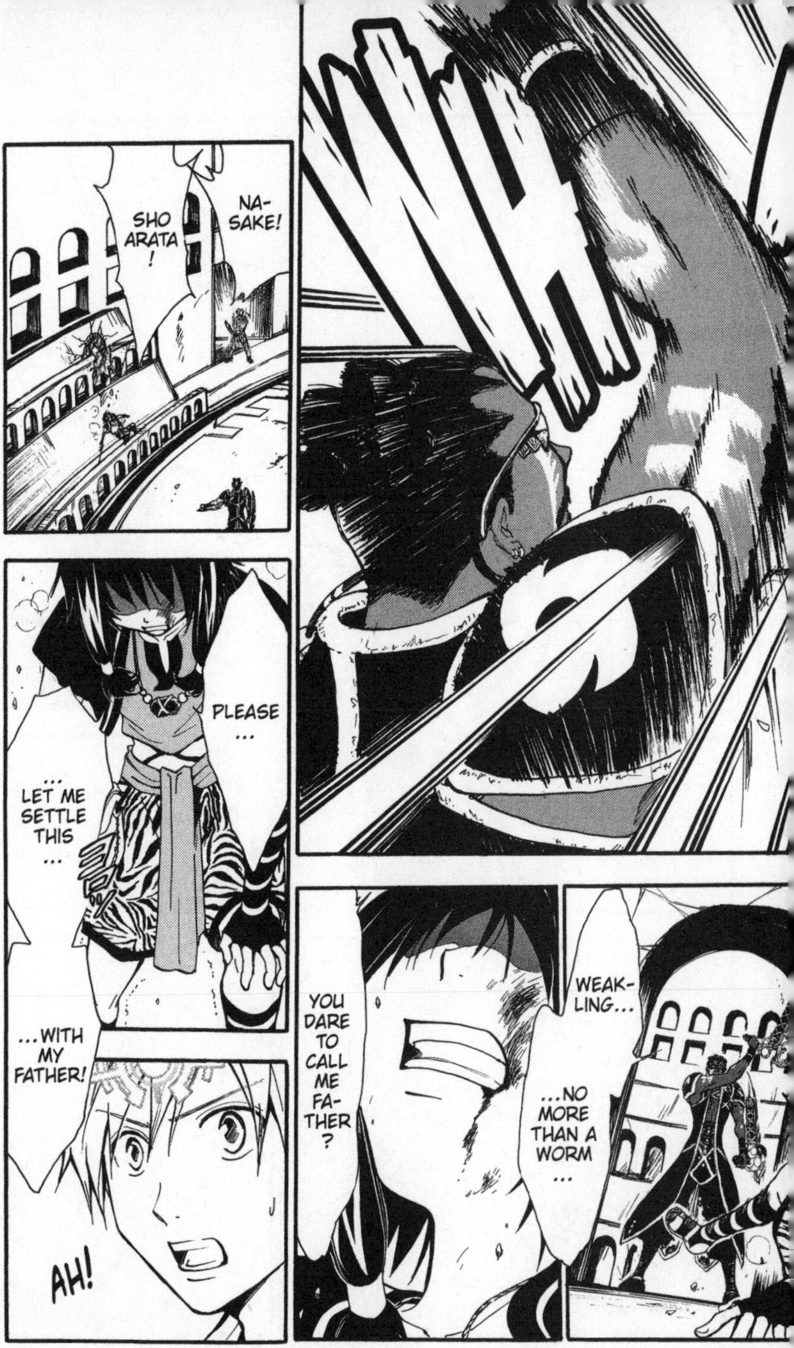
WEAK-LING...
...NO MORE THAN A WORM...
YOU DARE TO CALL ME FA-THER?
NA-SAKE!
SHO ARATA!
PLEASE...
...LET ME SETTLE THIS...
...WITH MY FATHER!
AH!

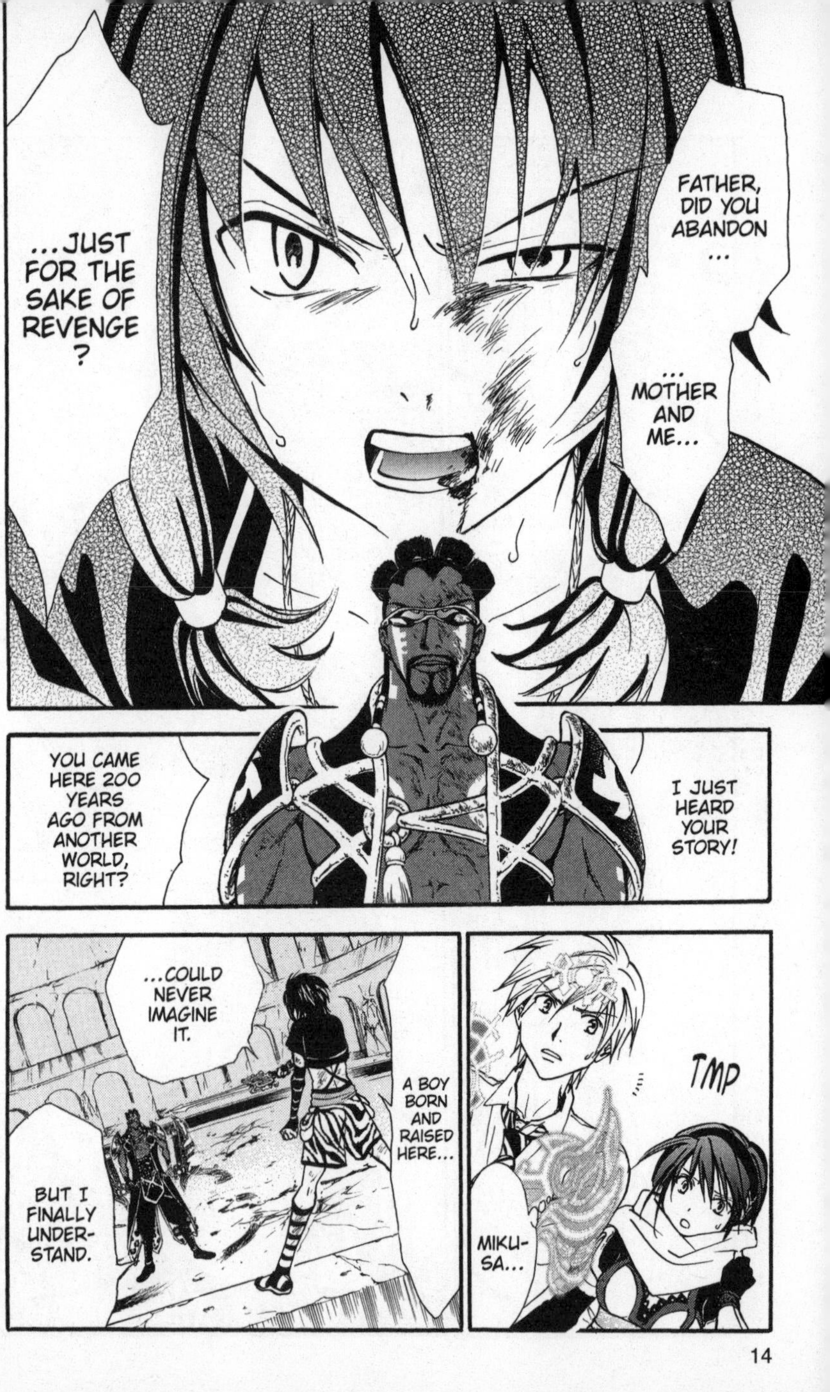

FATHER, DID YOU ABANDON ...
... MOTHER AND ME...
...JUST FOR THE SAKE OF REVENGE ?
I JUST HEARD YOUR STORY!
YOU CAME HERE 200 YEARS AGO FROM ANOTHER WORLD, RIGHT?
TMP
MIKU-SA...
A BOY BORN AND RAISED HERE...
...COULD NEVER IMAGINE IT.
BUT I FINALLY UNDER-STAND.

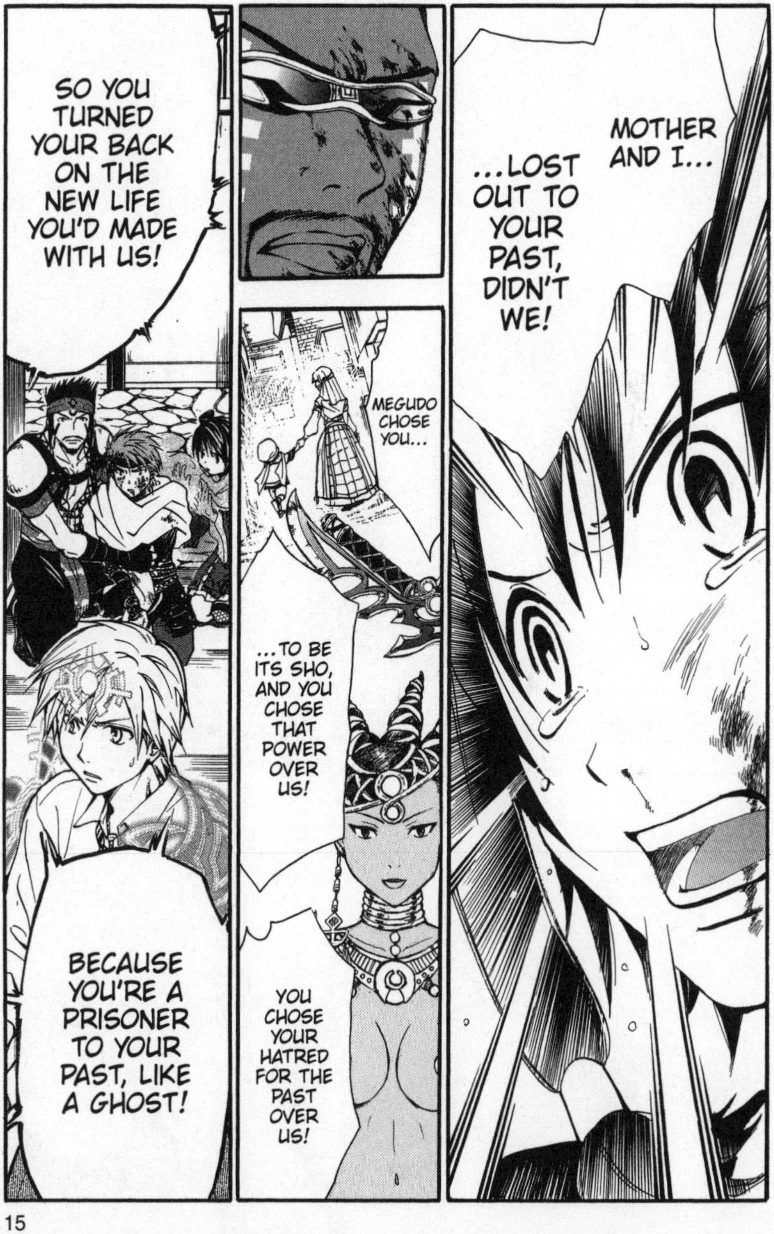
MOTHER AND I...
...LOST OUT TO YOUR PAST, DIDN'T WE!
MEGUDO CHOSE YOU...
...TO BE ITS SHO, AND YOU CHOSE THAT POWER OVER US!
YOU CHOSE YOUR HATRED FOR THE PAST OVER US!
SO YOU TURNED YOUR BACK ON THE NEW LIFE YOU'D MADE WITH US!
BECAUSE YOU'RE A PRISONER TO YOUR PAST, LIKE A GHOST!

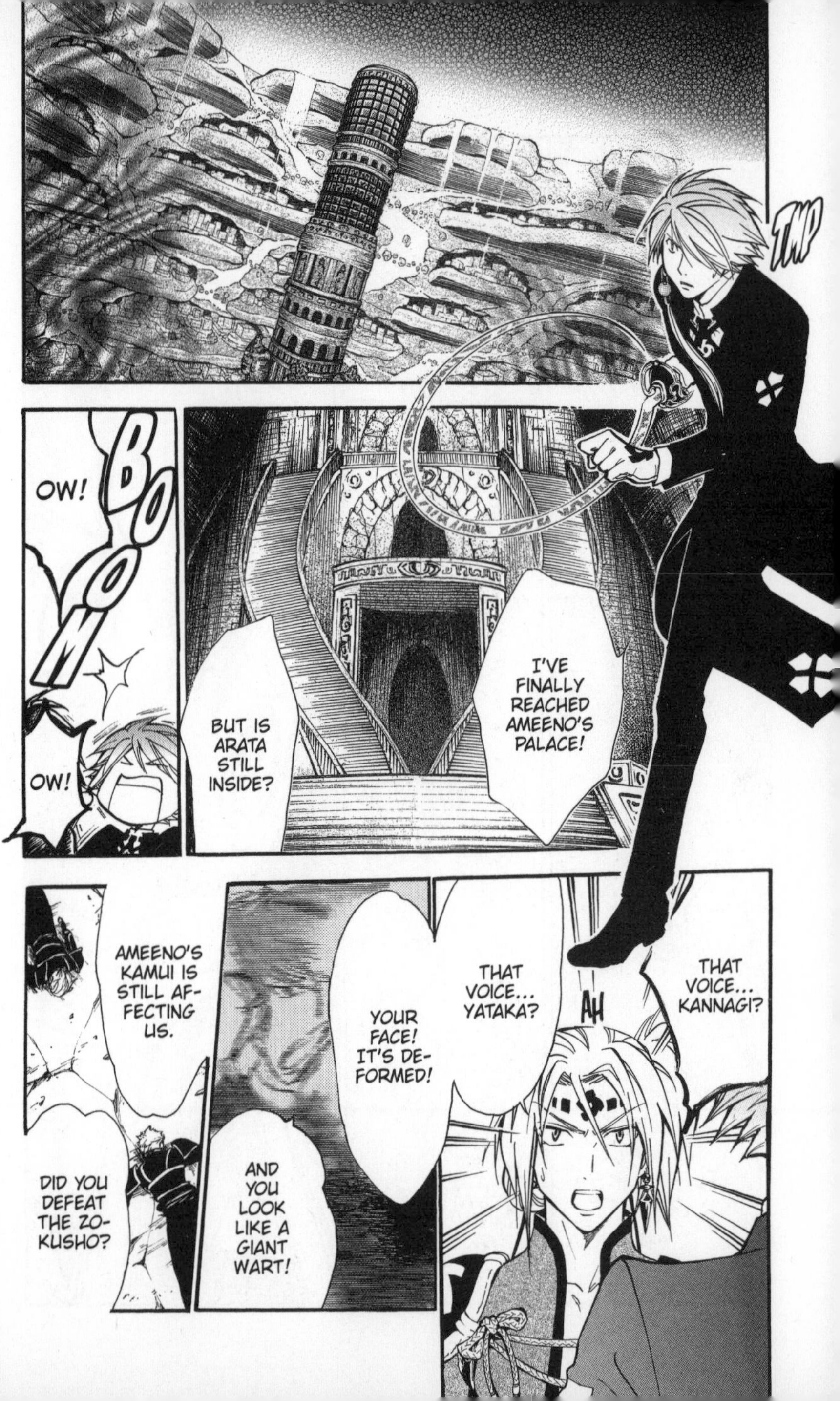
TMP
I'VE FINALLY REACHED AMEENO'S PALACE!
BUT IS ARATA STILL INSIDE?
BOOOM
OW!
OW!
THAT VOICE... KANNAGI?
AH
THAT VOICE... YATAKA?
YOUR FACE! IT'S DEFORMED!
AND YOU LOOK LIKE A GIANT WART!
AMEENO'S KAMUI IS STILL AFFECTING US.
DID YOU DEFEAT THE ZOKUSHO?

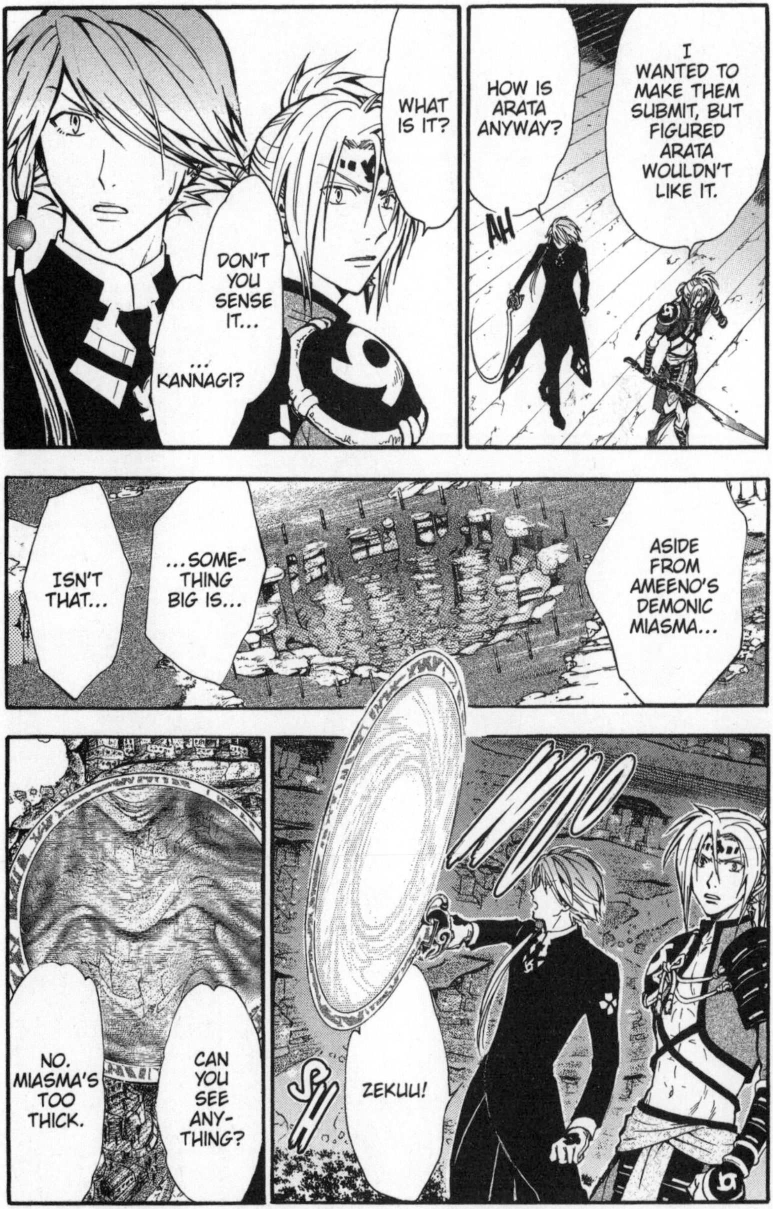
I WANTED TO MAKE THEM SUBMIT, BUT FIGURED ARATA WOULDN'T LIKE IT.
HOW IS ARATA ANYWAY?
AH
WHAT IS IT?
DON'T YOU SENSE IT...
...KANNAGI?
ASIDE FROM AMEENO'S DEMONIC MIASMA...
...SOME-THING BIG IS...
ISN'T THAT...
ZEKUU!
SH
CAN YOU SEE ANY-THING?
NO. MIASMA'S TOO THICK.

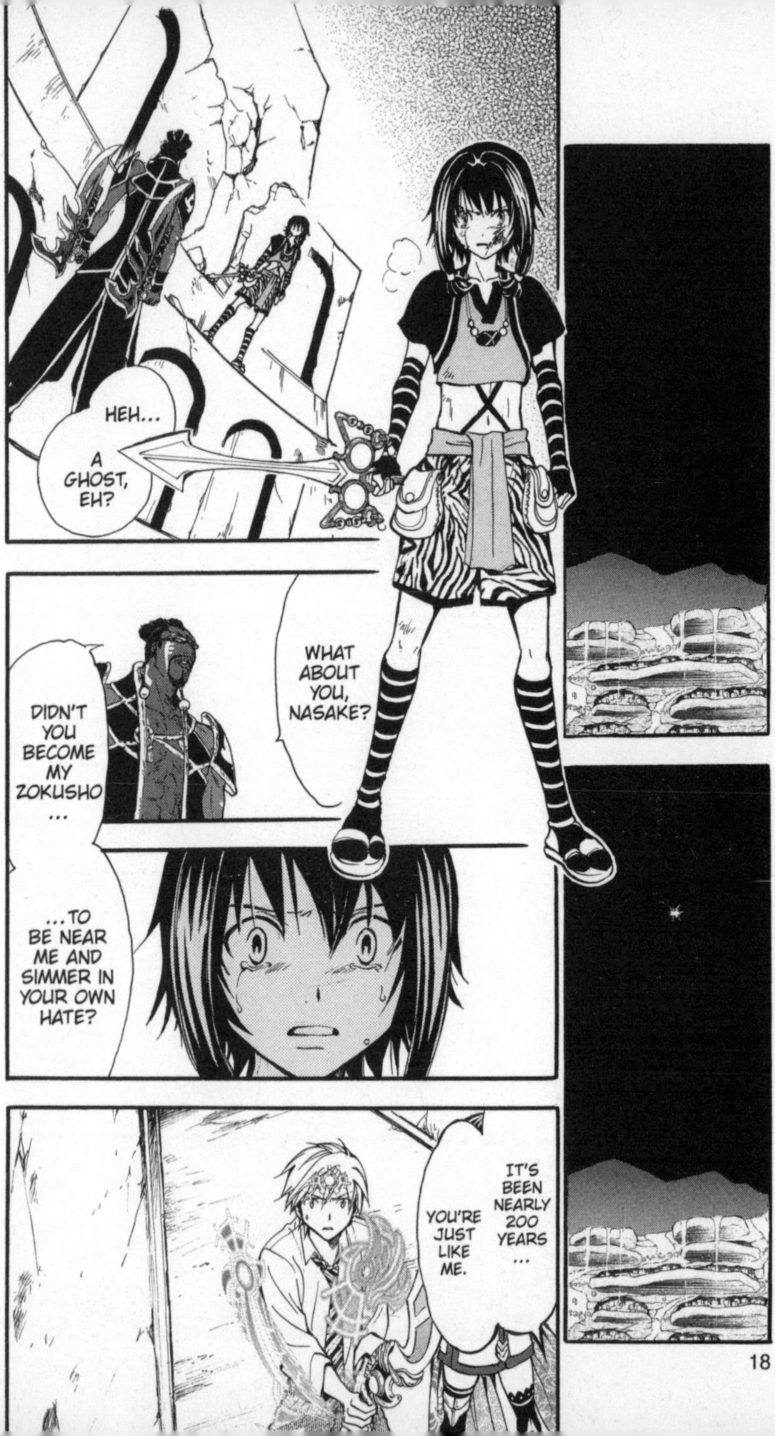
HEH... A GHOST, EH?
WHAT ABOUT YOU, NASAKE?
DIDN'T YOU BECOME MY ZOKUSHO...
...TO BE NEAR ME AND SIMMER IN YOUR OWN HATE?
IT'S BEEN NEARLY 200 YEARS...
YOU'RE JUST LIKE ME.

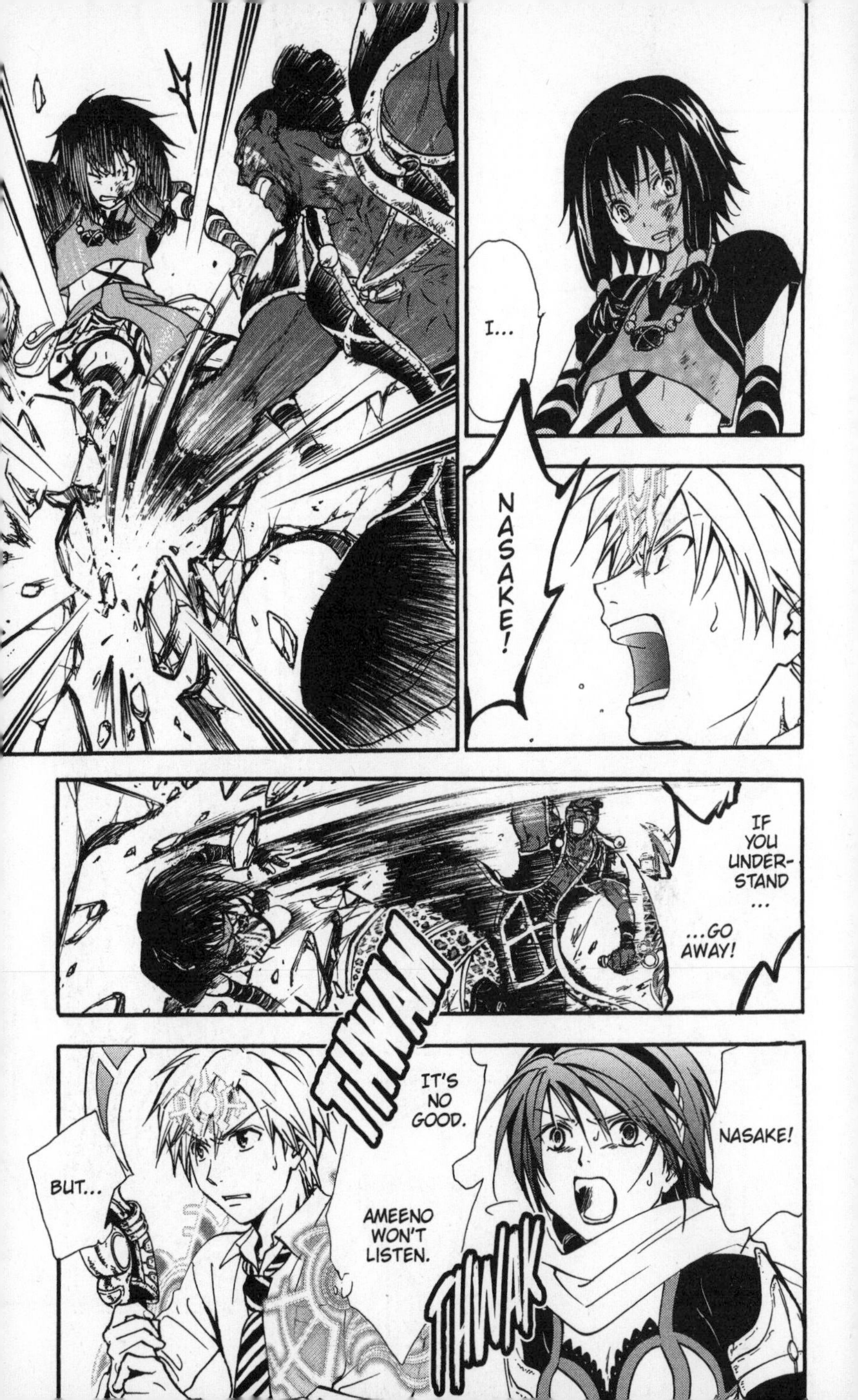
I...
NASAKE!
IF YOU UNDERSTAND...
...GO AWAY!
THWAM
NASAKE!
IT'S NO GOOD.
AMEENO WON'T LISTEN.
BUT...
THWAK

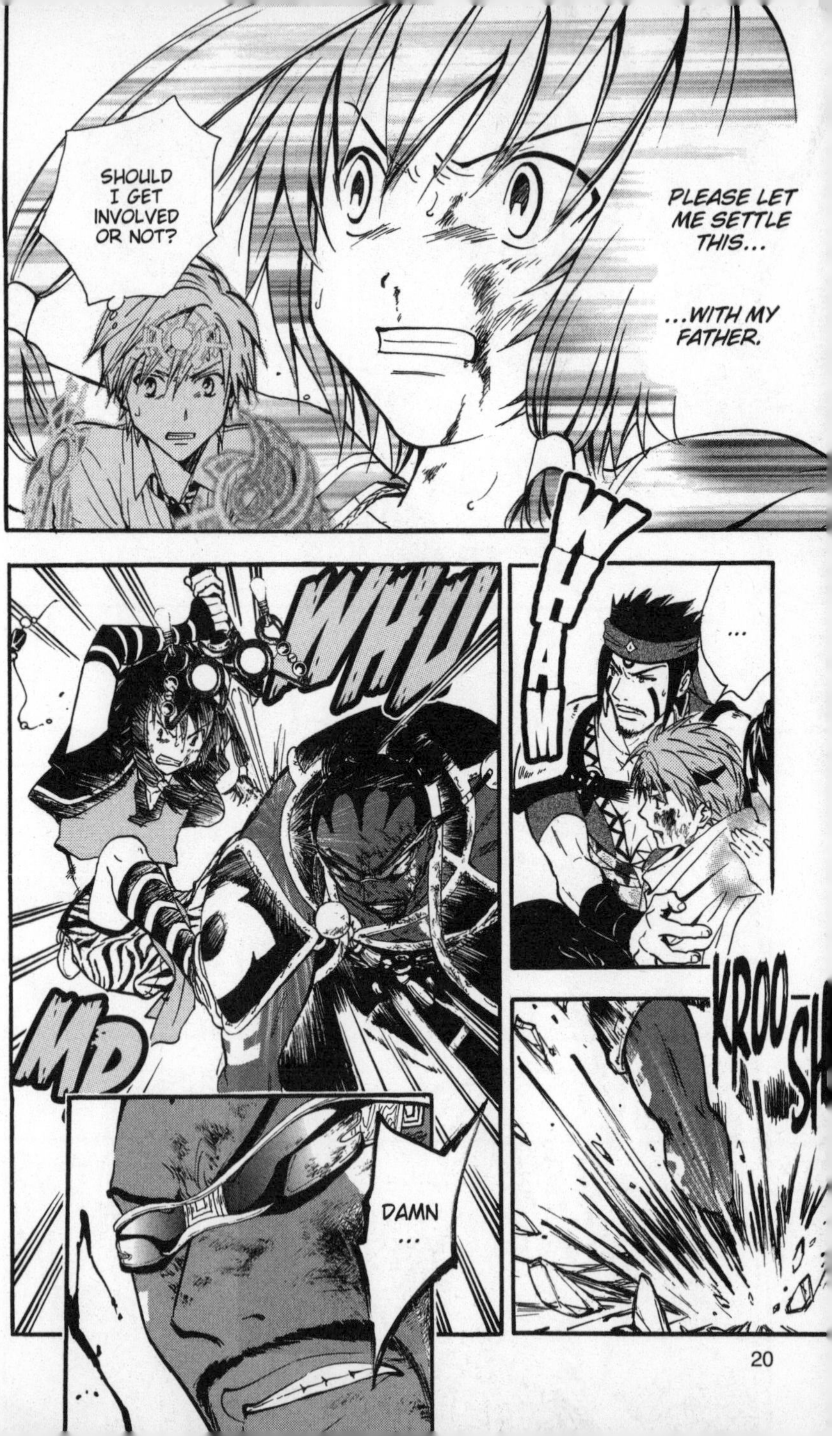
PLEASE LET ME SETTLE THIS...
...WITH MY FATHER.
SHOULD I GET INVOLVED OR NOT?
WHAM
...
WHU
MP
KROO-SH
DAMN ...

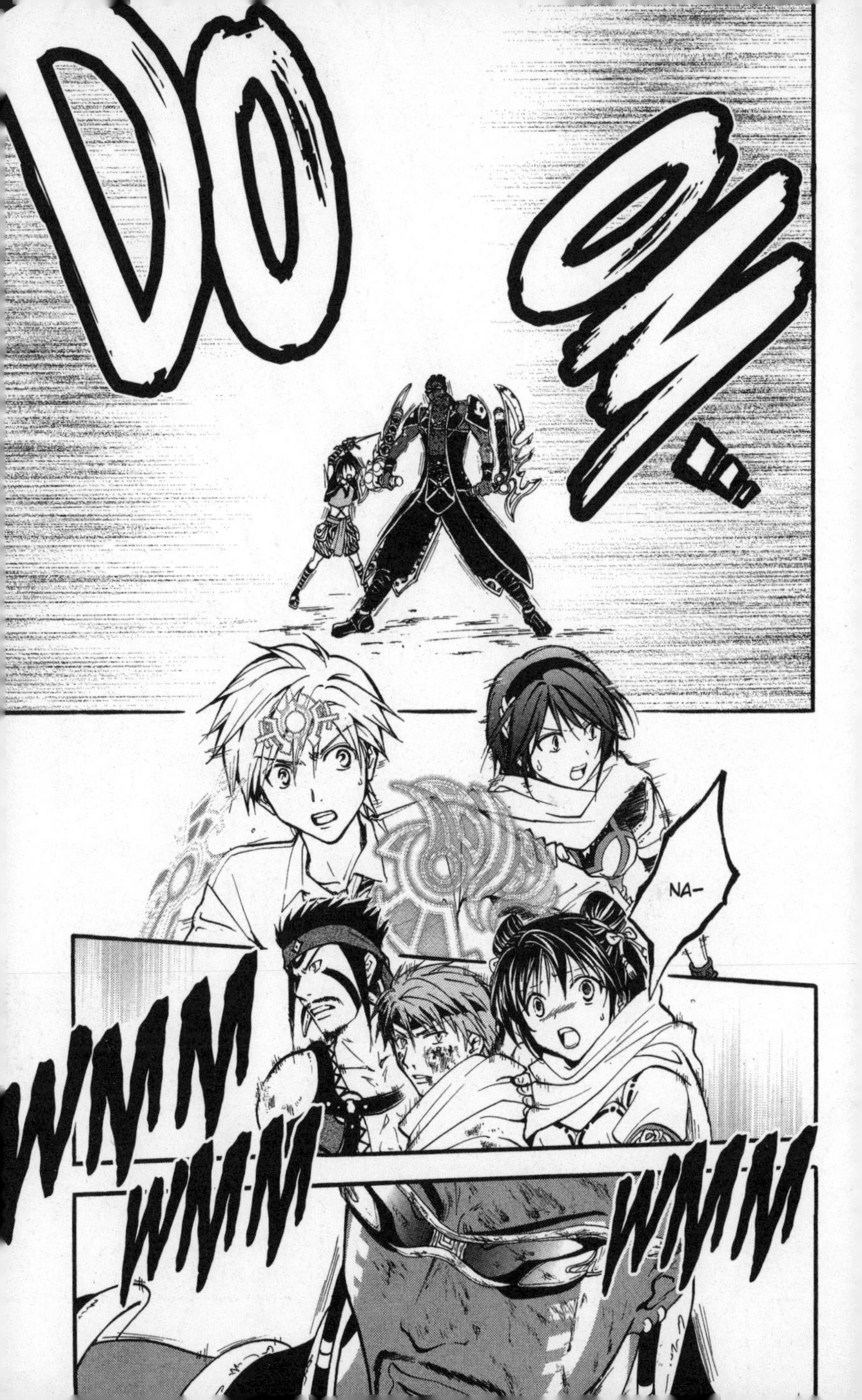
DOOM...
NA-
WMM
WMM
WMM

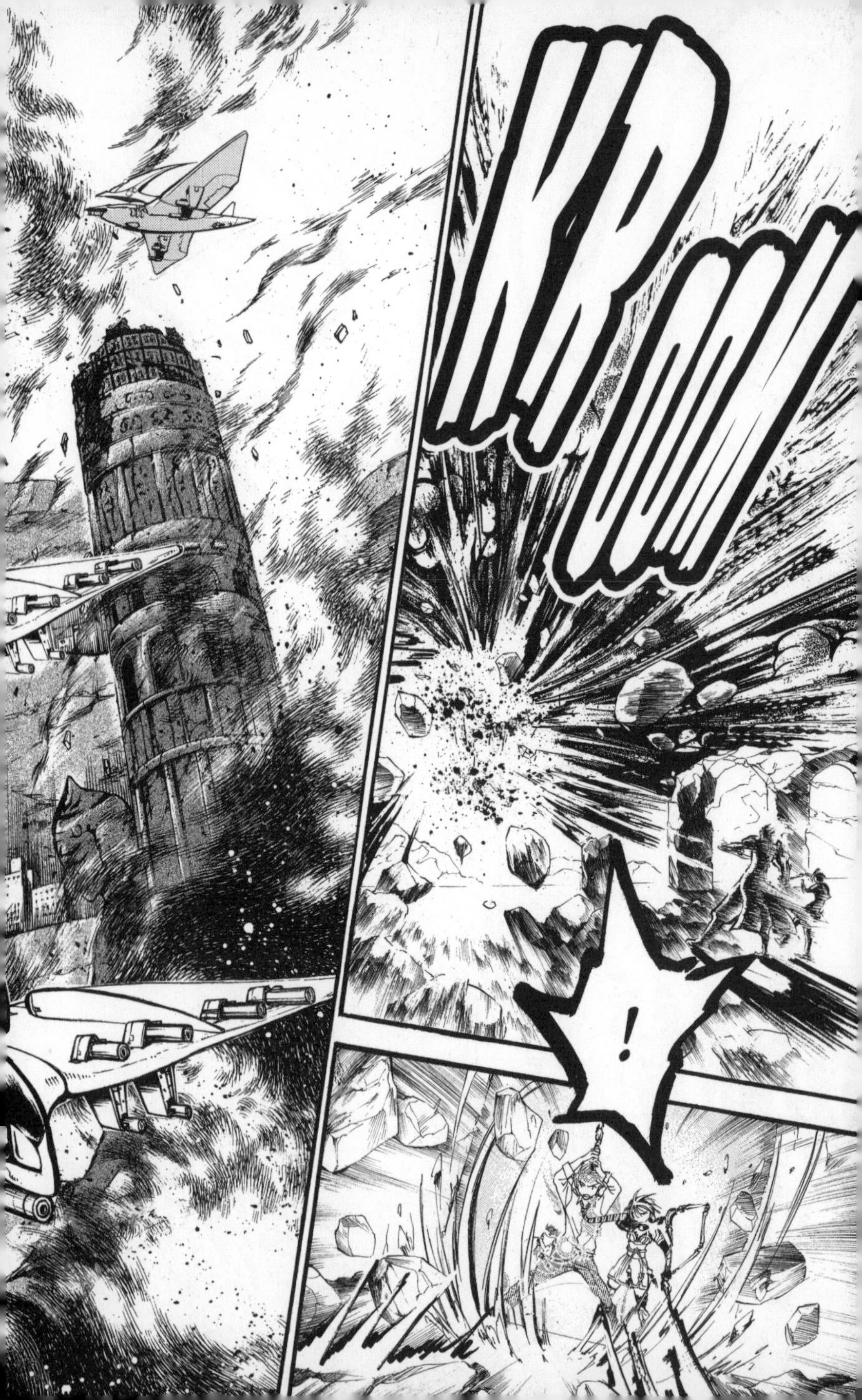
KABOOM
!

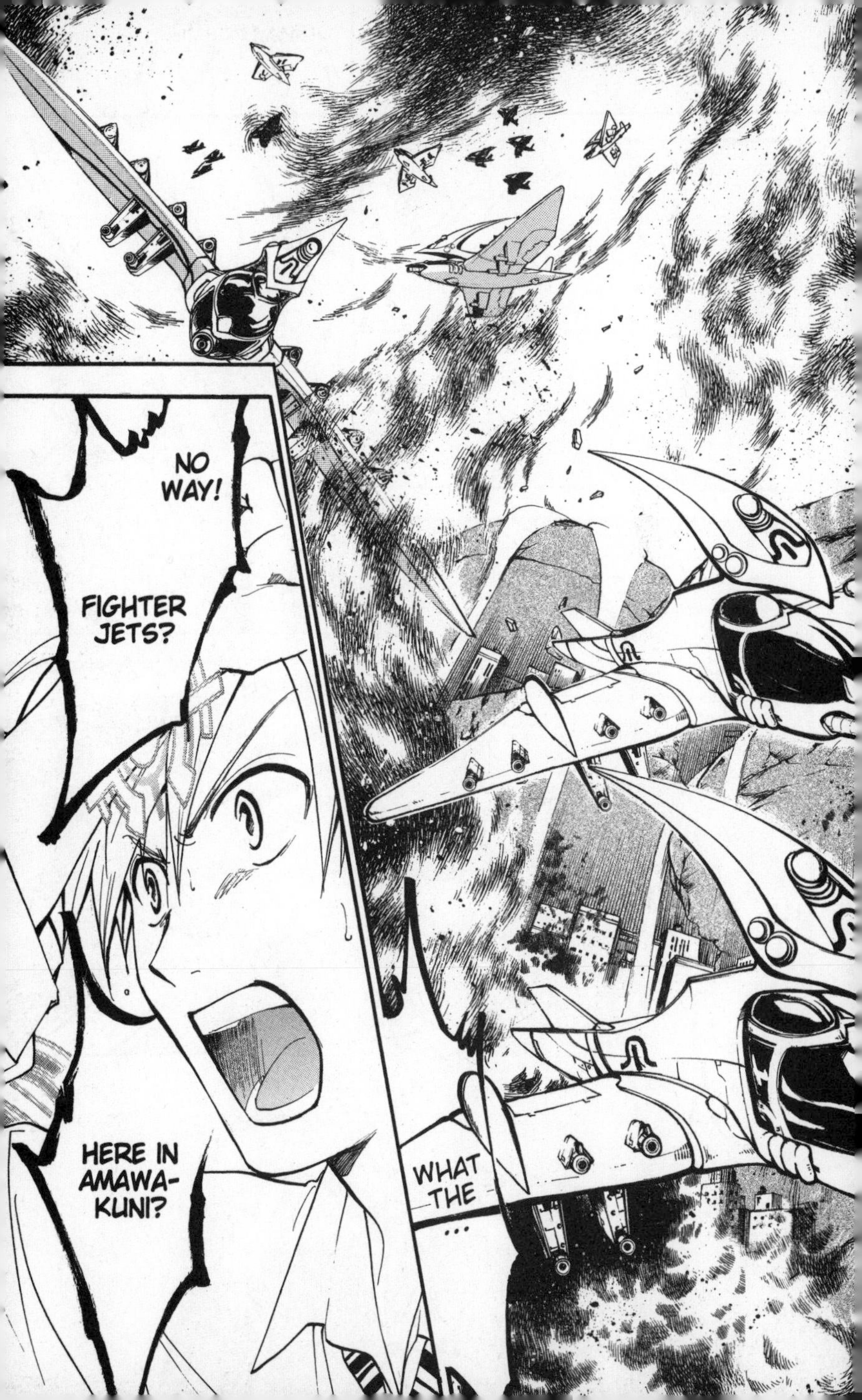
WHAT THE ...
NO WAY!
FIGHTER JETS?
HERE IN AMAWA-KUNI?

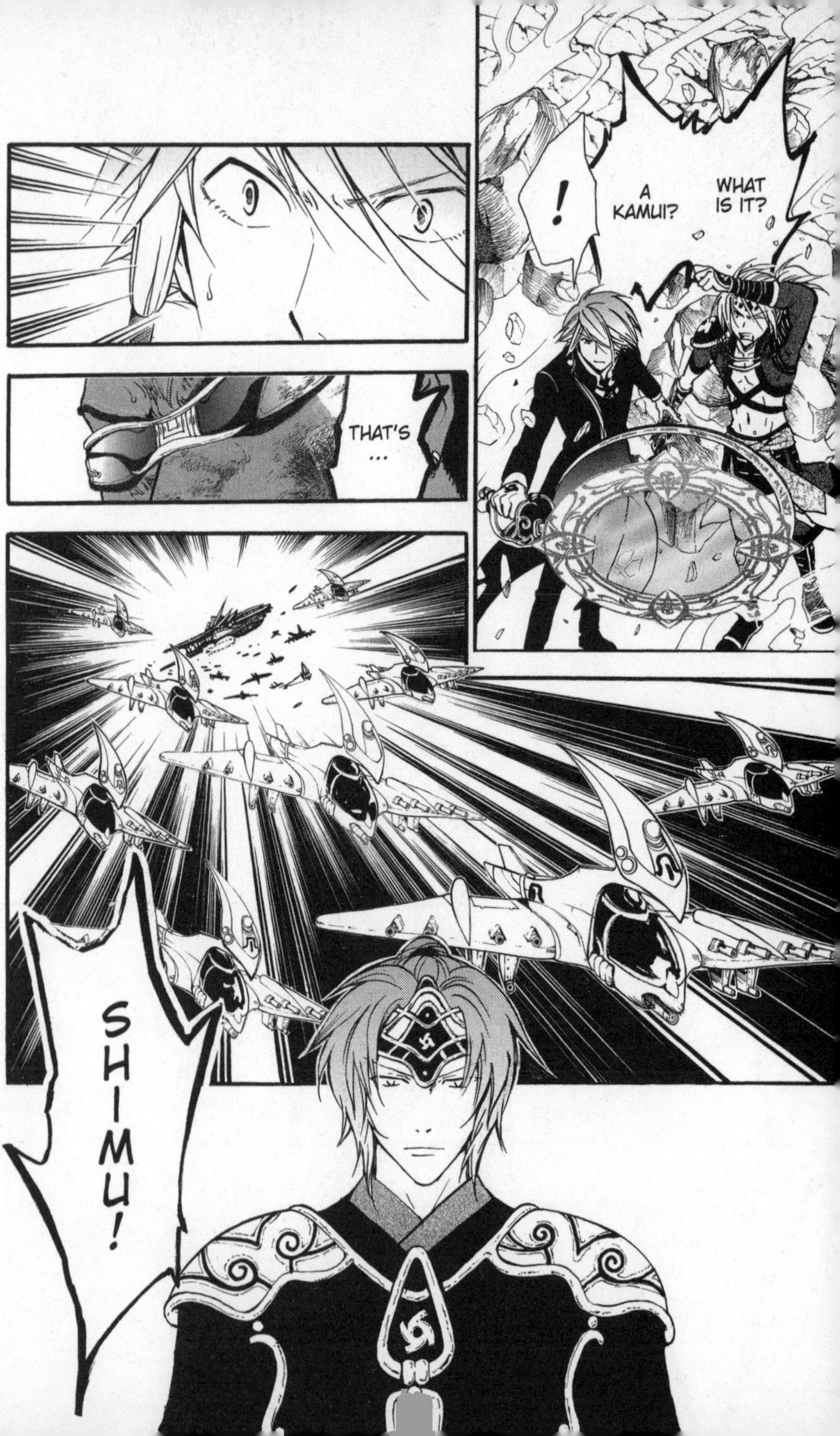
WHAT IS IT?
A KAMUI?
!
THAT'S ...
SHIMU!

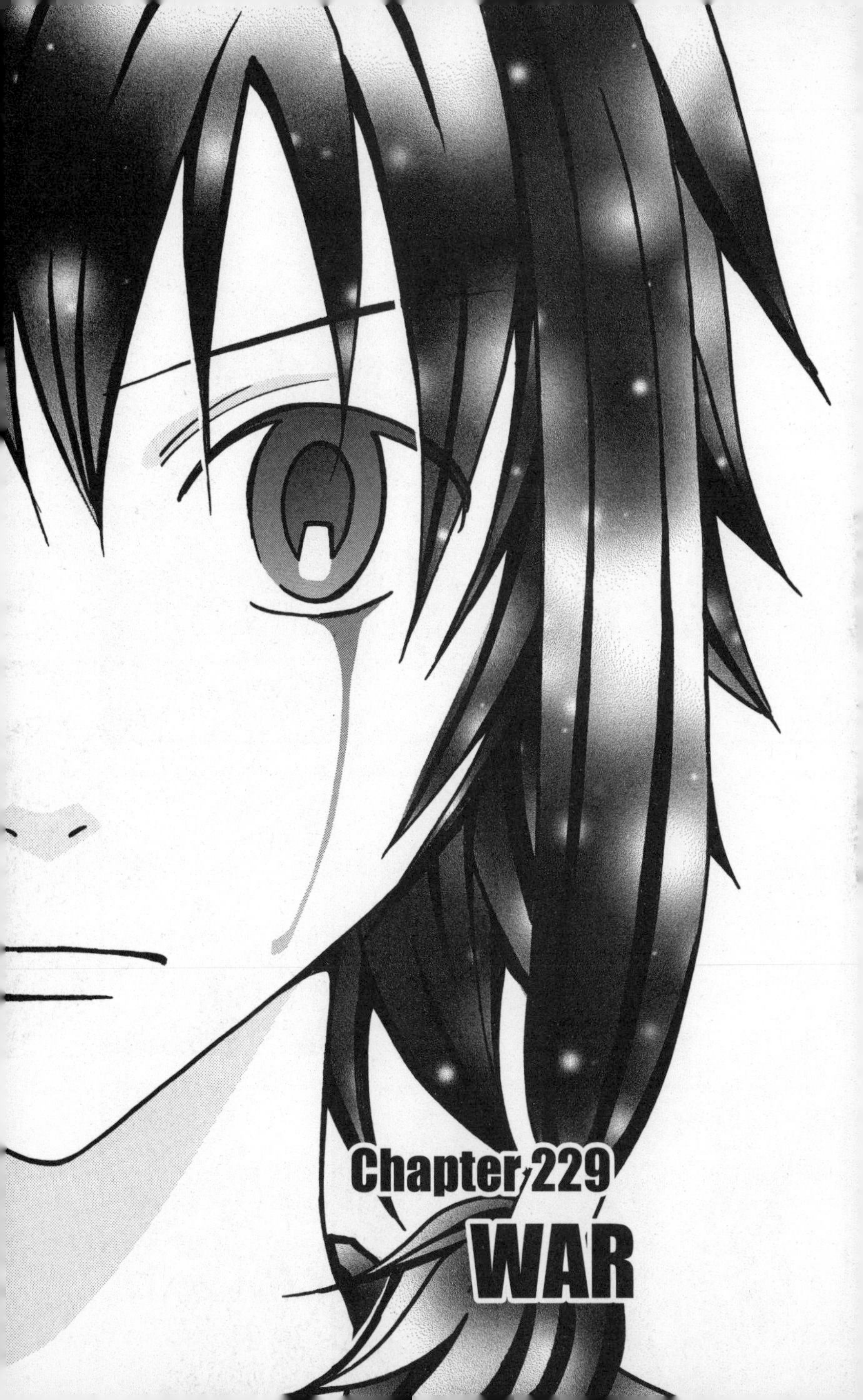
Chapter 229
WAR

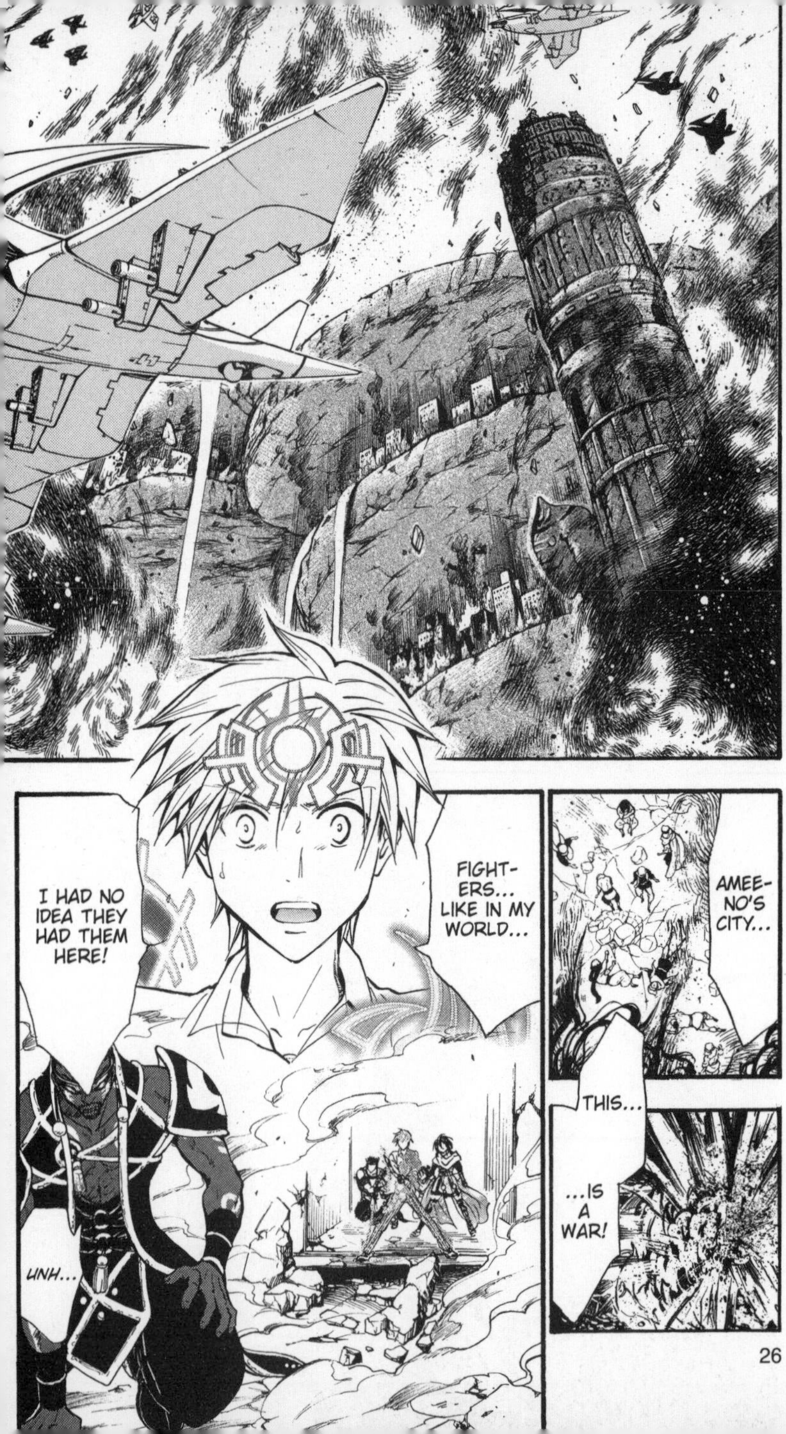
AMEE-NO'S CITY...
THIS...
...IS A WAR!
FIGHT-ERS... LIKE IN MY WORLD...
I HAD NO IDEA THEY HAD THEM HERE!
UNH...

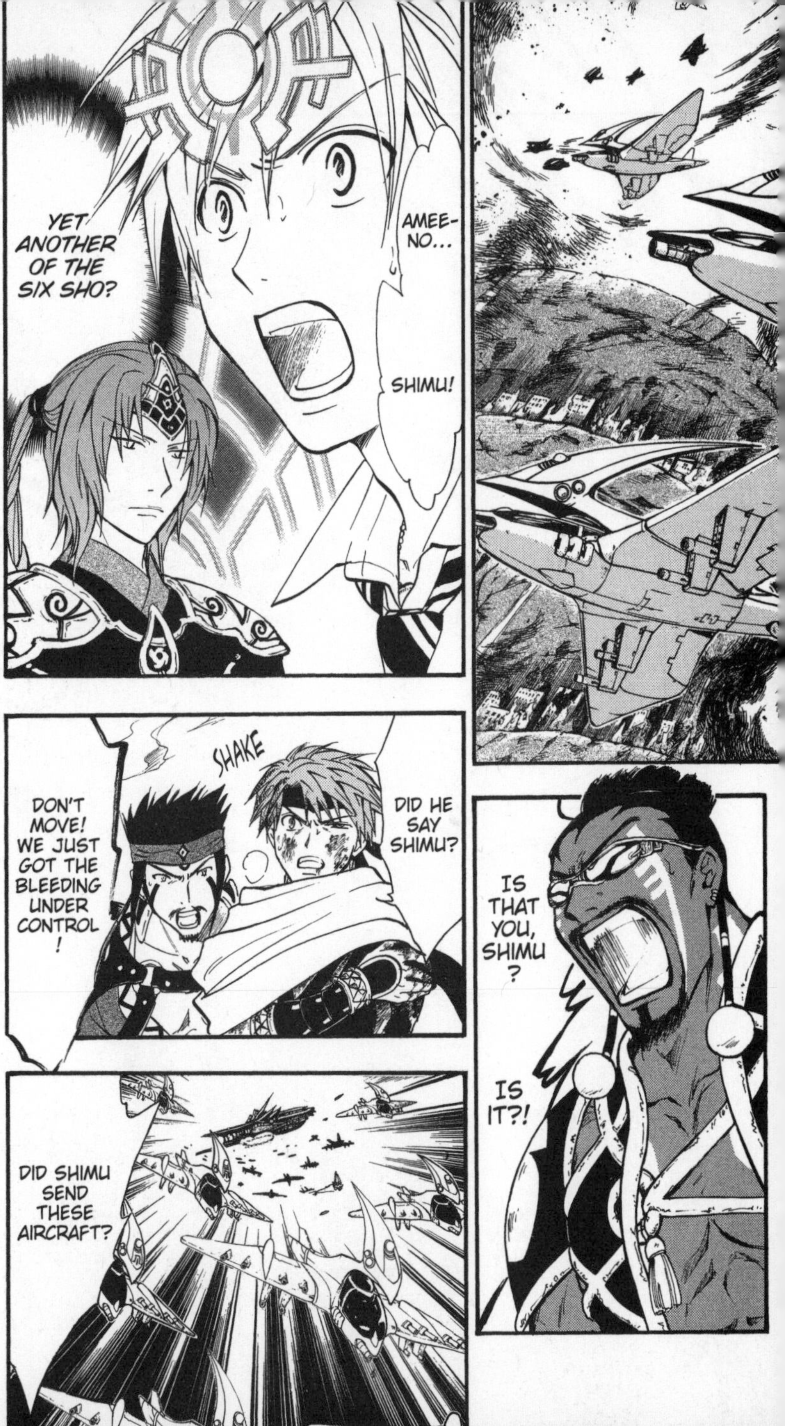
AMEE-NO...
SHIMU!
YET ANOTHER OF THE SIX SHO?
IS THAT YOU, SHIMU?
IS IT?!
DID HE SAY SHIMU?
SHAKE
DON'T MOVE! WE JUST GOT THE BLEEDING UNDER CONTROL!
DID SHIMU SEND THESE AIRCRAFT?

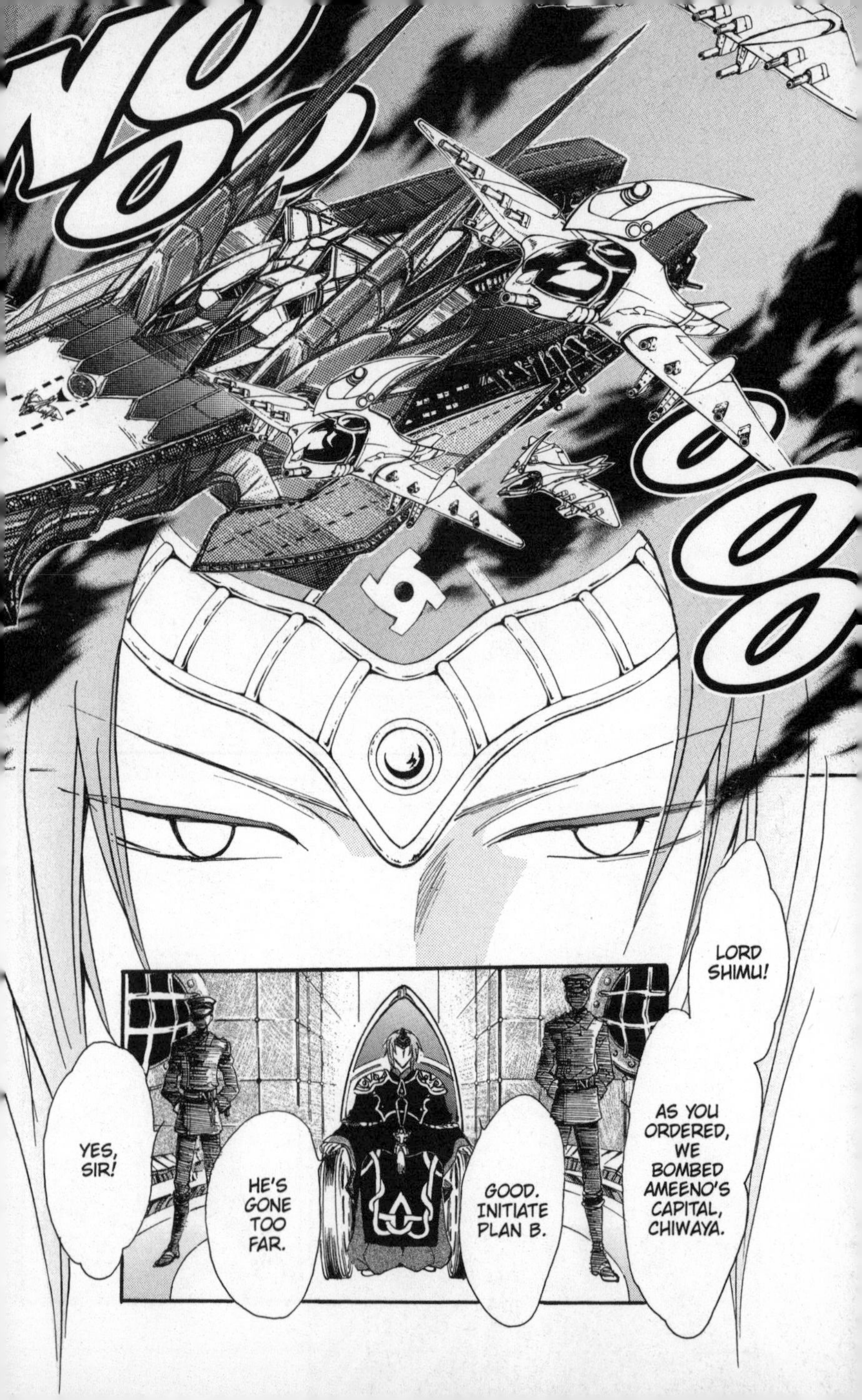
LORD SHIMU!
AS YOU ORDERED, WE BOMBED AMEENO'S CAPITAL, CHIWAYA.
GOOD. INITIATE PLAN B.
HE'S GONE TOO FAR.
YES, SIR!

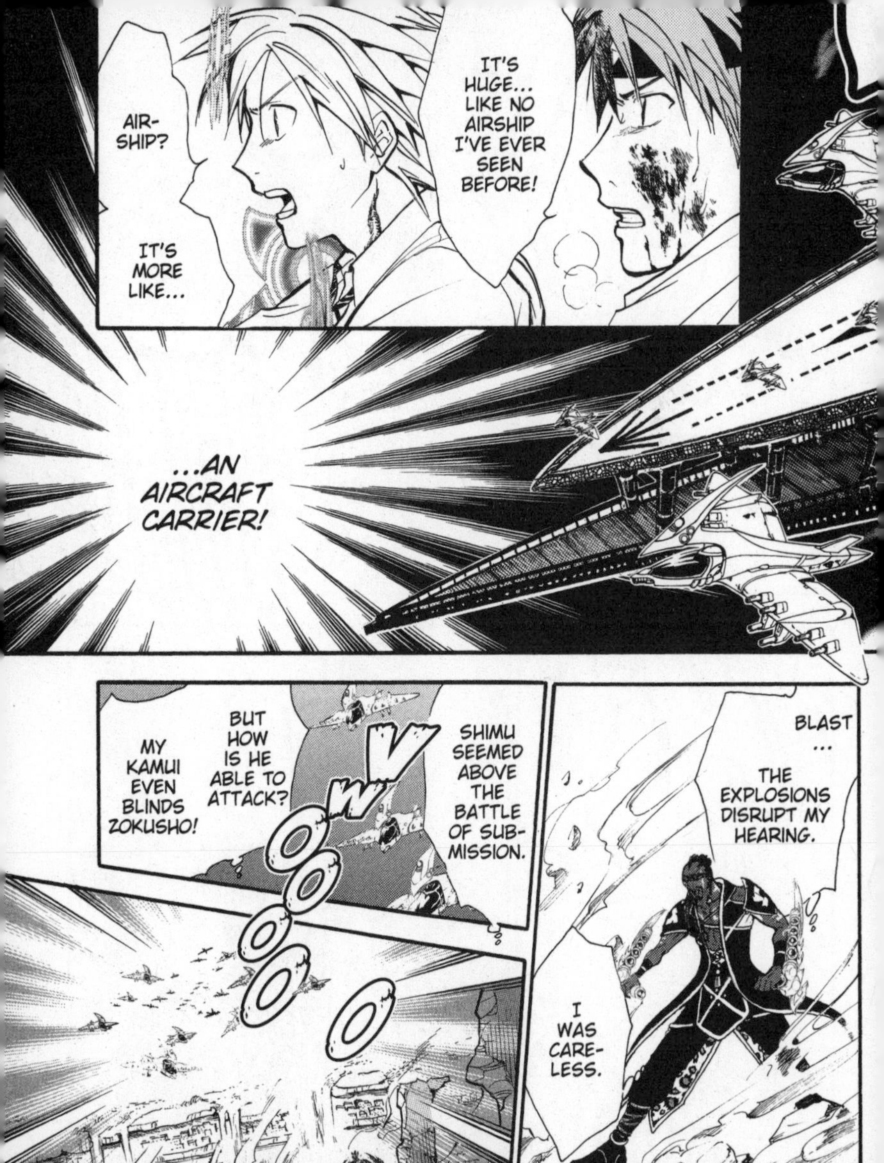
IT'S HUGE... LIKE NO AIRSHIP I'VE EVER SEEN BEFORE!
AIR-SHIP?
IT'S MORE LIKE...
...AN AIRCRAFT CARRIER!
BLAST...
THE EXPLOSIONS DISRUPT MY HEARING.
I WAS CARE-LESS.
SHIMU SEEMED ABOVE THE BATTLE OF SUB-MISSION.
BUT HOW IS HE ABLE TO ATTACK?
MY KAMUI EVEN BLINDS ZOKUSHO!
VWOOOOO

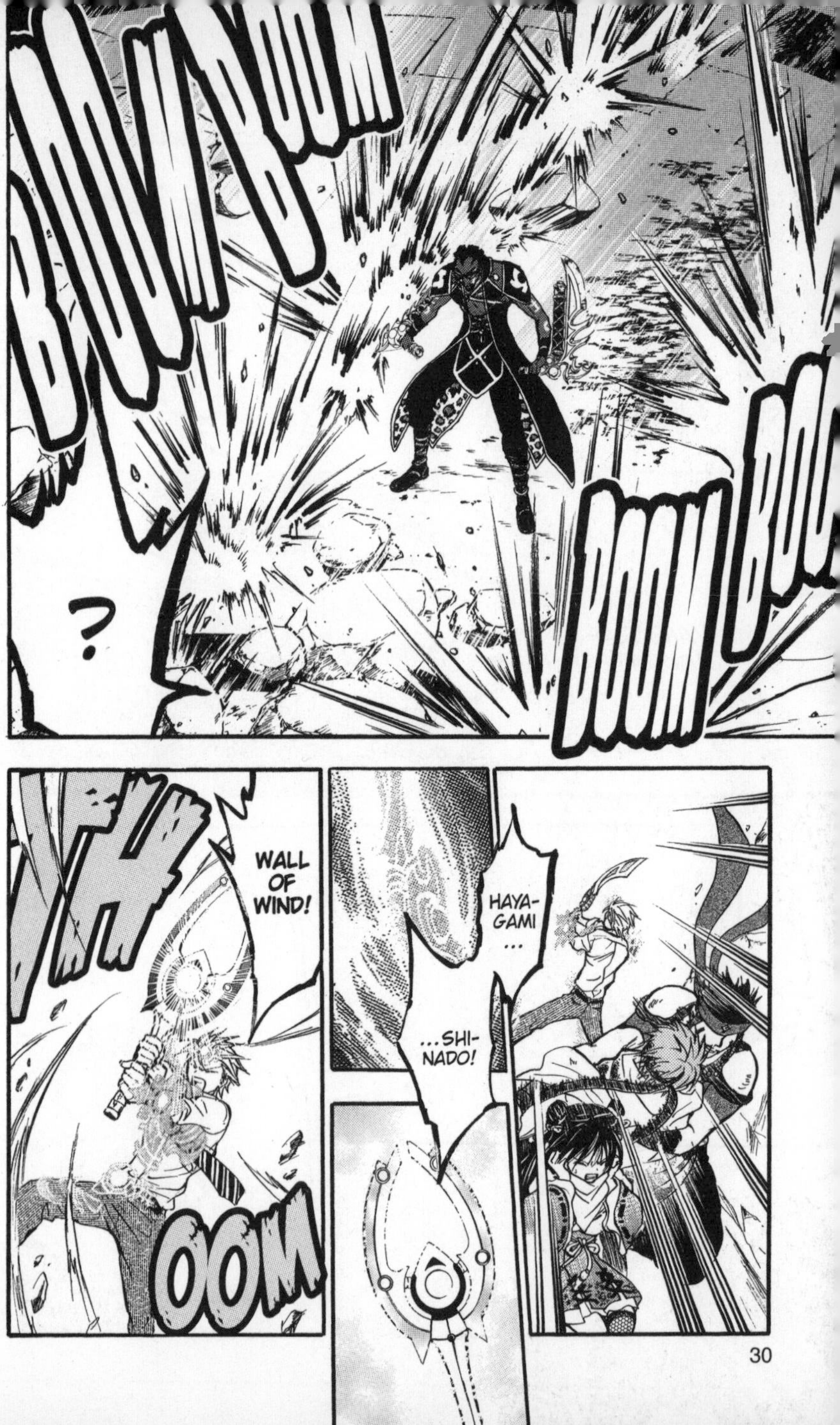
BOOM BOO
BOOM BOOM
?
HAYA-GAMI ...
...SHI-NADO!
WALL OF WIND!
OOM

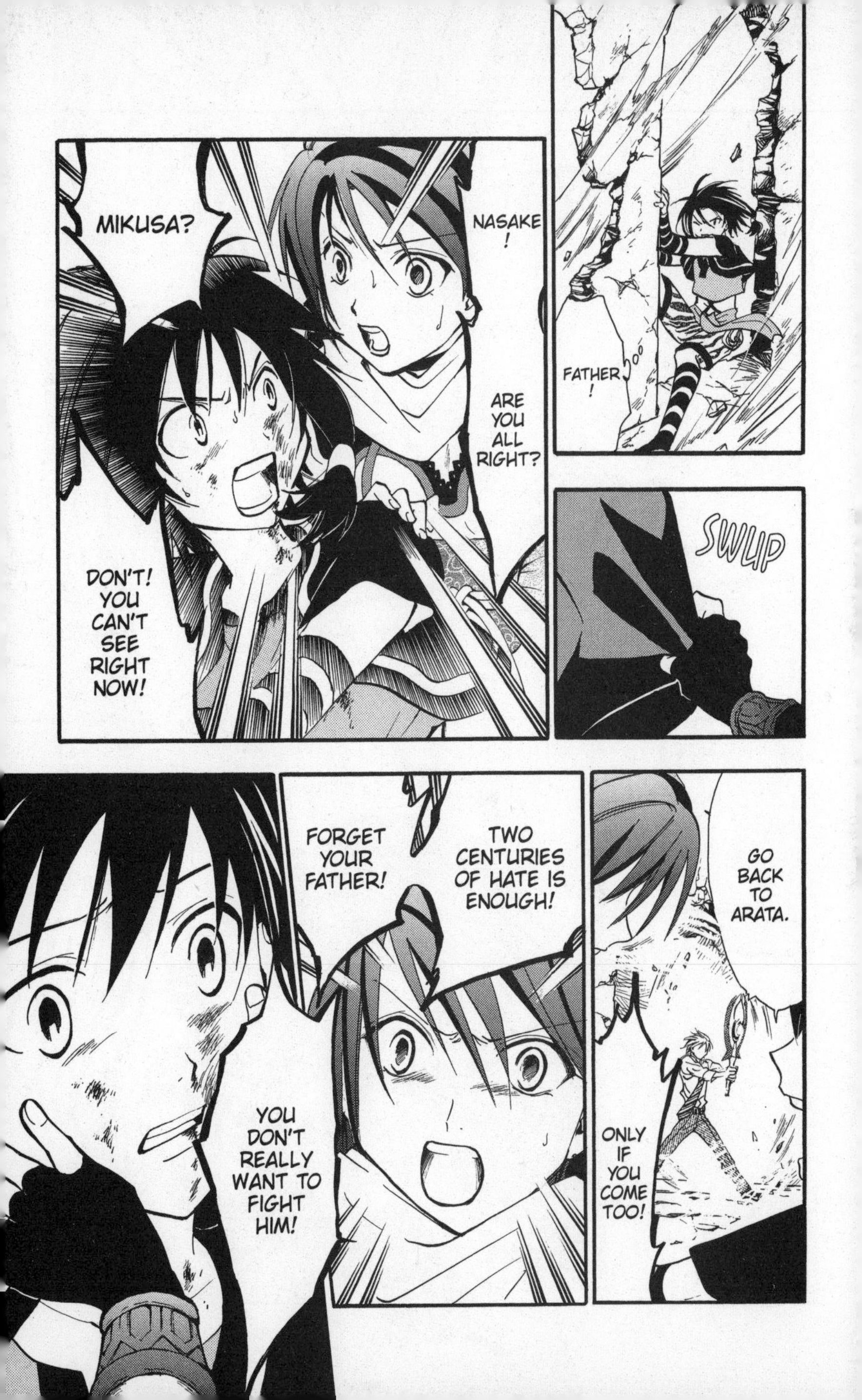
FATHER!
SWUP
NASAKE!
MIKUSA?
ARE YOU ALL RIGHT?
DON'T! YOU CAN'T SEE RIGHT NOW!
GO BACK TO ARATA.
ONLY IF YOU COME TOO!
TWO CENTURIES OF HATE IS ENOUGH!
FORGET YOUR FATHER!
YOU DON'T REALLY WANT TO FIGHT HIM!

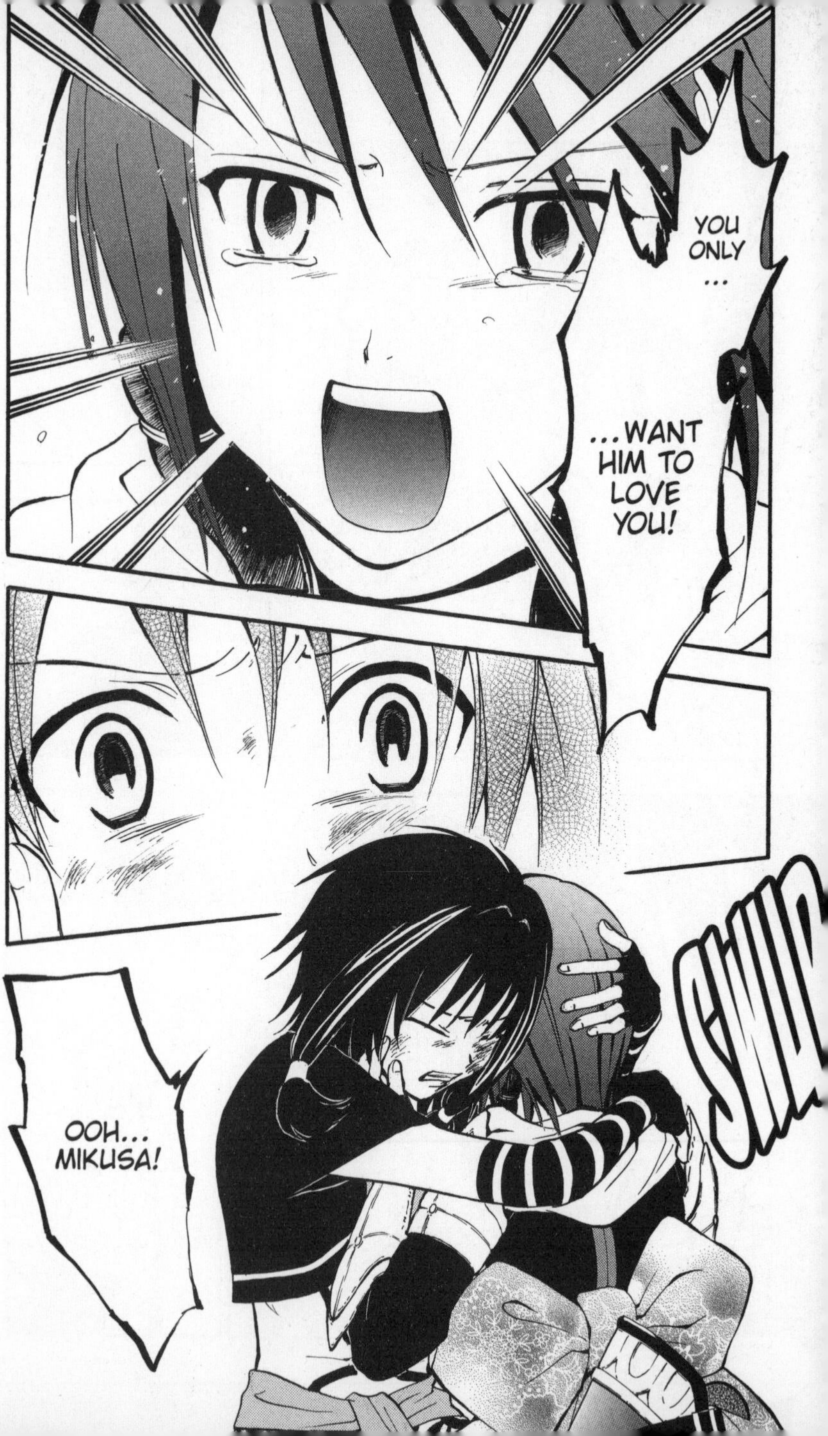
YOU ONLY ...
...WANT HIM TO LOVE YOU!
OOH... MIKUSA!

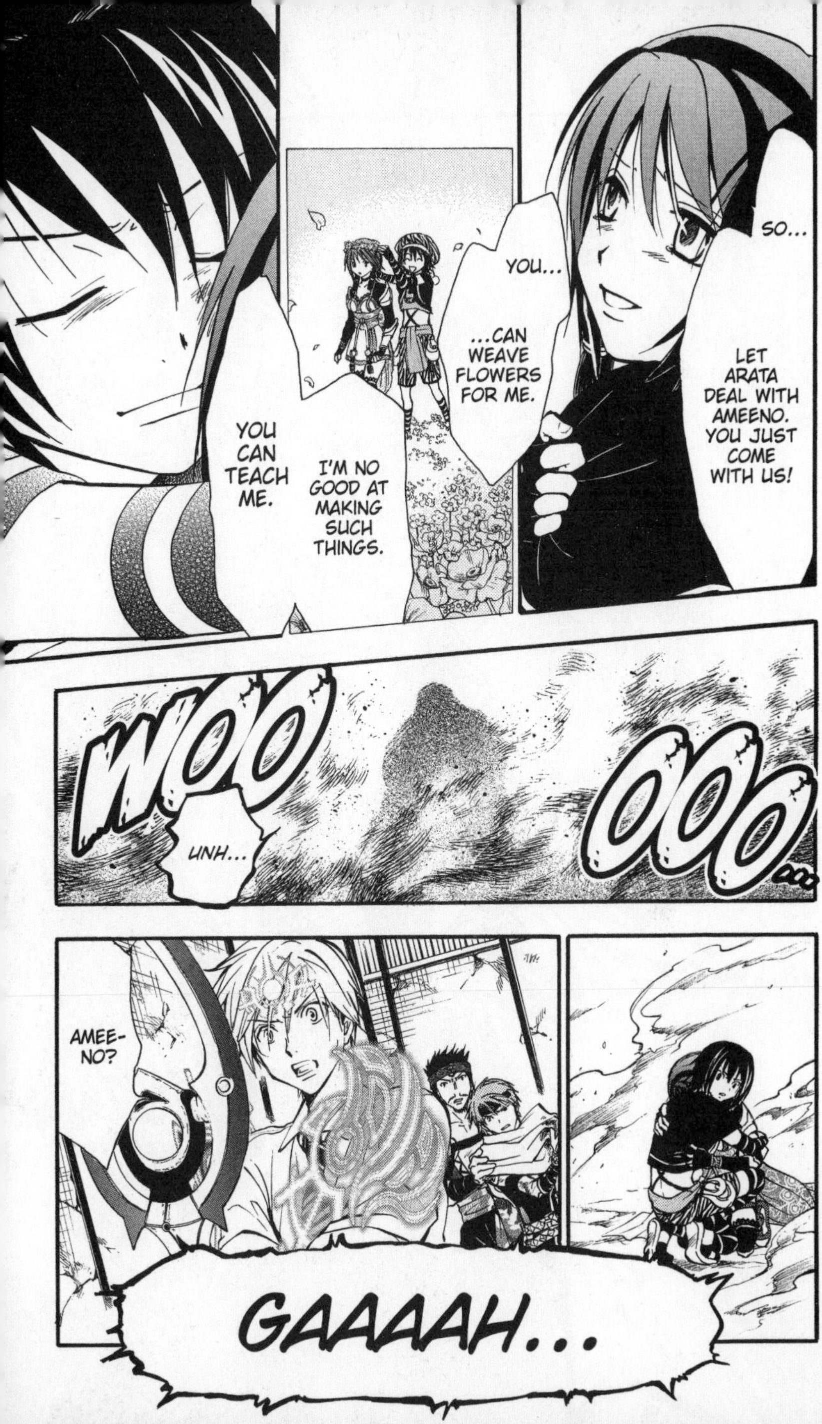
SO...
LET ARATA DEAL WITH AMEENO. YOU JUST COME WITH US!
YOU...
...CAN WEAVE FLOWERS FOR ME.
I'M NO GOOD AT MAKING SUCH THINGS.
YOU CAN TEACH ME.
WOOOOOOO
UNH...
AMEE-NO?
GAAAAH...

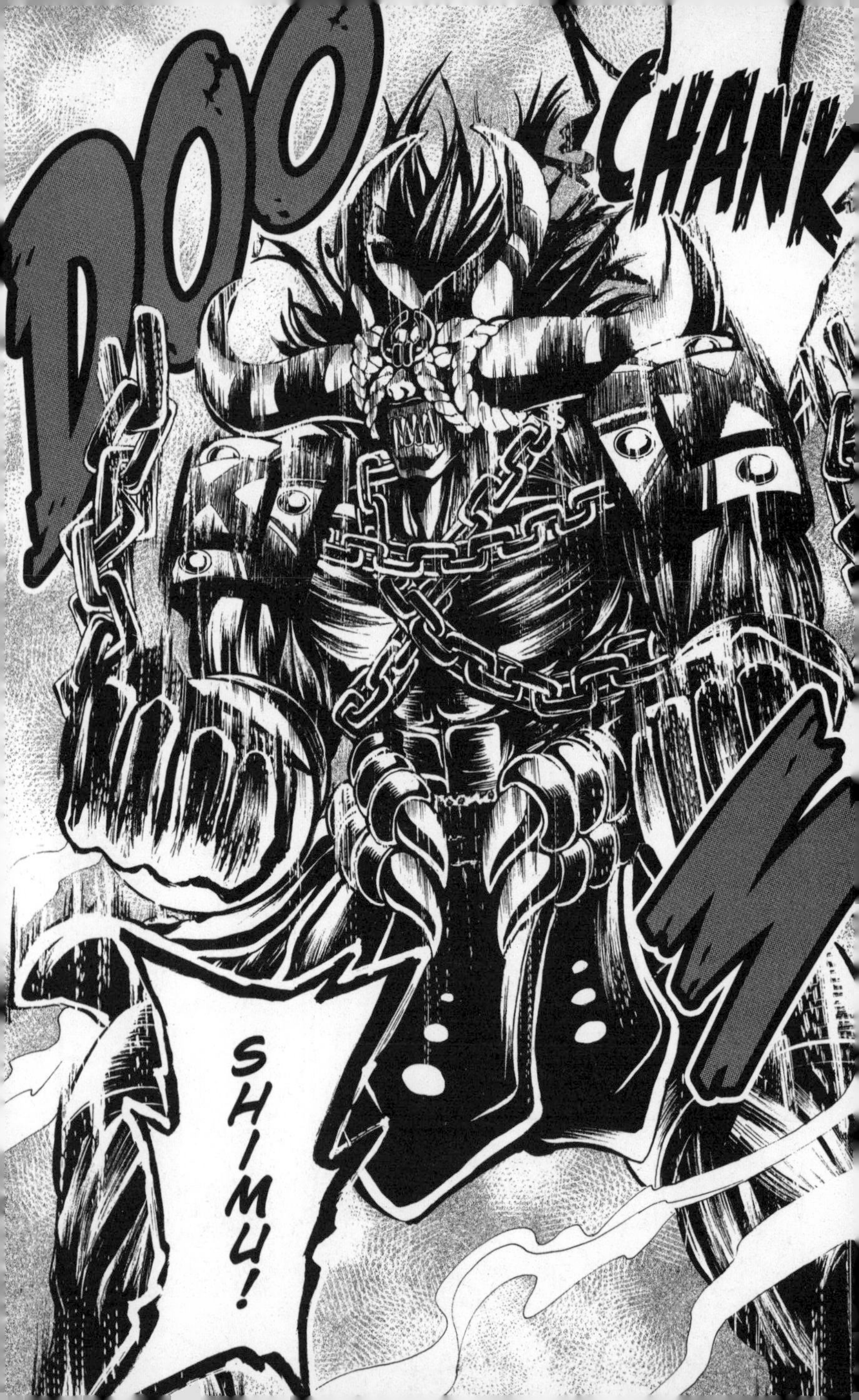
CHANK
DOOO
SHIMU!

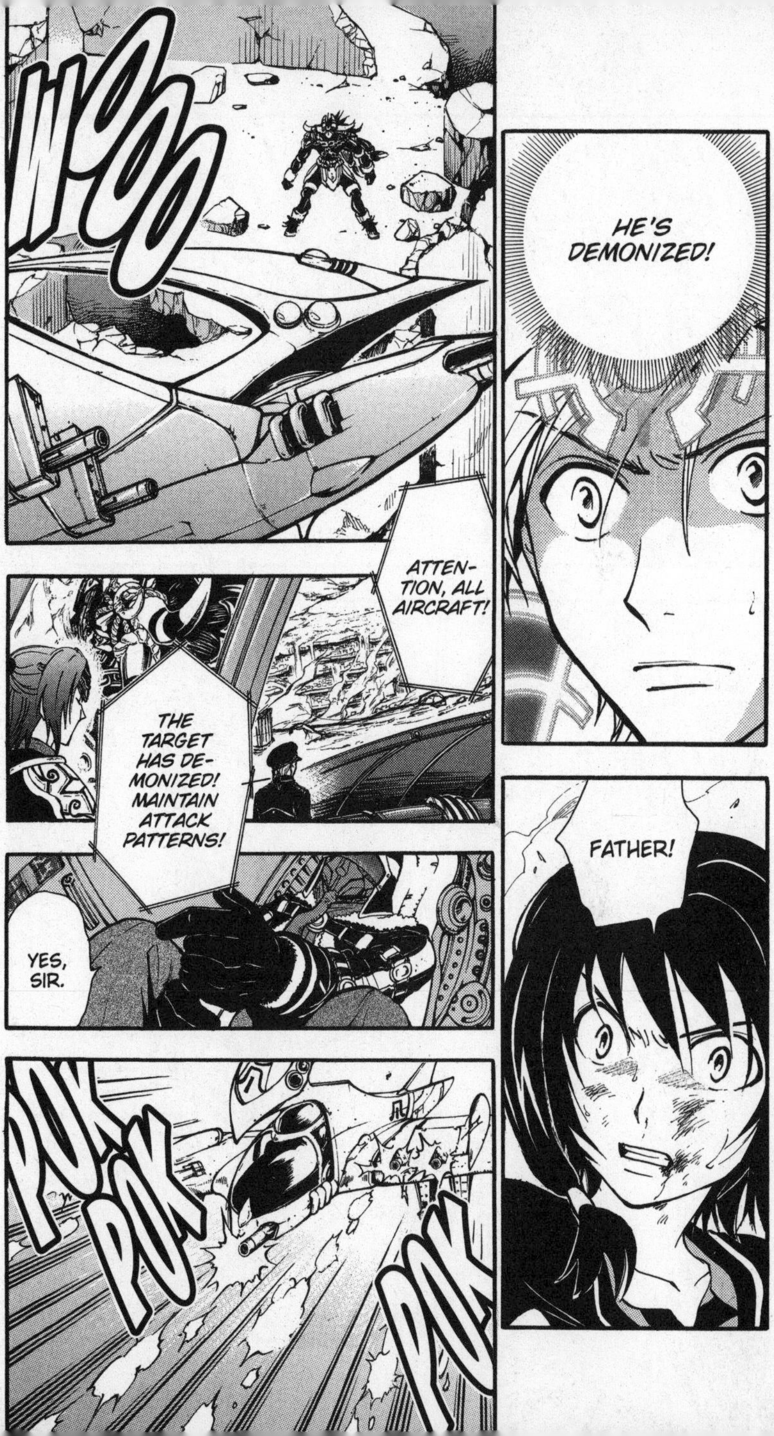
HE'S DEMONIZED!
WOOO
ATTENTION, ALL AIRCRAFT!
THE TARGET HAS DEMONIZED! MAINTAIN ATTACK PATTERNS!
YES, SIR.
FATHER!
POK POK
POK

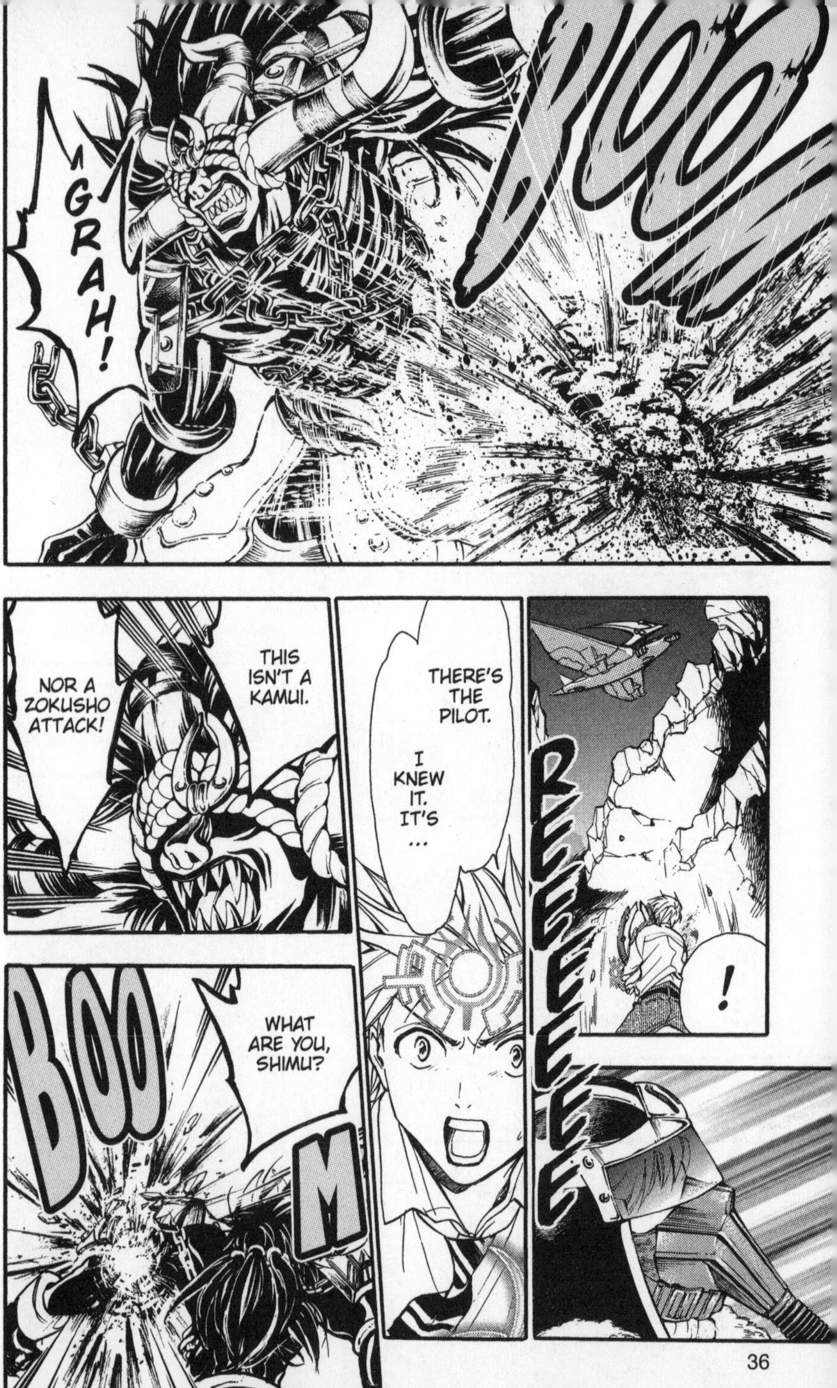
GRAH!
!
THERE'S THE PILOT.
I KNEW IT. IT'S ...
THIS ISN'T A KAMUI.
NOR A ZOKUSHO ATTACK!
WHAT ARE YOU, SHIMU?
BOOM

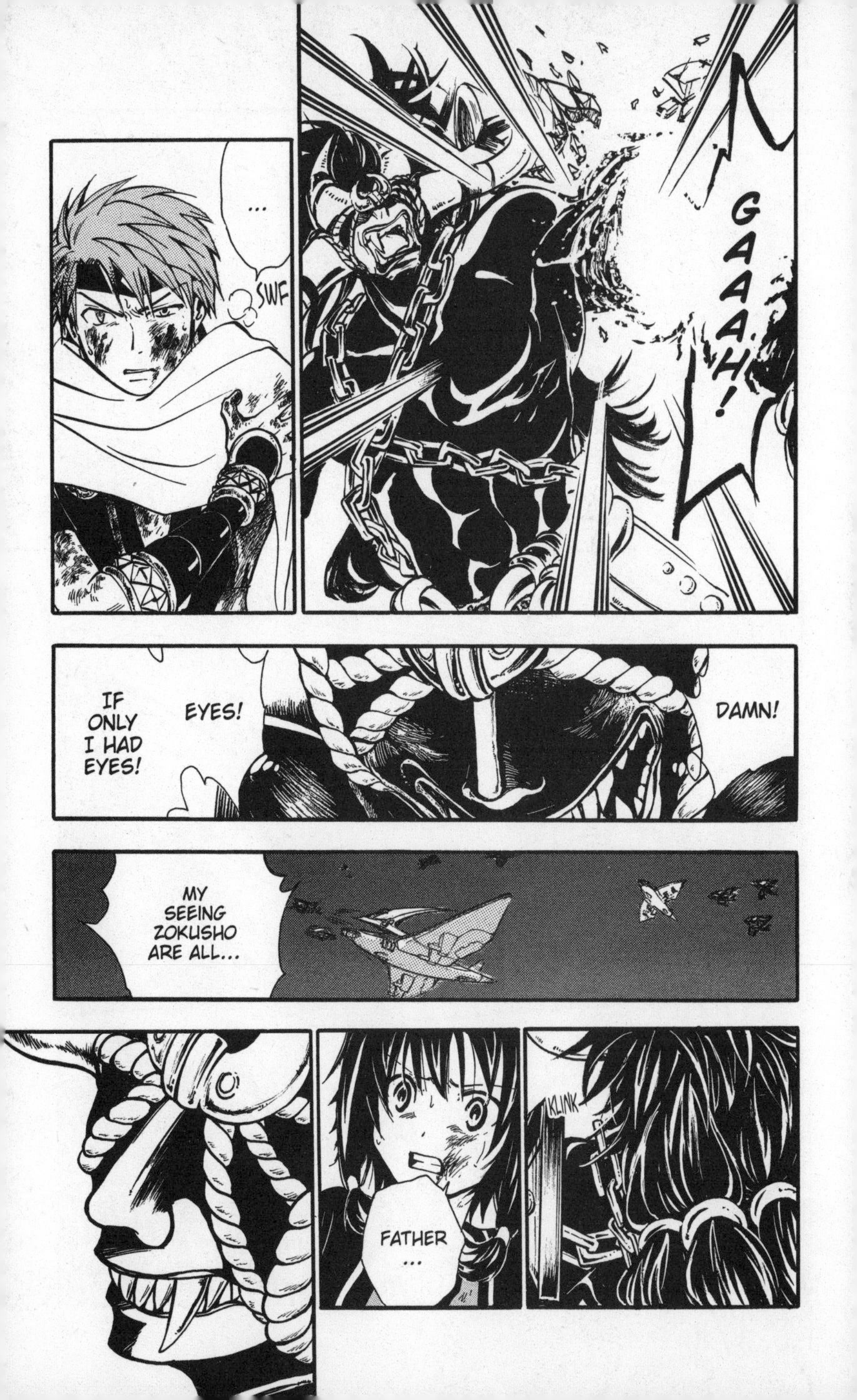
GAAAAH!
...
SWF
DAMN!
EYES!
IF ONLY I HAD EYES!
MY SEEING ZOKUSHO ARE ALL...
KLINK
FATHER ...

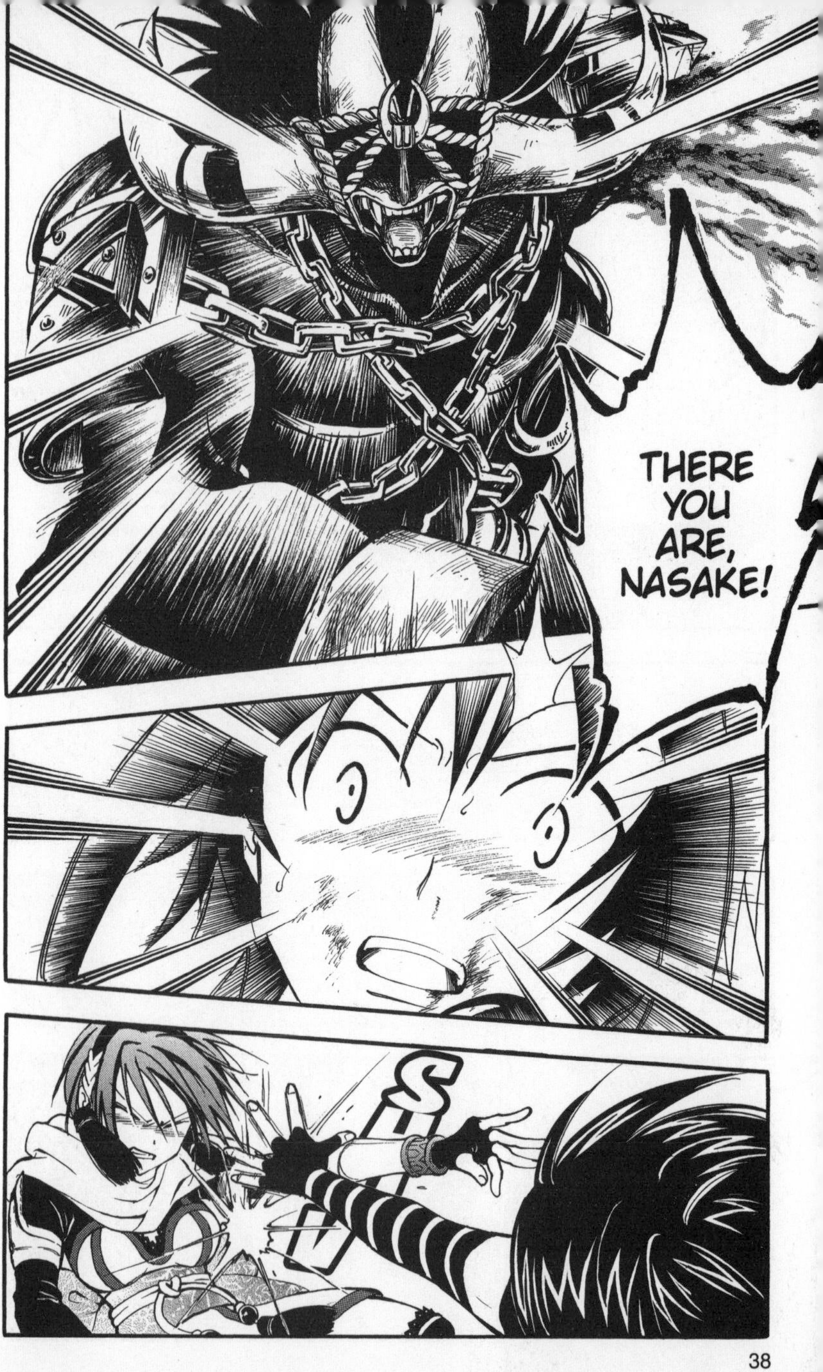
THERE YOU ARE, NASAKE!

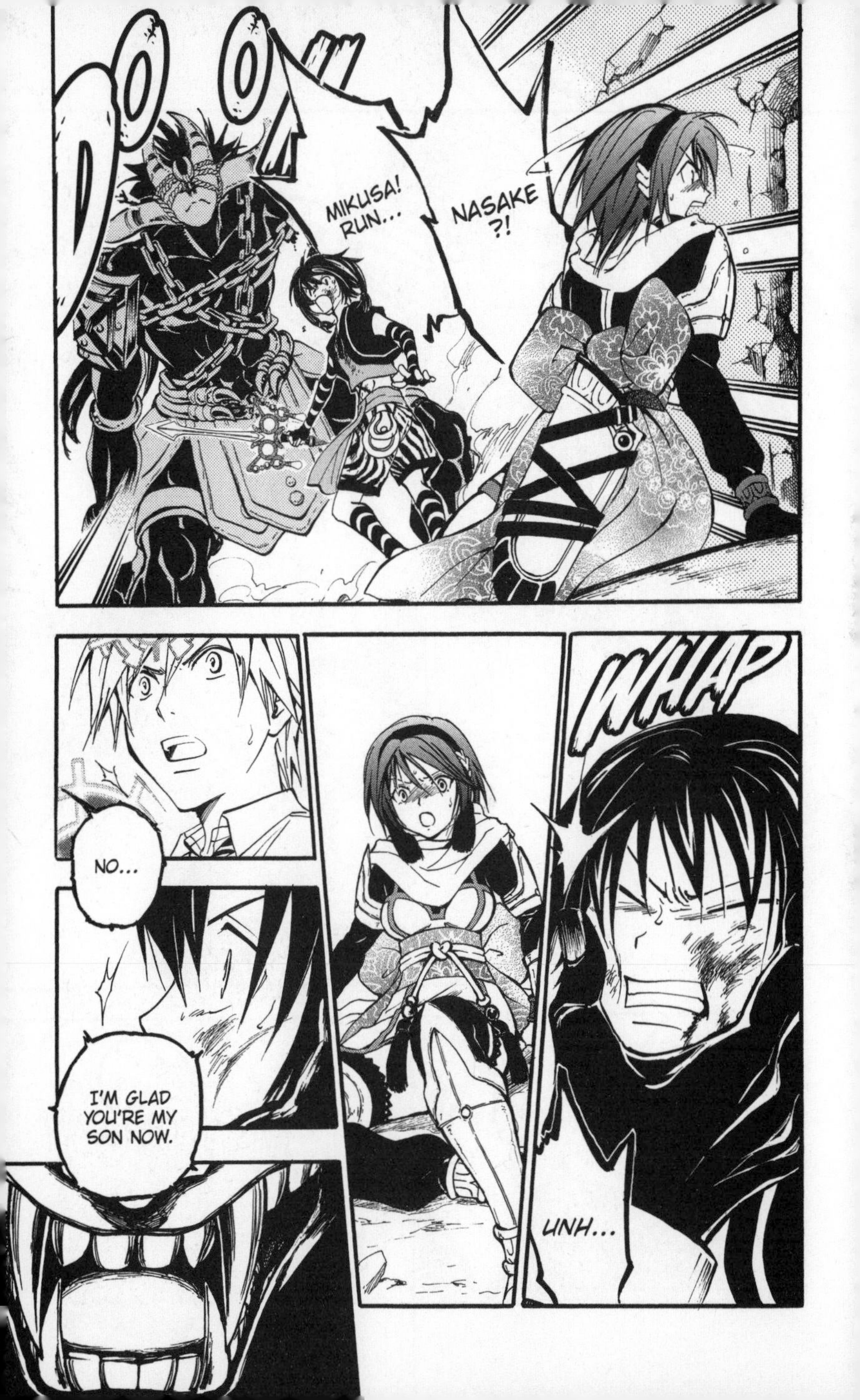
NASAKE ?!
MIKUSA! RUN...
DOO
WHAP
UNH...
NO...
I'M GLAD YOU'RE MY SON NOW.

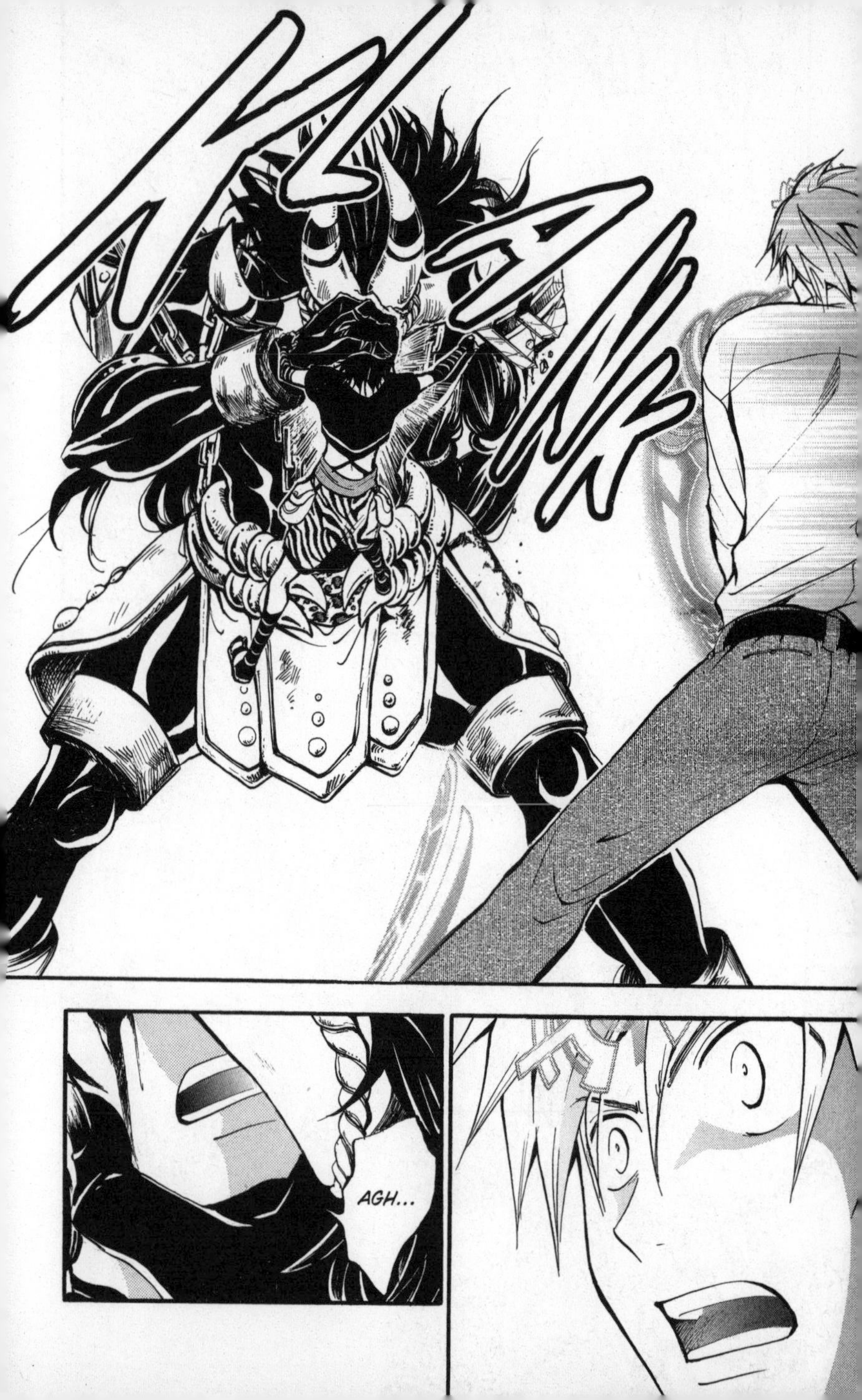
AGH...

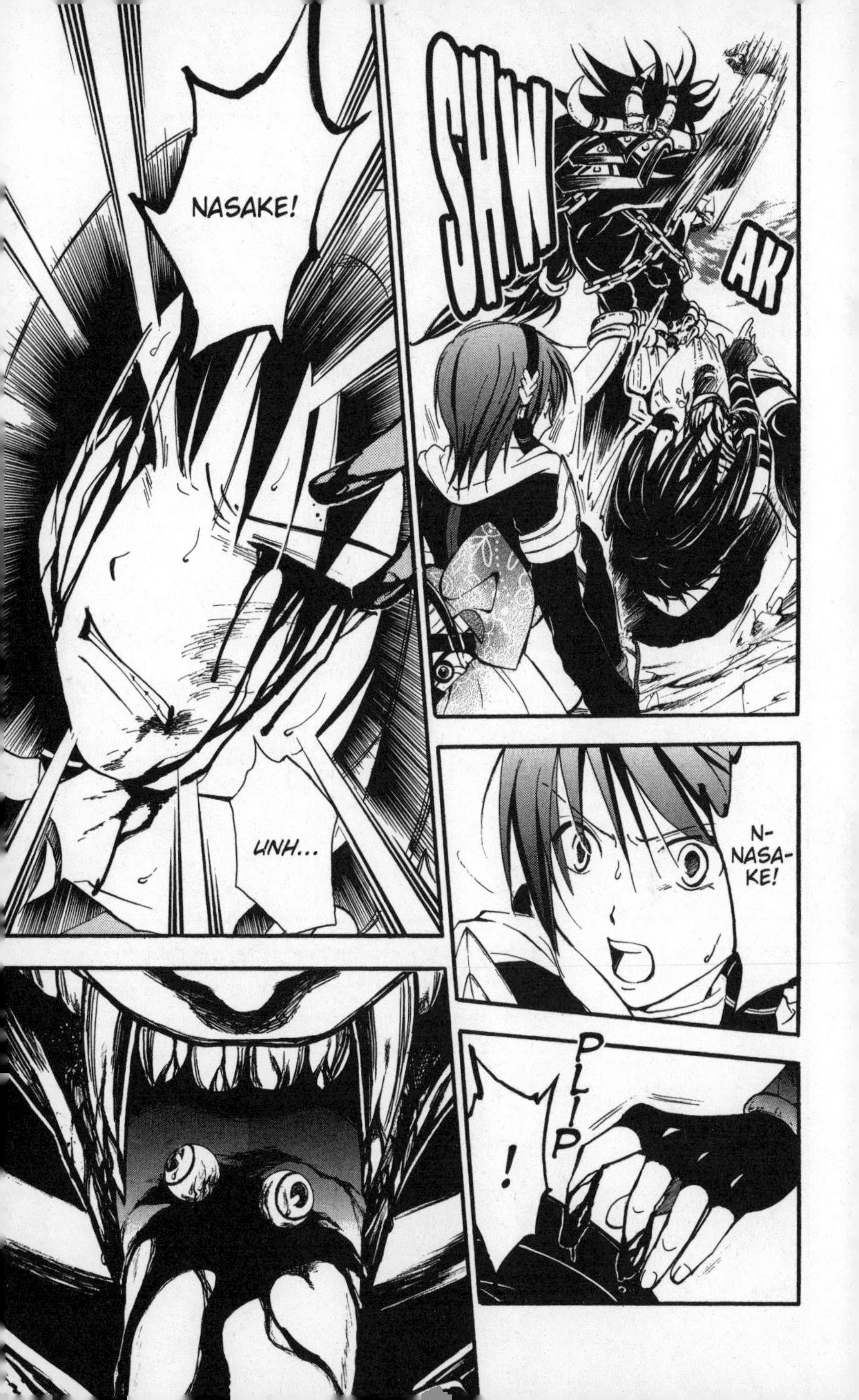
SHWN
AK
NASAKE!
UNH...
N-NASA-KE!
PLIP
!

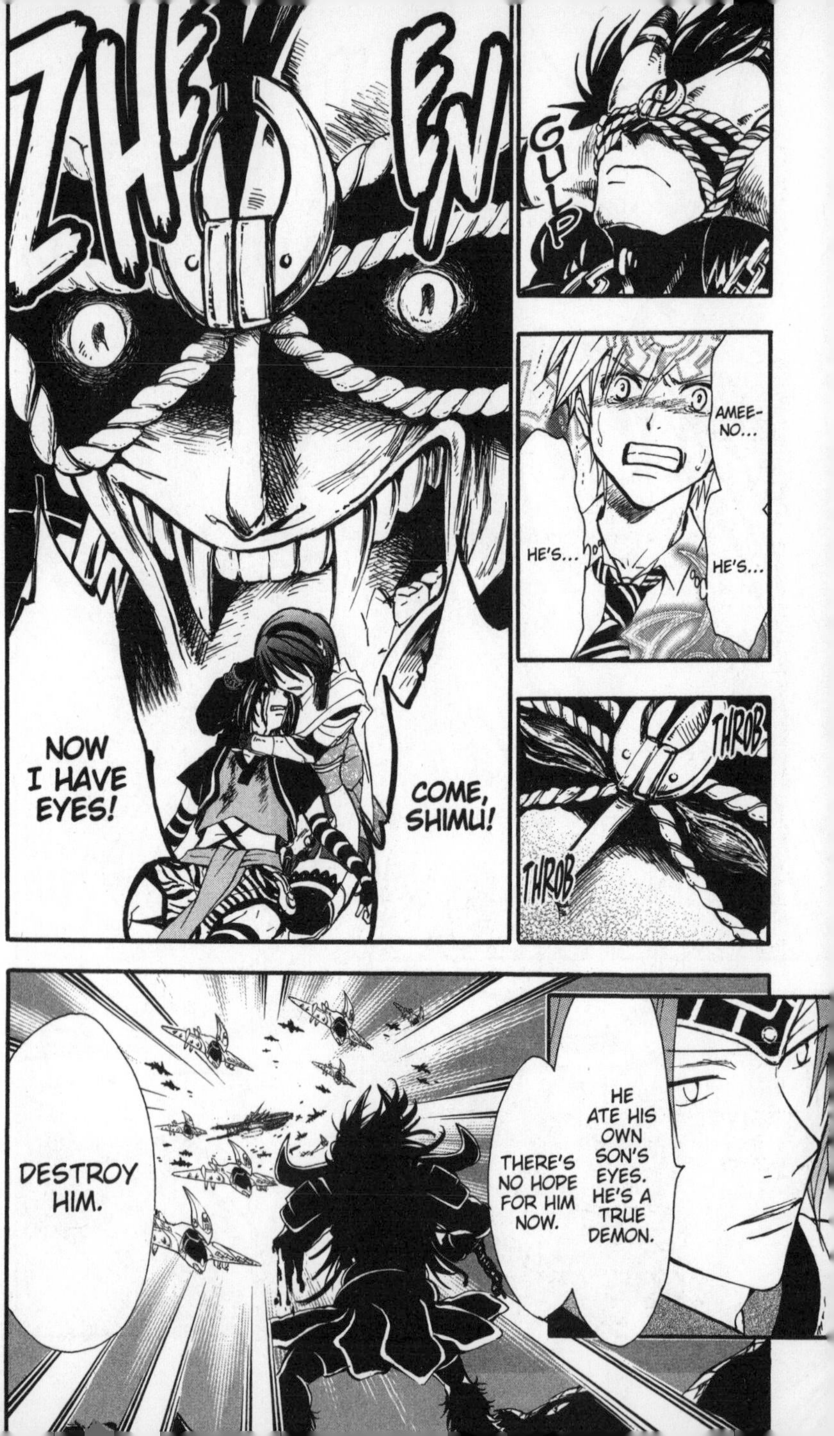
GULP
AMEE-NO...
HE'S...
HE'S...
THROB
THROB
ZHEEN
COME, SHIMU!
NOW I HAVE EYES!
HE ATE HIS OWN SON'S EYES. HE'S A TRUE DEMON.
THERE'S NO HOPE FOR HIM NOW.
DESTROY HIM.

Chapter.230
WARMTH

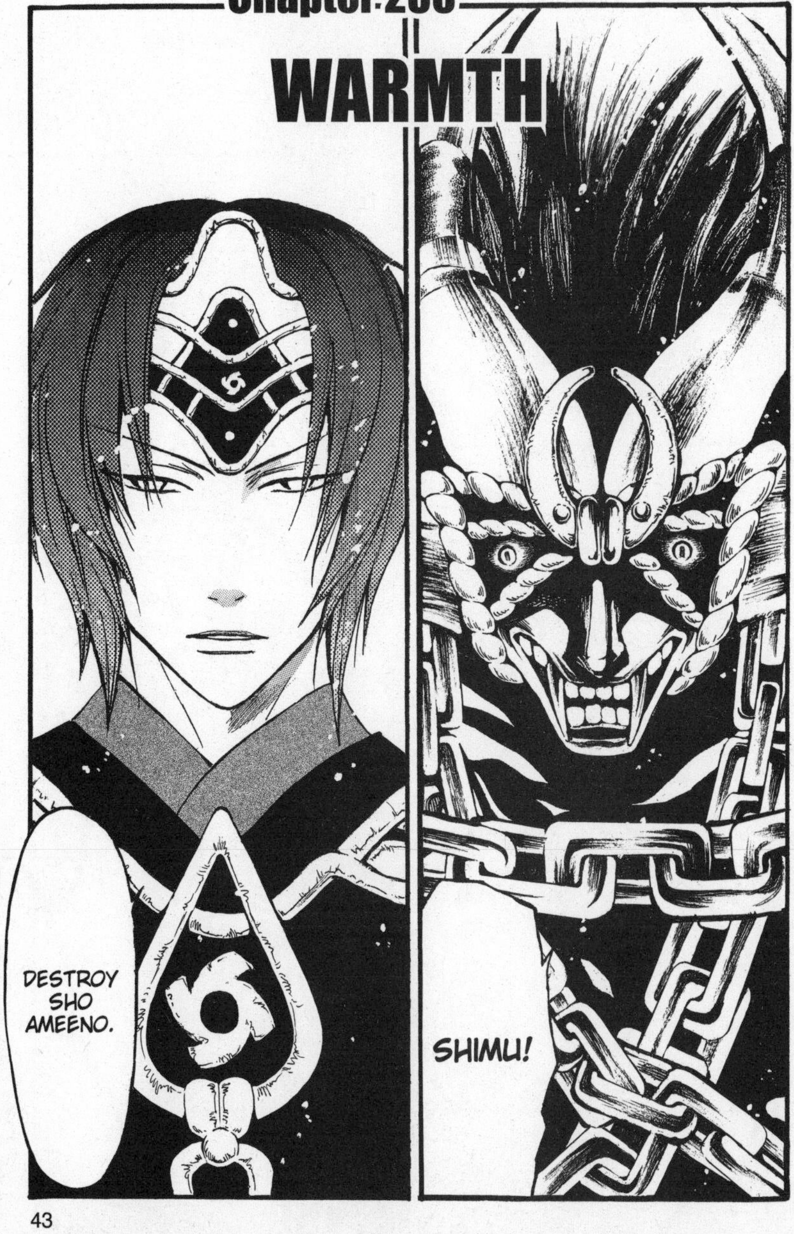
SHIMU!
DESTROY SHO AMEENO.

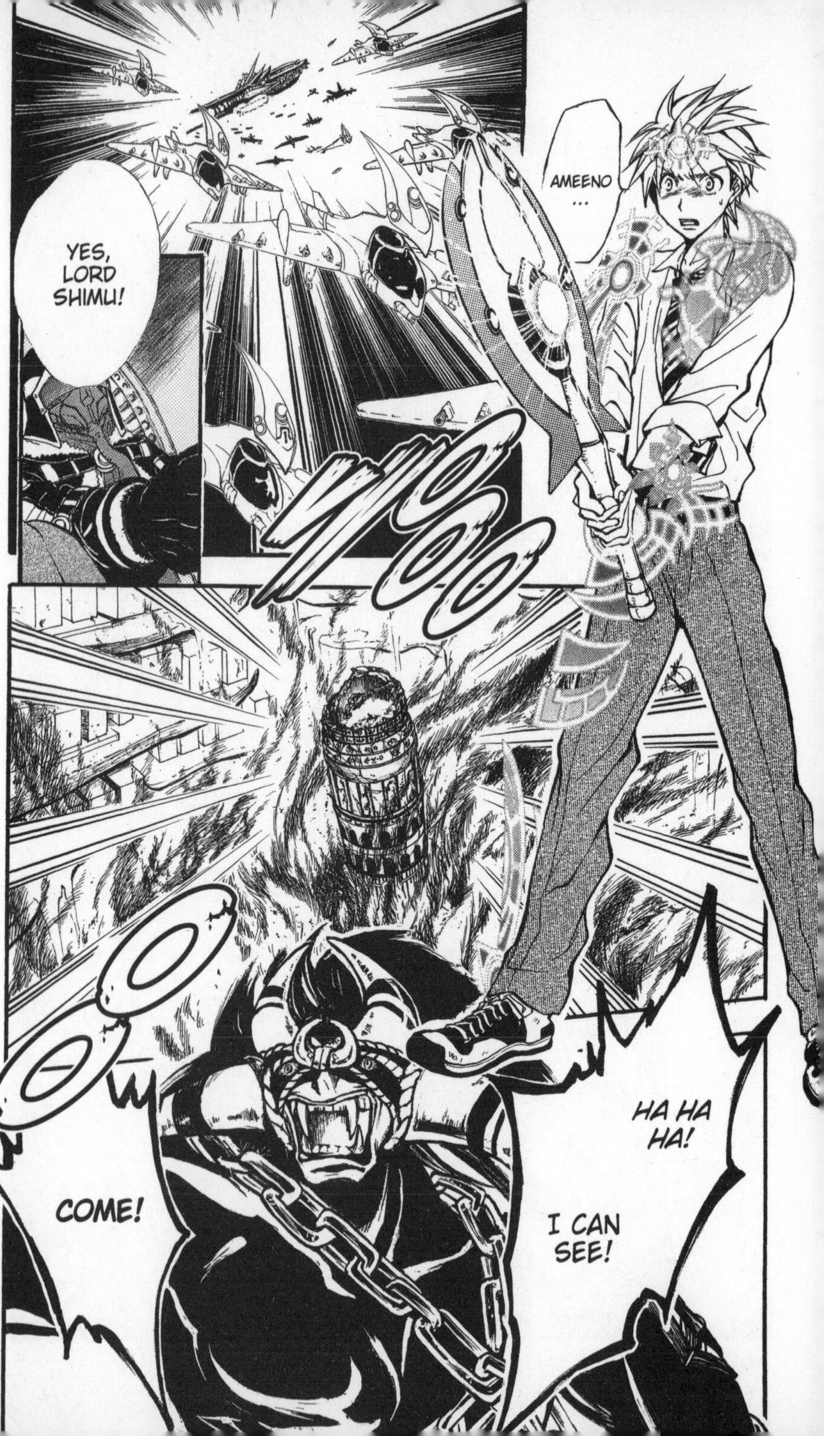
AMEENO ...
YES, LORD SHIMU!
HA HA HA!
I CAN SEE!
COME!

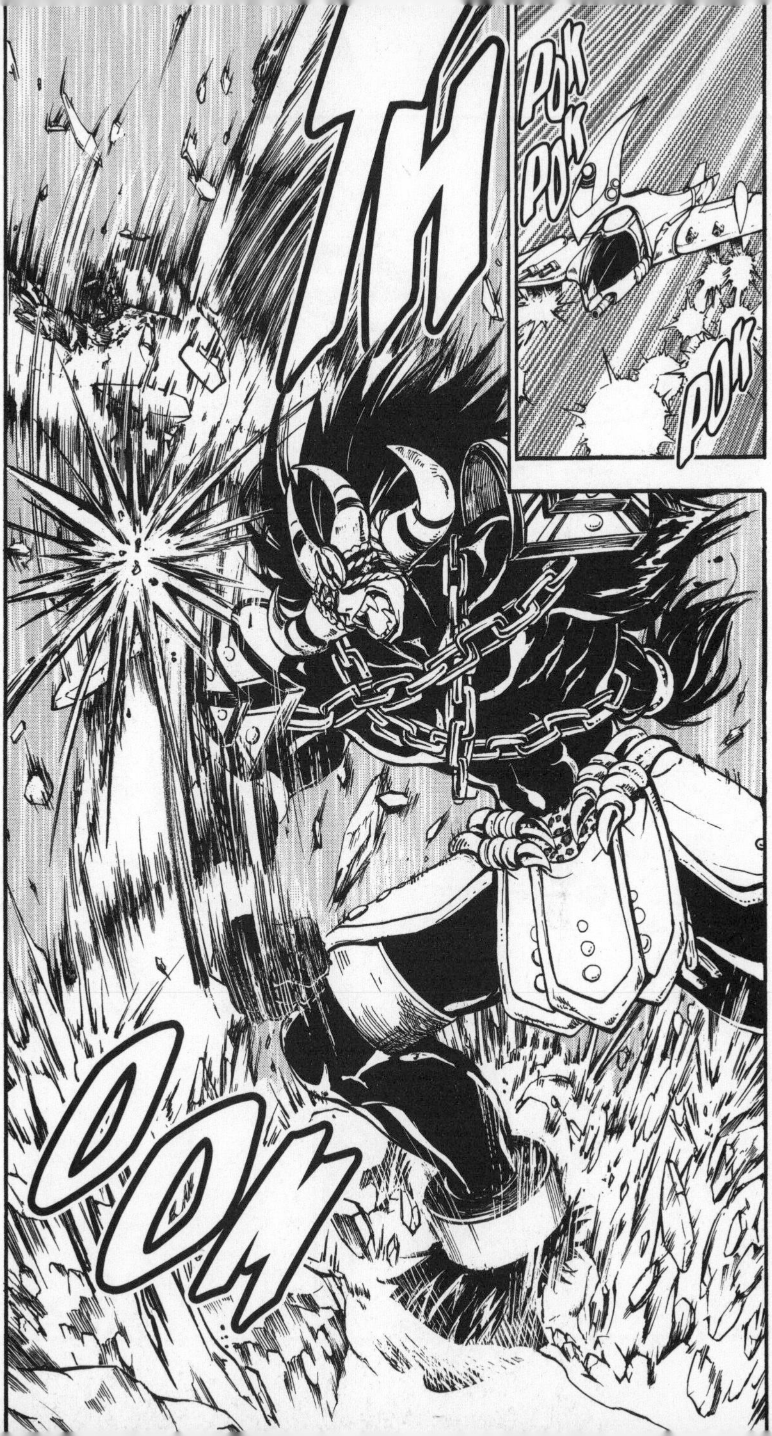
POK POK
POK
TH
DOOM

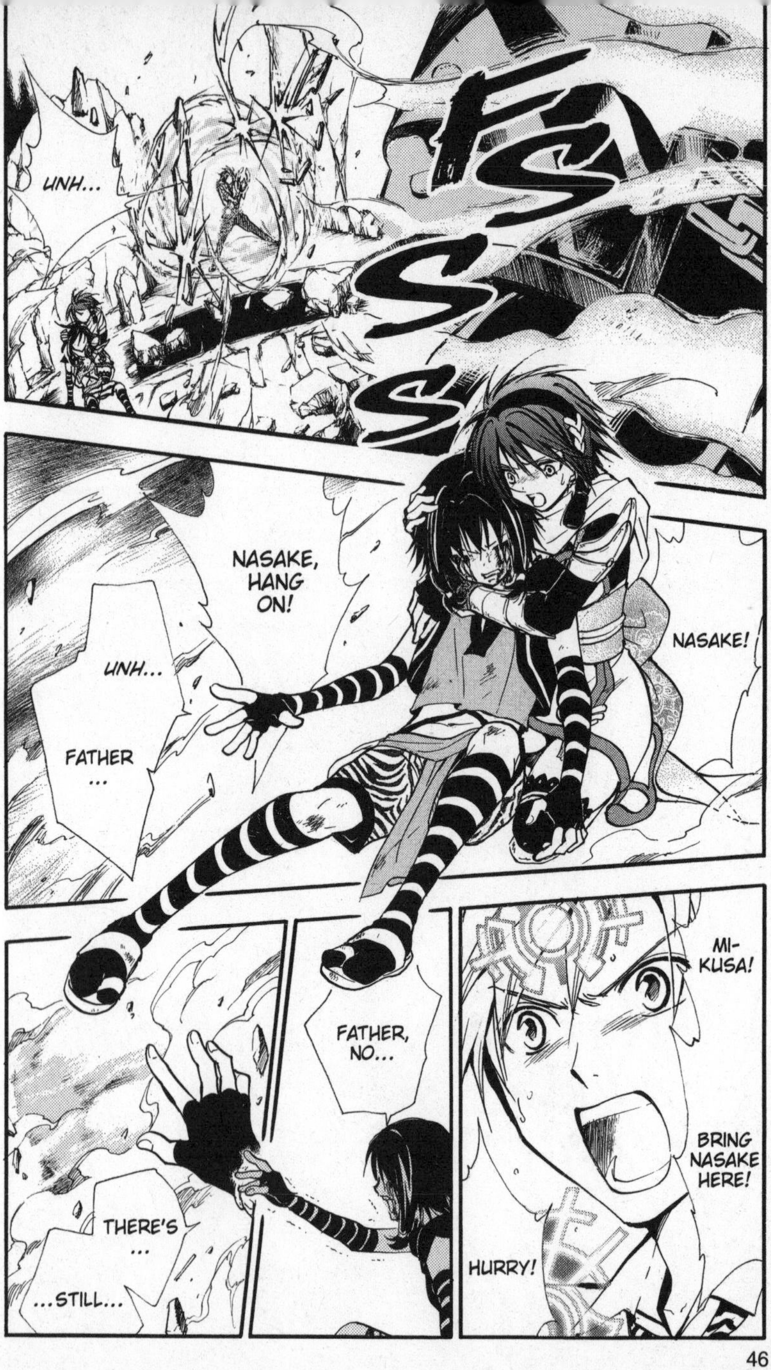
FSSS
UNH...
NASAKE!
NASAKE, HANG ON!
UNH...
FATHER ...
MI-KUSA!
BRING NASAKE HERE!
HURRY!
FATHER, NO...
THERE'S ...
...STILL...

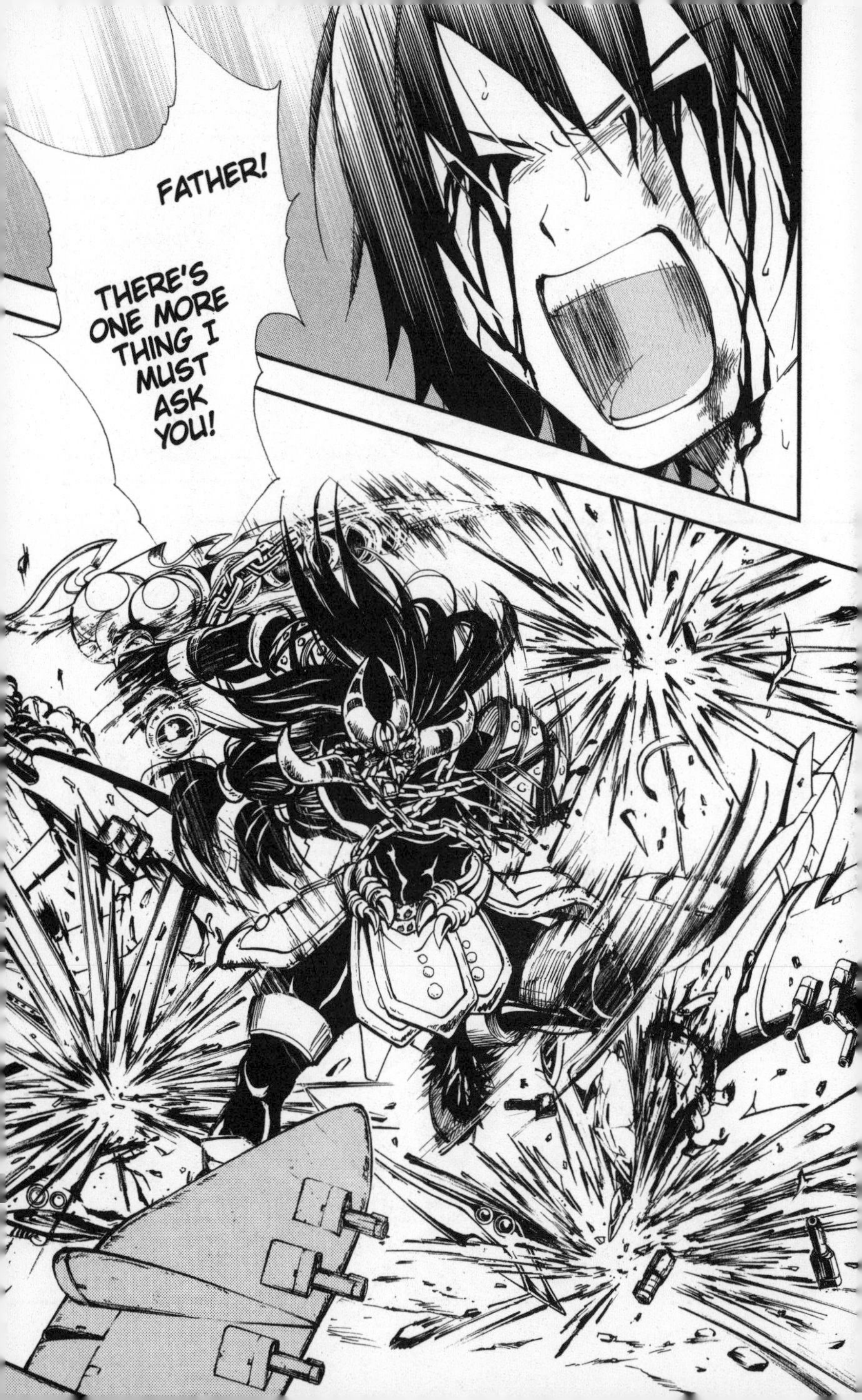
FATHER!
THERE'S ONE MORE THING I MUST ASK YOU!

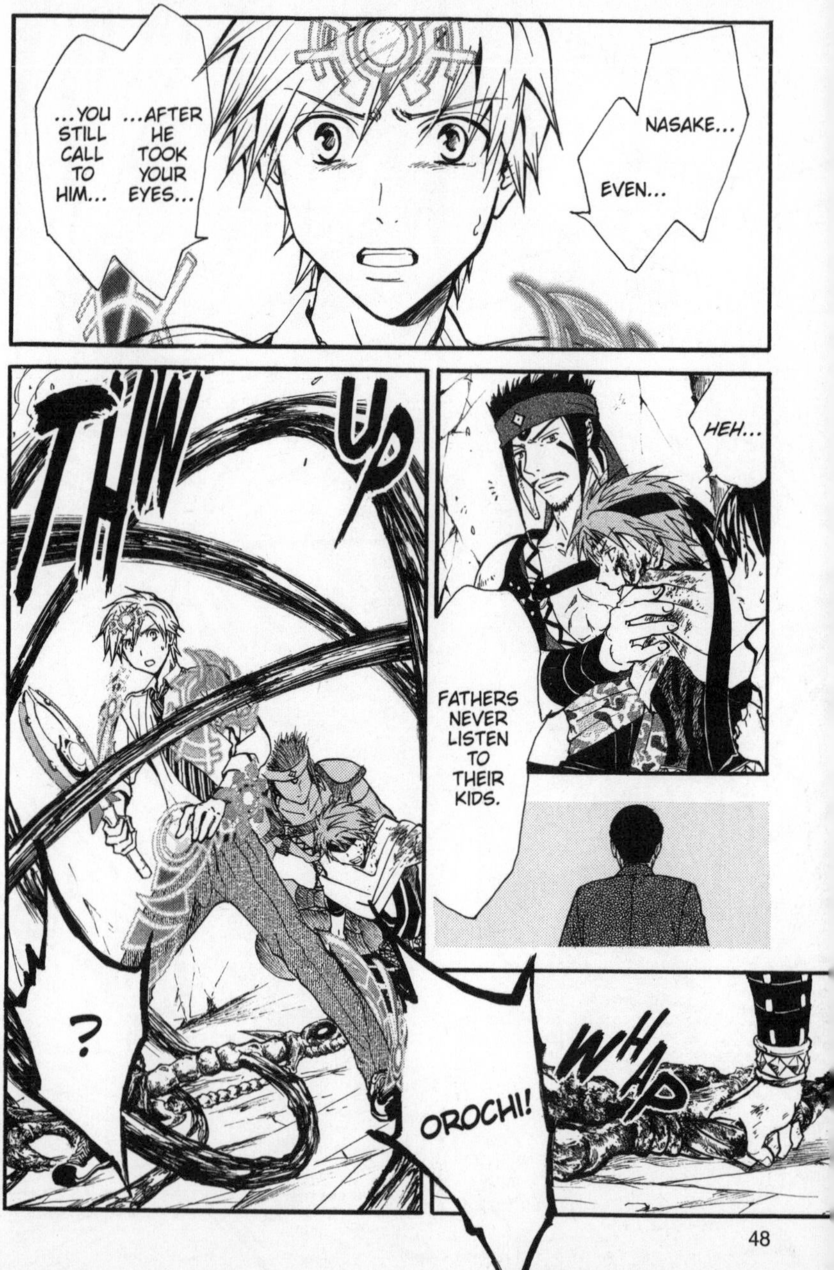
NASAKE...
EVEN...
...AFTER HE TOOK YOUR EYES...
...YOU STILL CALL TO HIM...
HEH...
FATHERS NEVER LISTEN TO THEIR KIDS.
WHAP
OROCHI!
THWUP
?

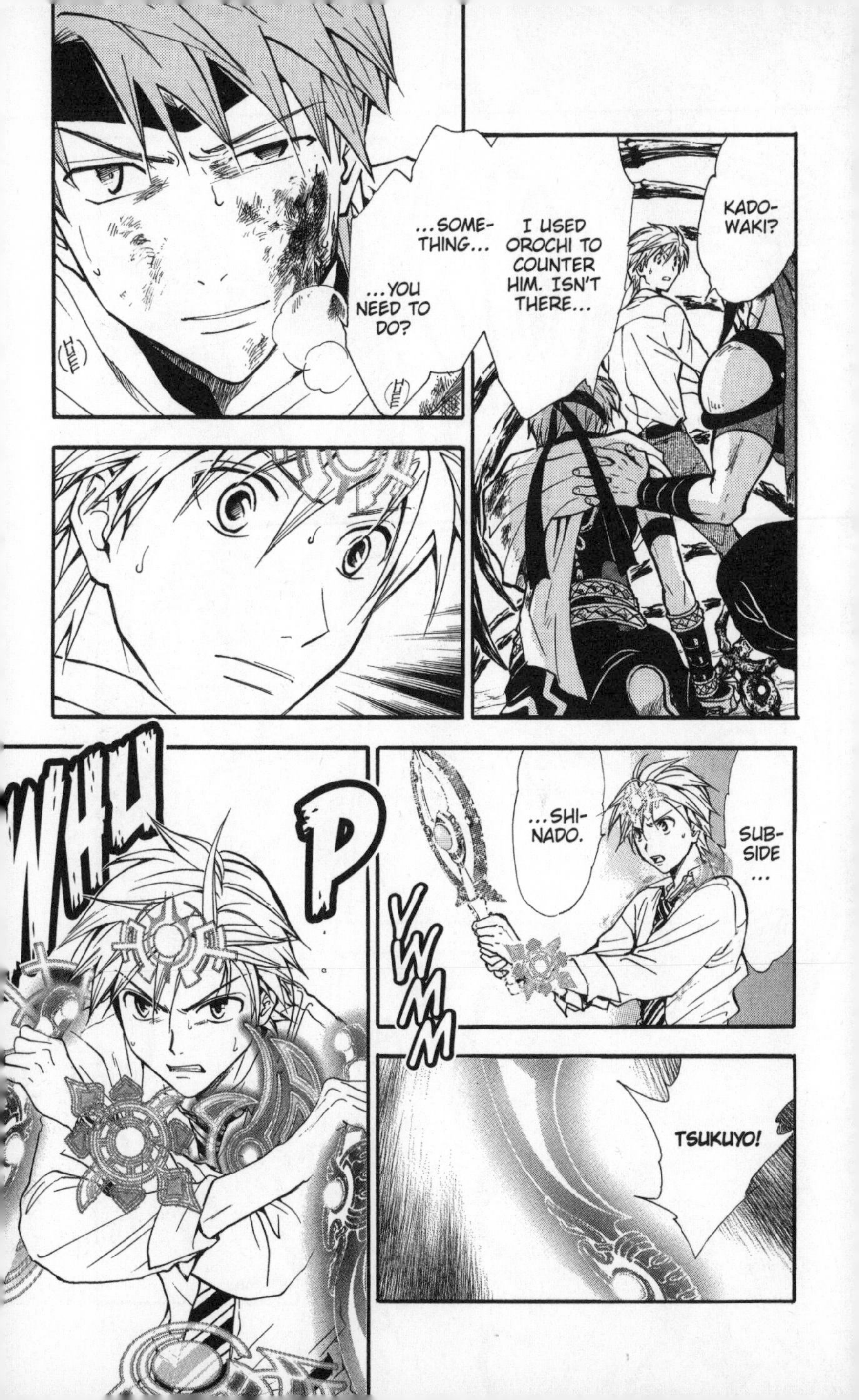
KADO-WAKI?
I USED OROCHI TO COUNTER HIM. ISN'T THERE...
...SOME-THING...
...YOU NEED TO DO?
SUB-SIDE...
...SHI-NADO.
VWMM
TSUKUYO!
WHUP

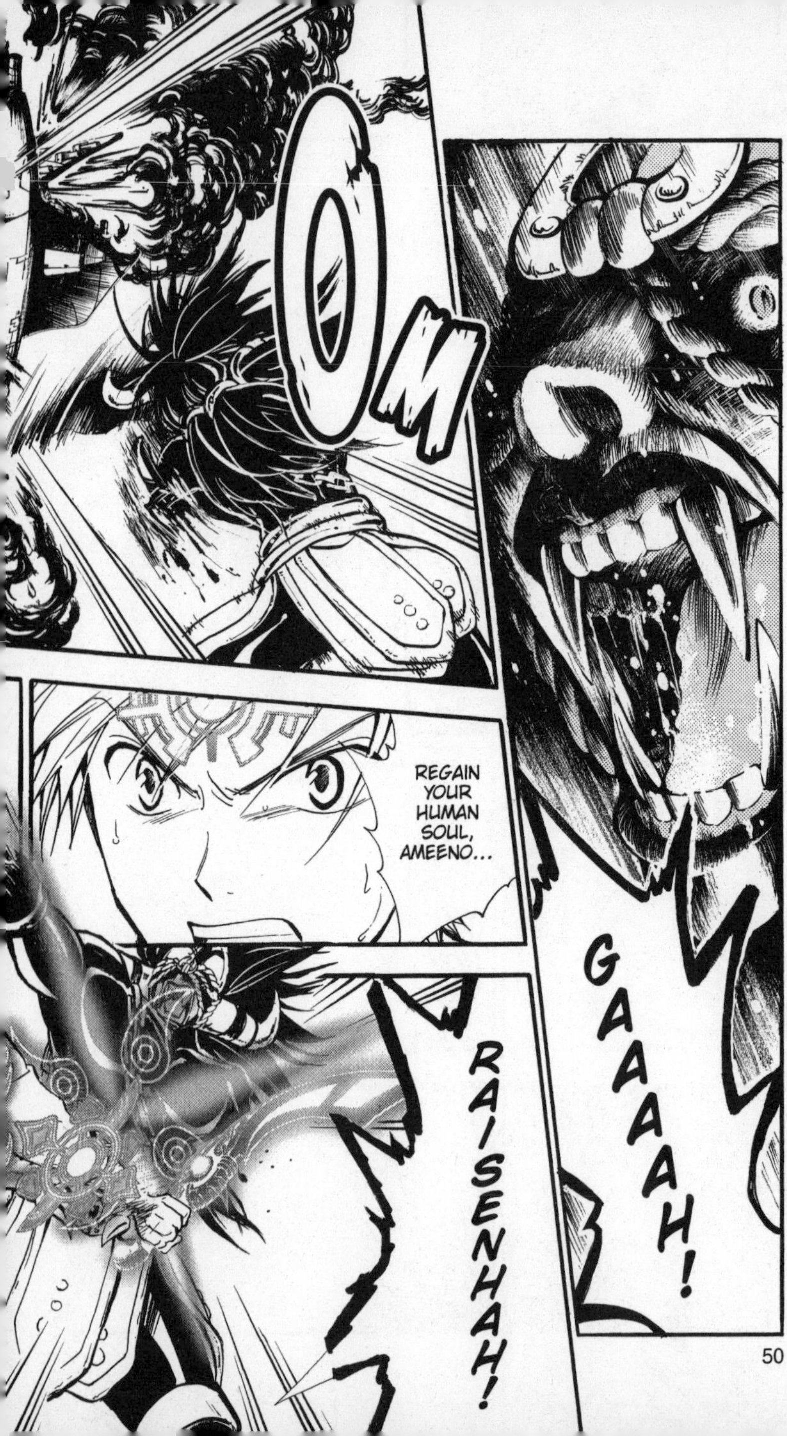
GAAAAH!
OOM
REGAIN YOUR HUMAN SOUL, AMEENO...
RAISENHAH!

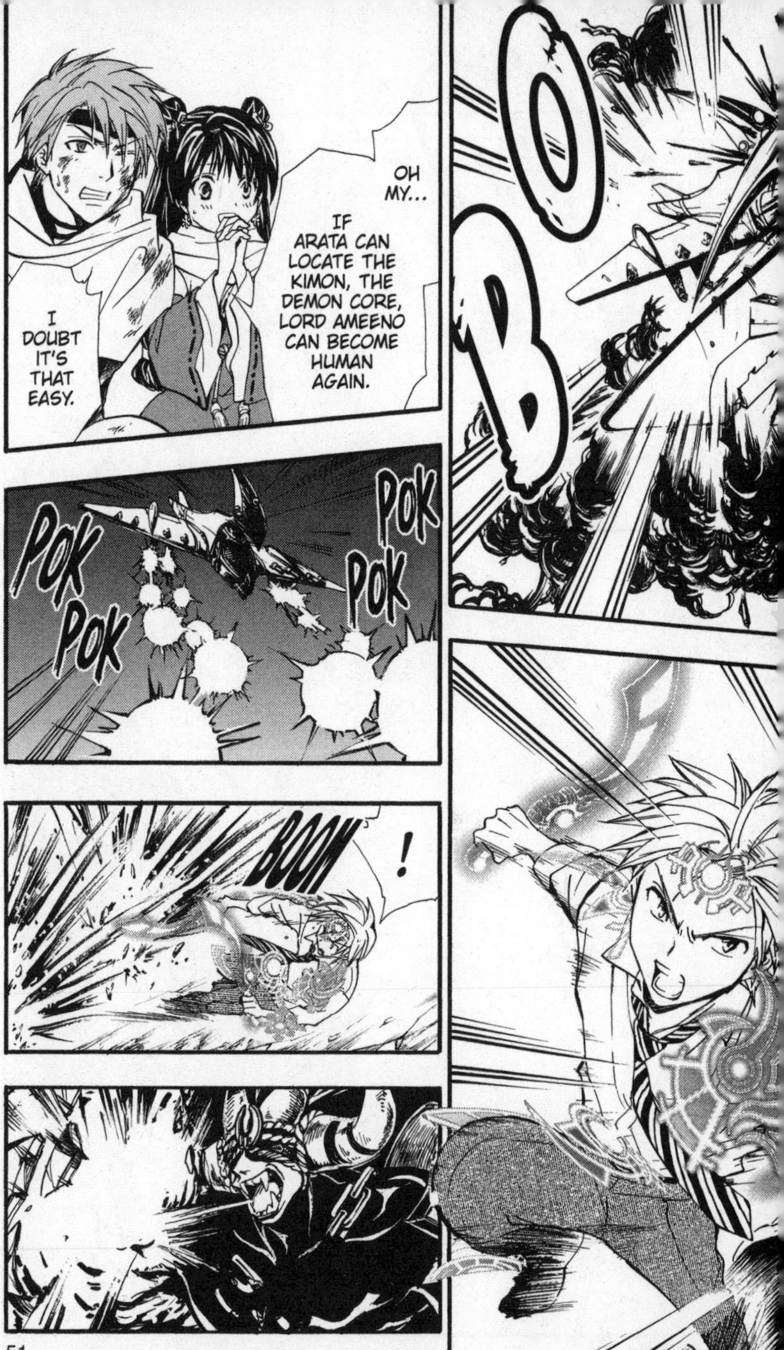
BOO
OH MY...
IF ARATA CAN LOCATE THE KIMON, THE DEMON CORE, LORD AMEENO CAN BECOME HUMAN AGAIN.
I DOUBT IT'S THAT EASY.
POK POK
POK POK
BOOM
!

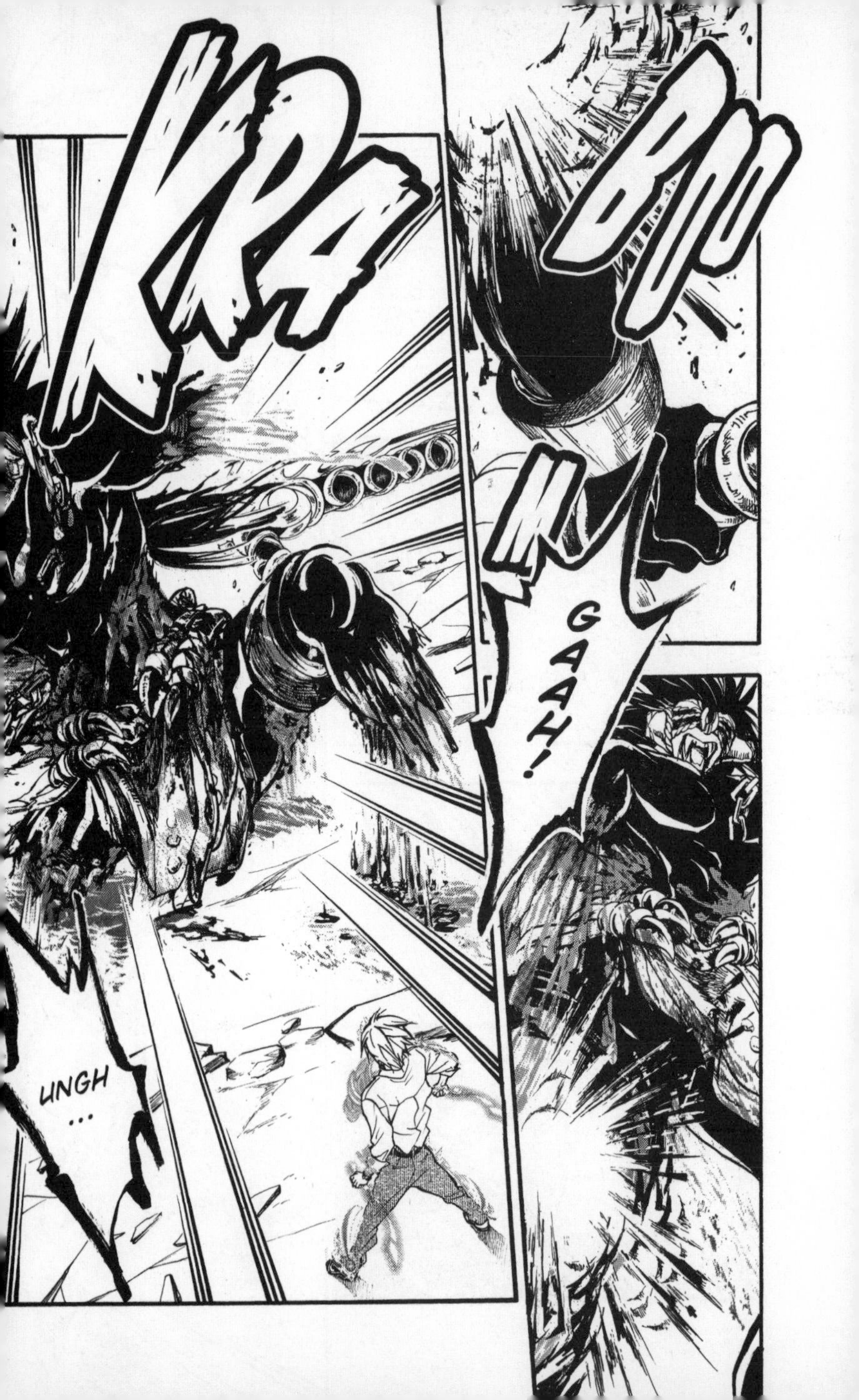
GAAH!
UNGH ...

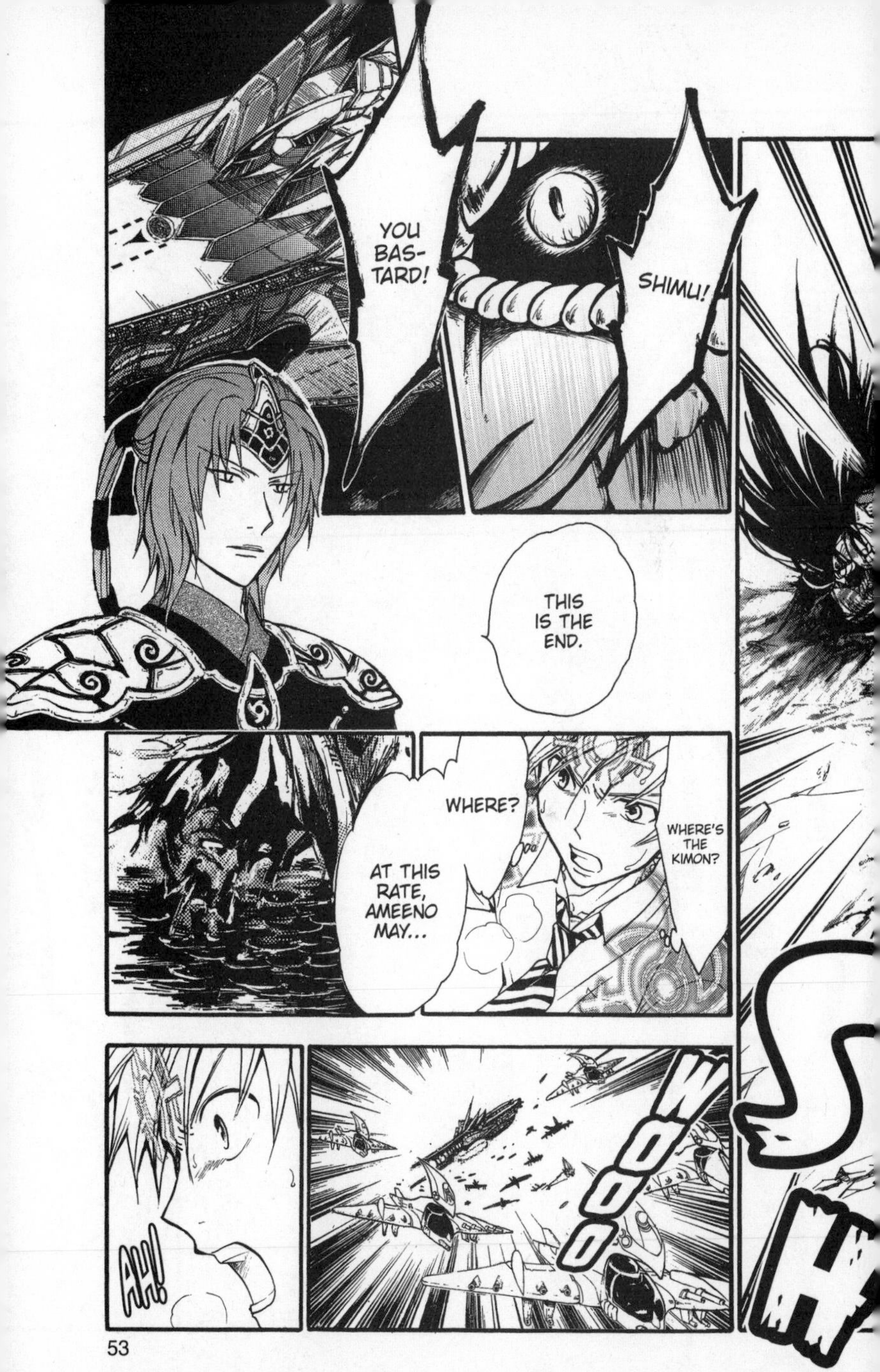
SHIMU!
YOU BAS-TARD!
THIS IS THE END.
WHERE'S THE KIMON?
WHERE?
AT THIS RATE, AMEENO MAY...
WOOOO
AH!

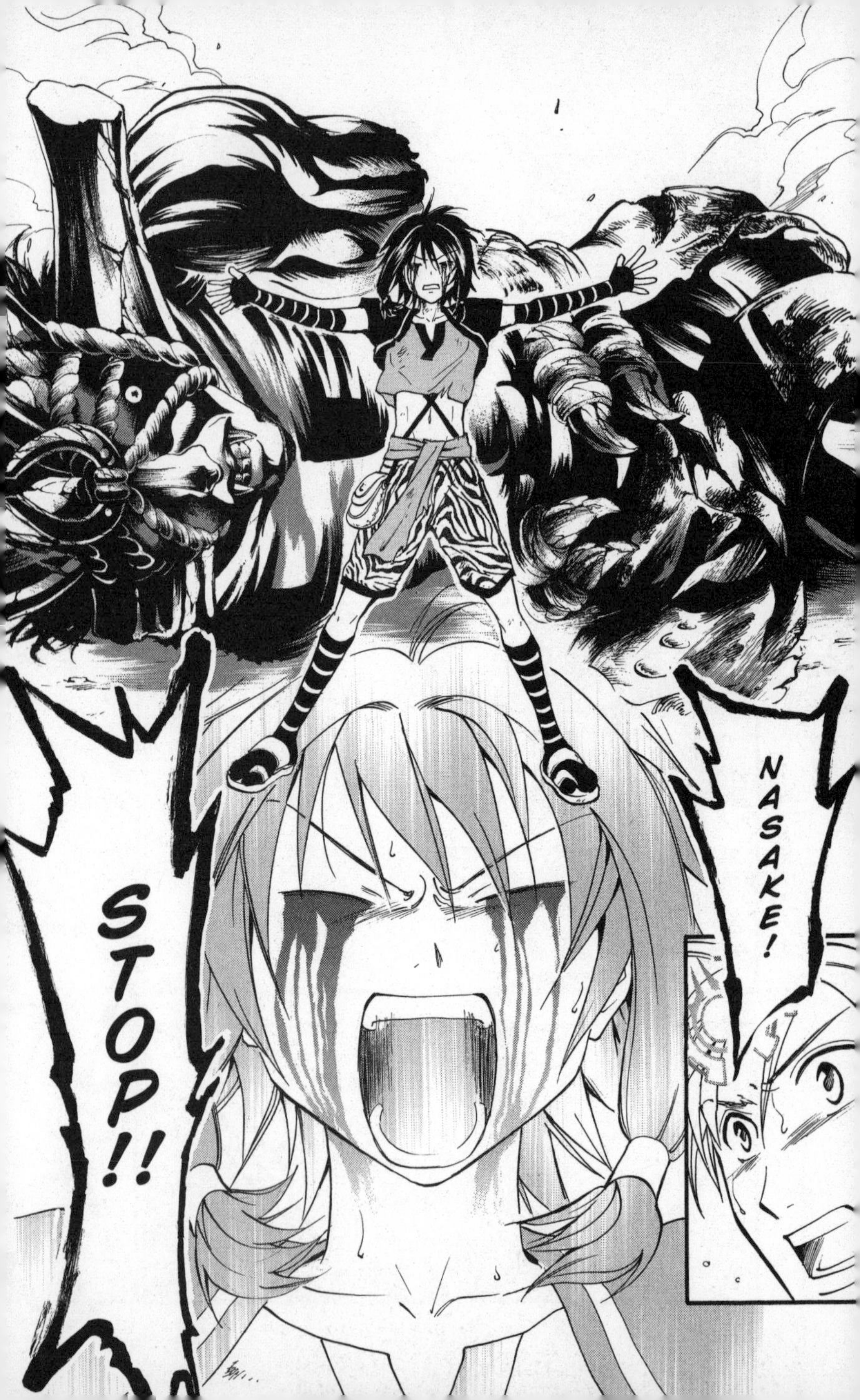
NASAKE!
STOP!!

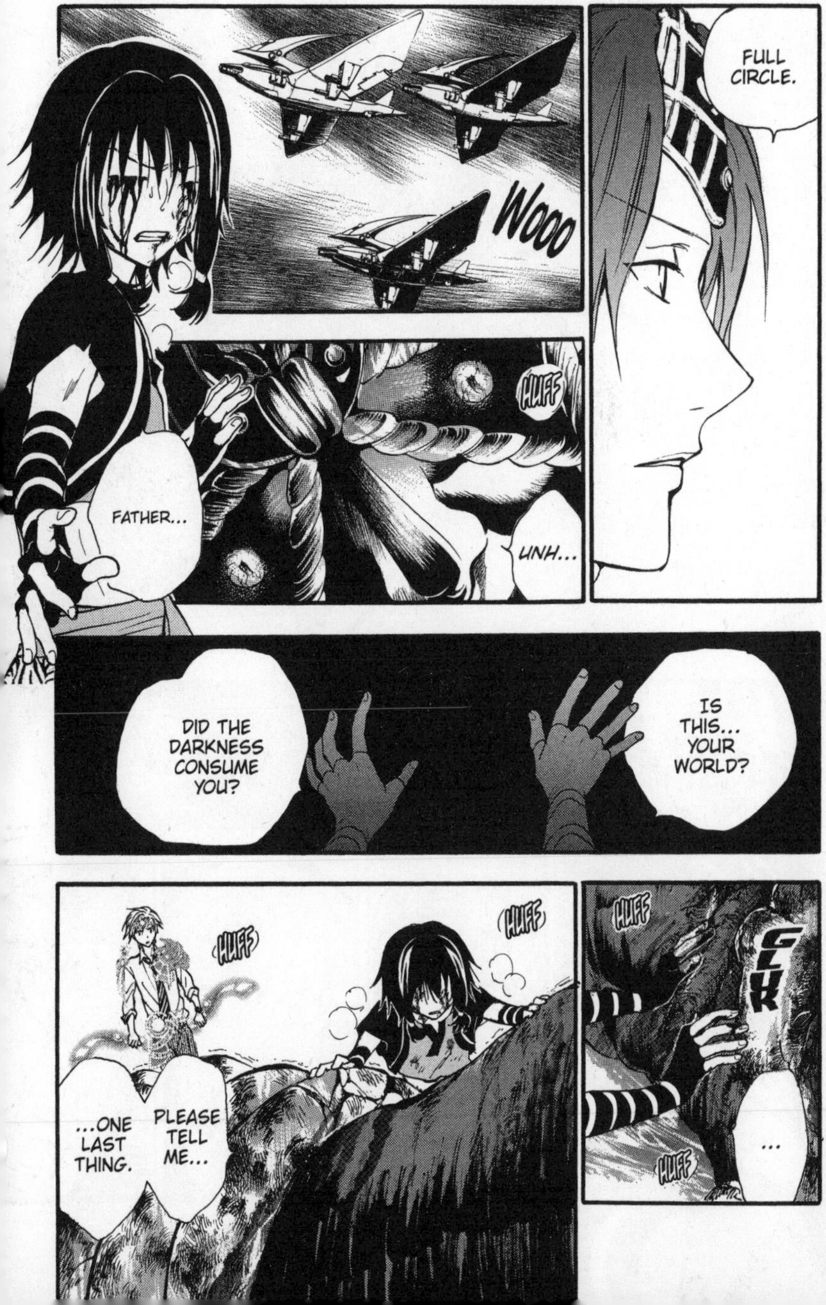
FULL CIRCLE.
WOOO
HUFF
UNH...
FATHER...
IS THIS... YOUR WORLD?
DID THE DARKNESS CONSUME YOU?
HUFF
GLUK
HUFF
...
HUFF
HUFF
PLEASE TELL ME...
...ONE LAST THING.

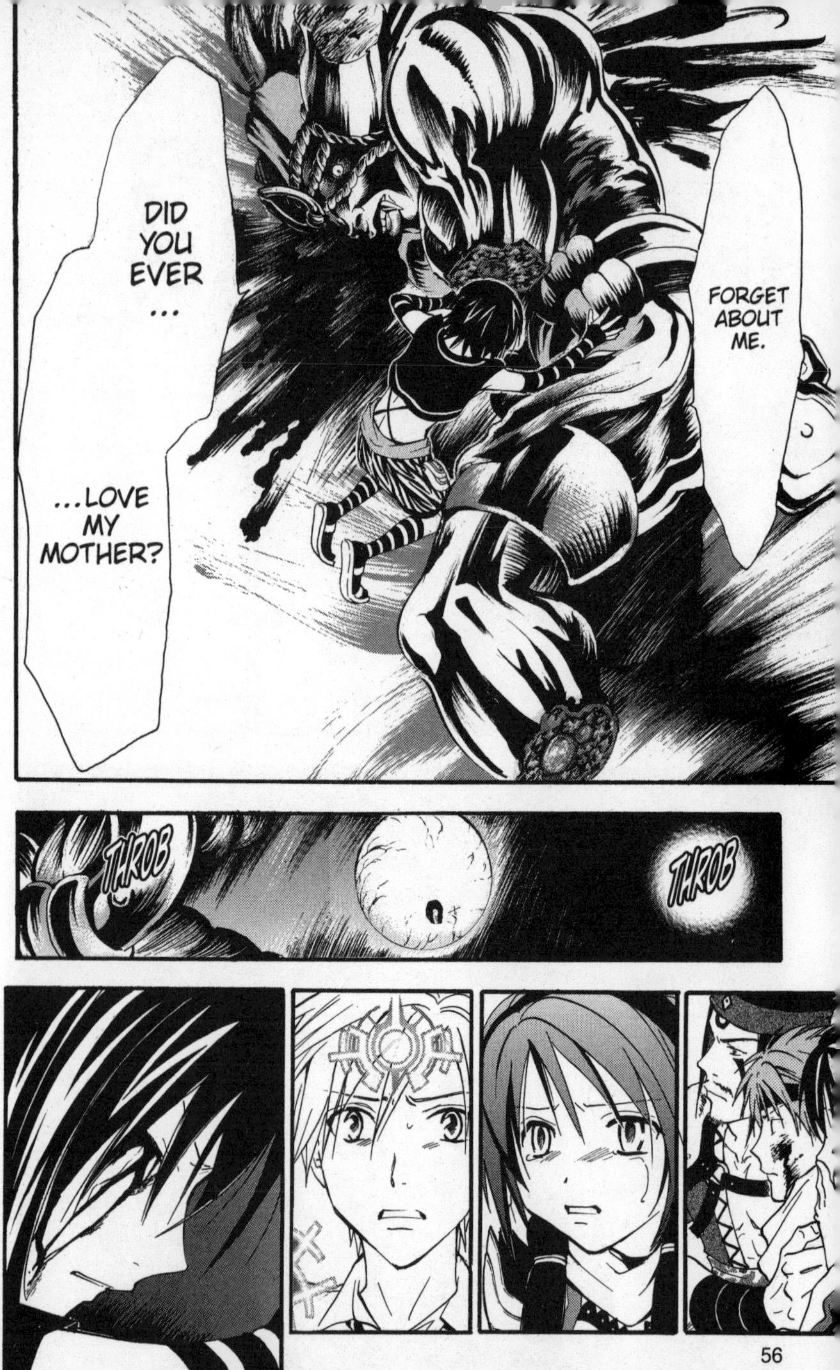
FORGET ABOUT ME.
DID YOU EVER ...
...LOVE MY MOTHER?
THROB
THROB

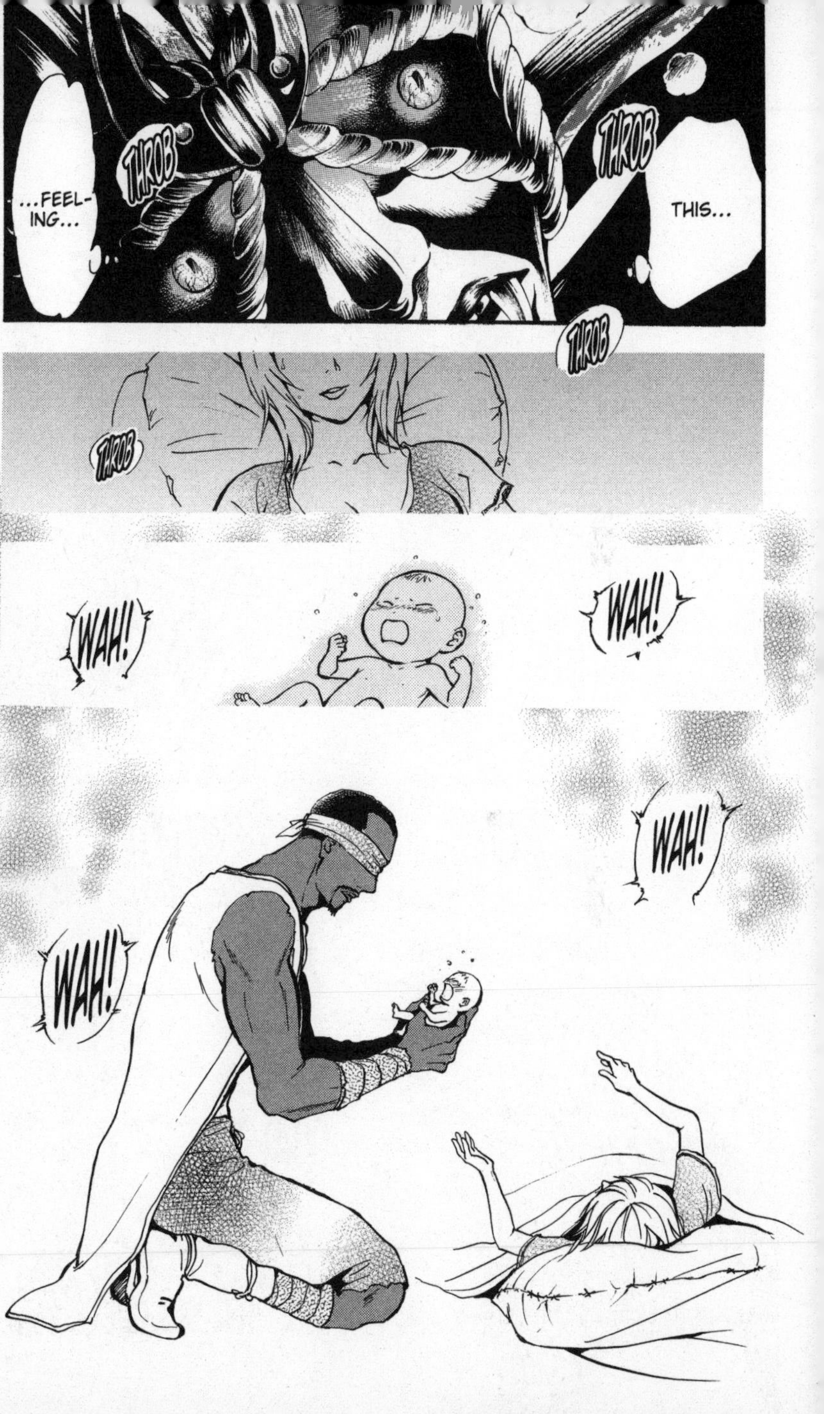
THIS...
THROB
...FEEL-
ING...
THROB
THROB
THROB
WAH!
WAH!
WAH!
WAH!

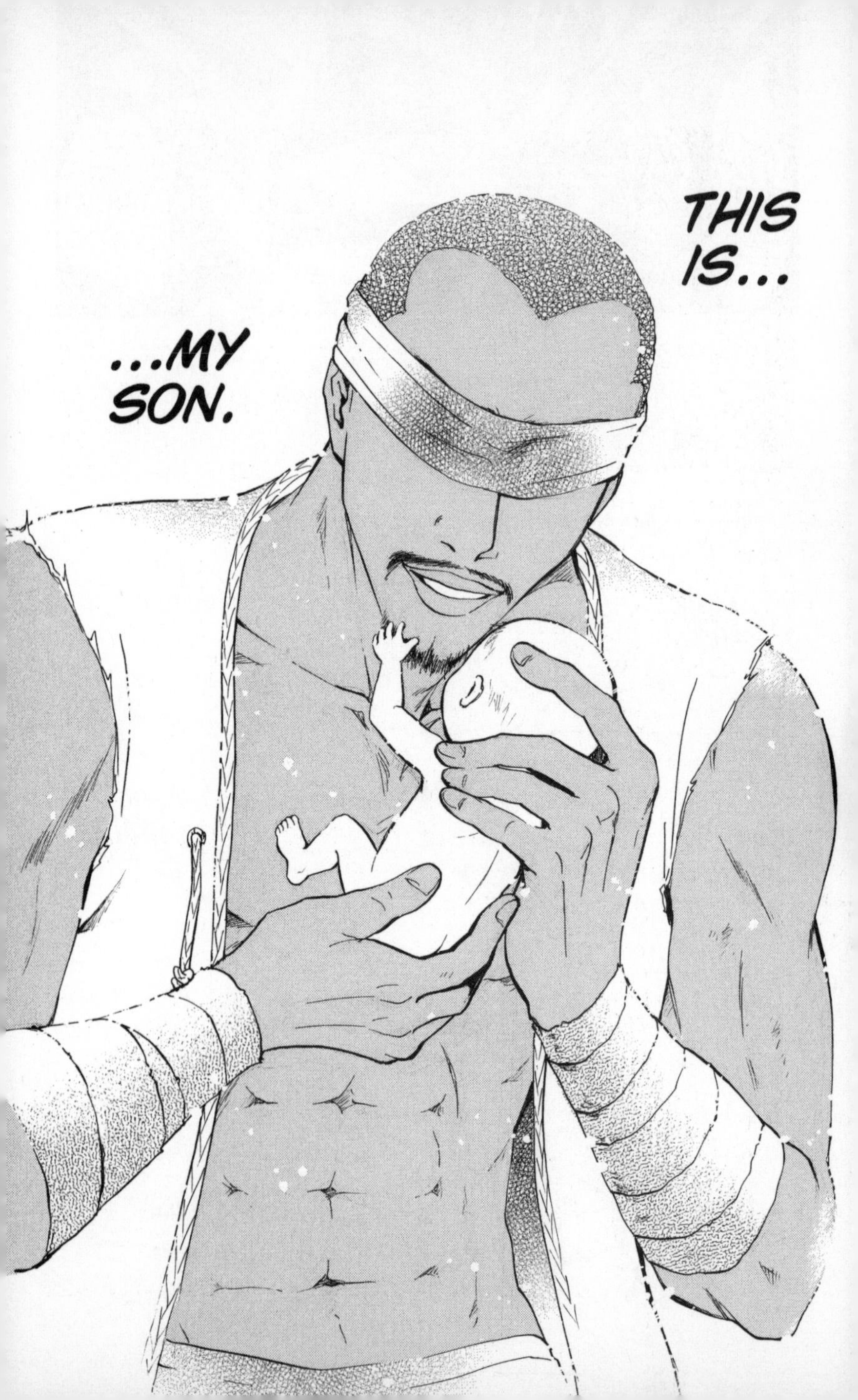
THIS IS...
...MY SON.

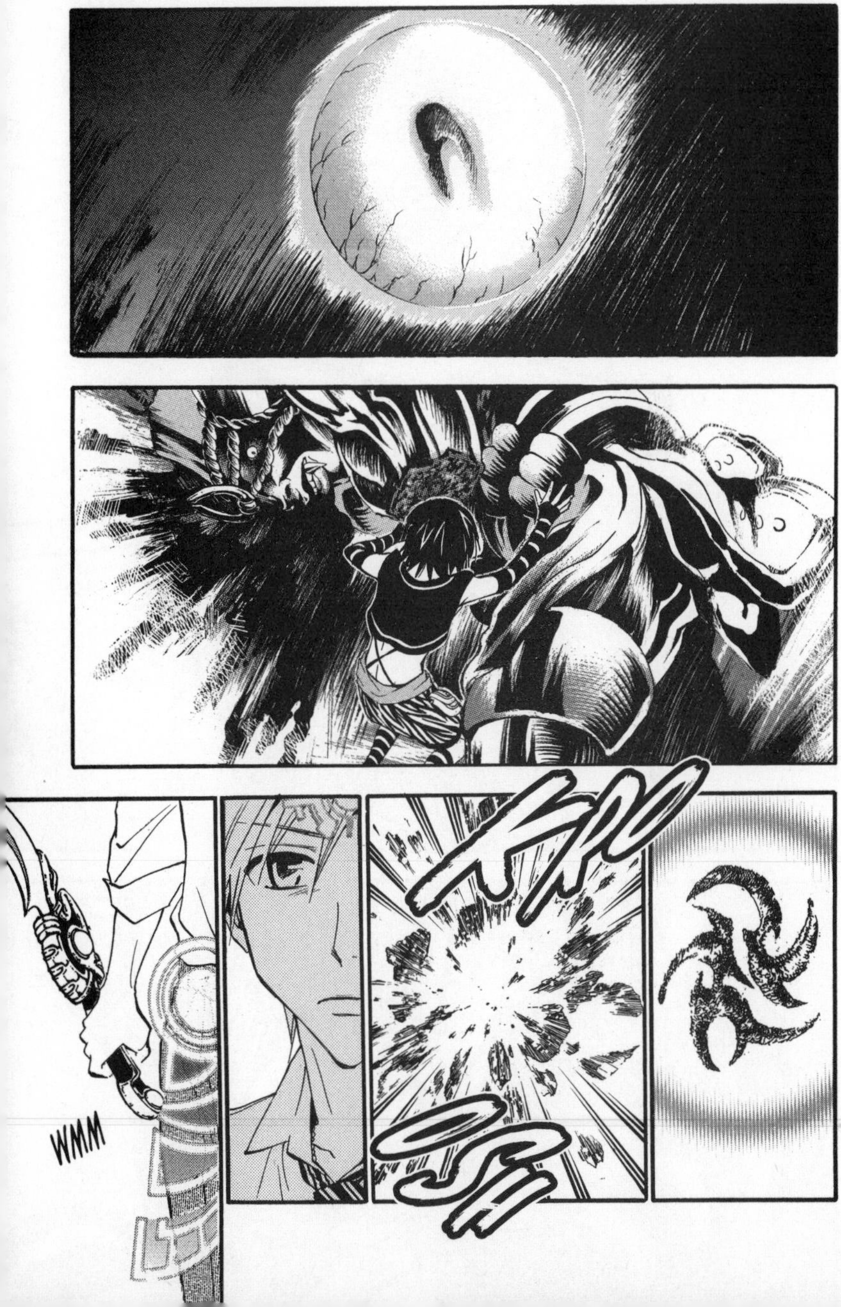
WMM

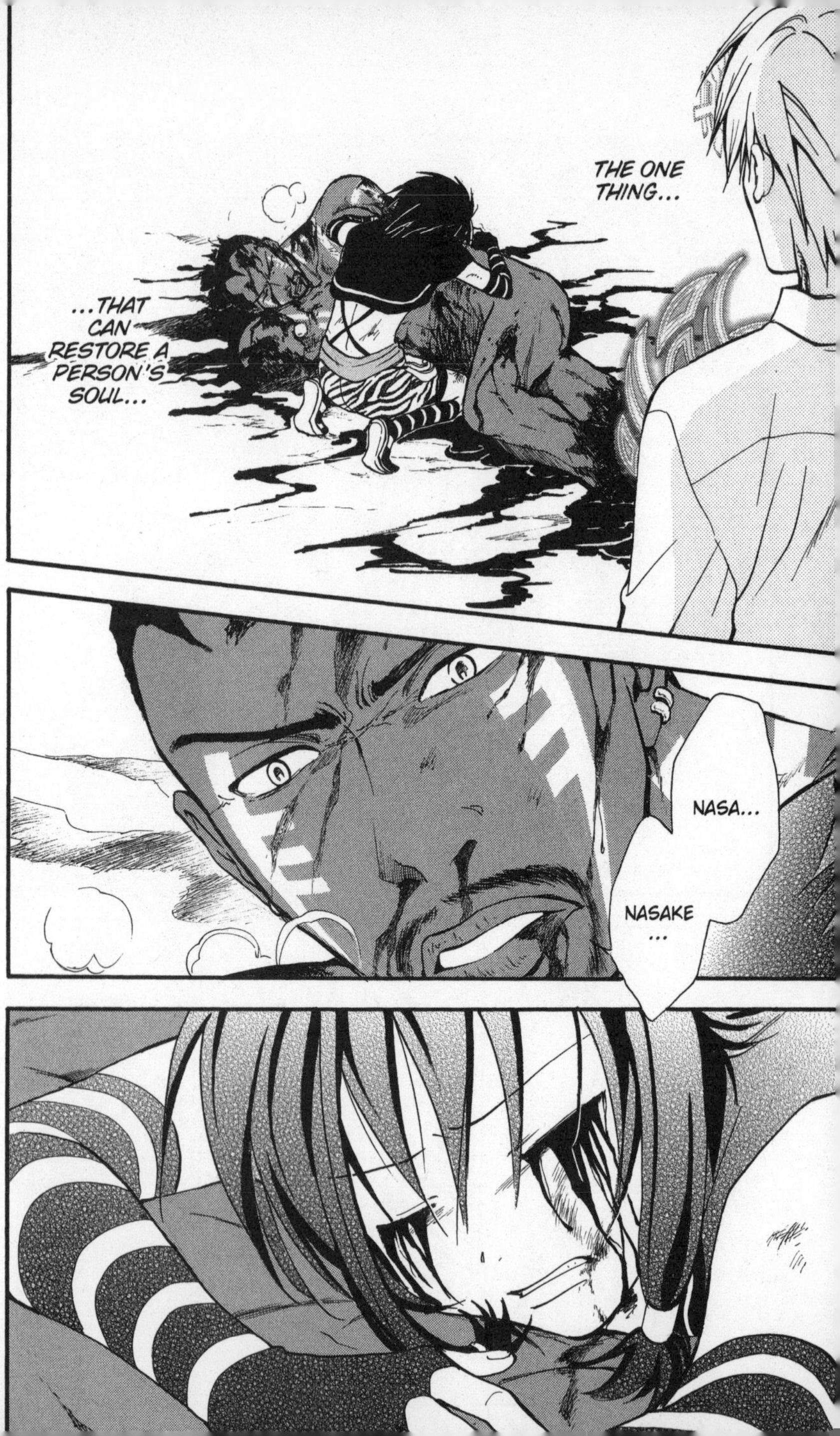
THE ONE THING...
...THAT CAN RESTORE A PERSON'S SOUL...
NASA...
NASAKE ...

Chapter 231

DEFEAT

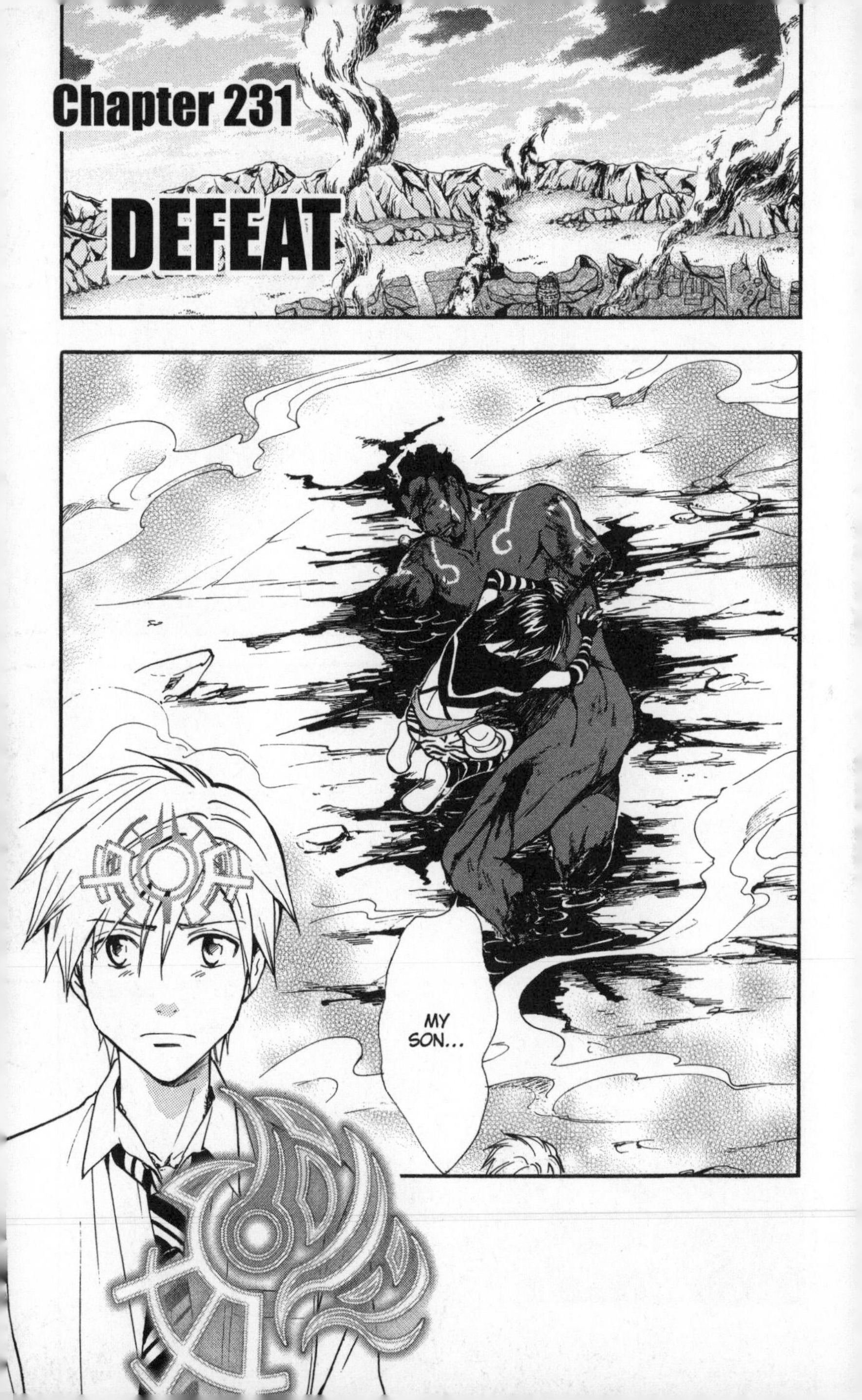
MY SON...

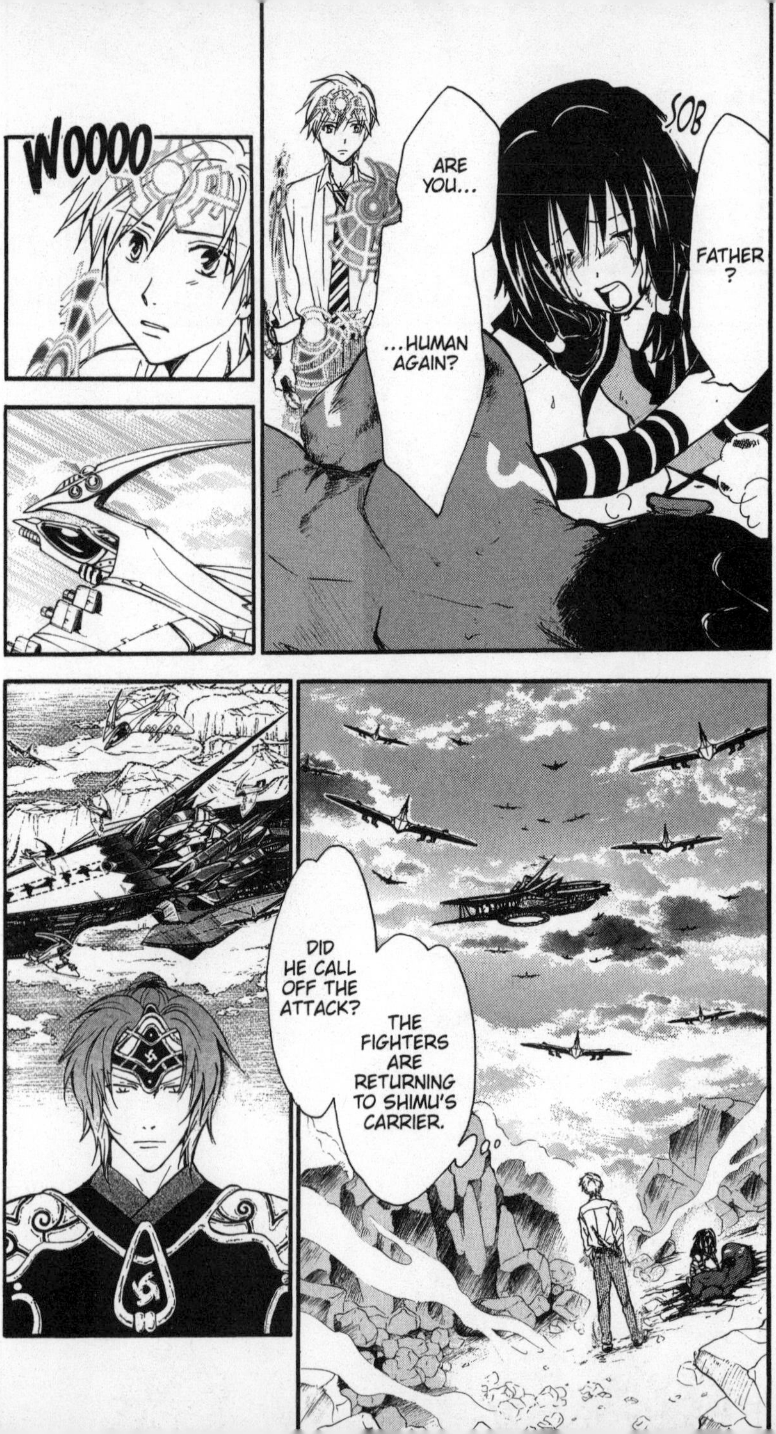
SOB
FATHER?
ARE YOU... ...HUMAN AGAIN?
WOOOO
DID HE CALL OFF THE ATTACK?
THE FIGHTERS ARE RETURNING TO SHIMU'S CARRIER.

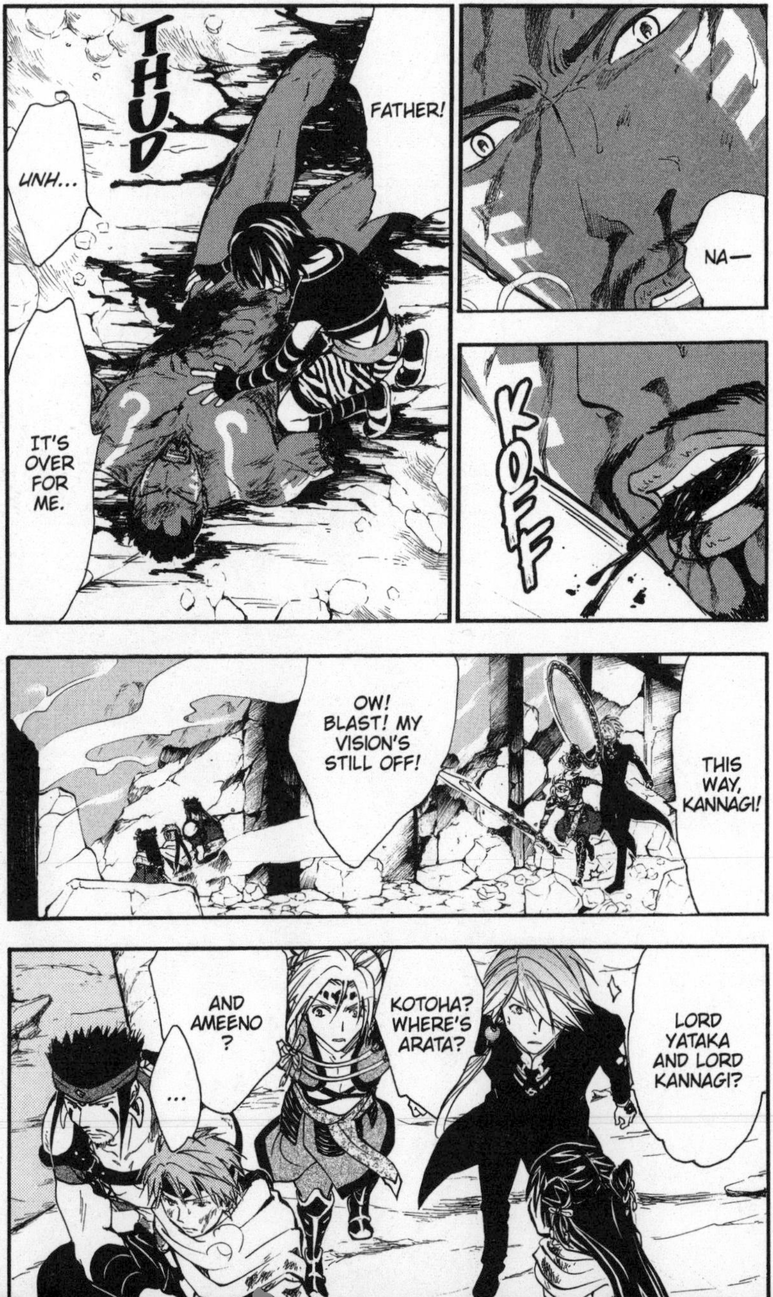
NA—
KOFF
FATHER!
THUD
UNH...
IT'S OVER FOR ME.
THIS WAY, KANNAGI!
OW! BLAST! MY VISION'S STILL OFF!
LORD YATAKA AND LORD KANNAGI?
KOTOHA? WHERE'S ARATA?
AND AMEENO?
...

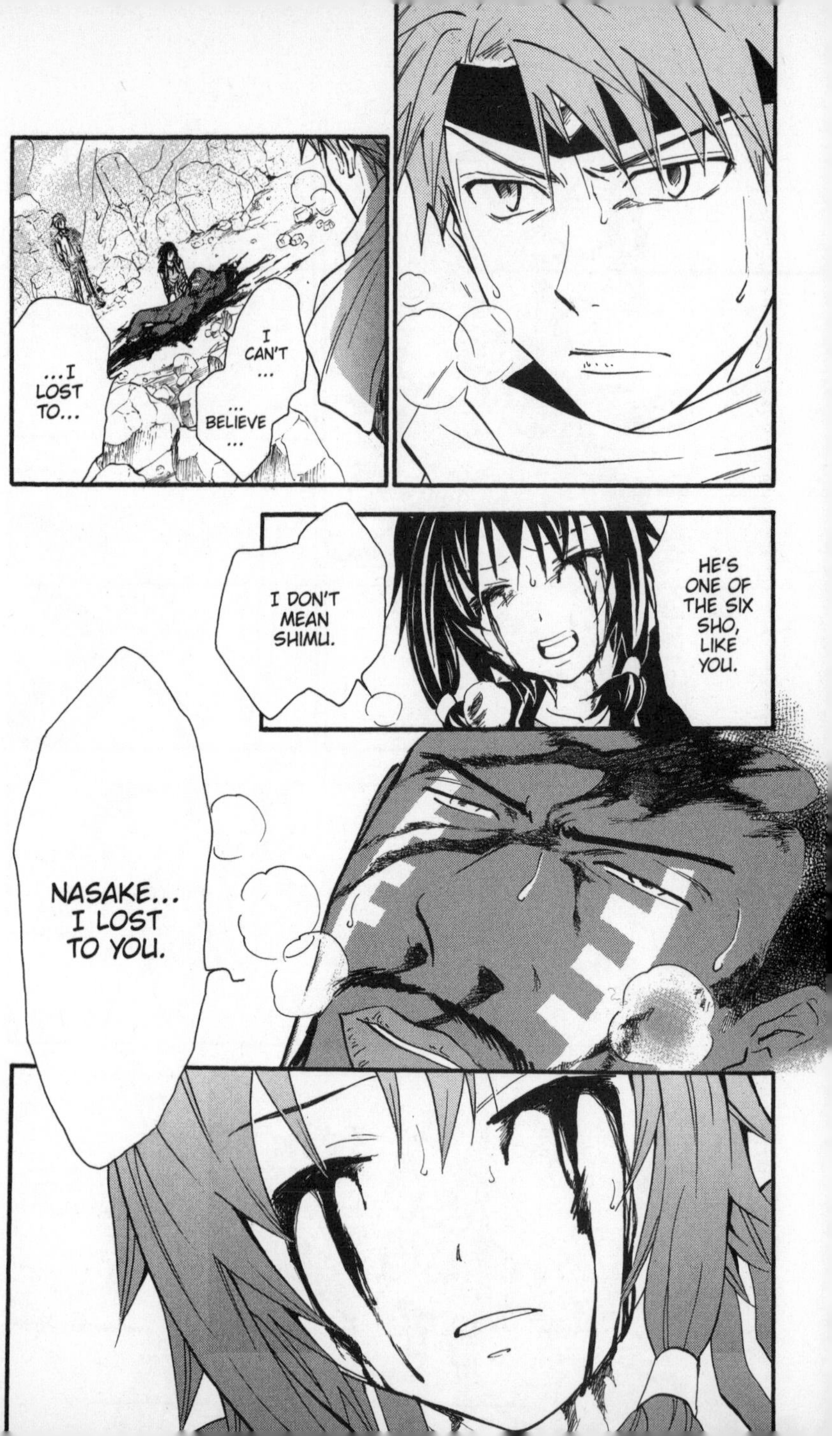
I CAN'T ...
... BELIEVE ...
...I LOST TO...
HE'S ONE OF THE SIX SHO, LIKE YOU.
I DON'T MEAN SHIMU.
NASAKE... I LOST TO YOU.

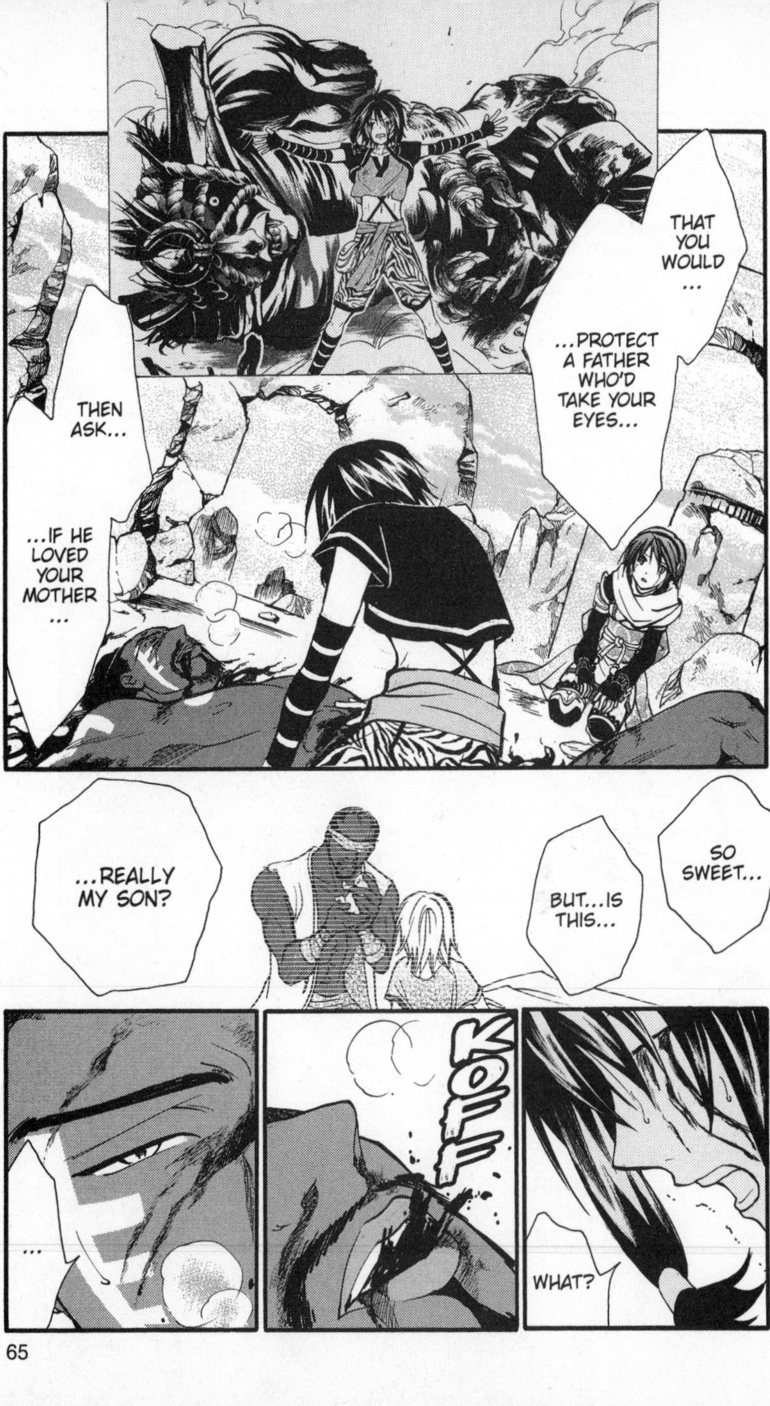
THAT YOU WOULD ...
...PROTECT A FATHER WHO'D TAKE YOUR EYES...
THEN ASK...
...IF HE LOVED YOUR MOTHER ...
SO SWEET...
BUT...IS THIS...
...REALLY MY SON?
WHAT?
KOFF
...

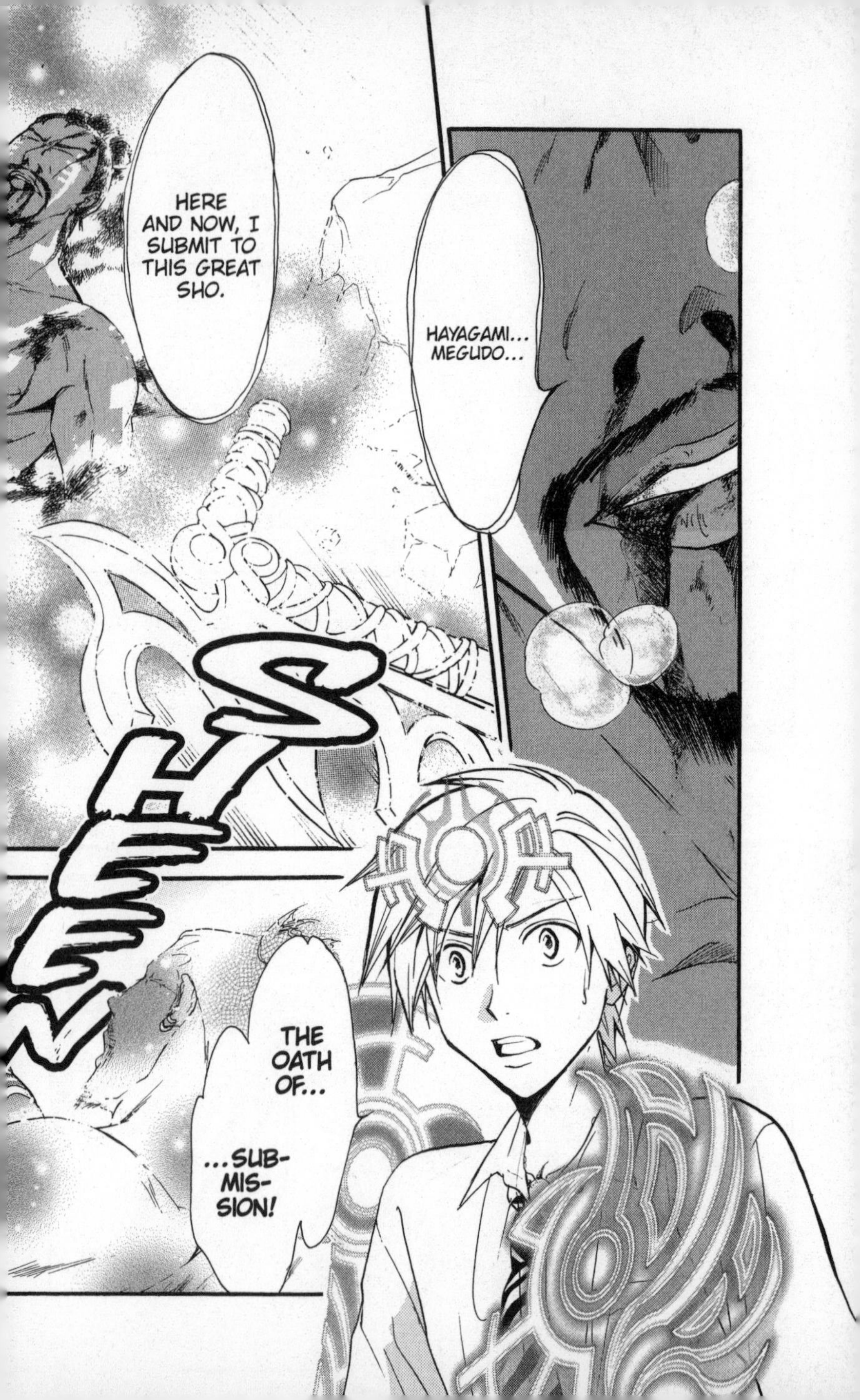
HAYAGAMI... MEGUDO...
HERE AND NOW, I SUBMIT TO THIS GREAT SHO.
SHEEN
THE OATH OF...
...SUB-MIS-SION!

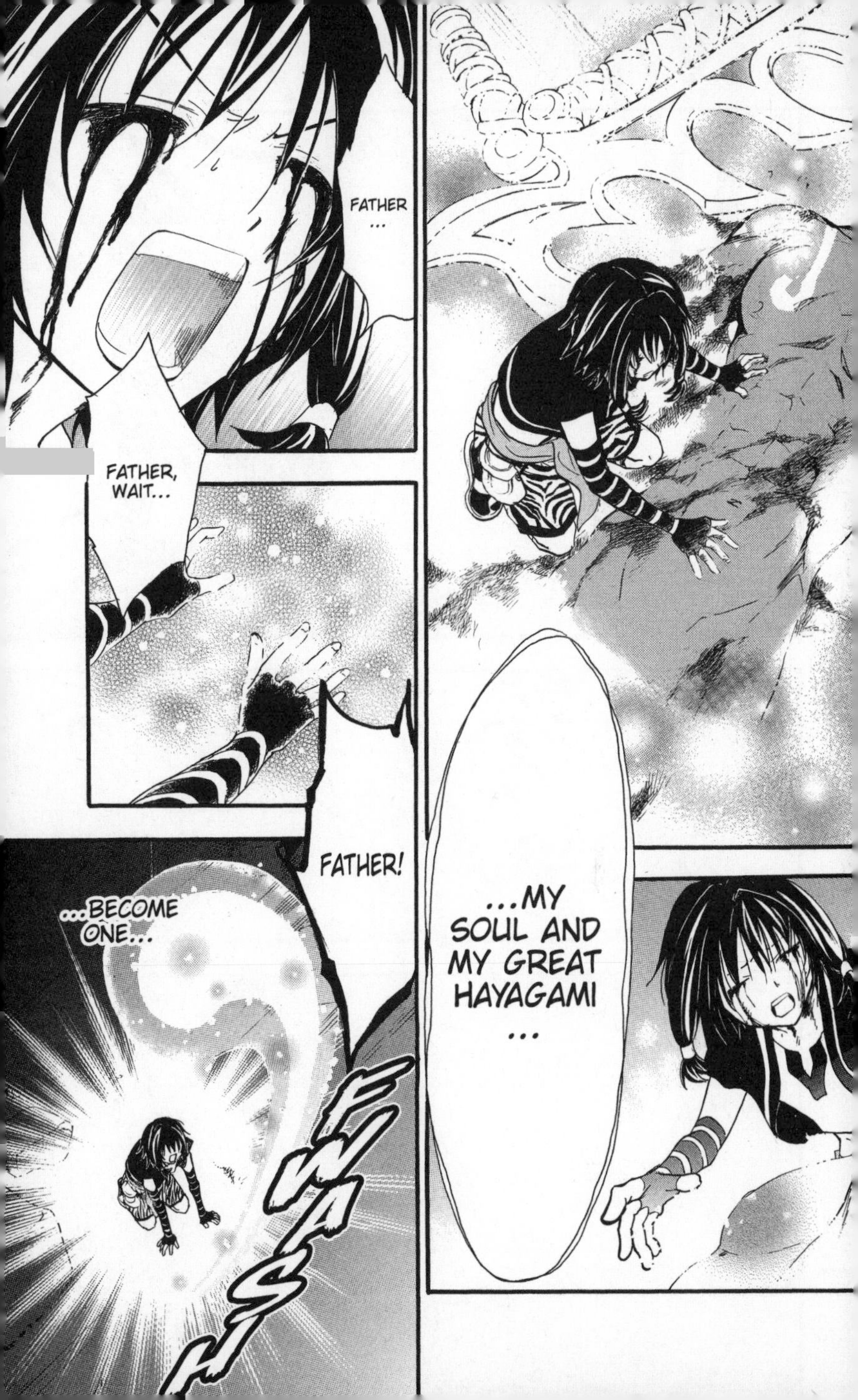
FATHER...
FATHER, WAIT...
FATHER!
...MY SOUL AND MY GREAT HAYAGAMI...
...BECOME ONE...
FWASH

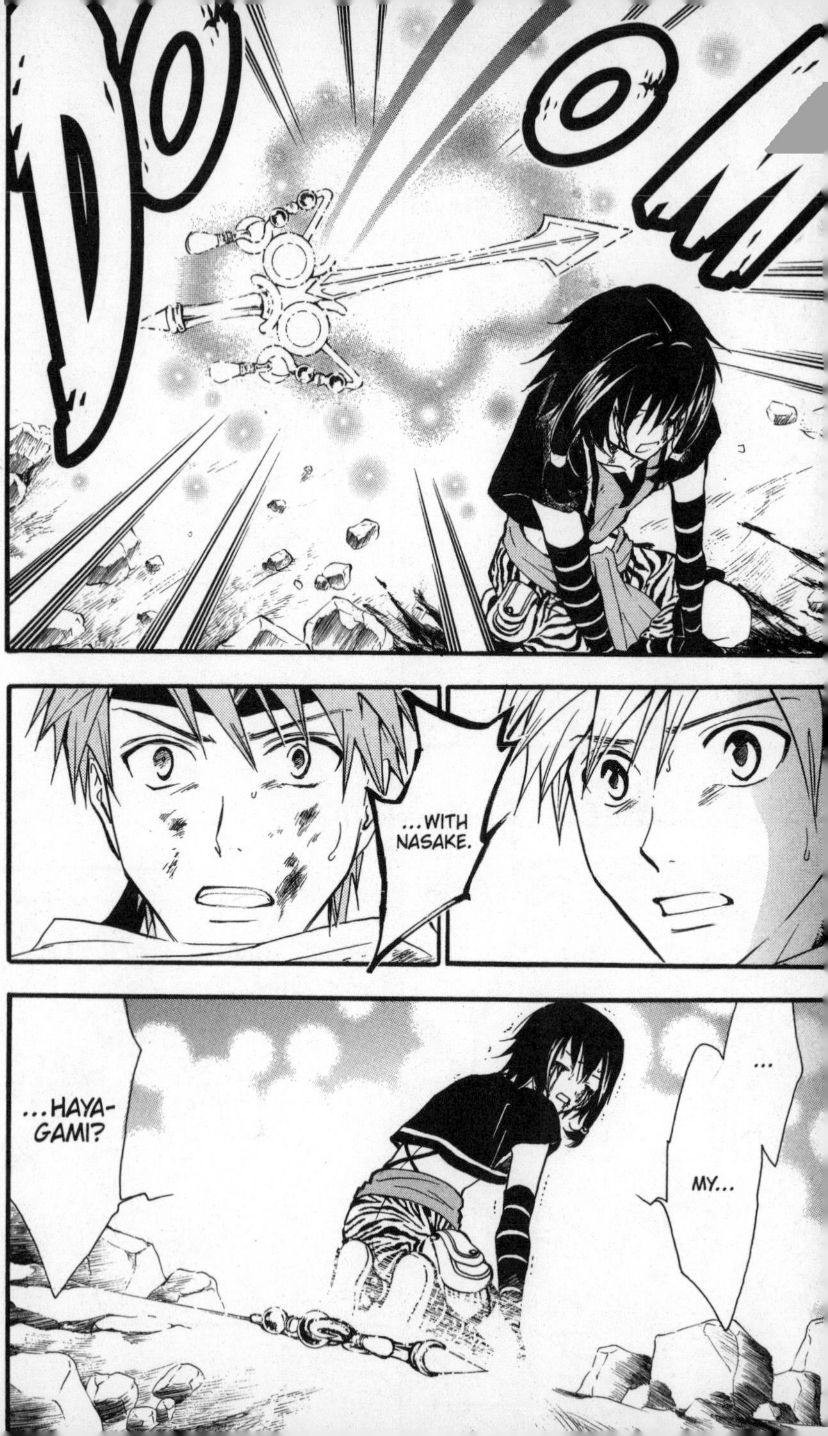
DOOM
...WITH NASAKE.
...
MY...
...HAYA-GAMI?

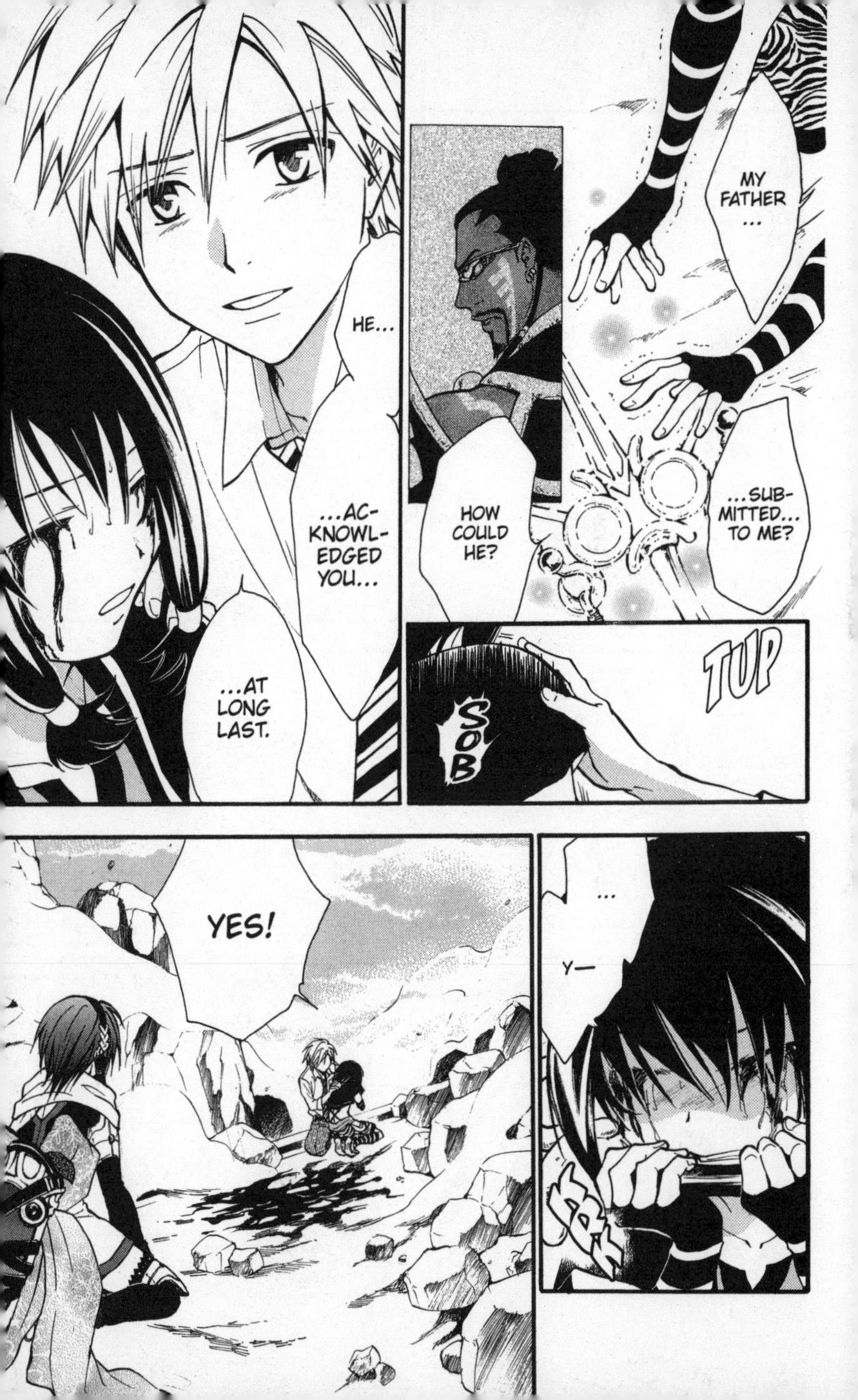

MY FATHER ...
...SUB-MITTED... TO ME?
HOW COULD HE?
TUP
SOB
HE...
...AC-KNOWL-EDGED YOU...
...AT LONG LAST.
...
Y—
YES!

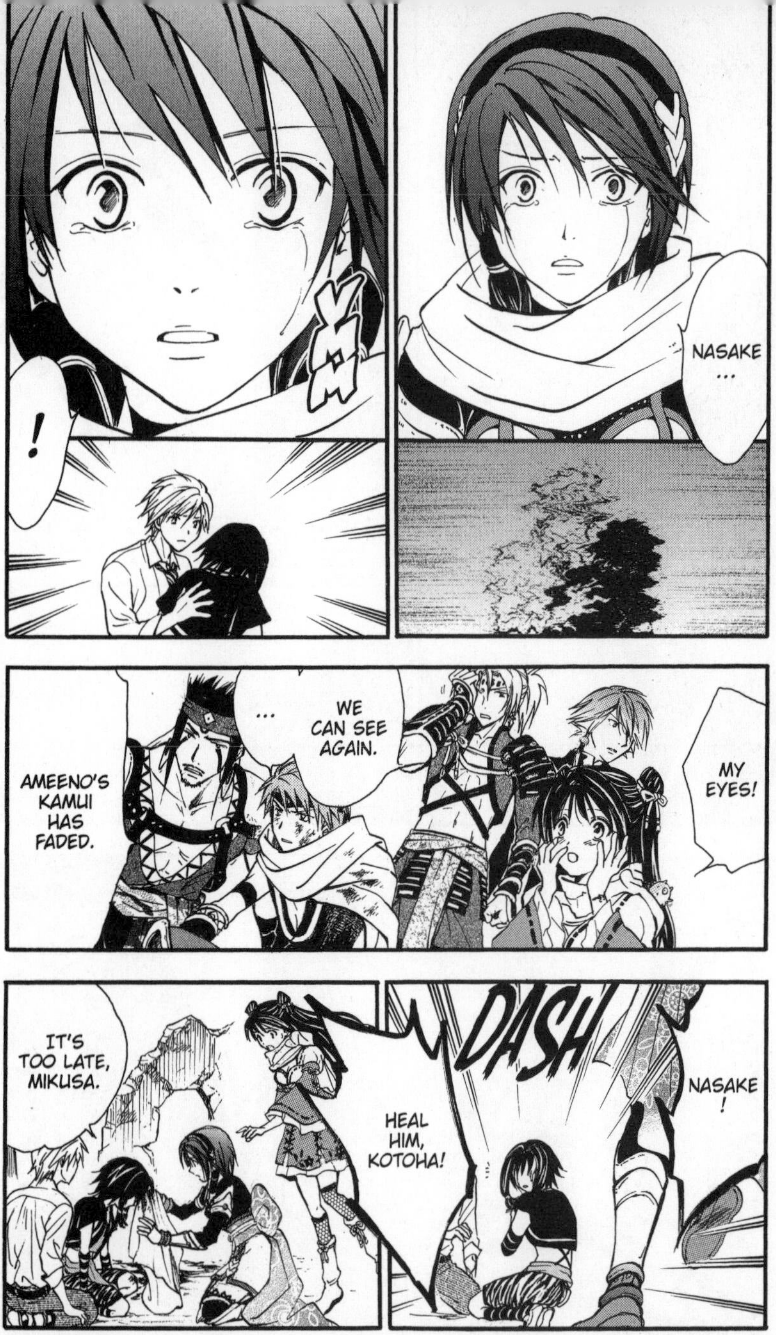
NASAKE ...
VOM
!
MY EYES!
... WE CAN SEE AGAIN.
AMEENO'S KAMUI HAS FADED.
NASAKE!
DASH
HEAL HIM, KOTOHA!
IT'S TOO LATE, MIKUSA.

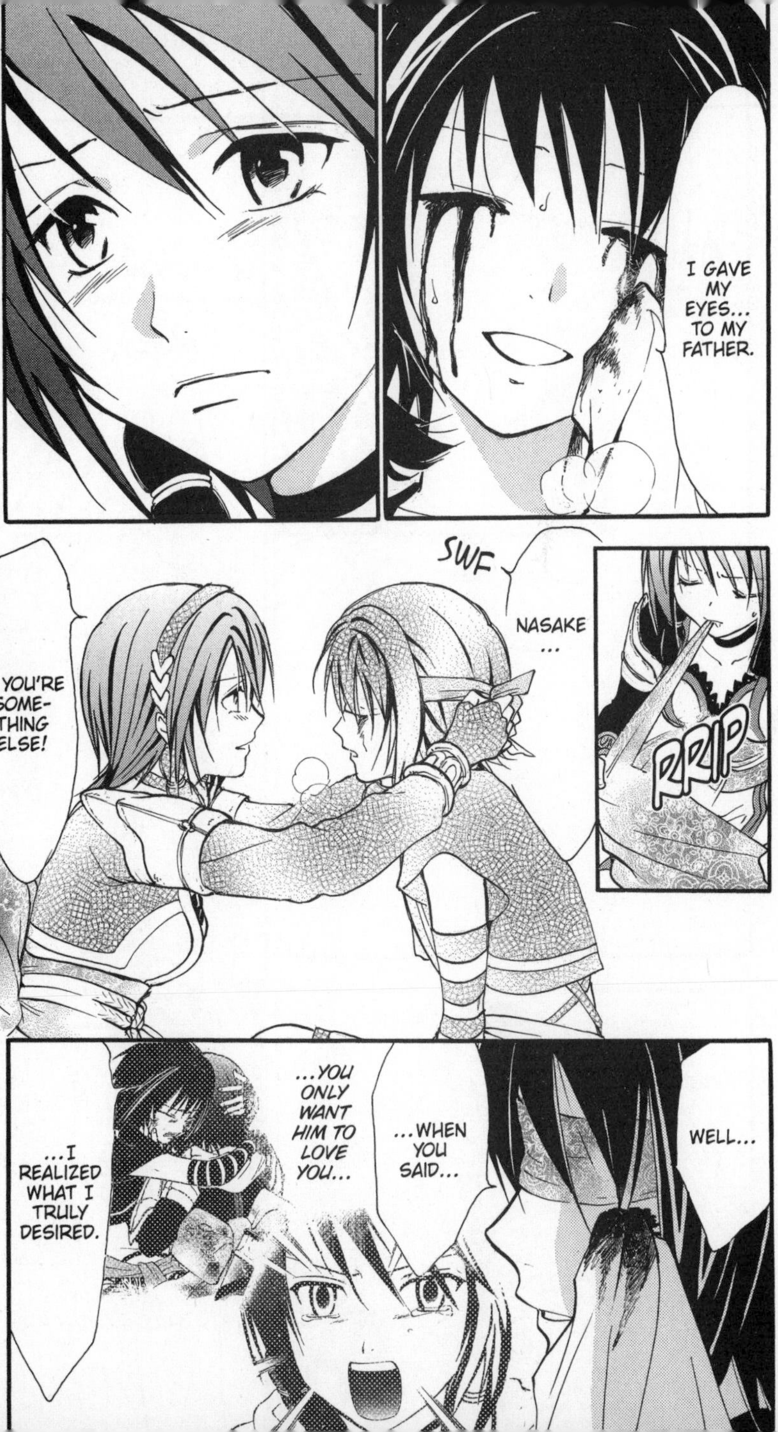
I GAVE MY EYES... TO MY FATHER.
RRIP
SWF
NASAKE ...
...YOU'RE SOME-THING ELSE!
WELL...
...WHEN YOU SAID...
...YOU ONLY WANT HIM TO LOVE YOU...
...I REALIZED WHAT I TRULY DESIRED.

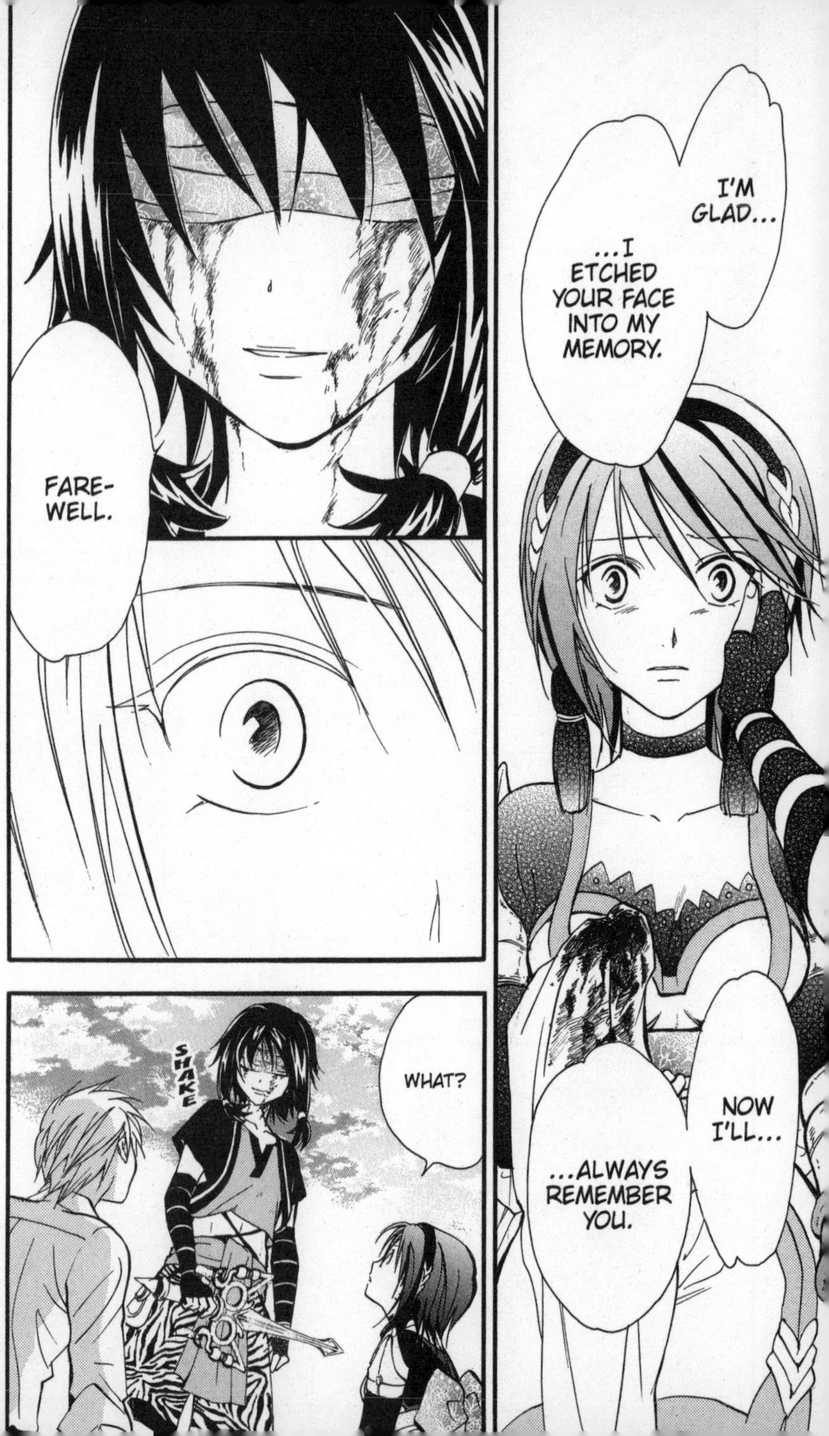
I'M GLAD...
...I ETCHED YOUR FACE INTO MY MEMORY.
NOW I'LL...
...ALWAYS REMEMBER YOU.
FARE-WELL.
WHAT?
SHAKE

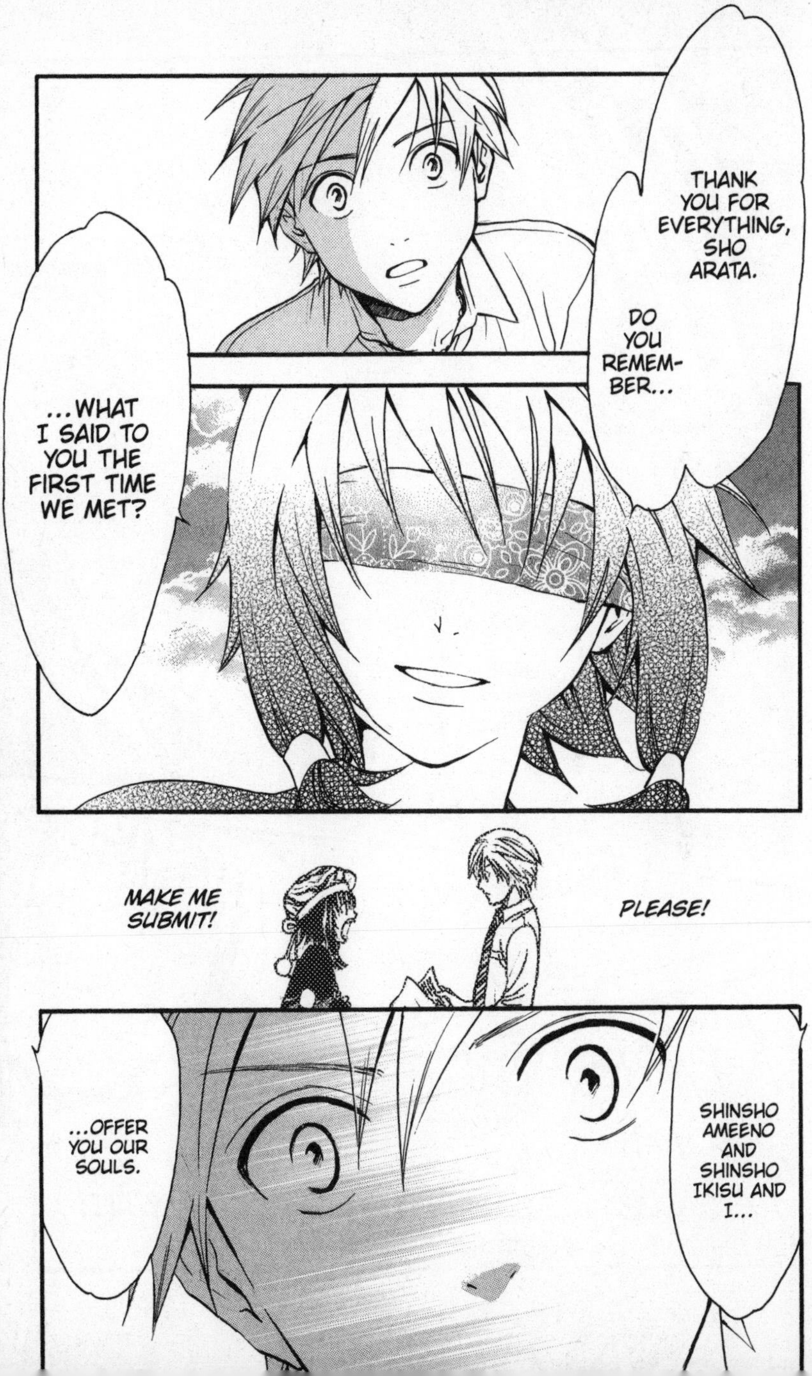
THANK YOU FOR EVERYTHING, SHO ARATA.
DO YOU REMEMBER...
...WHAT I SAID TO YOU THE FIRST TIME WE MET?
PLEASE!
MAKE ME SUBMIT!
SHINSHO AMEENO AND SHINSHO IKISU AND I...
...OFFER YOU OUR SOULS.

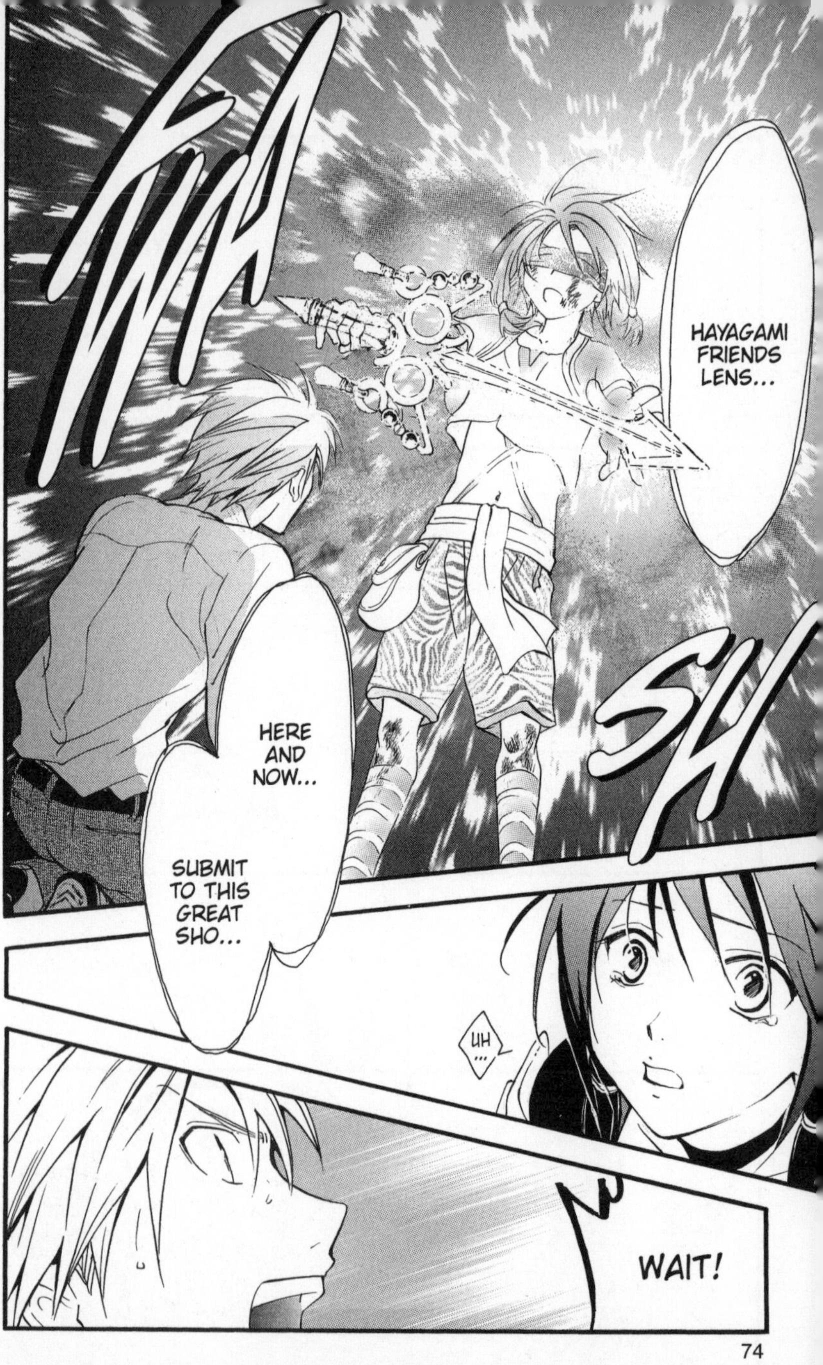
HAYAGAMI FRIENDS LENS...
SH
HERE AND NOW...
SUBMIT TO THIS GREAT SHO...
UH...
WAIT!

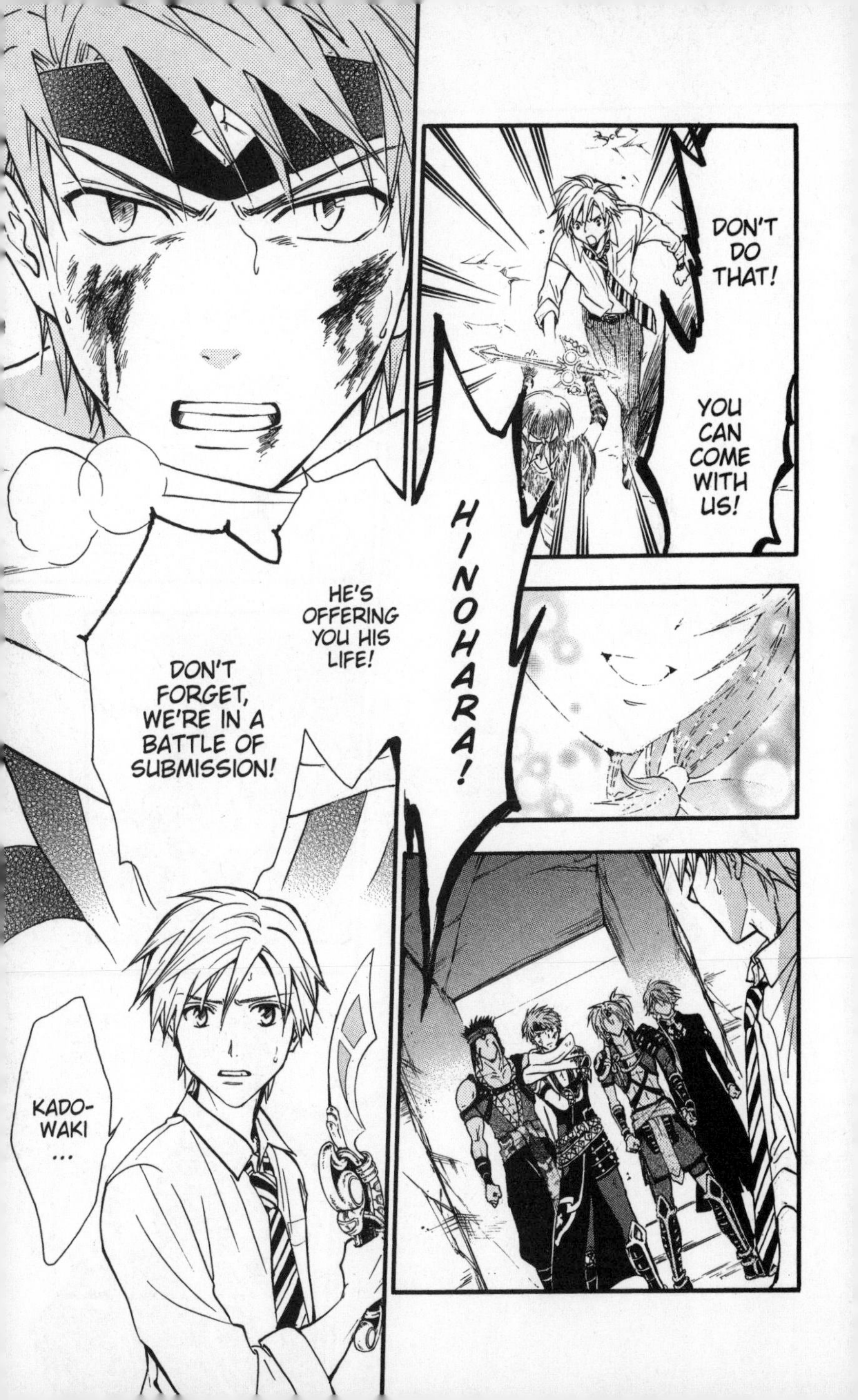

DON'T DO THAT!
YOU CAN COME WITH US!
HINOHARA!
HE'S OFFERING YOU HIS LIFE!
DON'T FORGET, WE'RE IN A BATTLE OF SUBMISSION!
KADO-WAKI ...

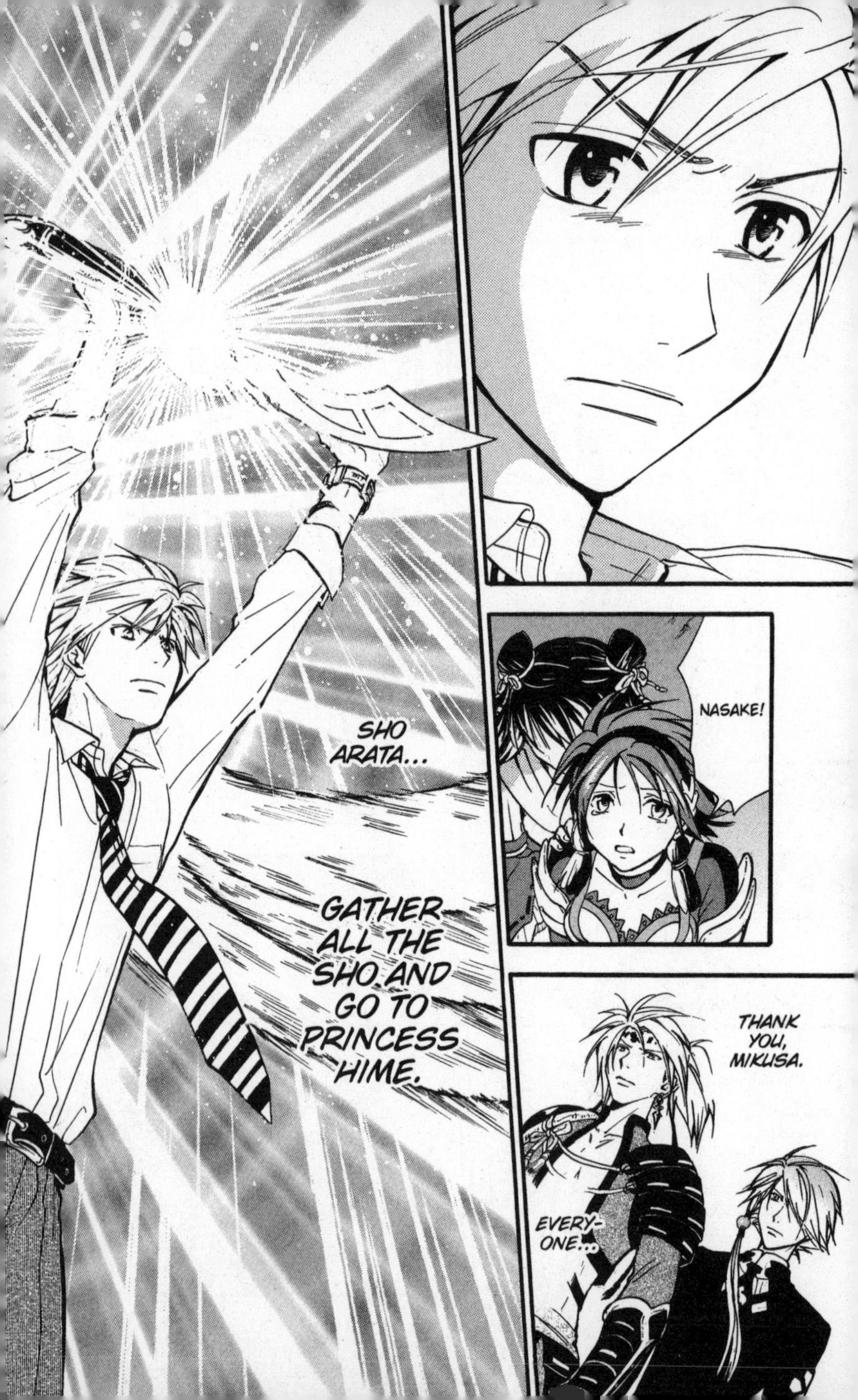
NASAKE!
THANK YOU, MIKUSA.
EVERY-ONE...
SHO ARATA...
GATHER ALL THE SHO AND GO TO PRINCESS HIME.

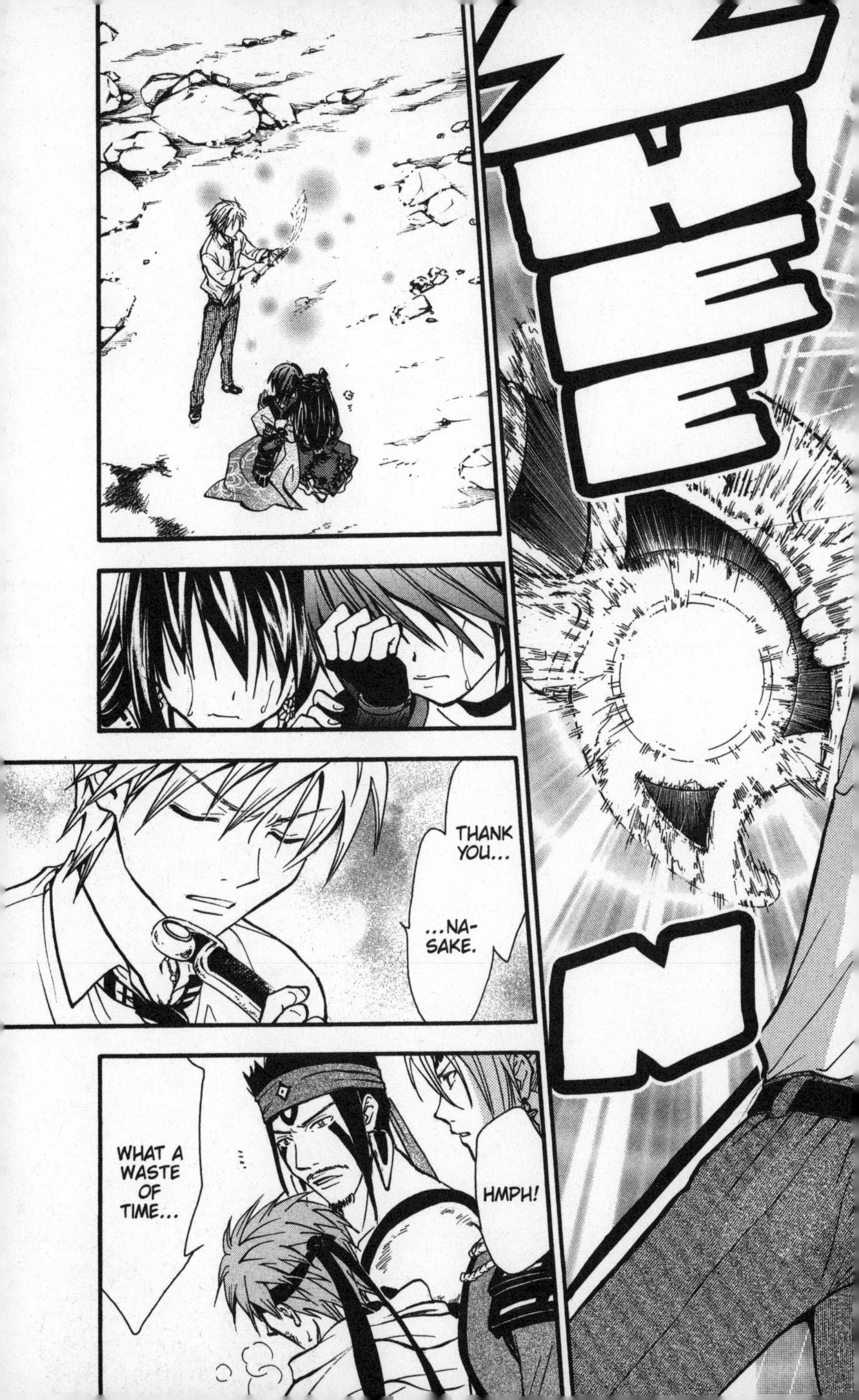
THANK YOU...
...NA-SAKE.
HMPH!
WHAT A WASTE OF TIME...

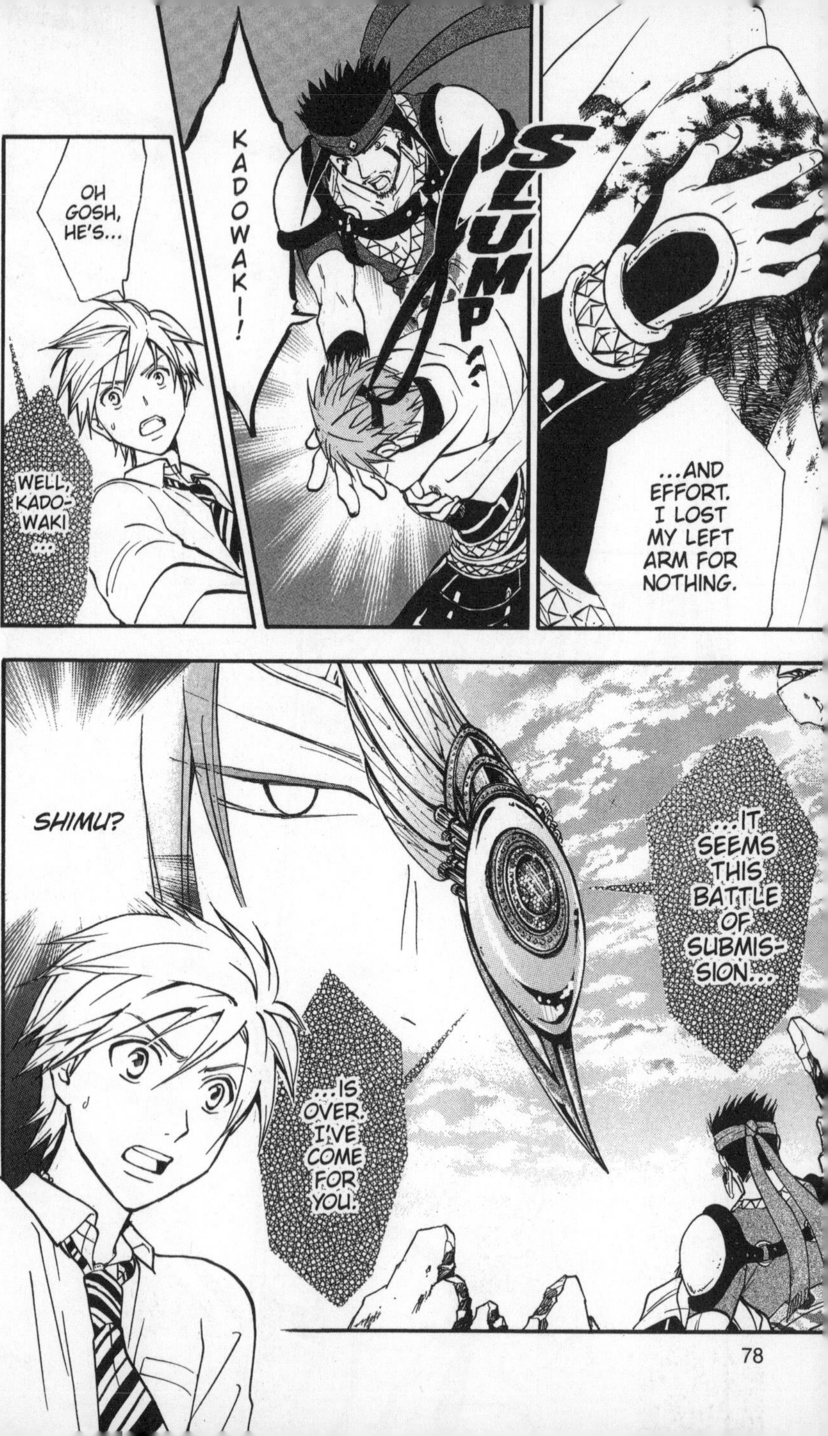
...AND EFFORT. I LOST MY LEFT ARM FOR NOTHING.
KADOWAKI!
SLUMP
OH GOSH, HE'S...
WELL, KADOWAKI...
...IT SEEMS THIS BATTLE OF SUBMISSION...
...IS OVER. I'VE COME FOR YOU.
SHIMU?

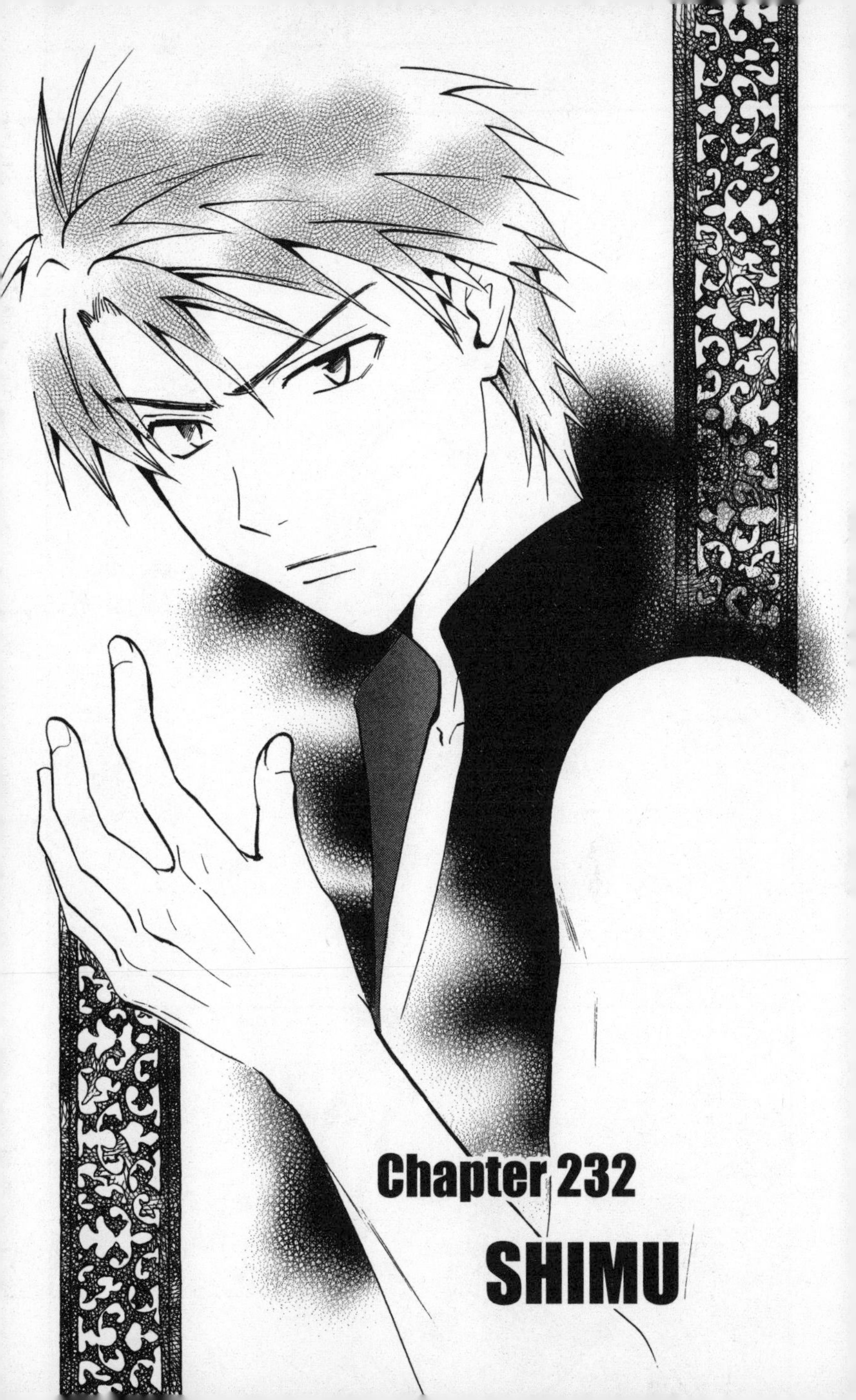
Chapter 232
SHIMU

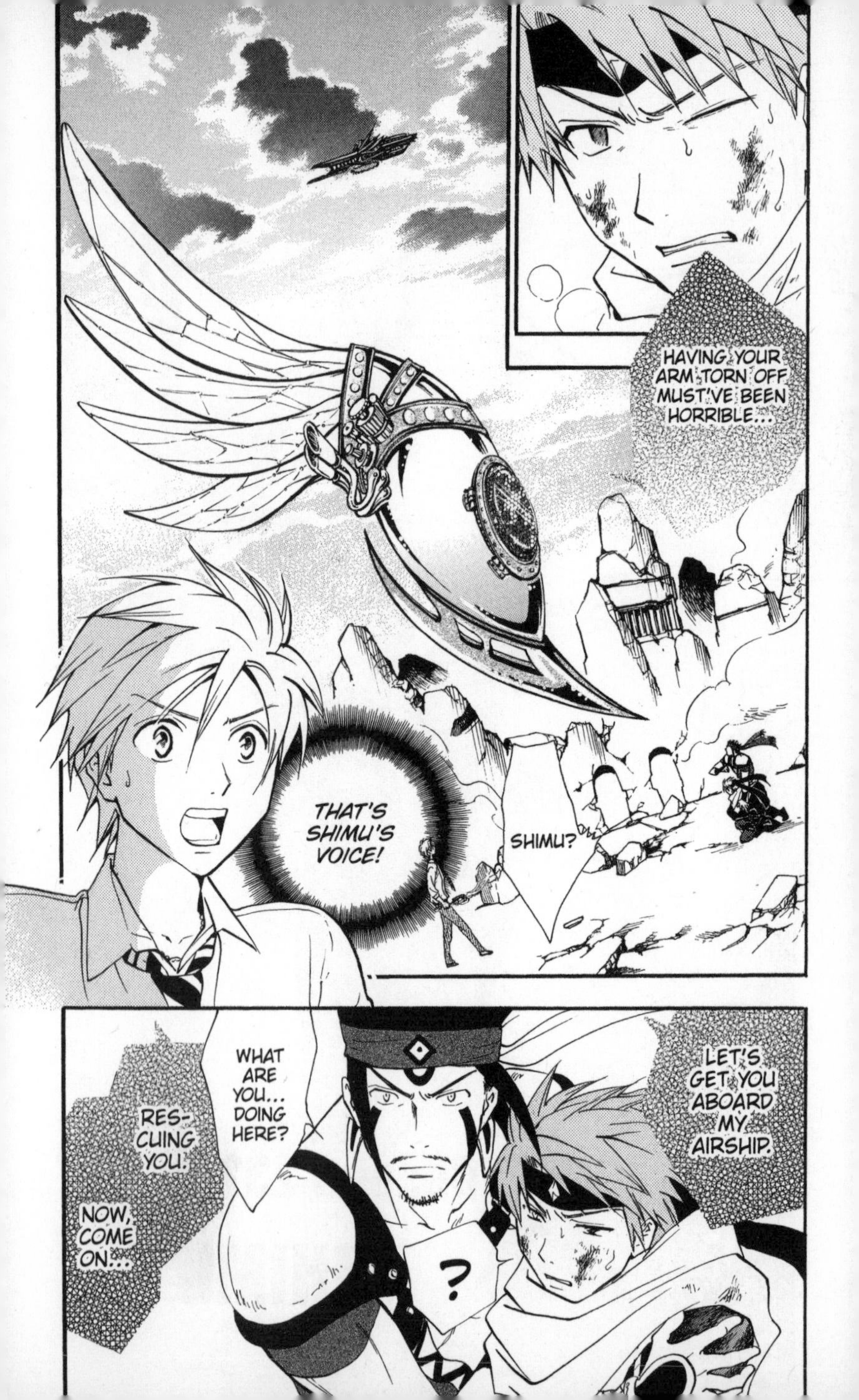
HAVING YOUR ARM TORN OFF MUST'VE BEEN HORRIBLE...
SHIMU?
THAT'S SHIMU'S VOICE!
LET'S GET YOU ABOARD MY AIRSHIP.
WHAT ARE YOU... DOING HERE?
RES-CUING YOU.
?
NOW, COME ON...

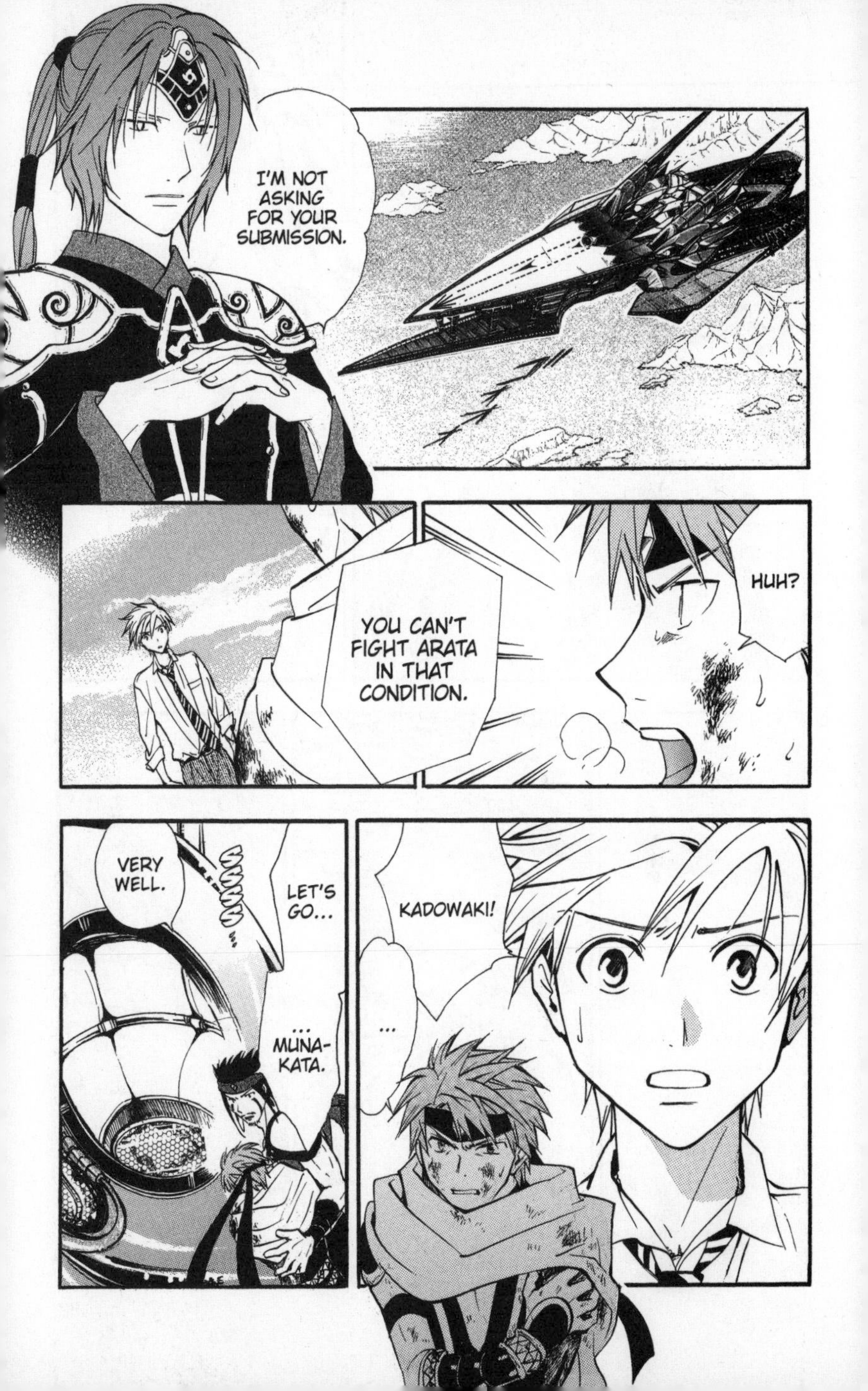
I'M NOT ASKING FOR YOUR SUBMISSION.
HUH?
YOU CAN'T FIGHT ARATA IN THAT CONDITION.
KADOWAKI!
...
LET'S GO...
... MUNA-KATA.
VERY WELL.

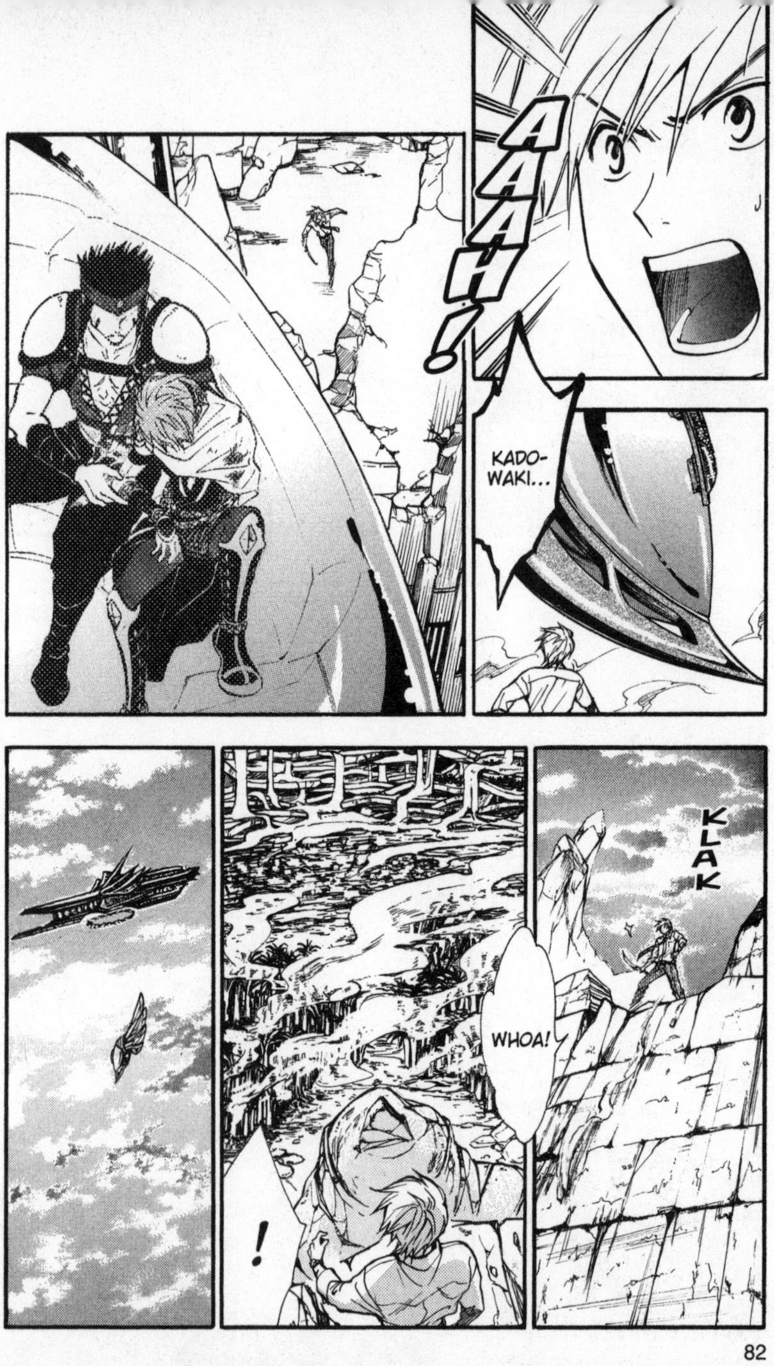
AAAAH!
KADO-WAKI...
KLAK
WHOA!
!

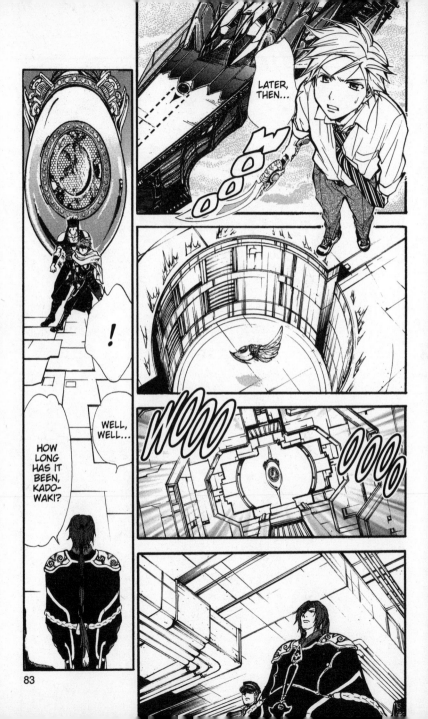

LATER, THEN...

!

WELL, WELL...

HOW LONG HAS IT BEEN, KADO-WAKI?

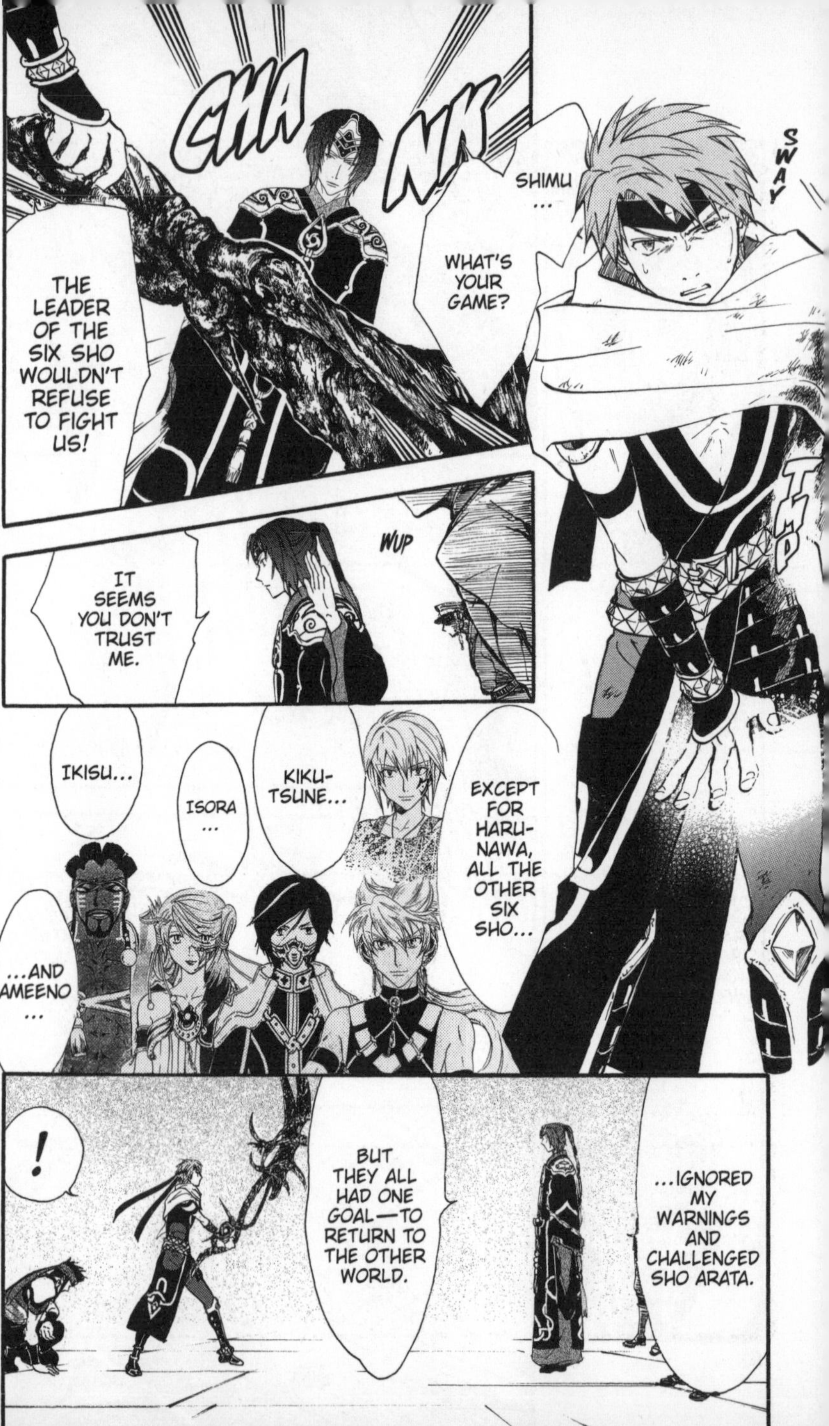
SWAY
SHIMU...
WHAT'S YOUR GAME?
TMP
CHANK
THE LEADER OF THE SIX SHO WOULDN'T REFUSE TO FIGHT US!
IT SEEMS YOU DON'T TRUST ME.
WUP
EXCEPT FOR HARU-NAWA, ALL THE OTHER SIX SHO...
KIKU-TSUNE...
ISORA...
IKISU...
...AND AMEENO...
...IGNORED MY WARNINGS AND CHALLENGED SHO ARATA.
BUT THEY ALL HAD ONE GOAL—TO RETURN TO THE OTHER WORLD.
!

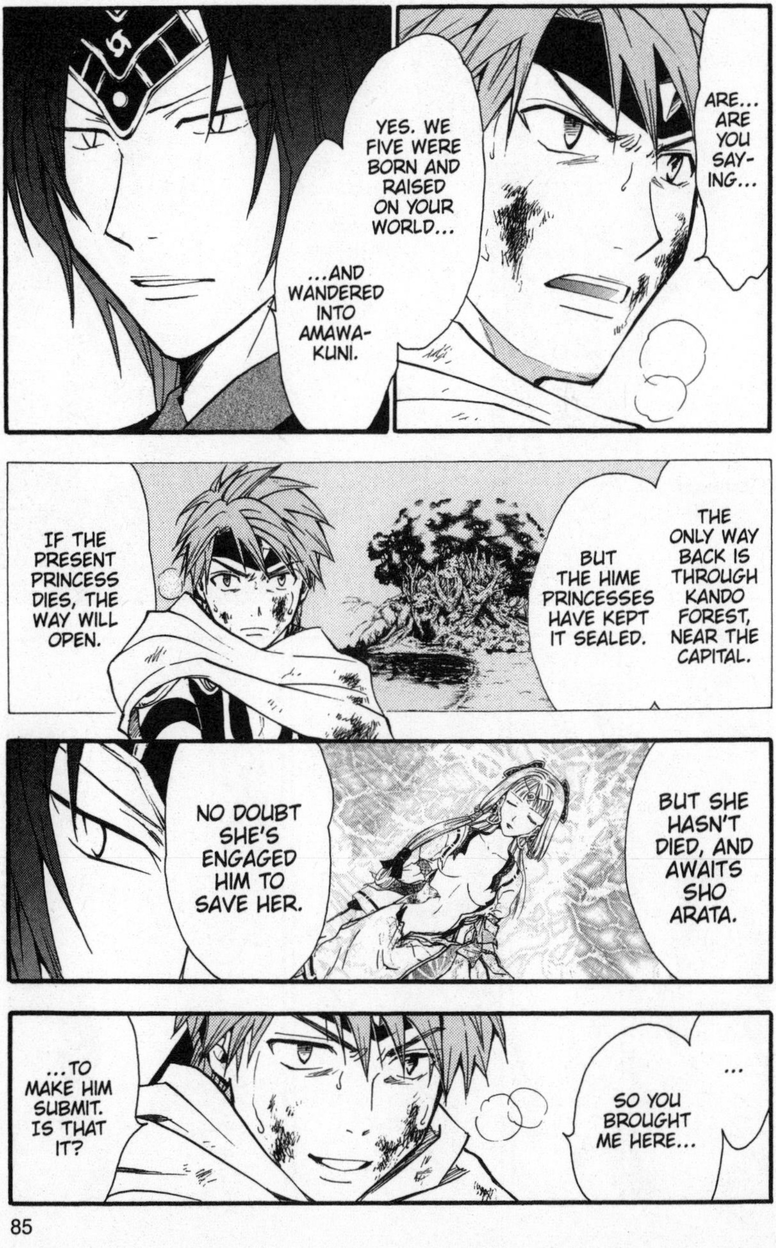
ARE... ARE YOU SAYING...
YES. WE FIVE WERE BORN AND RAISED ON YOUR WORLD...
...AND WANDERED INTO AMAWA-KUNI.
THE ONLY WAY BACK IS THROUGH KANDO FOREST, NEAR THE CAPITAL.
BUT THE HIME PRINCESSES HAVE KEPT IT SEALED.
IF THE PRESENT PRINCESS DIES, THE WAY WILL OPEN.
BUT SHE HASN'T DIED, AND AWAITS SHO ARATA.
NO DOUBT SHE'S ENGAGED HIM TO SAVE HER.
...
SO YOU BROUGHT ME HERE...
...TO MAKE HIM SUBMIT. IS THAT IT?

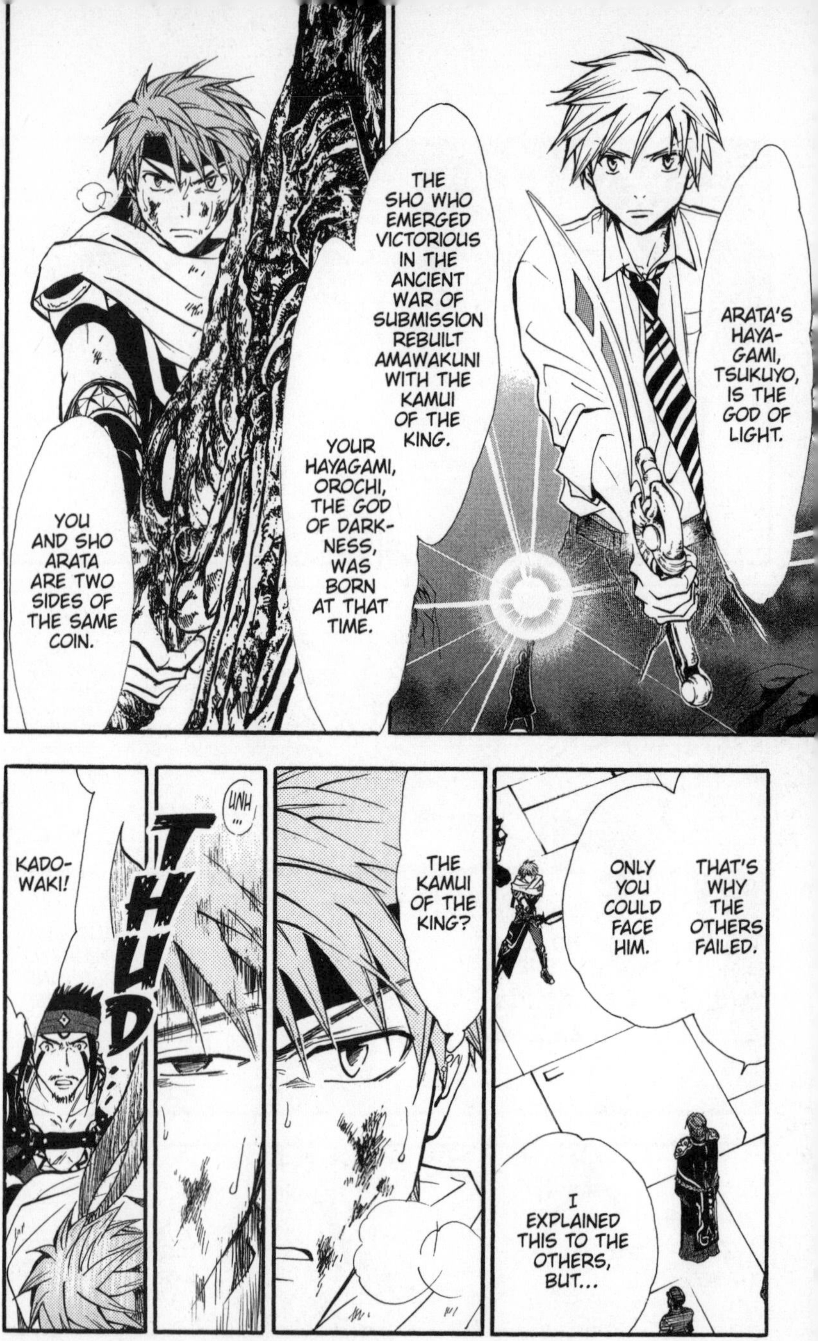
ARATA'S HAYA-GAMI, TSUKUYO, IS THE GOD OF LIGHT.
THE SHO WHO EMERGED VICTORIOUS IN THE ANCIENT WAR OF SUBMISSION REBUILT AMAWAKUNI WITH THE KAMUI OF THE KING.
YOUR HAYAGAMI, OROCHI, THE GOD OF DARK-NESS, WAS BORN AT THAT TIME.
YOU AND SHO ARATA ARE TWO SIDES OF THE SAME COIN.
THAT'S WHY THE OTHERS FAILED.
ONLY YOU COULD FACE HIM.
I EXPLAINED THIS TO THE OTHERS, BUT...
THE KAMUI OF THE KING?
UNH...
THUD
KADO-WAKI!

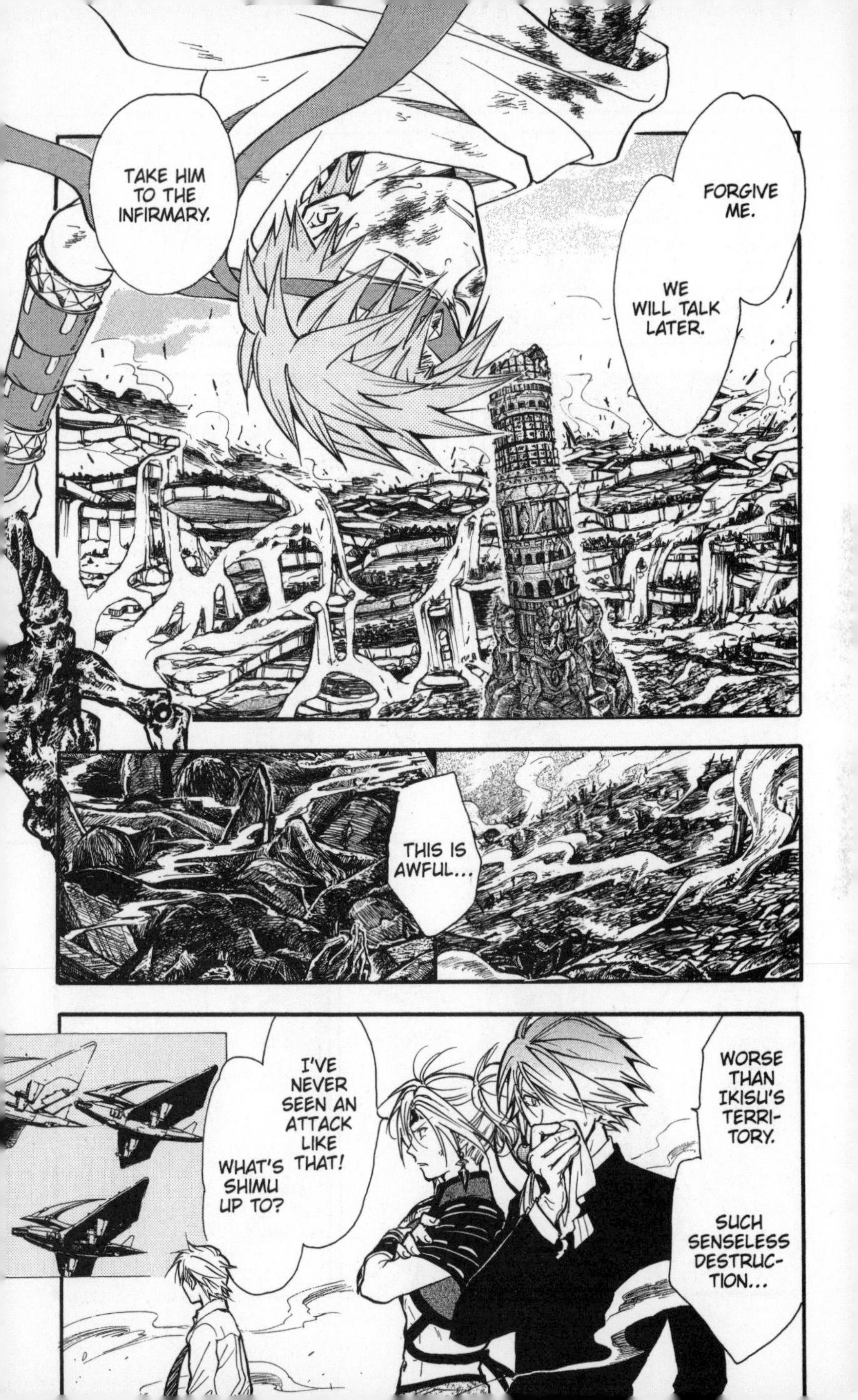
FORGIVE ME.
WE WILL TALK LATER.
TAKE HIM TO THE INFIRMARY.
THIS IS AWFUL...
WORSE THAN IKISU'S TERRITORY.
SUCH SENSELESS DESTRUCTION...
I'VE NEVER SEEN AN ATTACK LIKE THAT!
WHAT'S SHIMU UP TO?

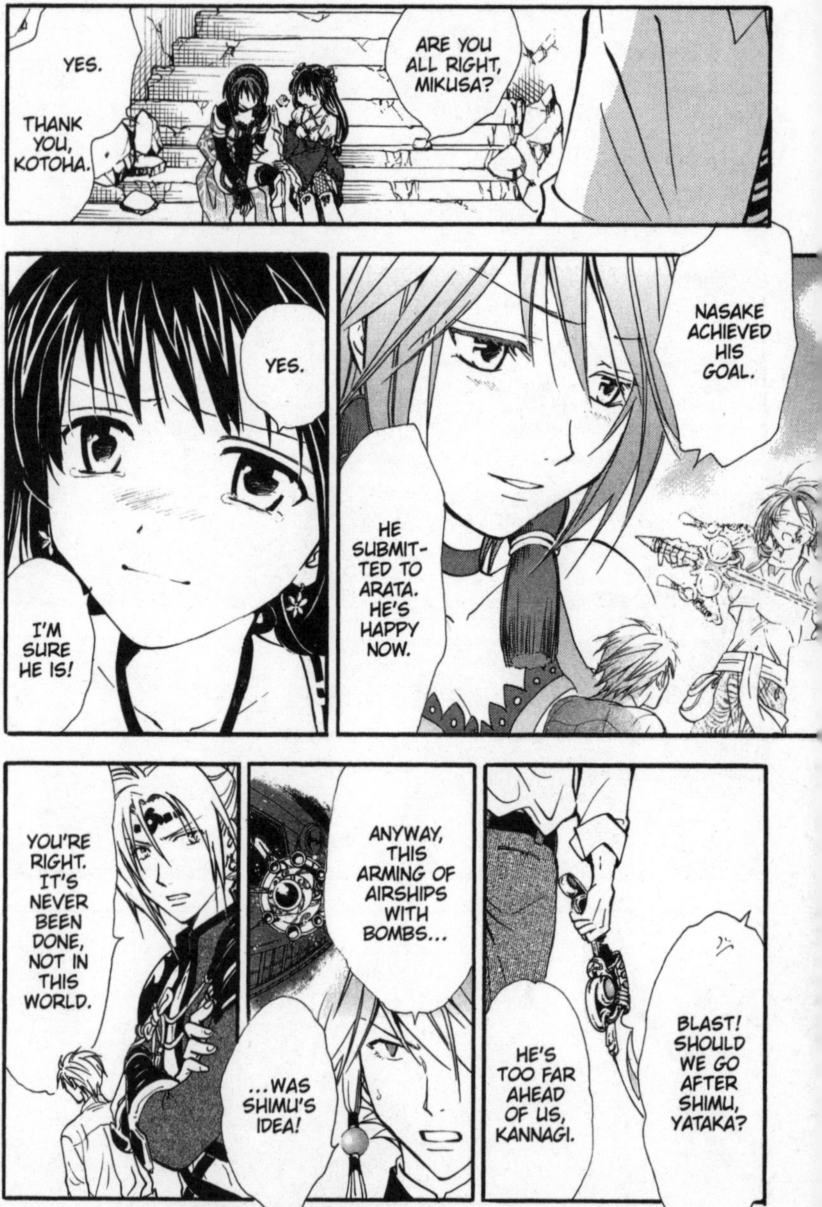
ARE YOU ALL RIGHT, MIKUSA?
YES.
THANK YOU, KOTOHA.
NASAKE ACHIEVED HIS GOAL.
HE SUBMIT-TED TO ARATA. HE'S HAPPY NOW.
YES.
I'M SURE HE IS!
BLAST! SHOULD WE GO AFTER SHIMU, YATAKA?
HE'S TOO FAR AHEAD OF US, KANNAGI.
ANYWAY, THIS ARMING OF AIRSHIPS WITH BOMBS...
...WAS SHIMU'S IDEA!
YOU'RE RIGHT. IT'S NEVER BEEN DONE, NOT IN THIS WORLD.

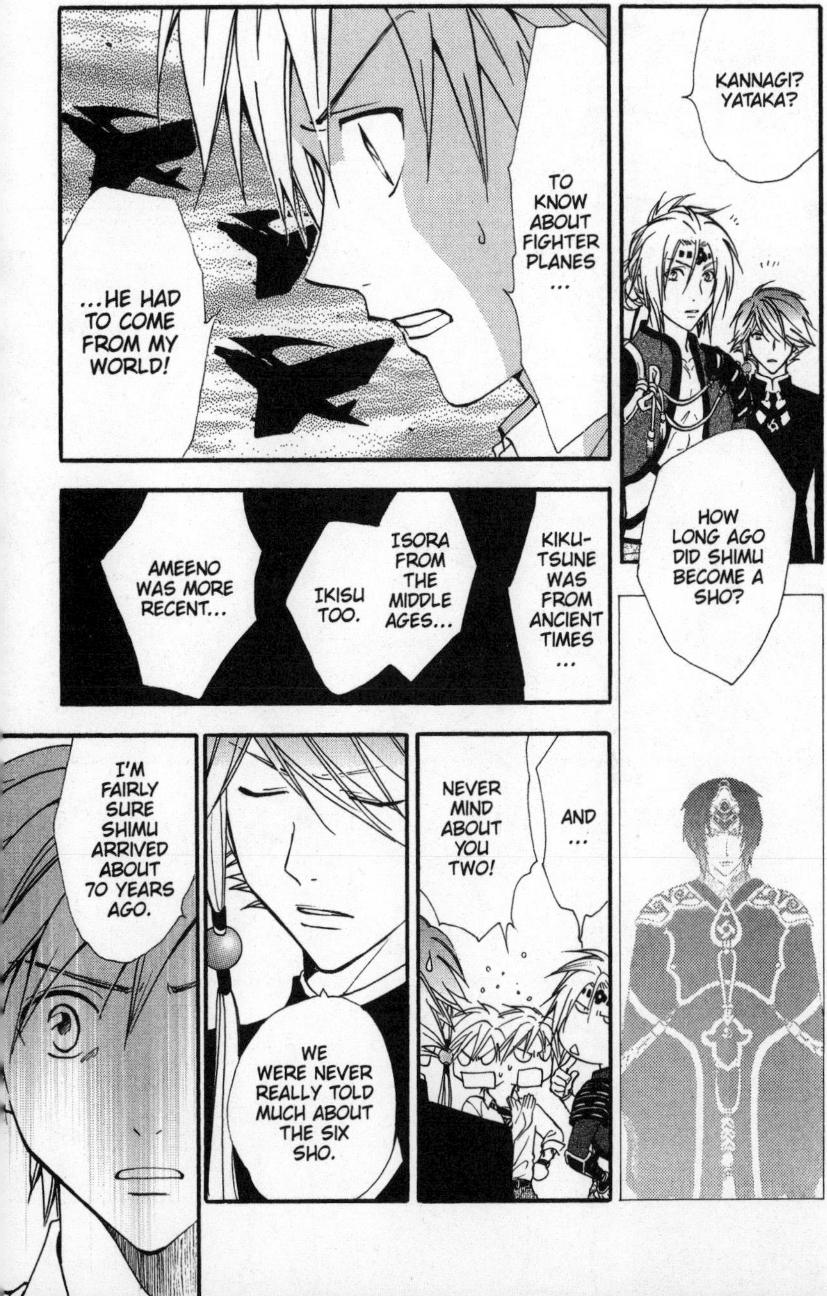
KANNAGI? YATAKA?
HOW LONG AGO DID SHIMU BECOME A SHO?
TO KNOW ABOUT FIGHTER PLANES...
...HE HAD TO COME FROM MY WORLD!
KIKU-TSUNE WAS FROM ANCIENT TIMES...
ISORA FROM THE MIDDLE AGES...
IKISU TOO.
AMEENO WAS MORE RECENT...
AND...
NEVER MIND ABOUT YOU TWO!
WE WERE NEVER REALLY TOLD MUCH ABOUT THE SIX SHO.
I'M FAIRLY SURE SHIMU ARRIVED ABOUT 70 YEARS AGO.

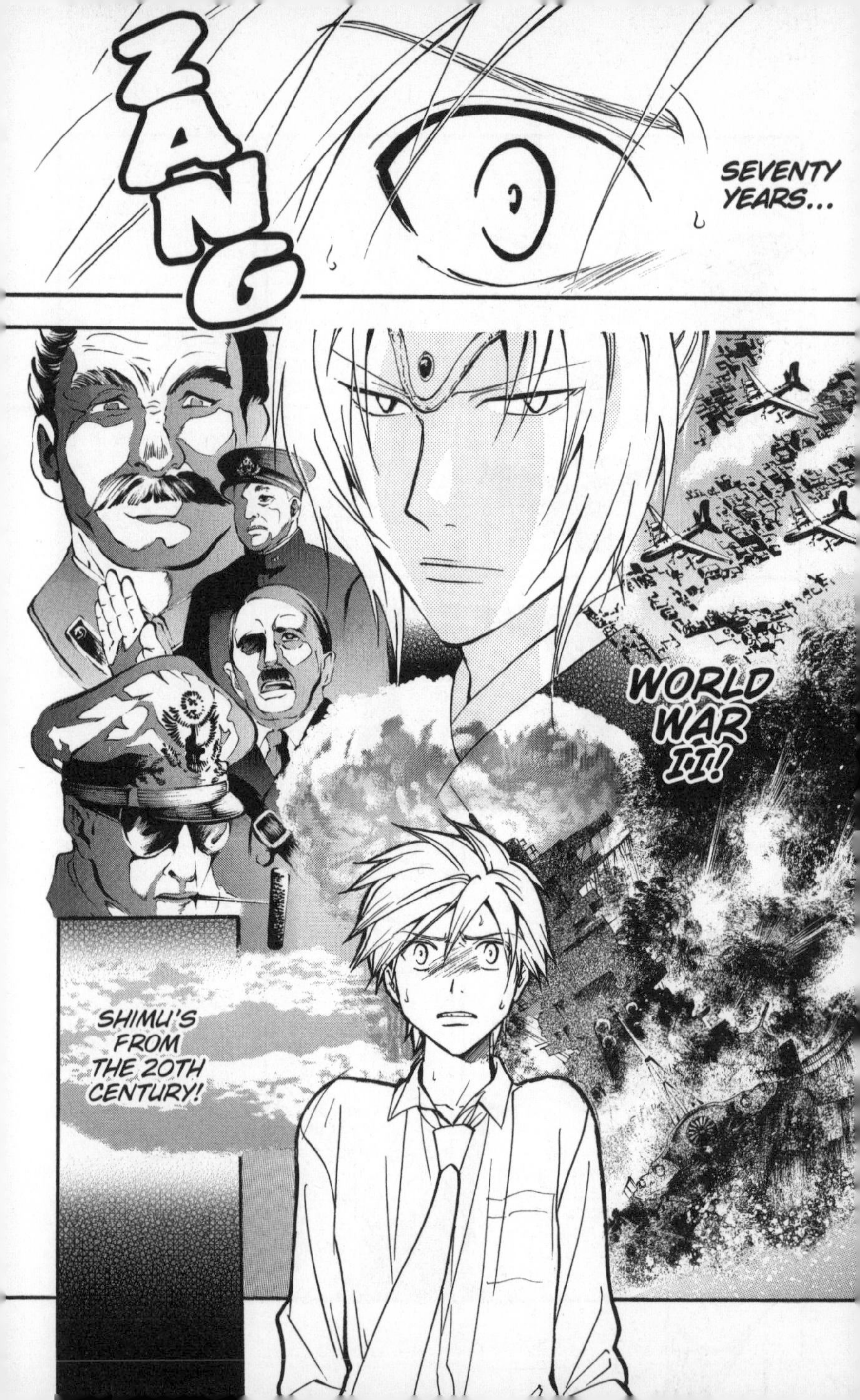
SEVENTY YEARS...
ZANG
WORLD WAR II!
SHIMU'S FROM THE 20TH CENTURY!

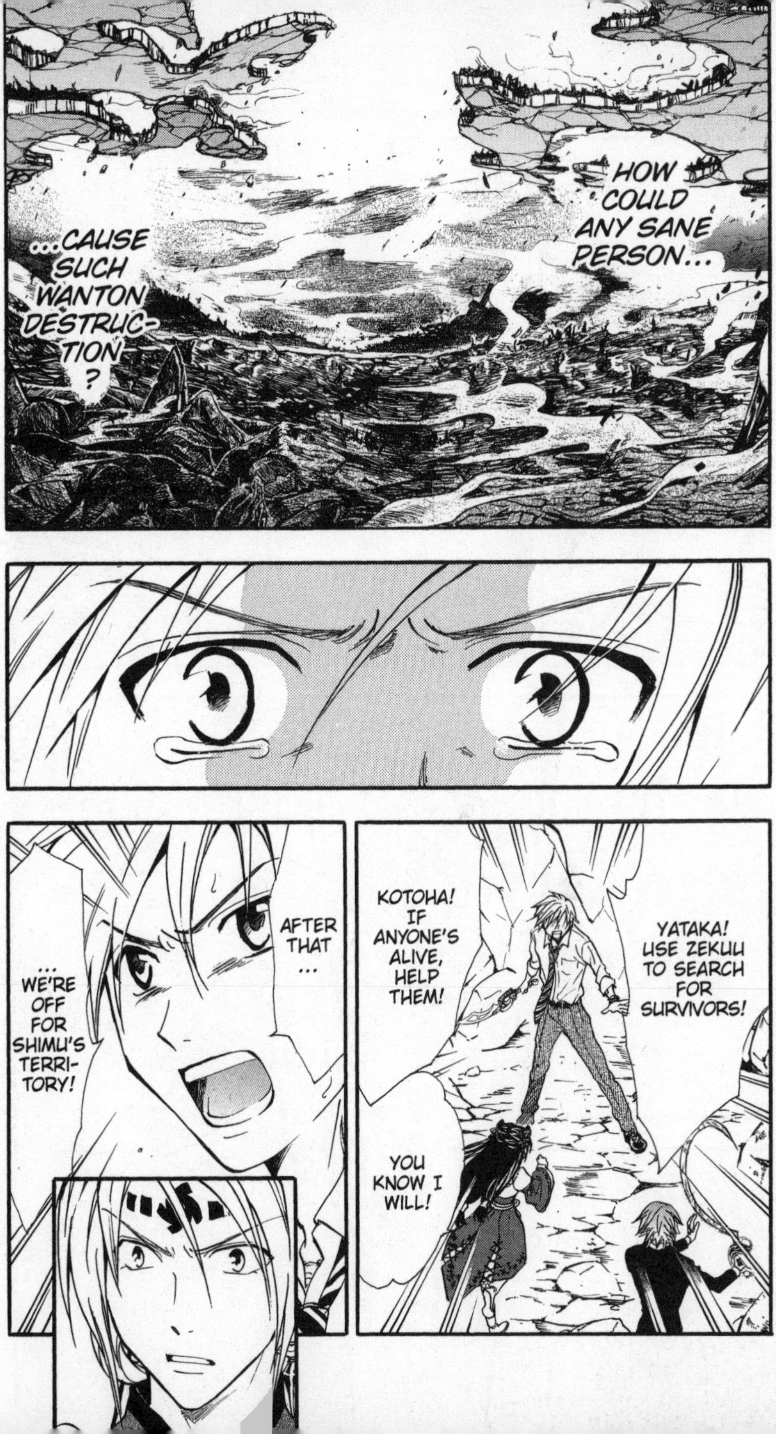
HOW COULD ANY SANE PERSON...
...CAUSE SUCH WANTON DESTRUCTION?
YATAKA! USE ZEKUU TO SEARCH FOR SURVIVORS!
KOTOHA! IF ANYONE'S ALIVE, HELP THEM!
YOU KNOW I WILL!
AFTER THAT...
...WE'RE OFF FOR SHIMU'S TERRITORY!

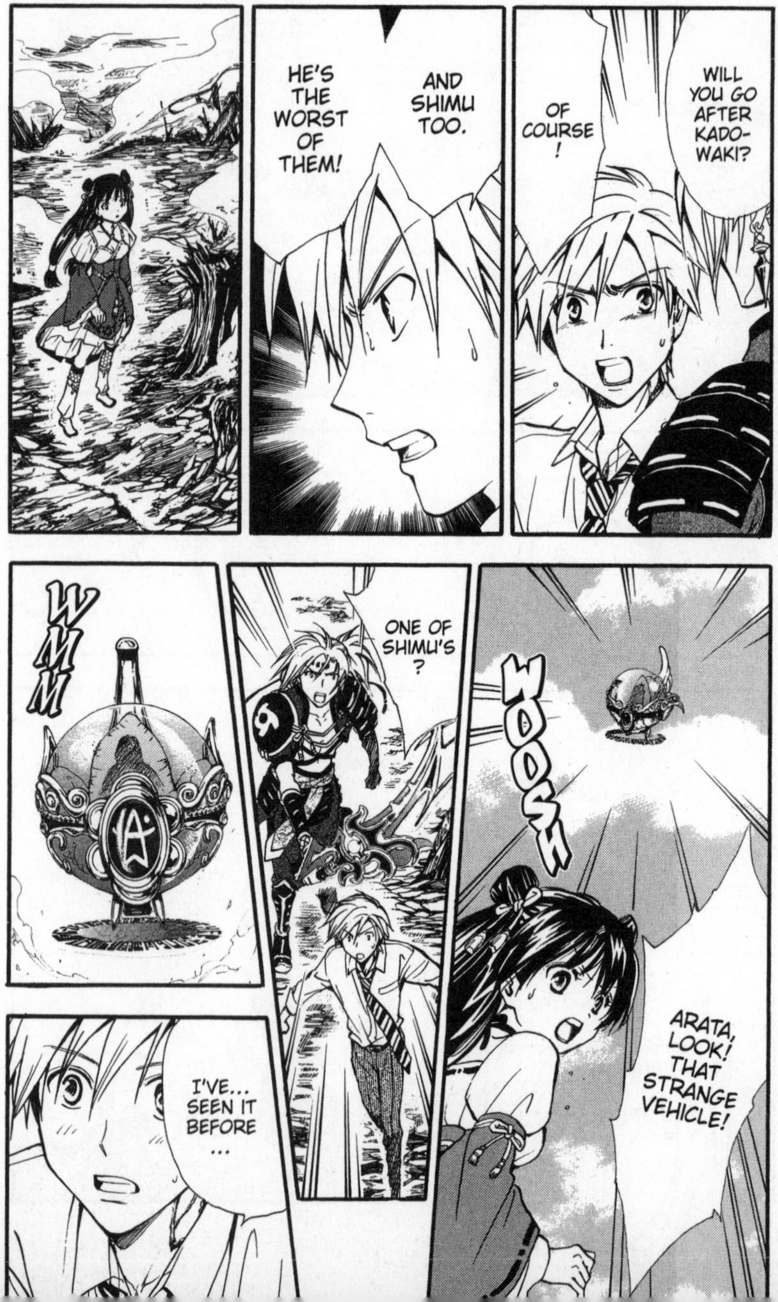
WILL YOU GO AFTER KADO-WAKI?
OF COURSE!
AND SHIMU TOO.
HE'S THE WORST OF THEM!
WOOSH
ARATA, LOOK! THAT STRANGE VEHICLE!
ONE OF SHIMU'S?
WMM
I'VE... SEEN IT BEFORE...

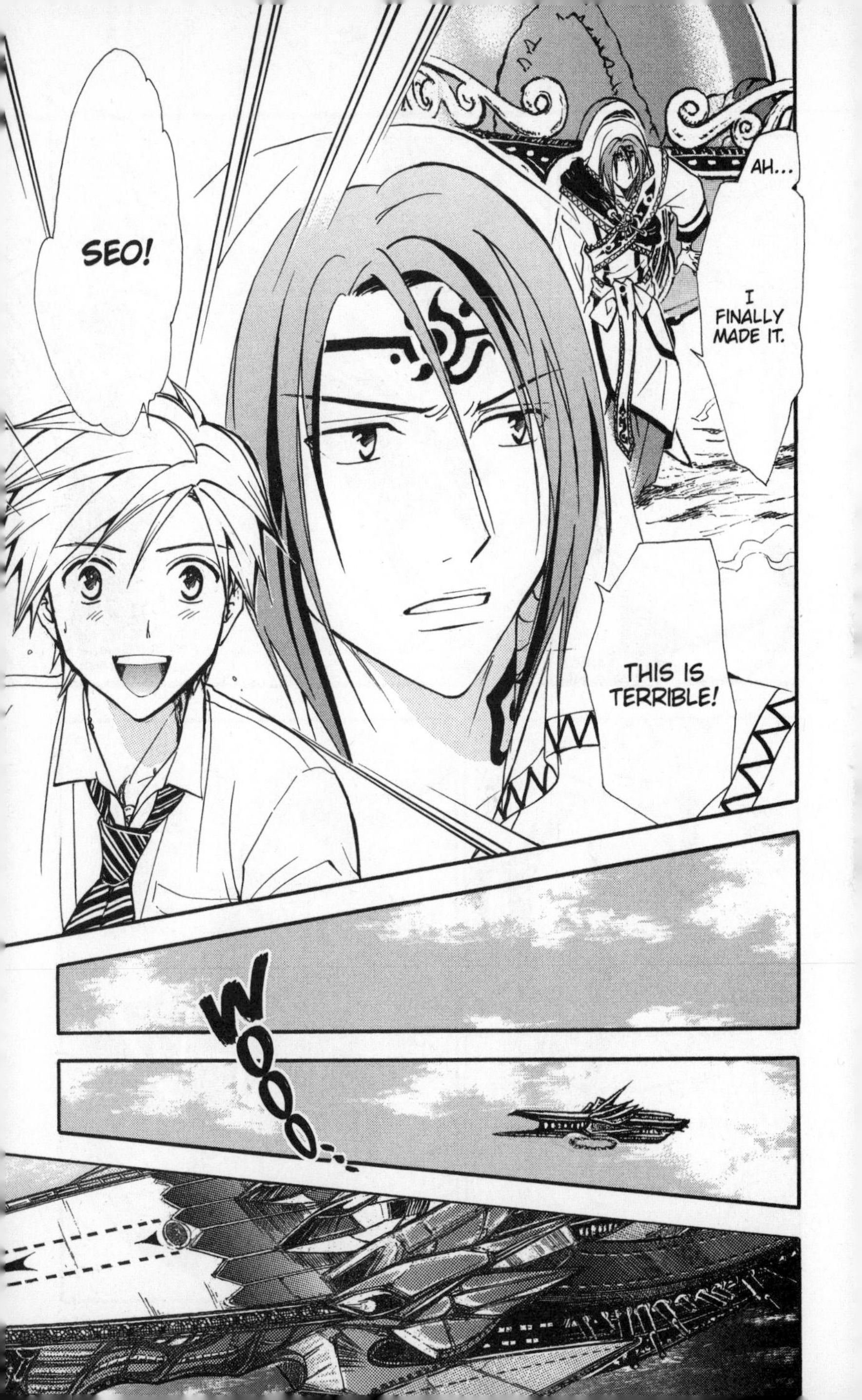
AH...
I FINALLY MADE IT.
SEO!
THIS IS TERRIBLE!
WOOO...

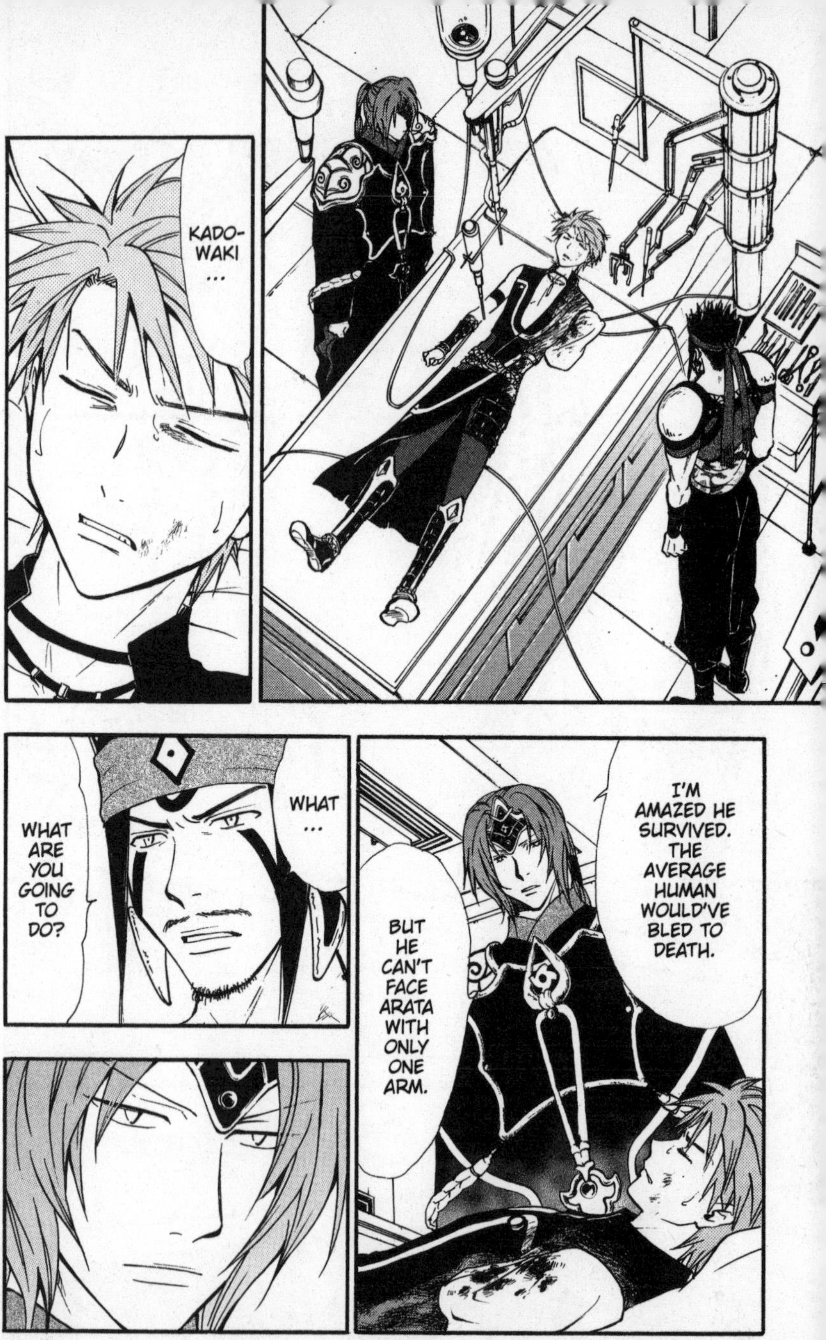
KADO-WAKI ...
I'M AMAZED HE SURVIVED. THE AVERAGE HUMAN WOULD'VE BLED TO DEATH.
BUT HE CAN'T FACE ARATA WITH ONLY ONE ARM.
WHAT ...
WHAT ARE YOU GOING TO DO?

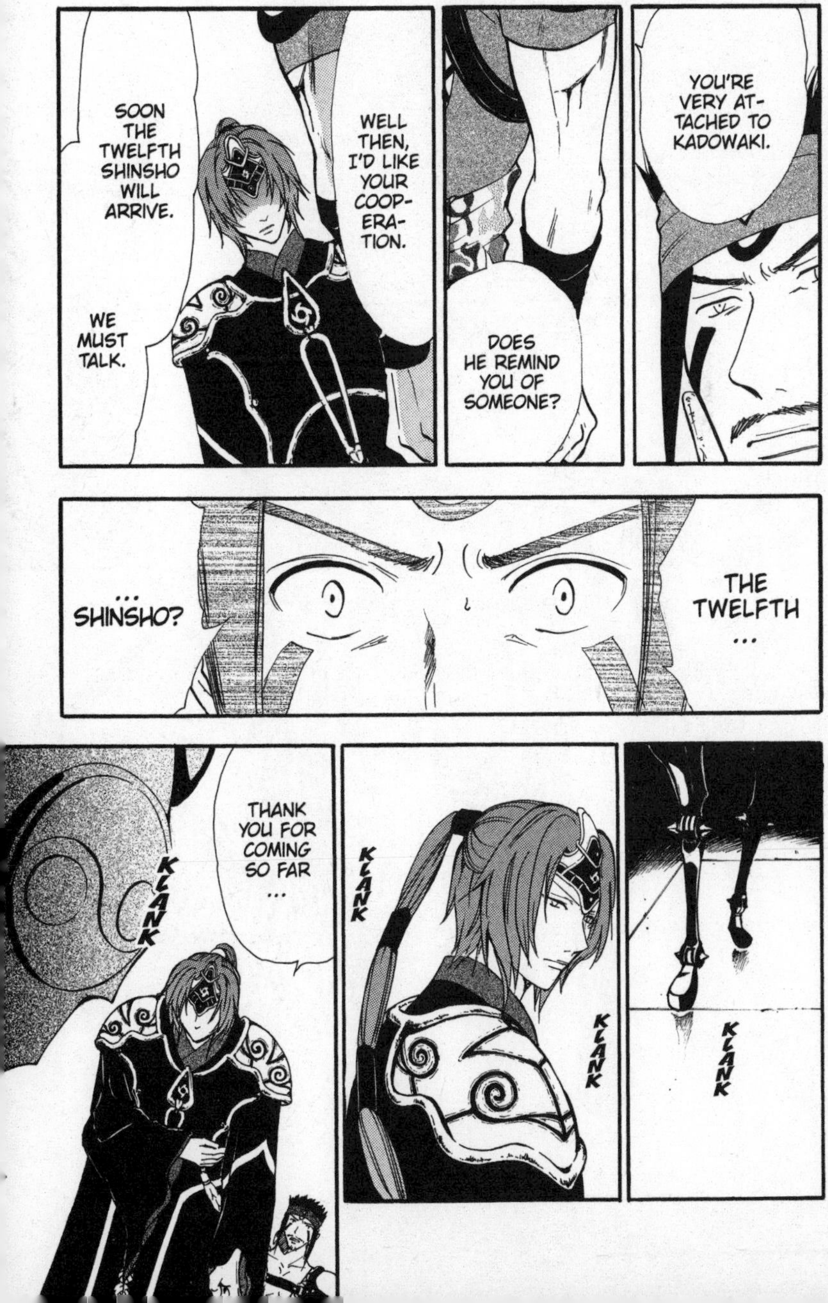
YOU'RE VERY AT-TACHED TO KADOWAKI.
DOES HE REMIND YOU OF SOMEONE?
WELL THEN, I'D LIKE YOUR COOP-ERATION.
SOON THE TWELFTH SHINSHO WILL ARRIVE.
WE MUST TALK.
THE TWELFTH ...
... SHINSHO?
KLANK
KLANK
KLANK
THANK YOU FOR COMING SO FAR ...
KLANK

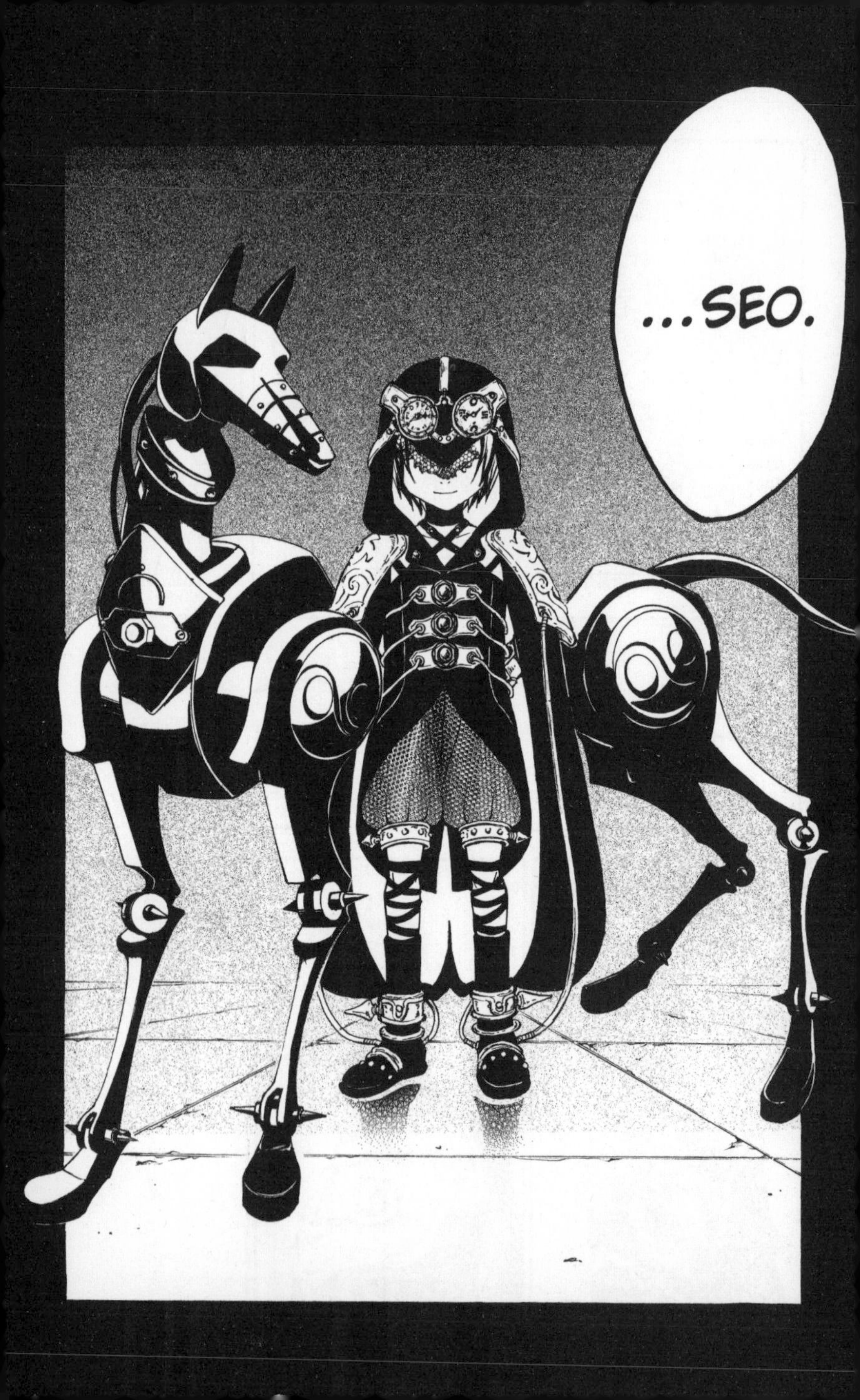
...SEO.

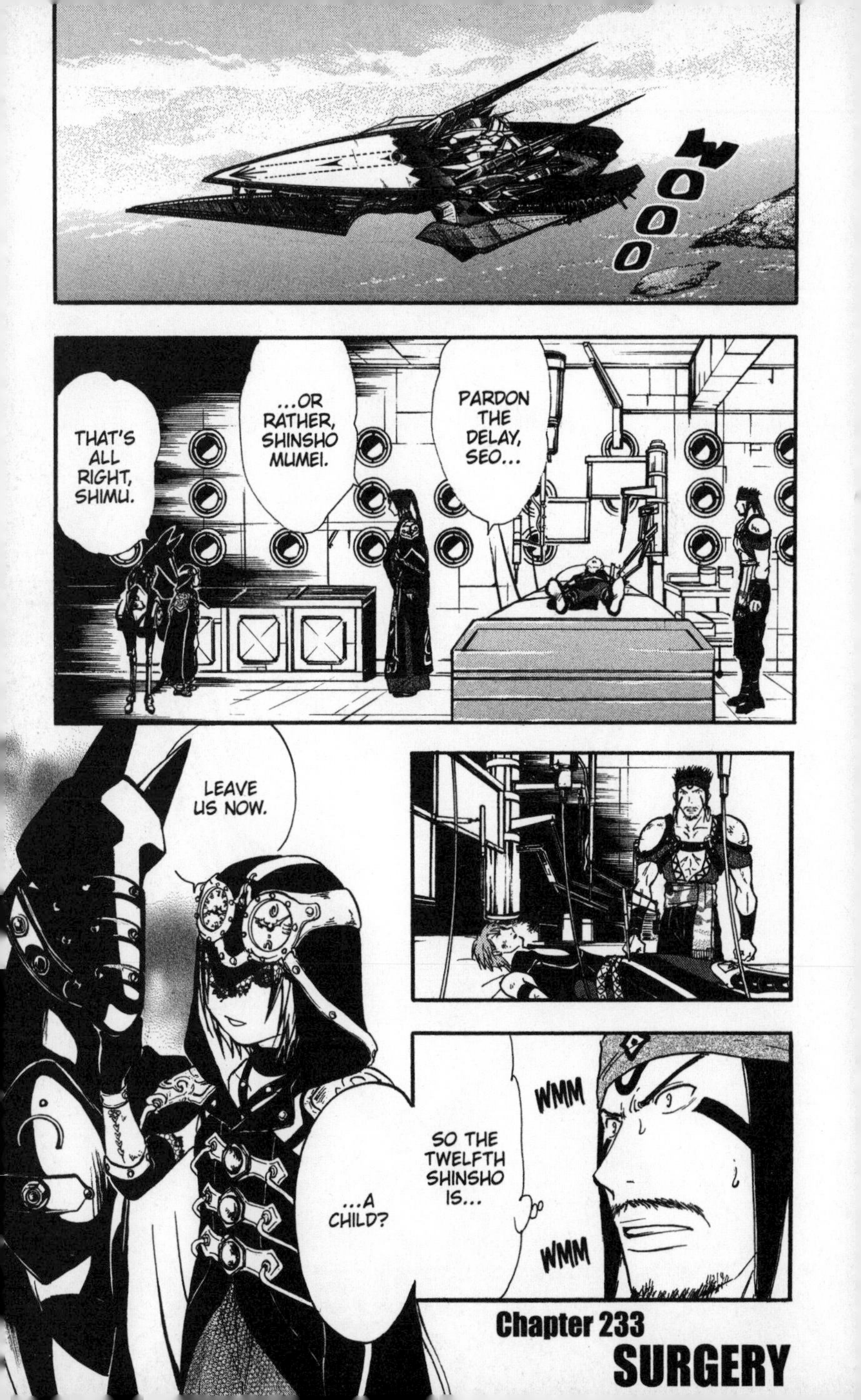
WOOOO
PARDON THE DELAY, SEO...
...OR RATHER, SHINSHO MUMEI.
THAT'S ALL RIGHT, SHIMU.
WMM
SO THE TWELFTH SHINSHO IS...
WMM
...A CHILD?
LEAVE US NOW.

Chapter 233
SURGERY

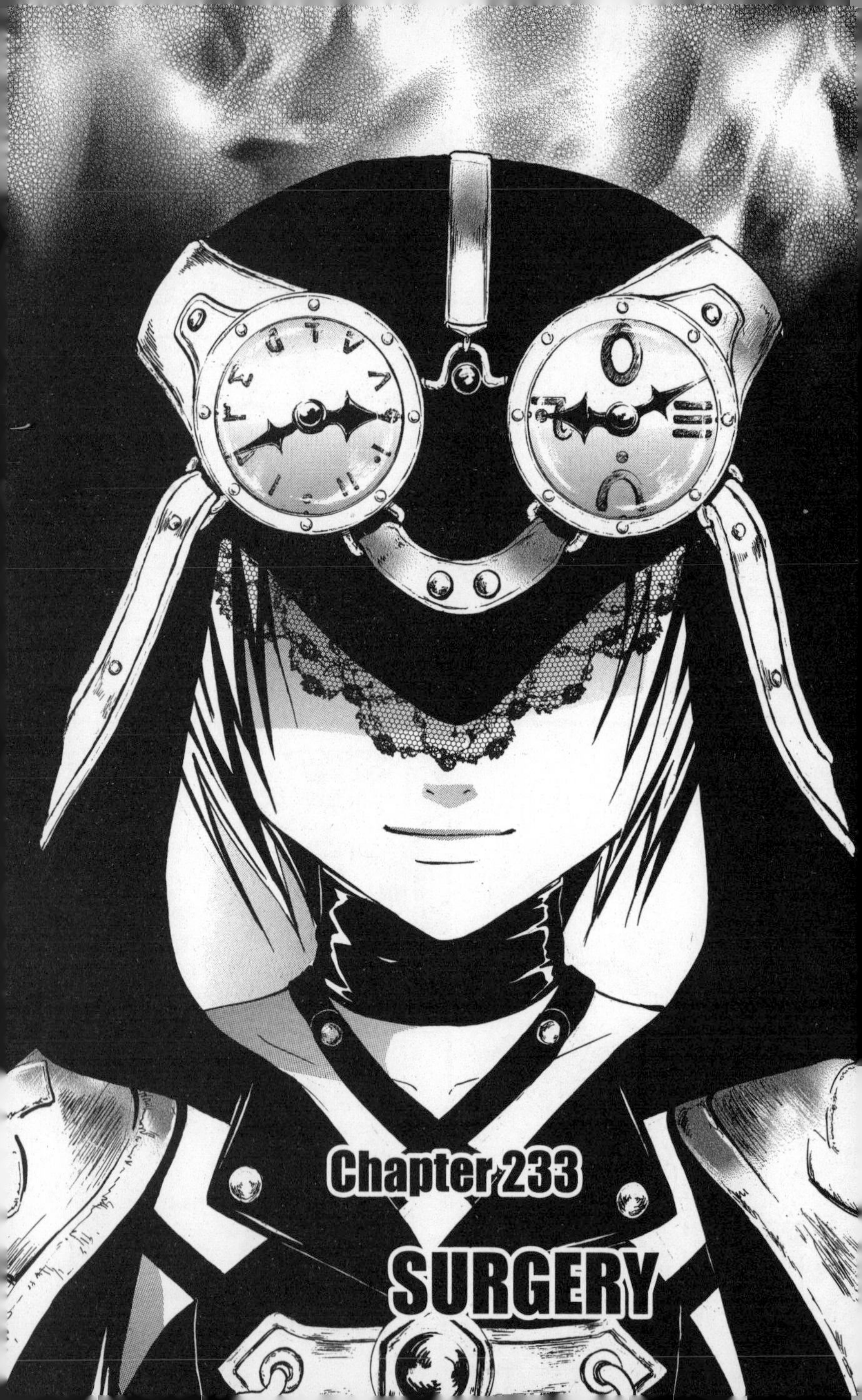
Chapter 233
SURGERY

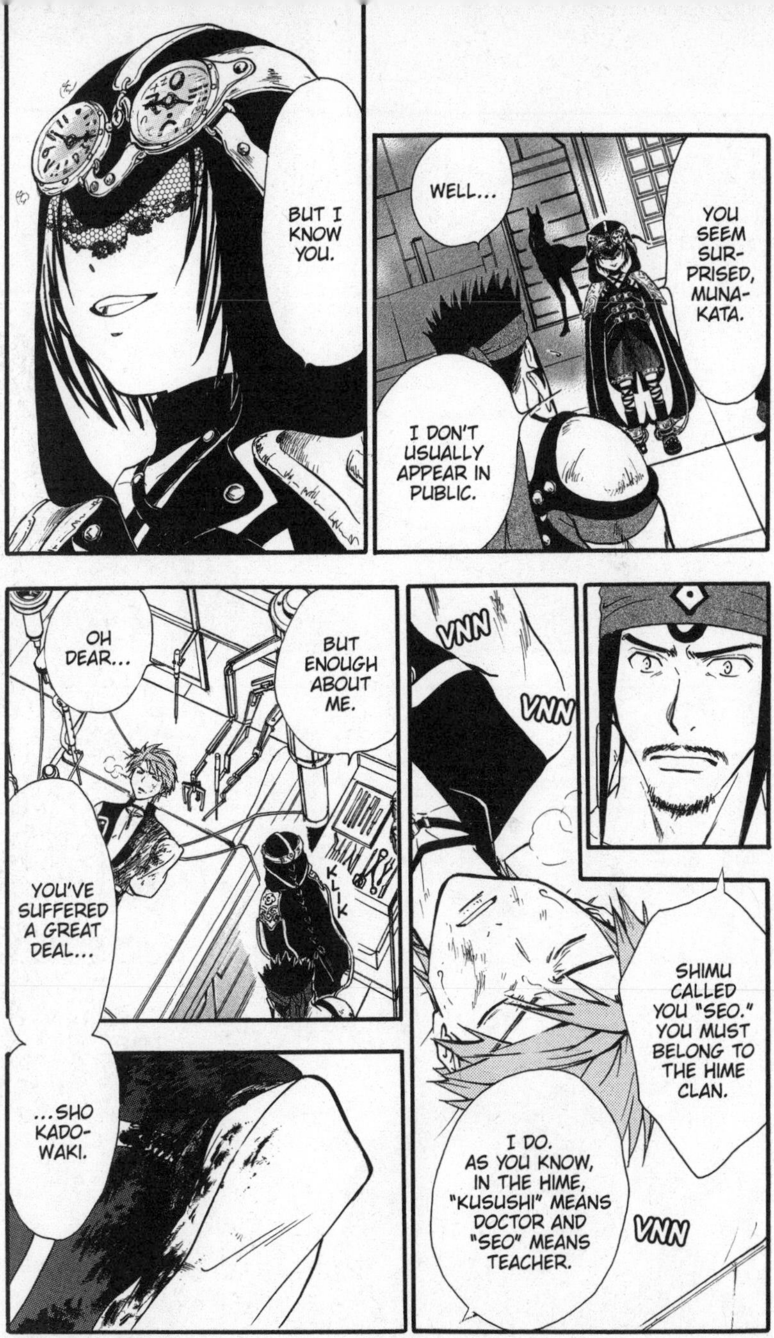
YOU SEEM SURPRISED, MUNAKATA.
WELL...
I DON'T USUALLY APPEAR IN PUBLIC.
BUT I KNOW YOU.
VNN
VNN
SHIMU CALLED YOU "SEO." YOU MUST BELONG TO THE HIME CLAN.
I DO. AS YOU KNOW, IN THE HIME, "KUSUSHI" MEANS DOCTOR AND "SEO" MEANS TEACHER.
VNN
OH DEAR...
BUT ENOUGH ABOUT ME.
KLIK
YOU'VE SUFFERED A GREAT DEAL...
...SHO KADOWAKI.

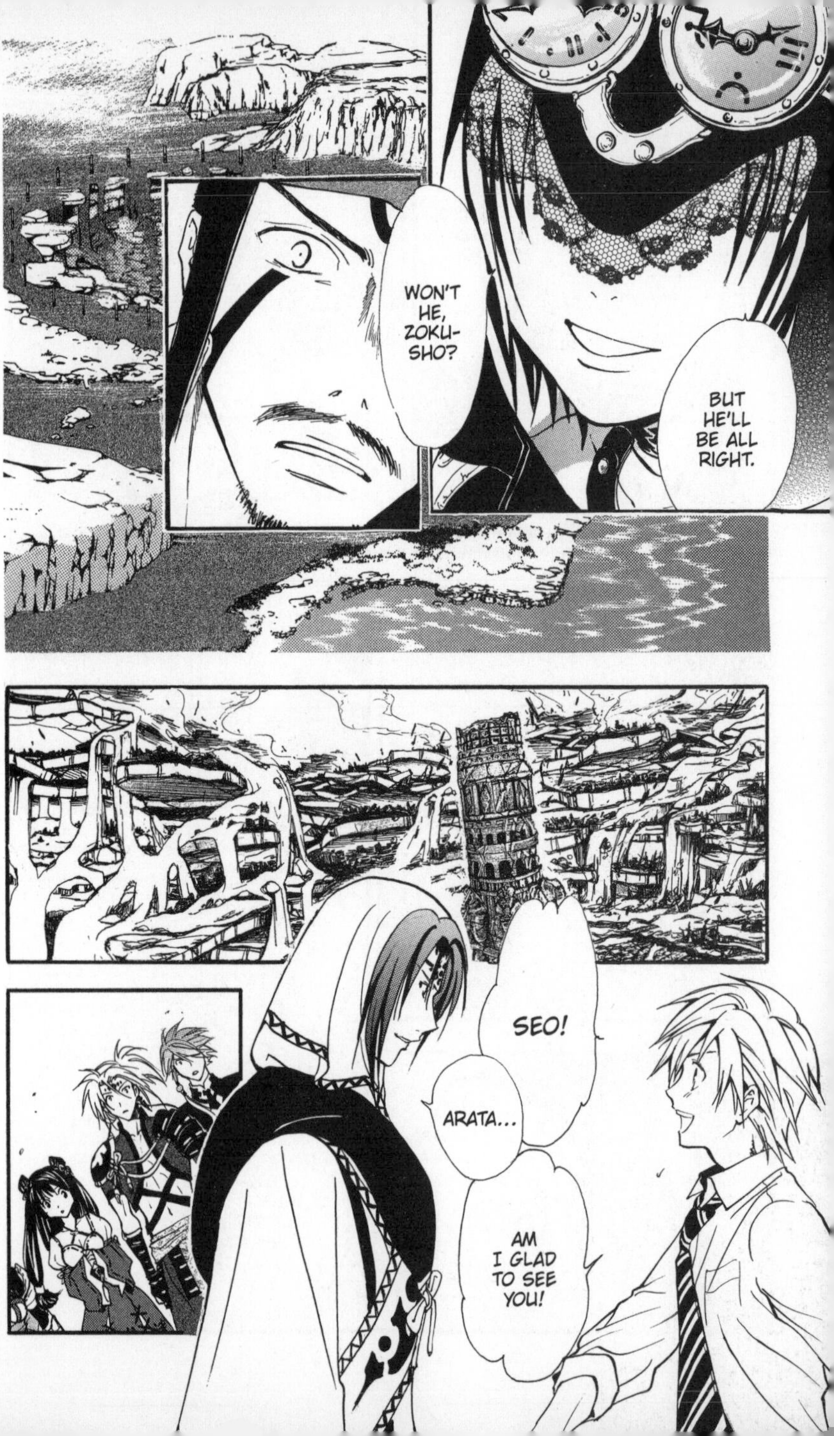
BUT HE'LL BE ALL RIGHT.
WON'T HE, ZOKU-SHO?
SEO!
ARATA...
AM I GLAD TO SEE YOU!

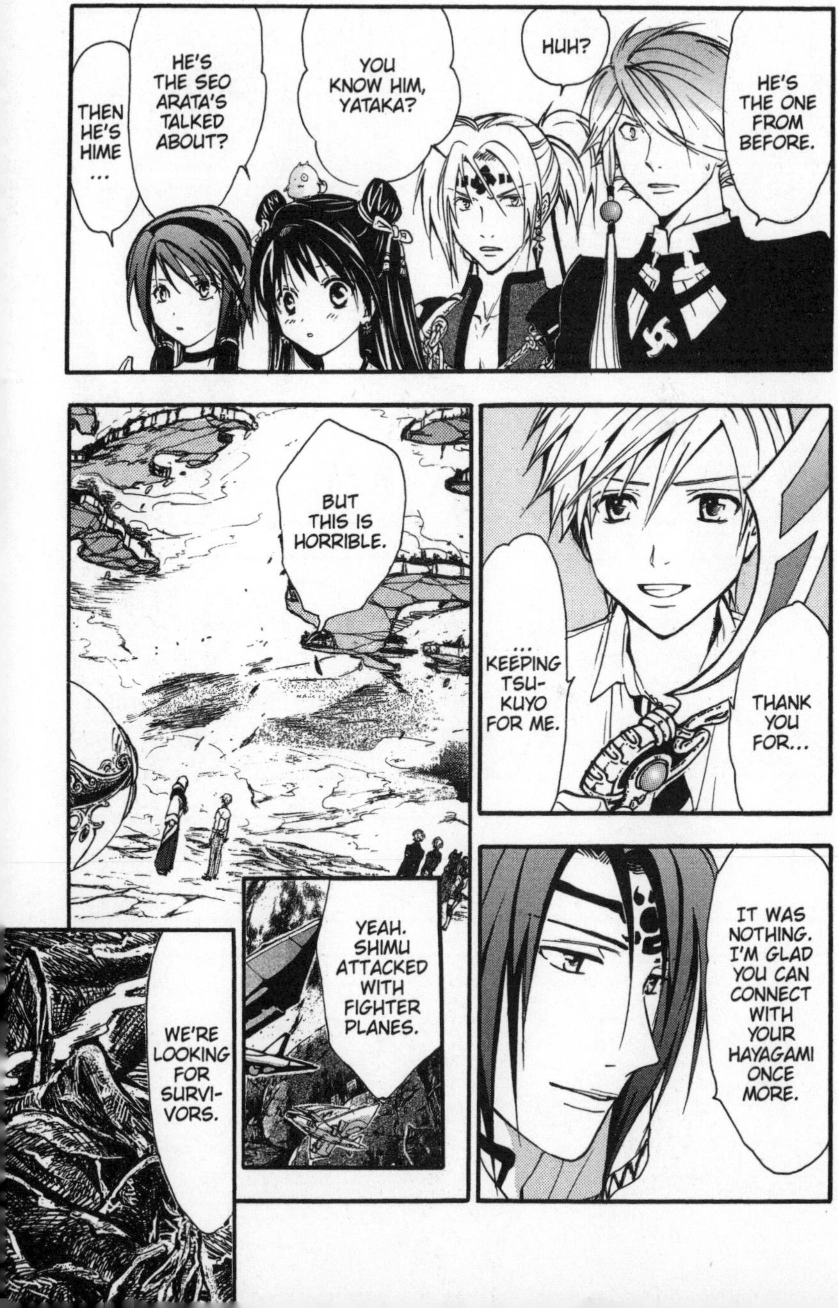
HE'S THE ONE FROM BEFORE.
HUH?
YOU KNOW HIM, YATAKA?
HE'S THE SEO ARATA'S TALKED ABOUT?
THEN HE'S HIME...
THANK YOU FOR...
...KEEPING TSU-KUYO FOR ME.
IT WAS NOTHING. I'M GLAD YOU CAN CONNECT WITH YOUR HAYAGAMI ONCE MORE.
BUT THIS IS HORRIBLE.
YEAH. SHIMU ATTACKED WITH FIGHTER PLANES.
WE'RE LOOKING FOR SURVIVORS.

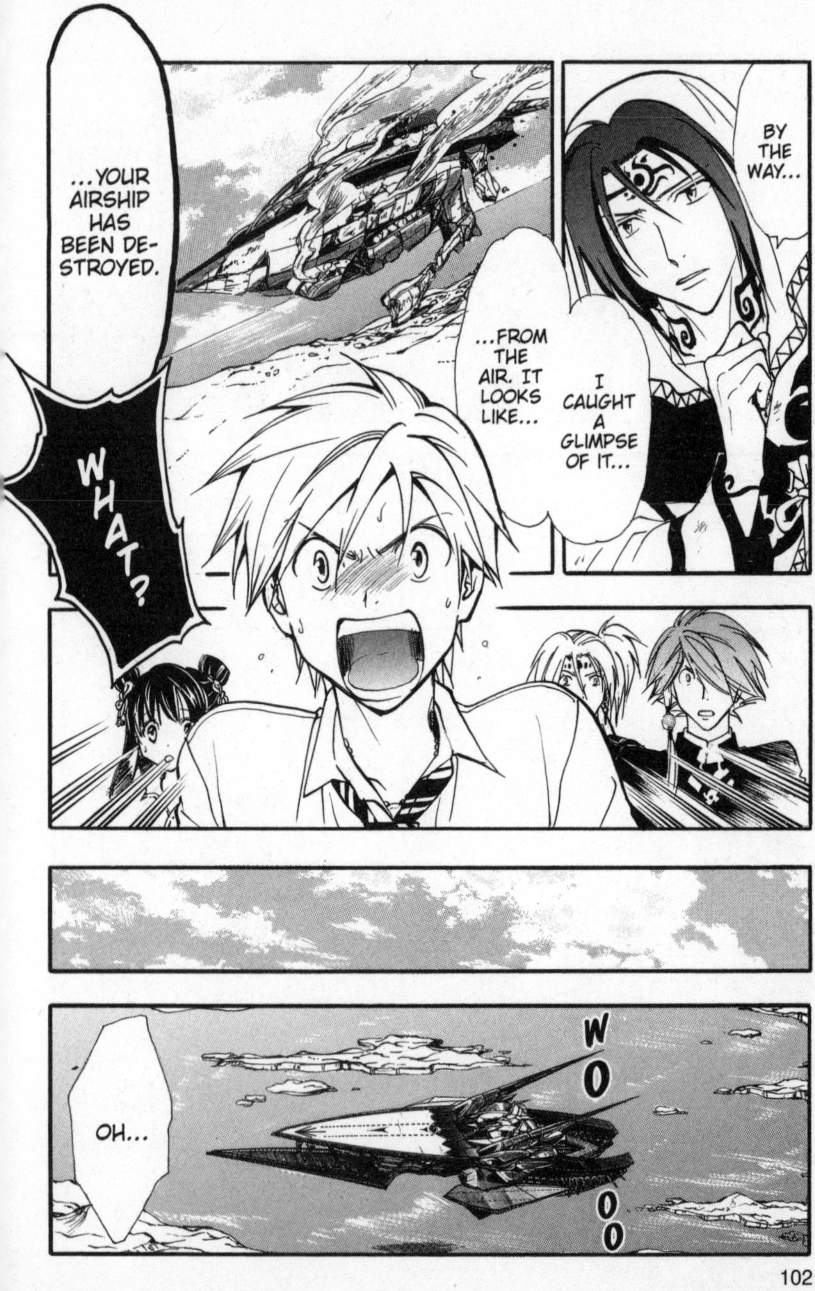
BY THE WAY...
I CAUGHT A GLIMPSE OF IT...
...FROM THE AIR. IT LOOKS LIKE...
...YOUR AIRSHIP HAS BEEN DE-STROYED.
WHAT?
OH...
WOOOO

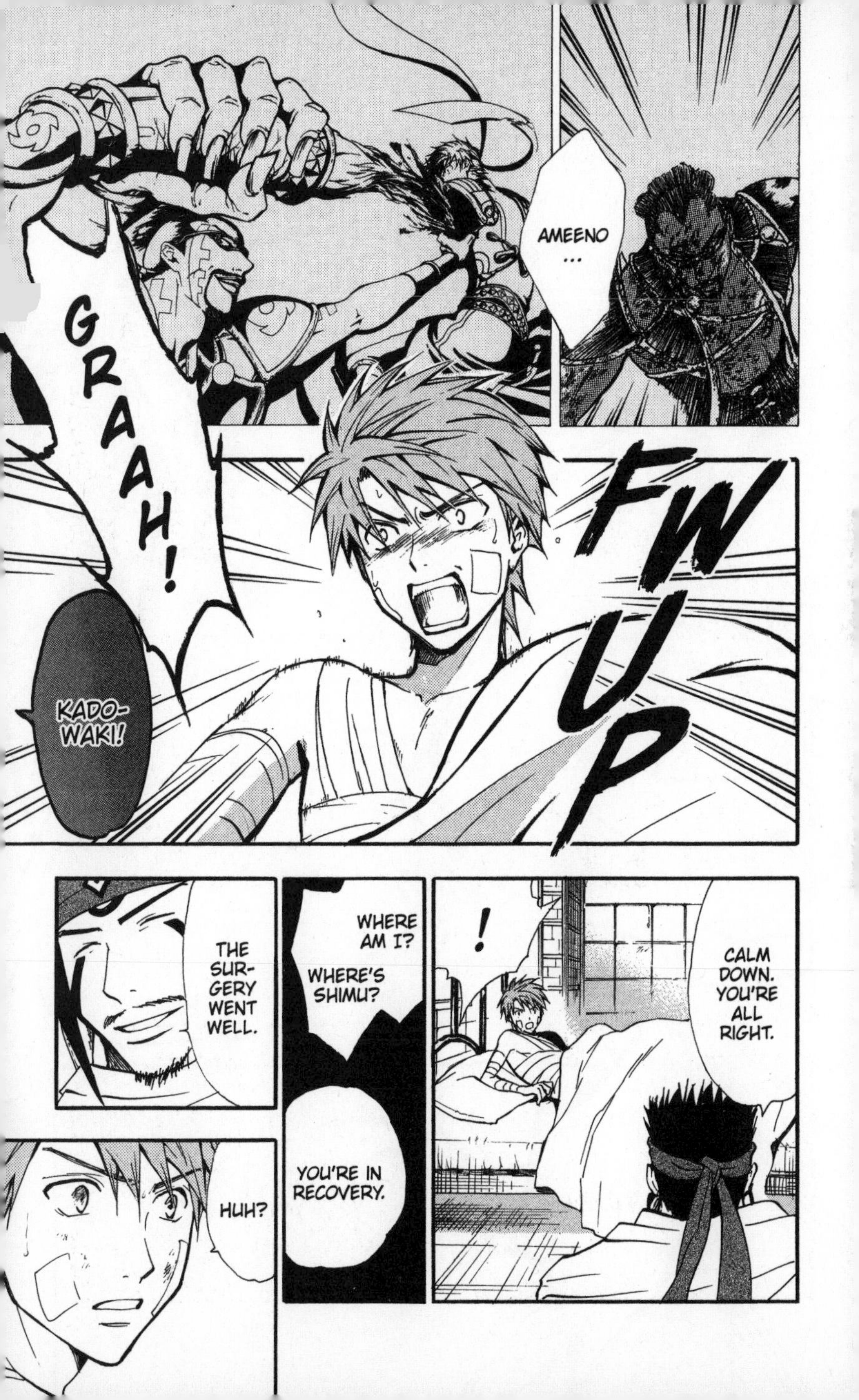
AMEENO ...
GRAAH!
FWUP
KADO-WAKI!
!
CALM DOWN. YOU'RE ALL RIGHT.
WHERE AM I?
WHERE'S SHIMU?
YOU'RE IN RECOVERY.
THE SUR-GERY WENT WELL.
HUH?

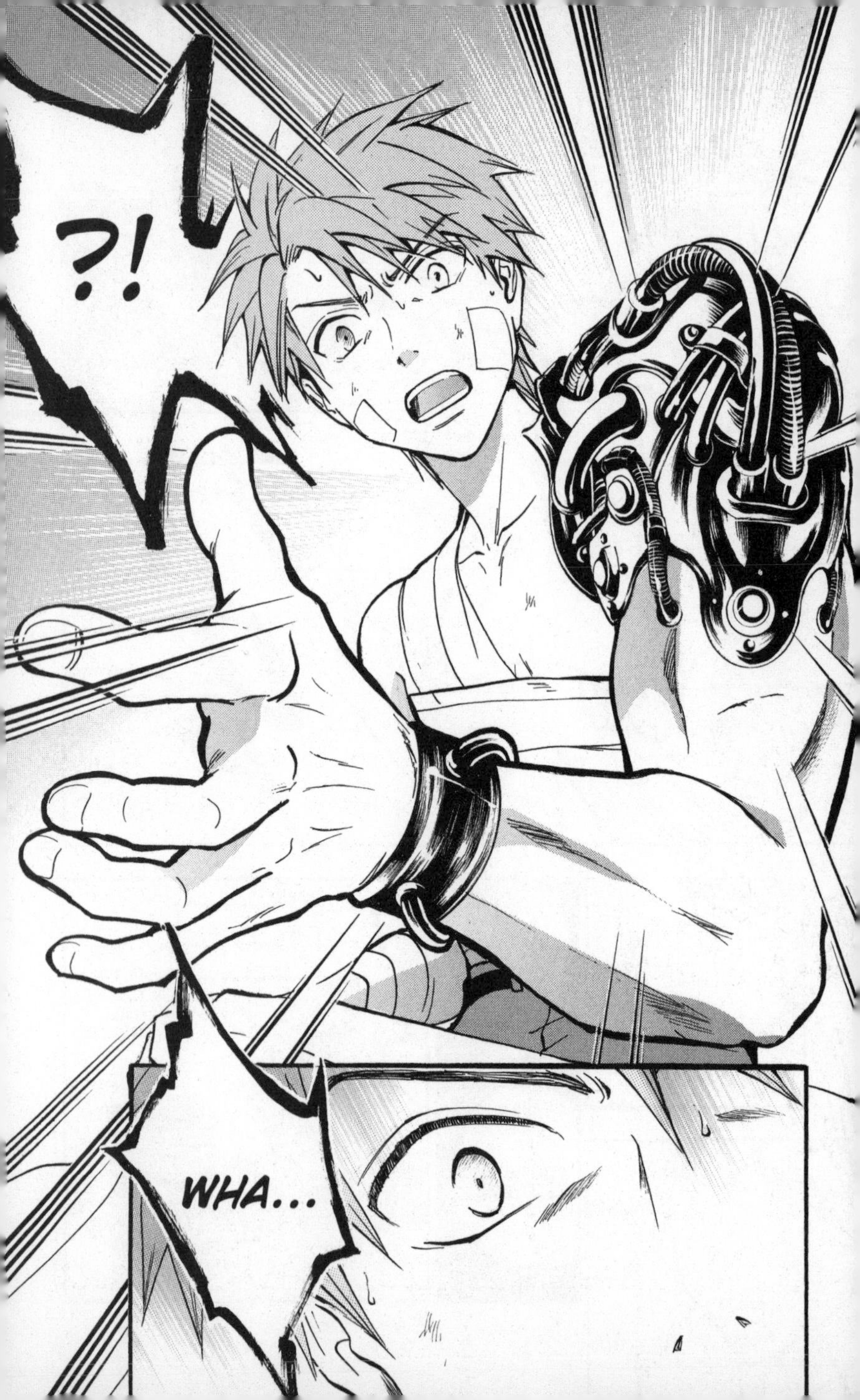
?!
WHA...

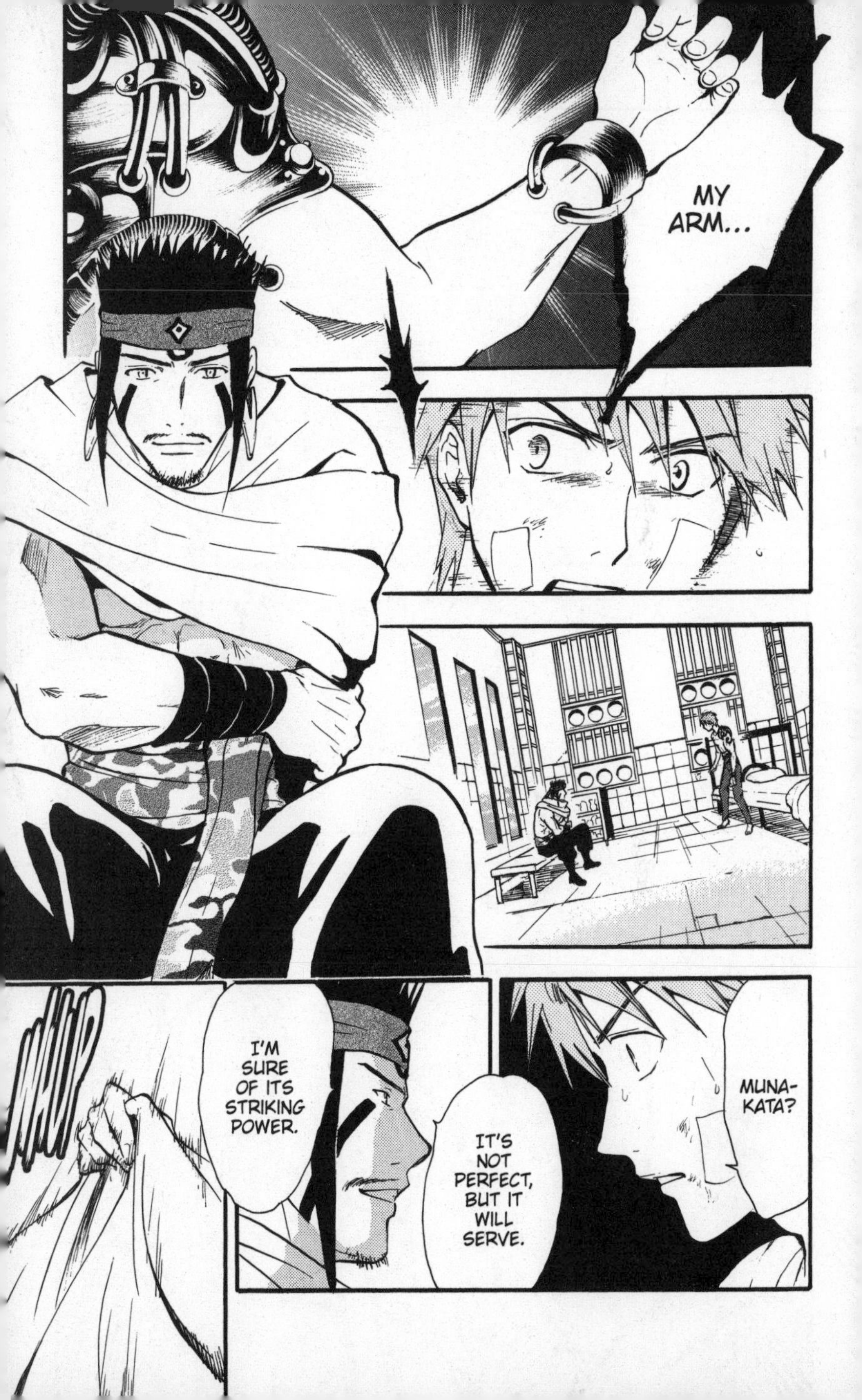
MY ARM...
MUNA-KATA?
IT'S NOT PERFECT, BUT IT WILL SERVE.
I'M SURE OF ITS STRIKING POWER.

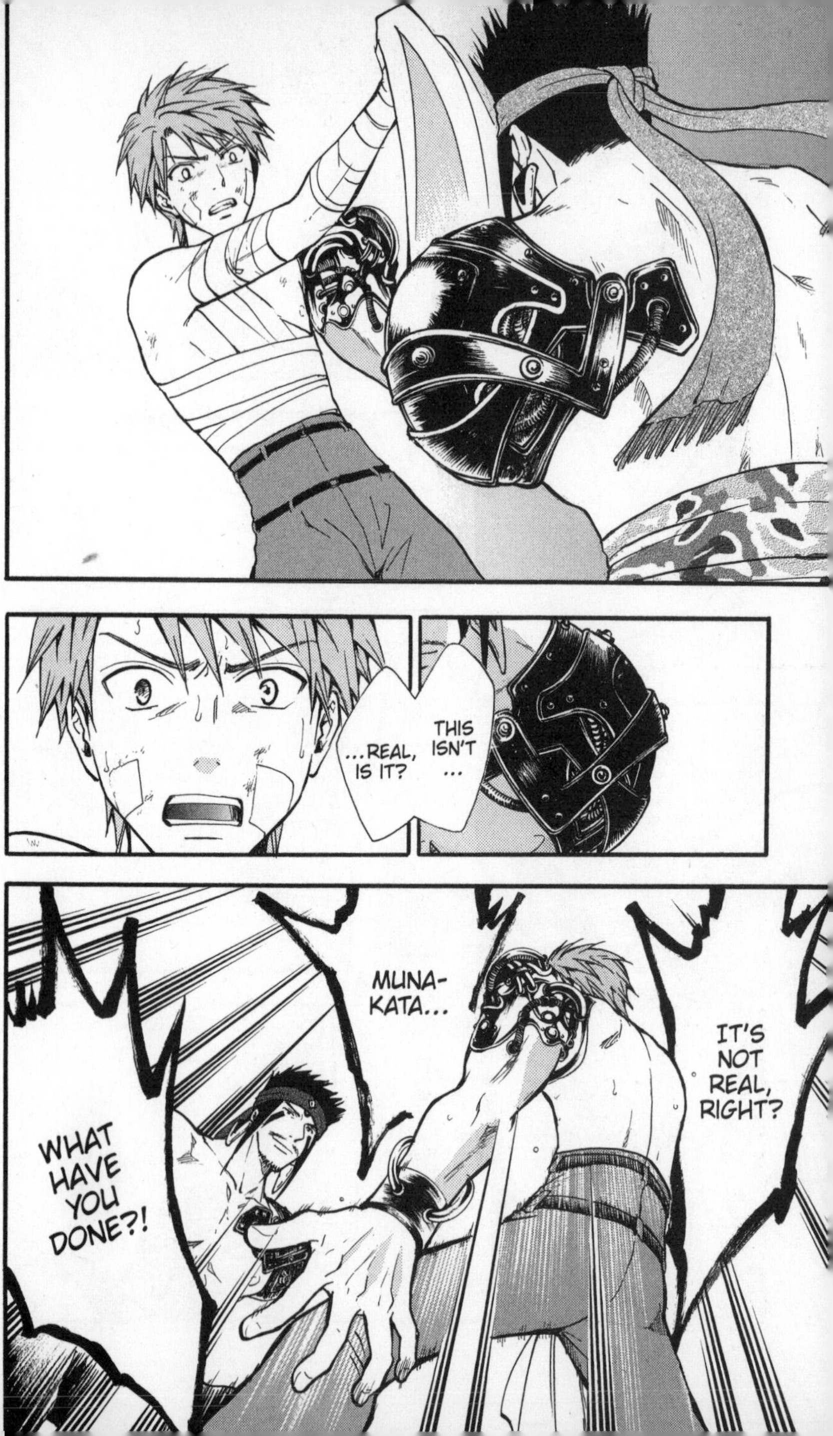
THIS ISN'T ...
...REAL, IS IT?
MUNA-KATA...
IT'S NOT REAL, RIGHT?
WHAT HAVE YOU DONE?!

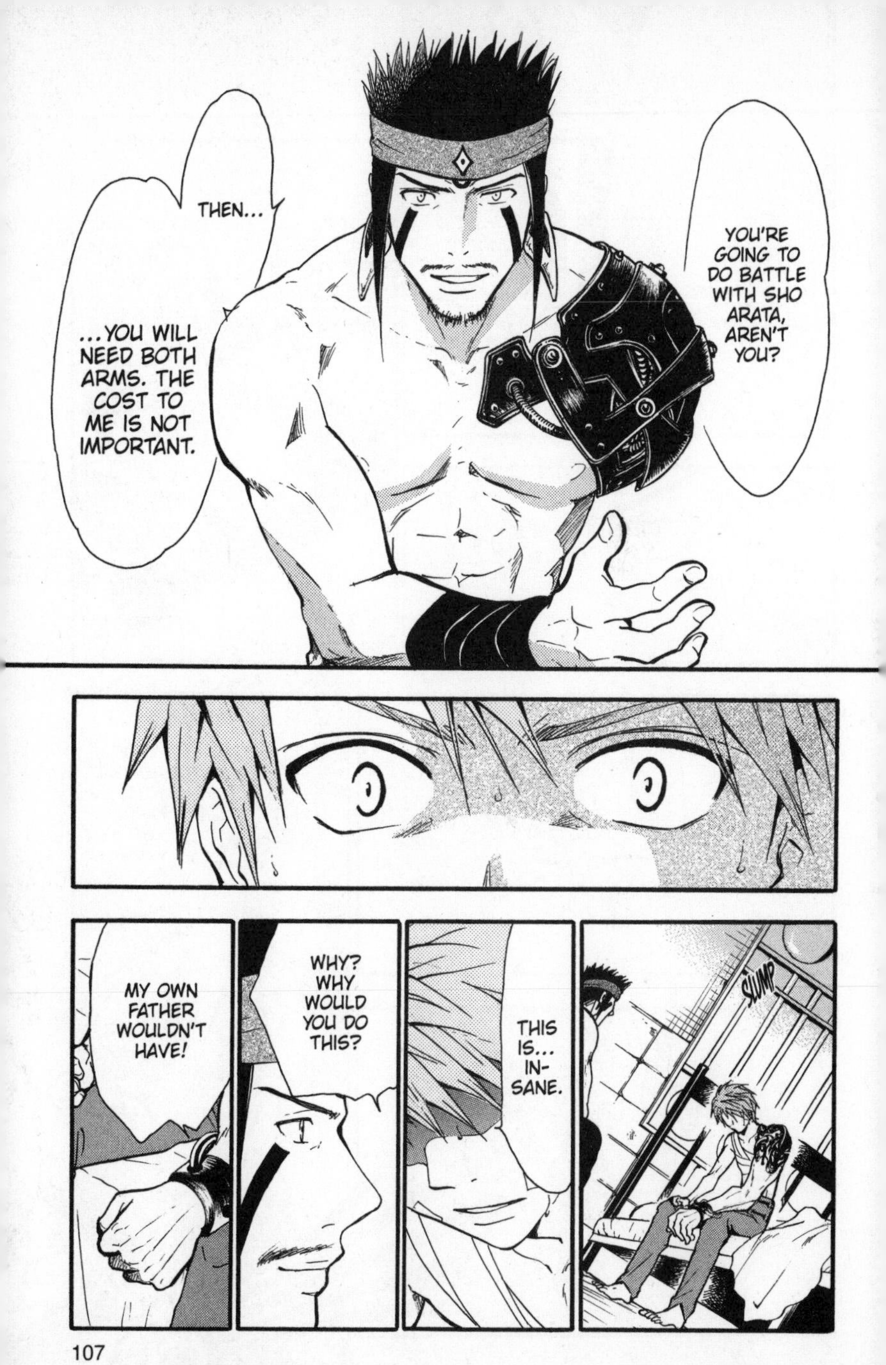
YOU'RE GOING TO DO BATTLE WITH SHO ARATA, AREN'T YOU?
THEN...
...YOU WILL NEED BOTH ARMS. THE COST TO ME IS NOT IMPORTANT.
SLUMP
THIS IS... IN-SANE.
WHY? WHY WOULD YOU DO THIS?
MY OWN FATHER WOULDN'T HAVE!

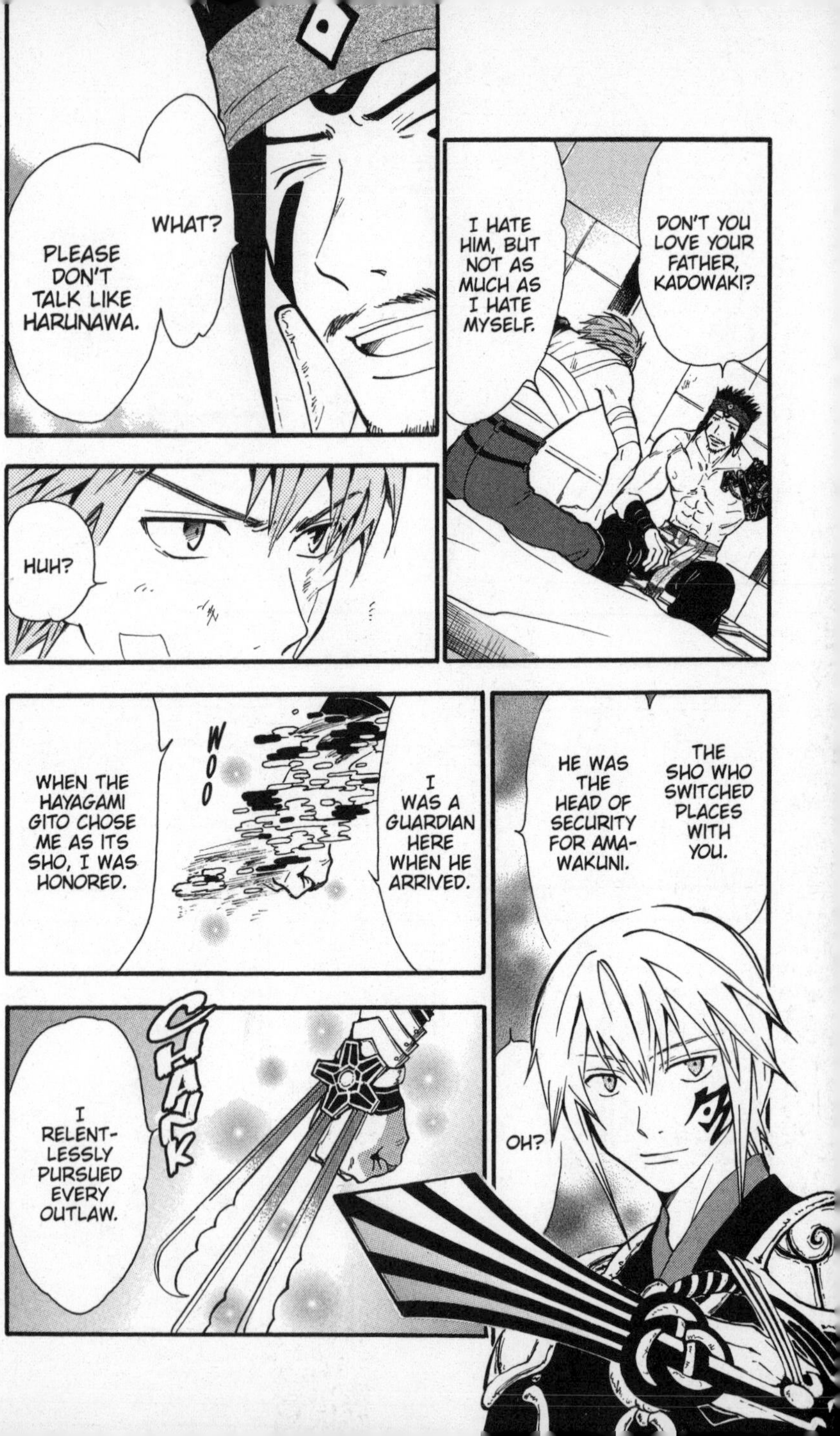
DON'T YOU LOVE YOUR FATHER, KADOWAKI?
I HATE HIM, BUT NOT AS MUCH AS I HATE MYSELF.
WHAT?
PLEASE DON'T TALK LIKE HARUNAWA.
HUH?
THE SHO WHO SWITCHED PLACES WITH YOU.
HE WAS THE HEAD OF SECURITY FOR AMA-WAKUNI.
OH?
I WAS A GUARDIAN HERE WHEN HE ARRIVED.
WOO
WHEN THE HAYAGAMI GITO CHOSE ME AS ITS SHO, I WAS HONORED.
CHAK
I RELENT-LESSLY PURSUED EVERY OUTLAW.

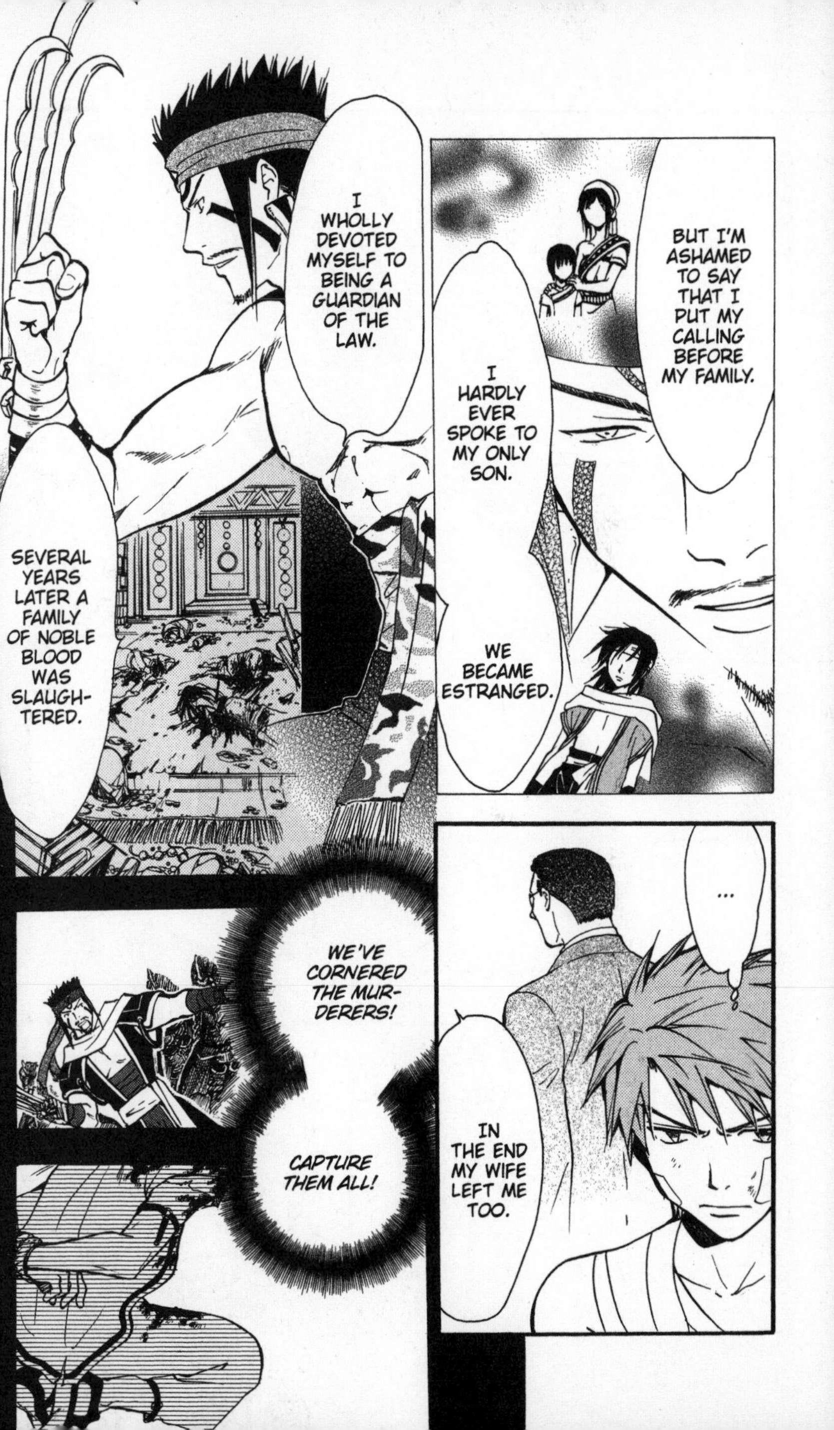
I WHOLLY DEVOTED MYSELF TO BEING A GUARDIAN OF THE LAW.
BUT I'M ASHAMED TO SAY THAT I PUT MY CALLING BEFORE MY FAMILY.
I HARDLY EVER SPOKE TO MY ONLY SON.
WE BECAME ESTRANGED.
...
IN THE END MY WIFE LEFT ME TOO.
SEVERAL YEARS LATER A FAMILY OF NOBLE BLOOD WAS SLAUGH-TERED.
WE'VE CORNERED THE MUR-DERERS!
CAPTURE THEM ALL!

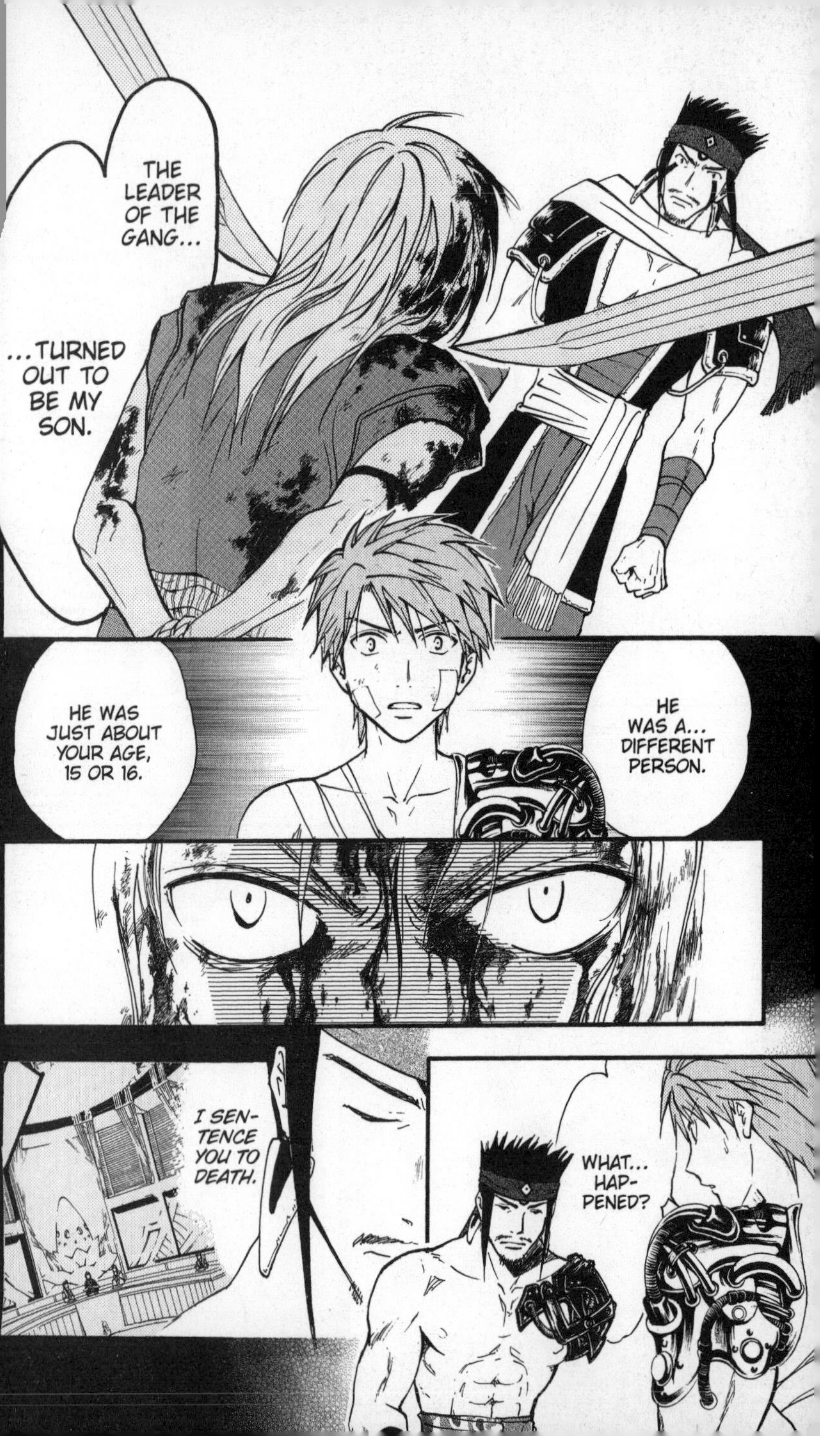
THE LEADER OF THE GANG...
...TURNED OUT TO BE MY SON.
HE WAS A... DIFFERENT PERSON.
HE WAS JUST ABOUT YOUR AGE, 15 OR 16.
WHAT... HAP-PENED?
I SEN-TENCE YOU TO DEATH.

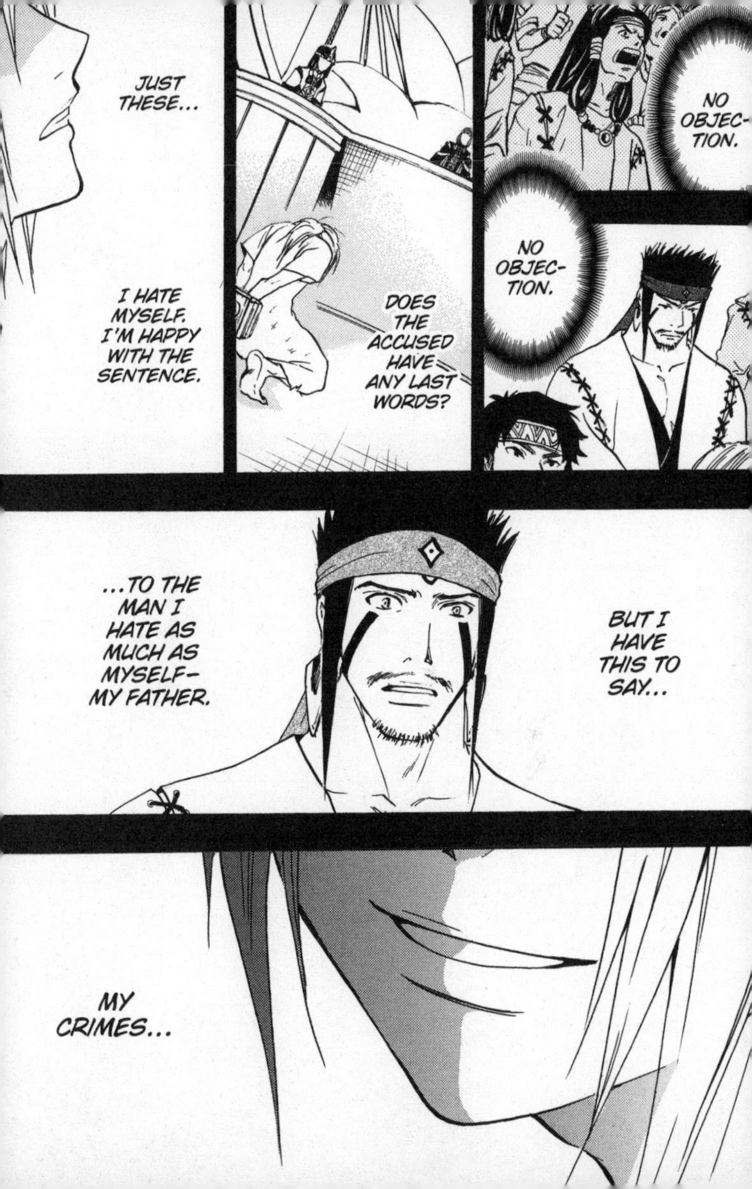
NO OBJECTION.
NO OBJECTION.
DOES THE ACCUSED HAVE ANY LAST WORDS?
JUST THESE...
I HATE MYSELF. I'M HAPPY WITH THE SENTENCE.
BUT I HAVE THIS TO SAY...
...TO THE MAN I HATE AS MUCH AS MYSELF- MY FATHER.
MY CRIMES...

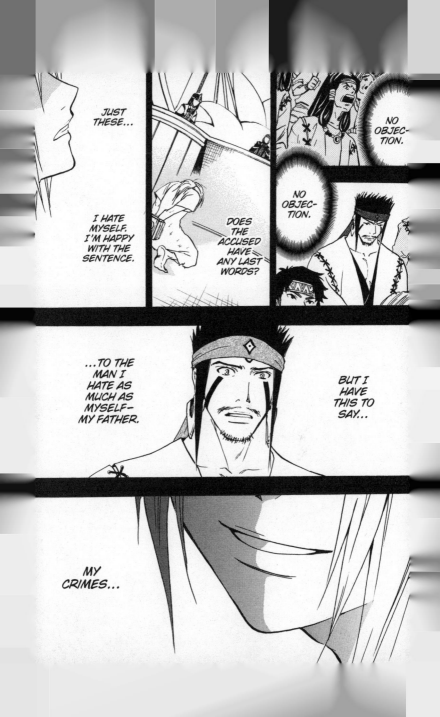

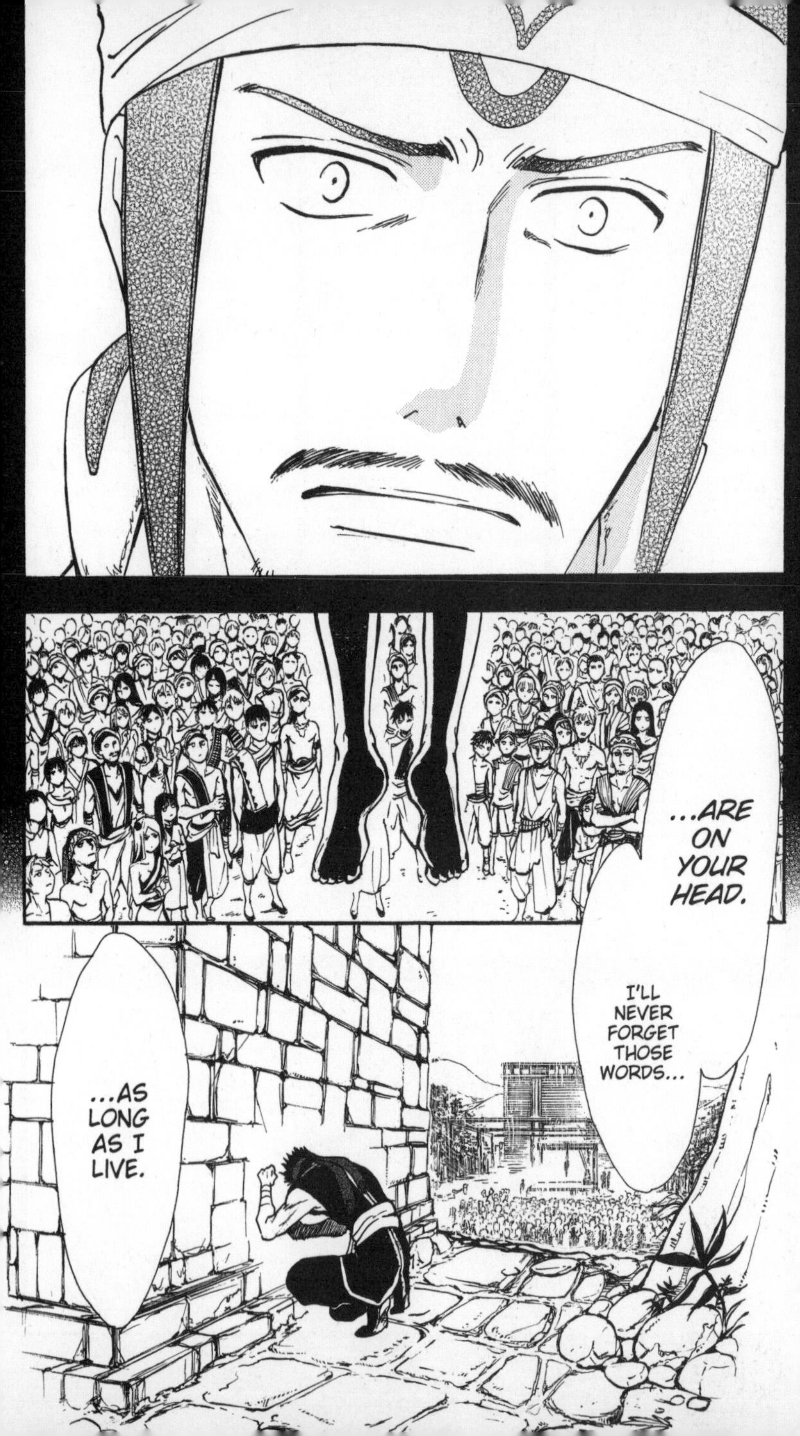
...ARE ON YOUR HEAD.
I'LL NEVER FORGET THOSE WORDS...
...AS LONG AS I LIVE.

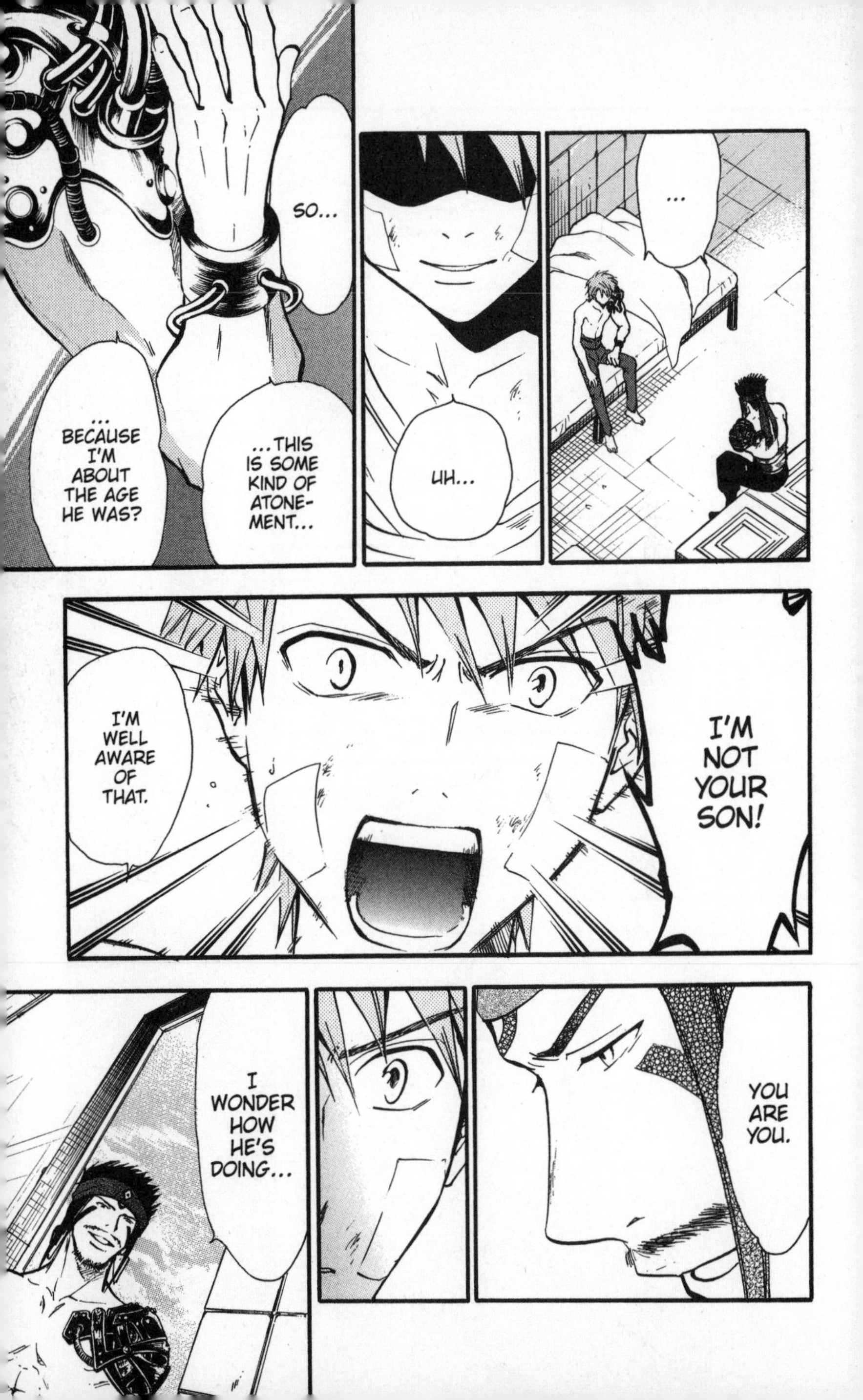
...
UH...
SO...
...THIS IS SOME KIND OF ATONEMENT...
...BECAUSE I'M ABOUT THE AGE HE WAS?
I'M NOT YOUR SON!
I'M WELL AWARE OF THAT.
YOU ARE YOU.
I WONDER HOW HE'S DOING...

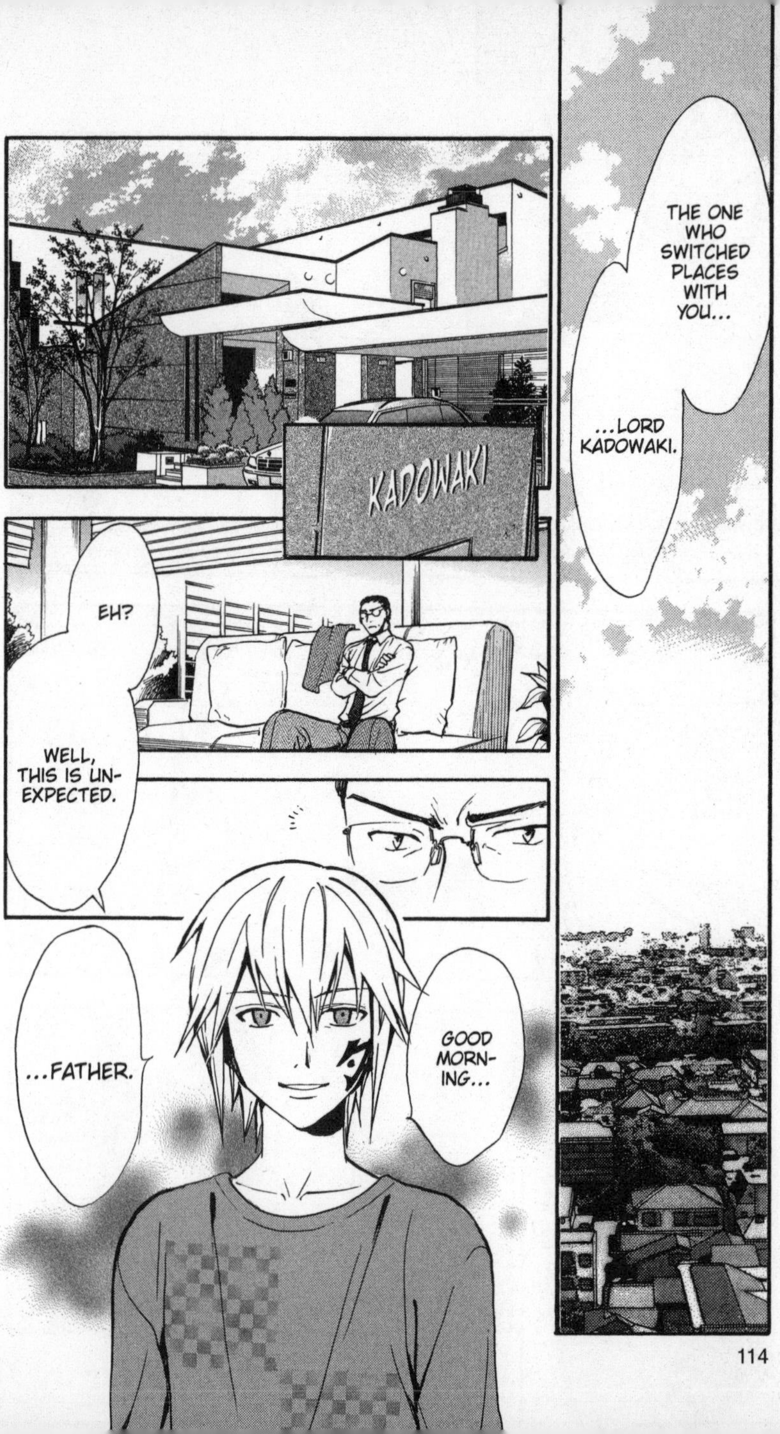
THE ONE WHO SWITCHED PLACES WITH YOU...
...LORD KADOWAKI.
KADOWAKI
EH?
WELL, THIS IS UN-EXPECTED.
GOOD MORN-ING...
...FATHER.

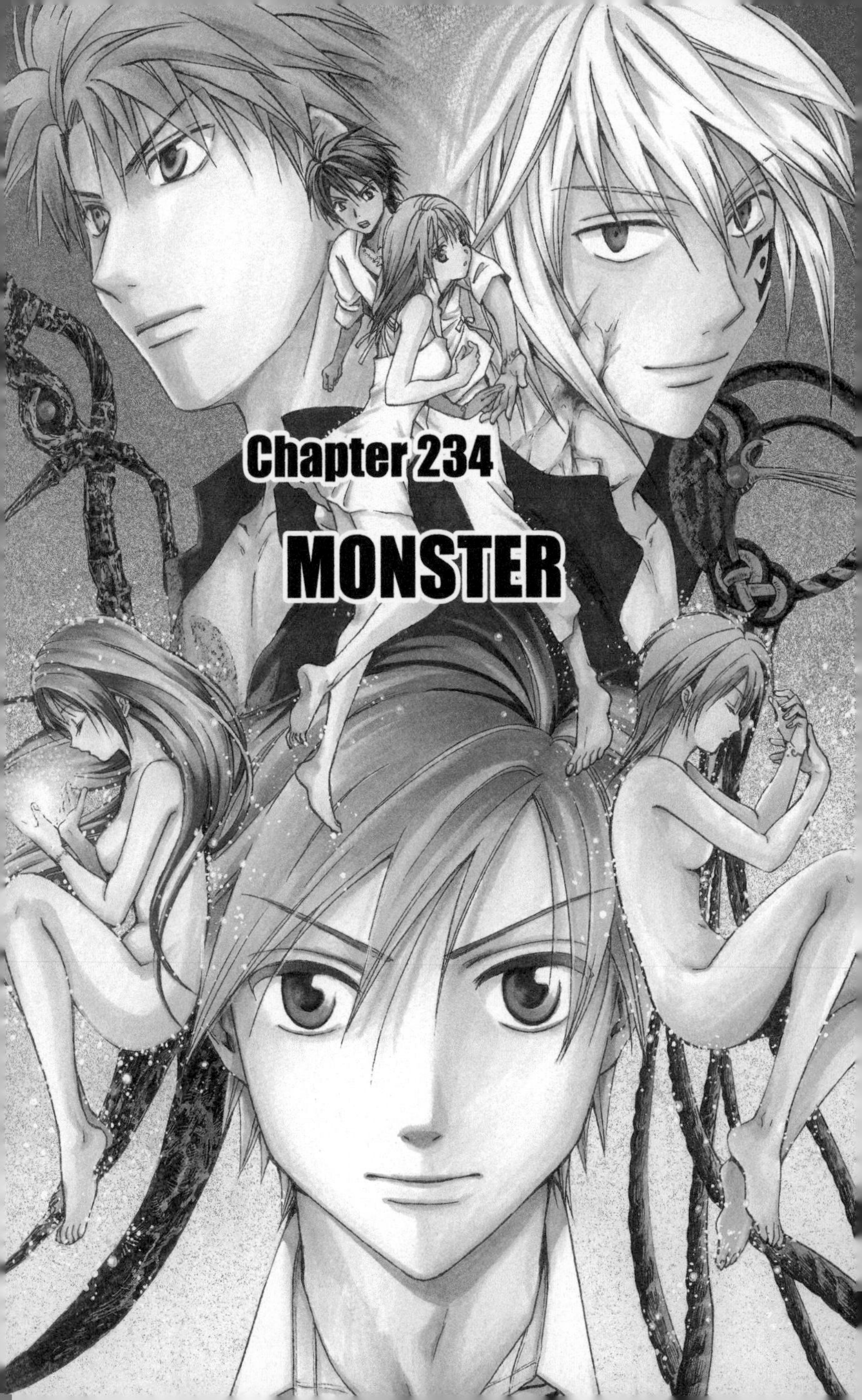
Chapter 234
MONSTER

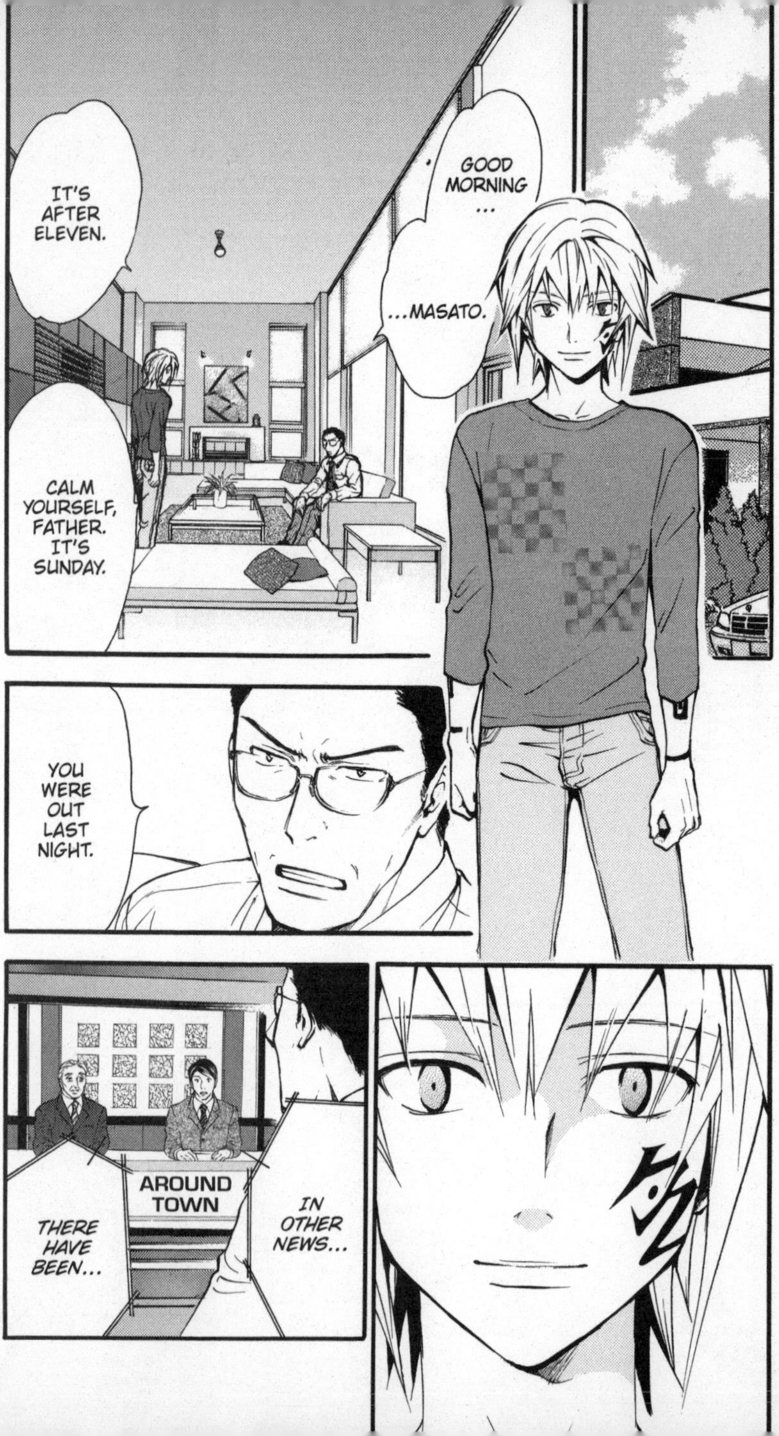
GOOD MORNING...
...MASATO.
IT'S AFTER ELEVEN.
CALM YOURSELF, FATHER. IT'S SUNDAY.
YOU WERE OUT LAST NIGHT.
AROUND TOWN
IN OTHER NEWS...
THERE HAVE BEEN...

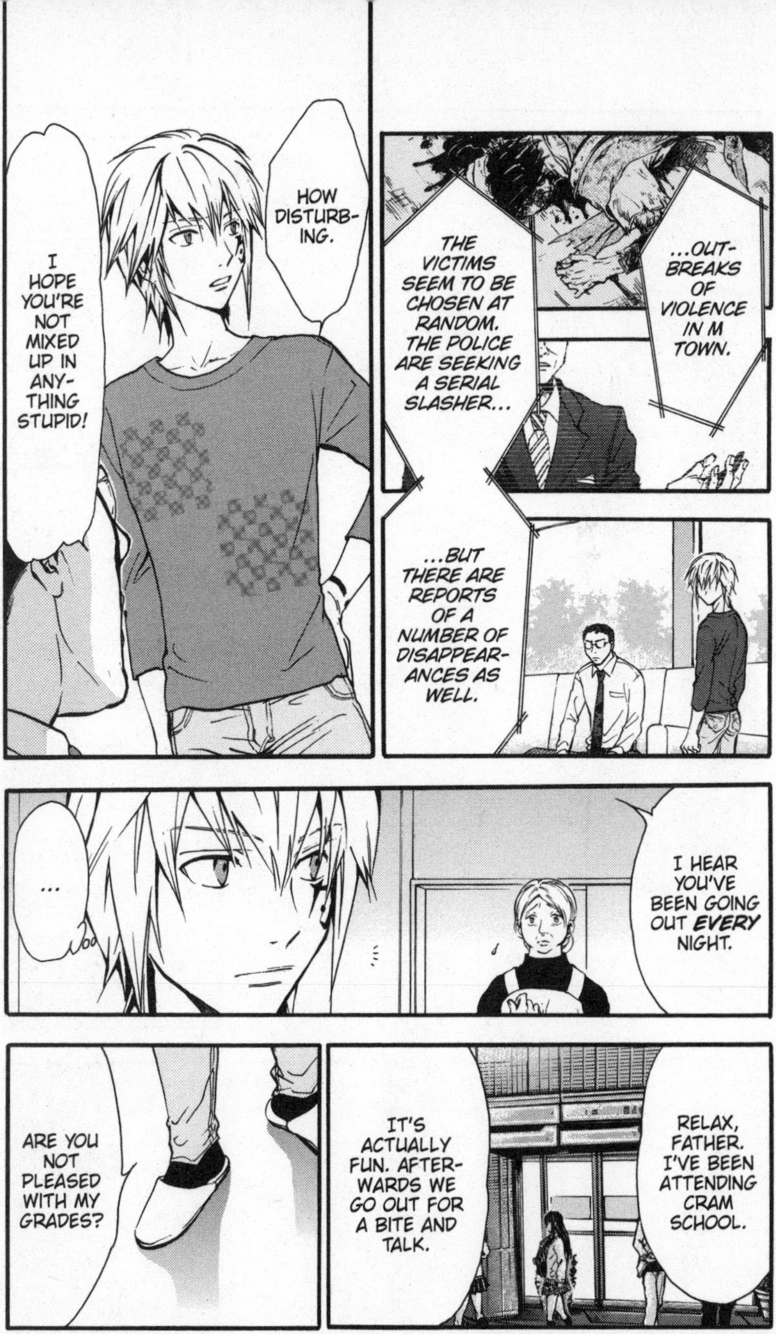
...OUT-BREAKS OF VIOLENCE IN M TOWN.
THE VICTIMS SEEM TO BE CHOSEN AT RANDOM. THE POLICE ARE SEEKING A SERIAL SLASHER...
...BUT THERE ARE REPORTS OF A NUMBER OF DISAPPEAR-ANCES AS WELL.
HOW DISTURB-ING.
I HOPE YOU'RE NOT MIXED UP IN ANY-THING STUPID!
I HEAR YOU'VE BEEN GOING OUT EVERY NIGHT.
...
RELAX, FATHER. I'VE BEEN ATTENDING CRAM SCHOOL.
IT'S ACTUALLY FUN. AFTER-WARDS WE GO OUT FOR A BITE AND TALK.
ARE YOU NOT PLEASED WITH MY GRADES?

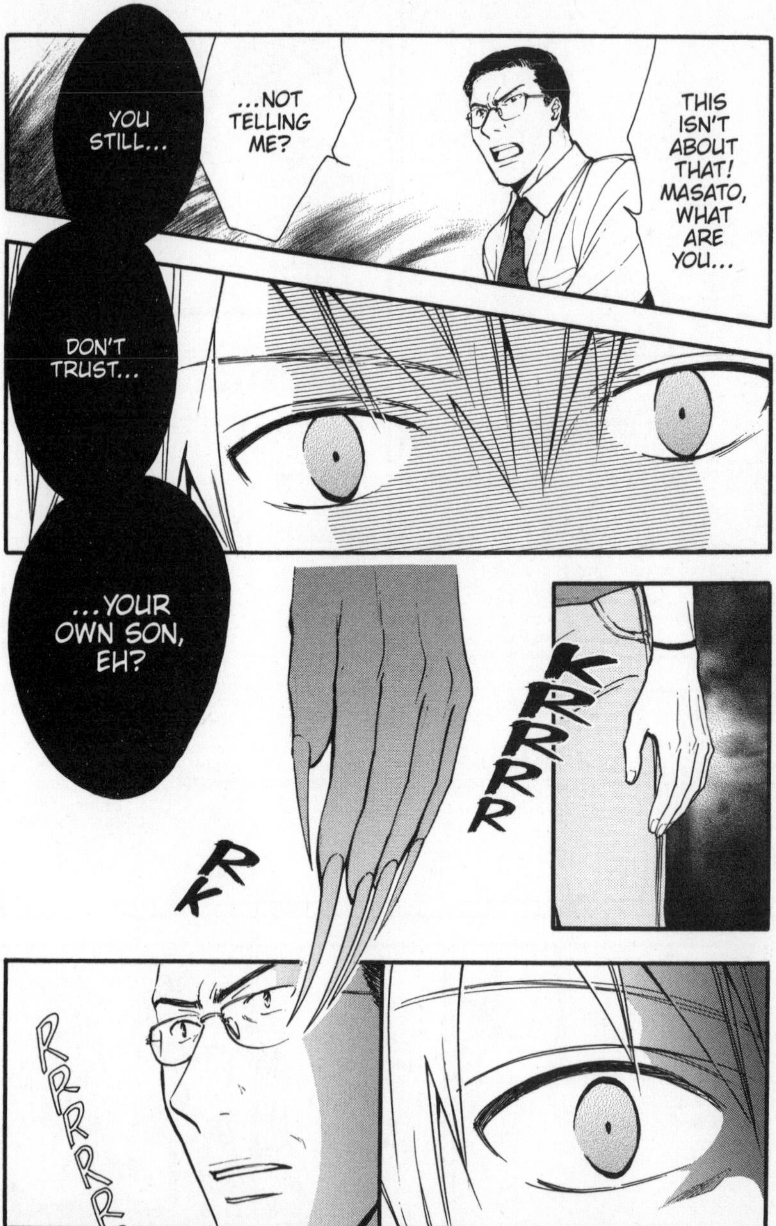
THIS ISN'T ABOUT THAT! MASATO, WHAT ARE YOU...
...NOT TELLING ME?
YOU STILL...
DON'T TRUST...
...YOUR OWN SON, EH?
KRRRRR
RK
RRRRRRR

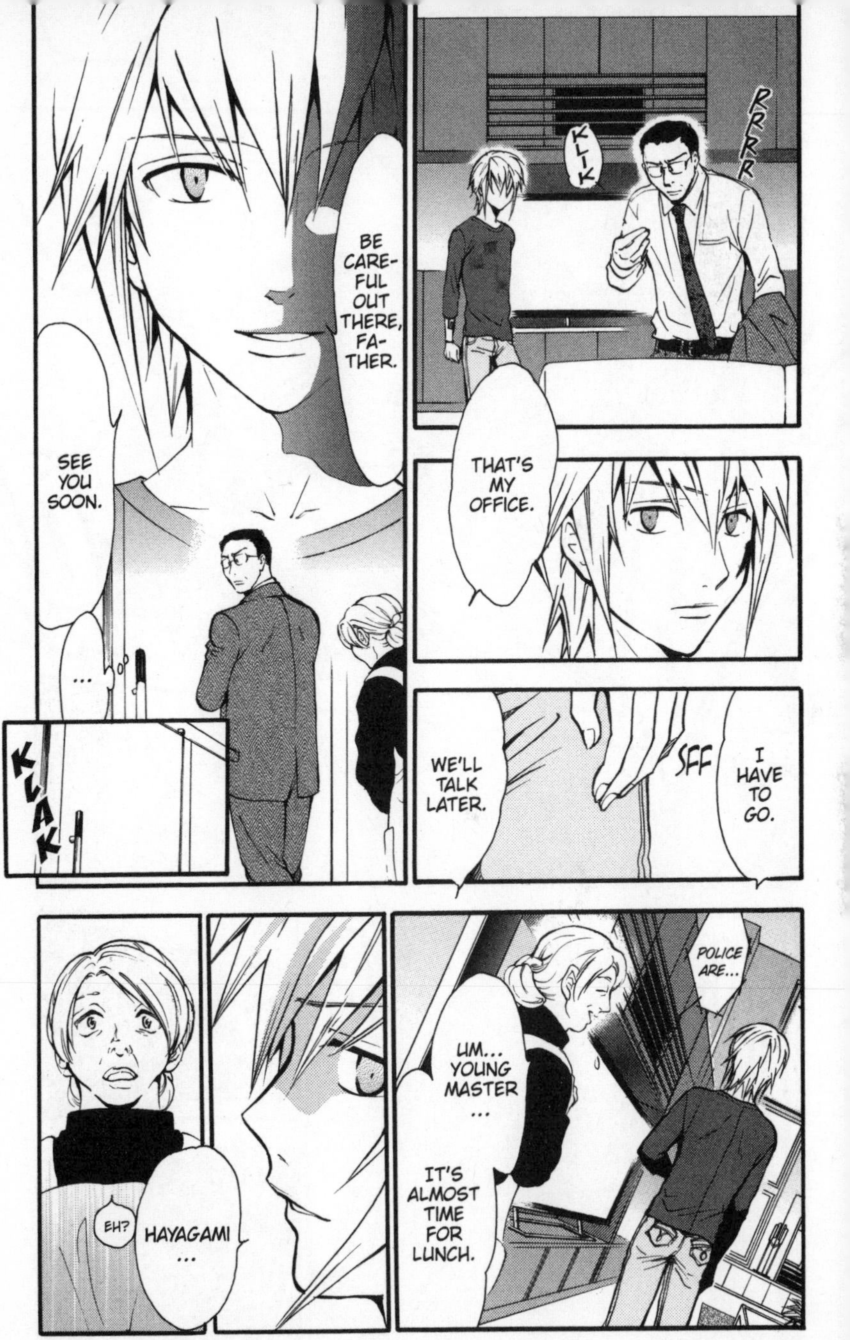
RRRR
KLIK
THAT'S MY OFFICE.
I HAVE TO GO.
SFF
WE'LL TALK LATER.
BE CAREFUL OUT THERE, FATHER.
SEE YOU SOON.
...
KLAK
POLICE ARE...
UM... YOUNG MASTER ...
IT'S ALMOST TIME FOR LUNCH.
HAYAGAMI ...
EH?

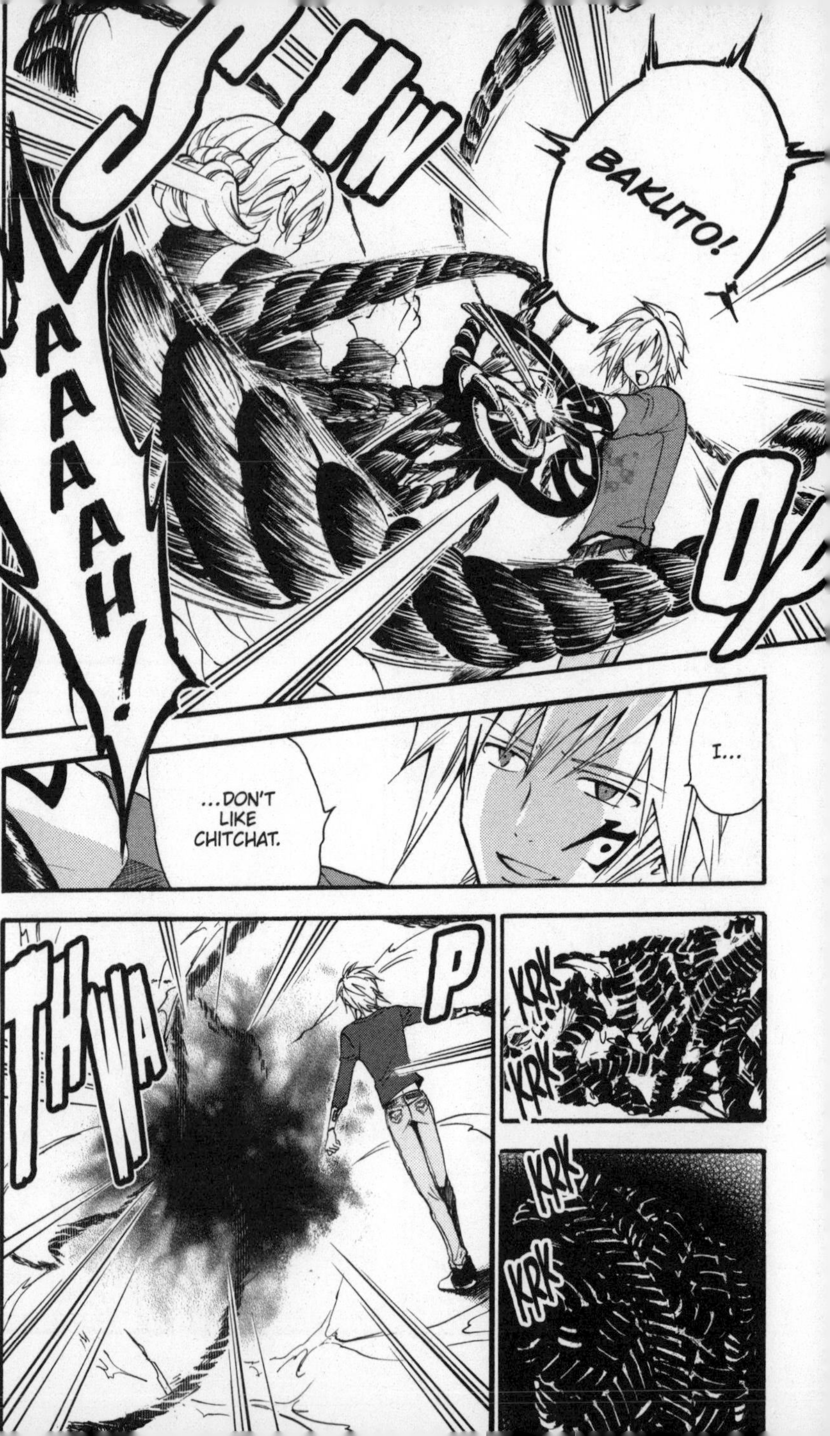
BAKUTO!
CHW
AAAAH!
I...
...DON'T LIKE CHITCHAT.
KRK KRK
P
THWA
KRK
KRK

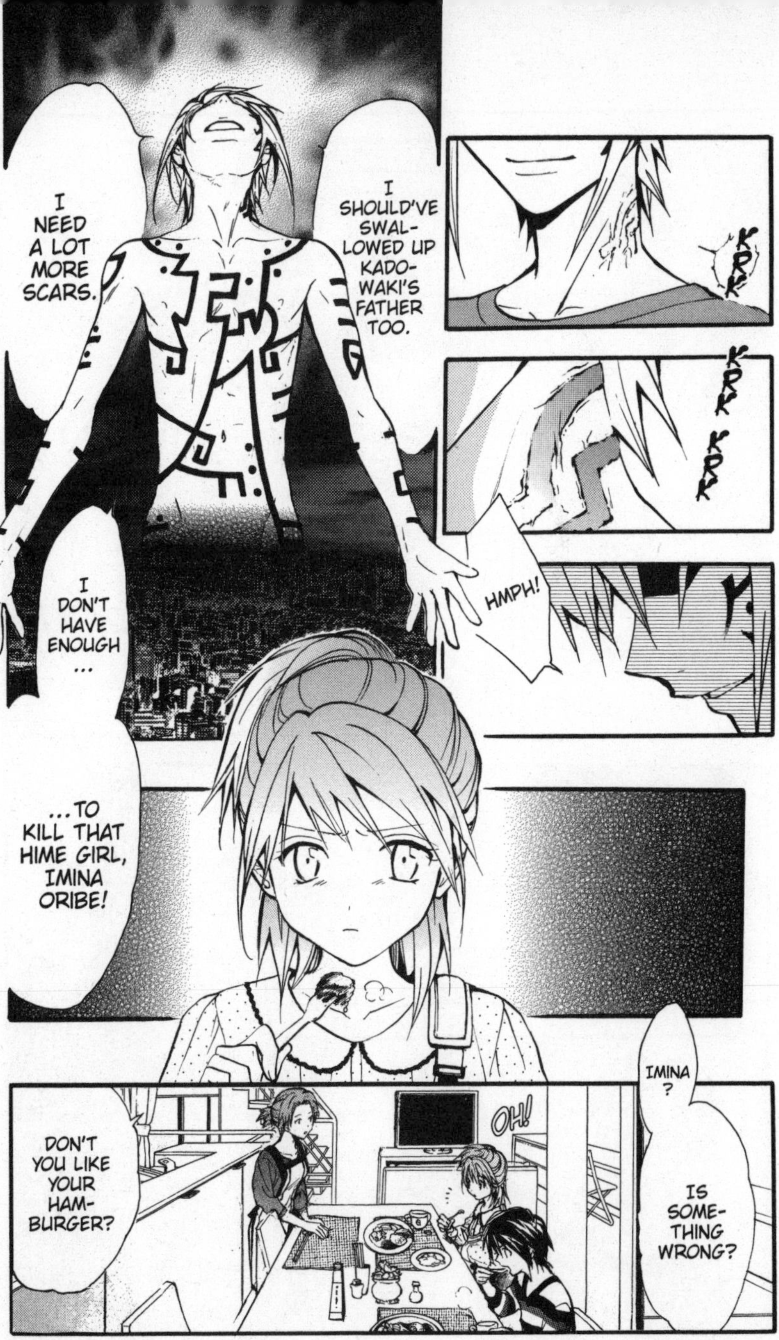
KRK
KRK KRK
HMPH!
I SHOULD'VE SWAL-LOWED UP KADO-WAKI'S FATHER TOO.
I NEED A LOT MORE SCARS.
I DON'T HAVE ENOUGH...
...TO KILL THAT HIME GIRL, IMINA ORIBE!
IMINA?
IS SOME-THING WRONG?
OH!
DON'T YOU LIKE YOUR HAM-BURGER?

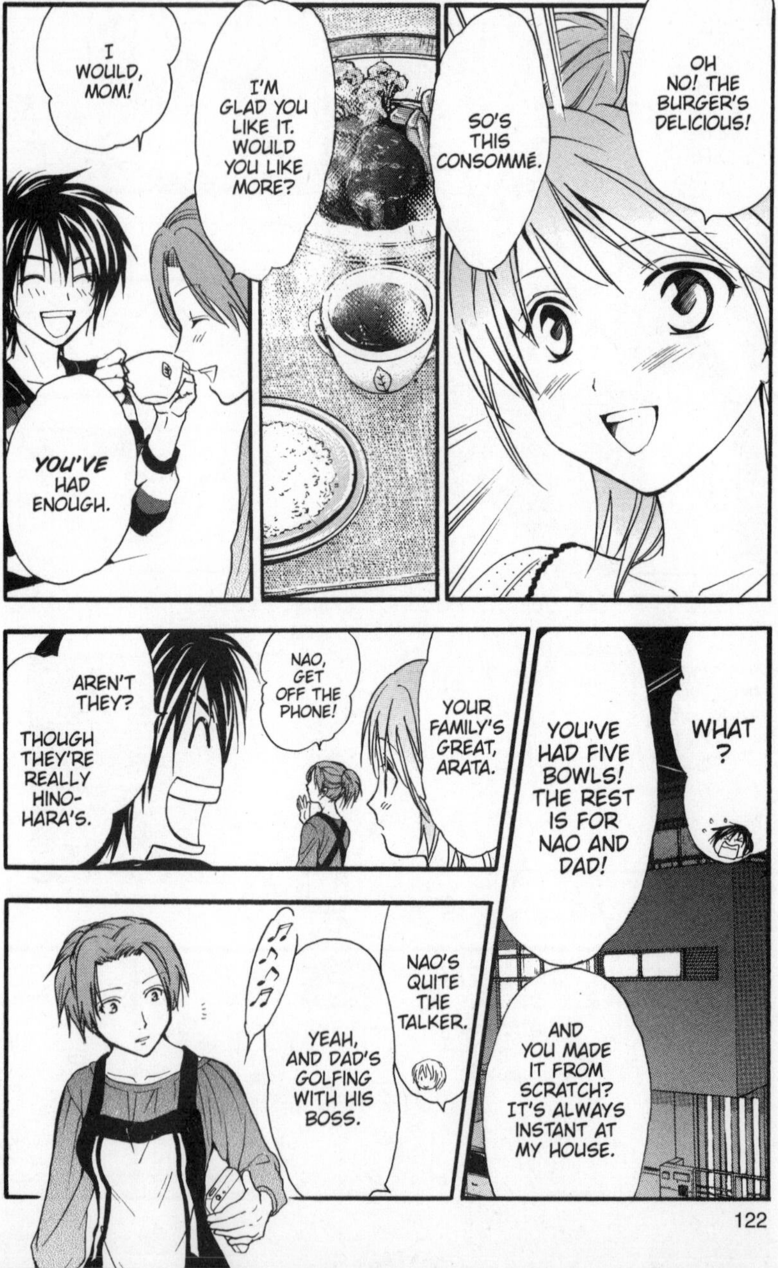
OH NO! THE BURGER'S DELICIOUS!
SO'S THIS CONSOMMÉ.
I'M GLAD YOU LIKE IT. WOULD YOU LIKE MORE?
I WOULD, MOM!
YOU'VE HAD ENOUGH.
WHAT?
YOU'VE HAD FIVE BOWLS! THE REST IS FOR NAO AND DAD!
AND YOU MADE IT FROM SCRATCH? IT'S ALWAYS INSTANT AT MY HOUSE.
YOUR FAMILY'S GREAT, ARATA.
NAO, GET OFF THE PHONE!
AREN'T THEY?
THOUGH THEY'RE REALLY HINO-HARA'S.
NAO'S QUITE THE TALKER.
YEAH, AND DAD'S GOLFING WITH HIS BOSS.

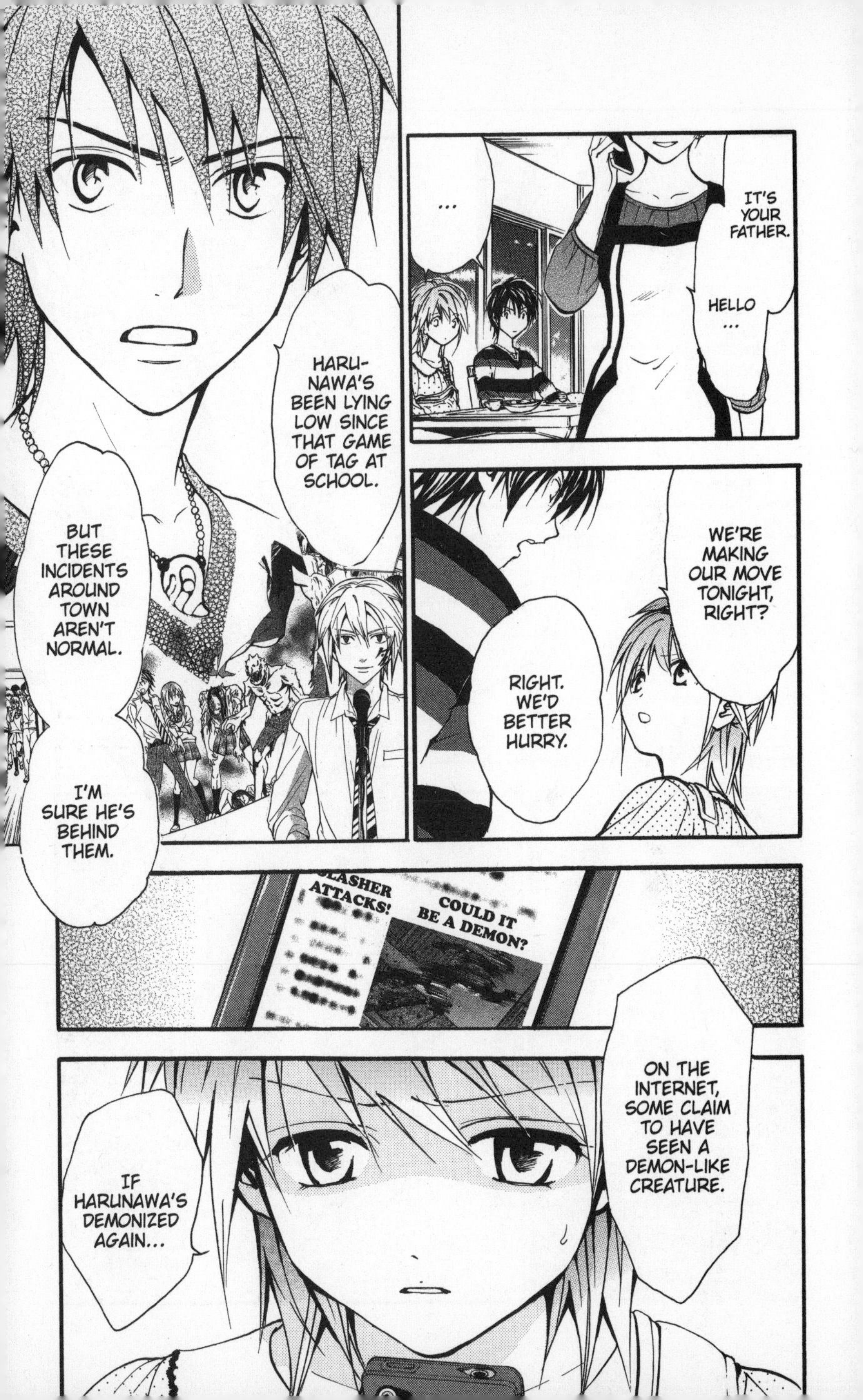
IT'S YOUR FATHER.
HELLO ...
...
WE'RE MAKING OUR MOVE TONIGHT, RIGHT?
RIGHT. WE'D BETTER HURRY.
HARUNAWA'S BEEN LYING LOW SINCE THAT GAME OF TAG AT SCHOOL.
BUT THESE INCIDENTS AROUND TOWN AREN'T NORMAL.
I'M SURE HE'S BEHIND THEM.
SLASHER ATTACKS!
COULD IT BE A DEMON?
ON THE INTERNET, SOME CLAIM TO HAVE SEEN A DEMON-LIKE CREATURE.
IF HARUNAWA'S DEMONIZED AGAIN...

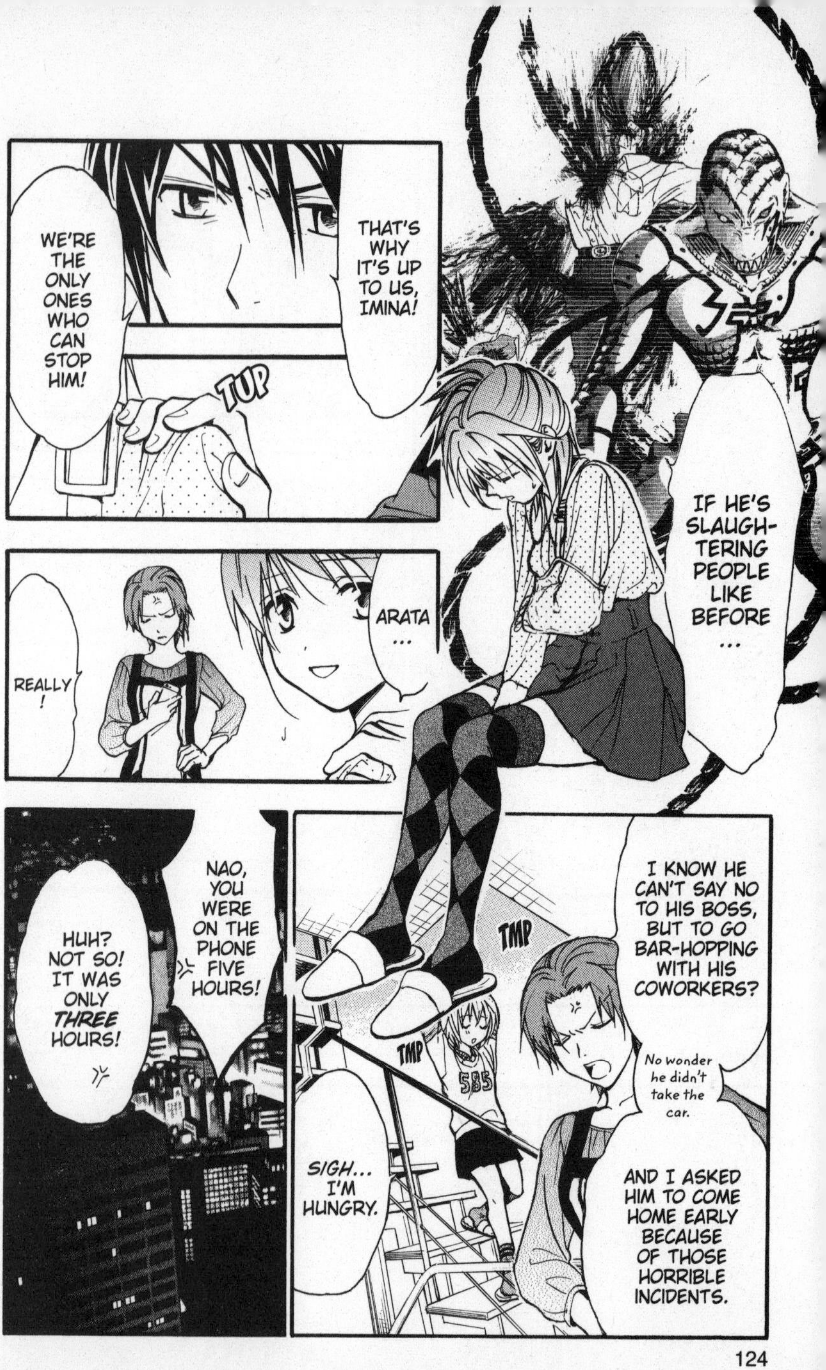
IF HE'S SLAUGHTERING PEOPLE LIKE BEFORE...
THAT'S WHY IT'S UP TO US, IMINA!
TUP
WE'RE THE ONLY ONES WHO CAN STOP HIM!
ARATA...
REALLY!
I KNOW HE CAN'T SAY NO TO HIS BOSS, BUT TO GO BAR-HOPPING WITH HIS COWORKERS?
TMP
No wonder he didn't take the car.
TMP
AND I ASKED HIM TO COME HOME EARLY BECAUSE OF THOSE HORRIBLE INCIDENTS.
SIGH... I'M HUNGRY.
NAO, YOU WERE ON THE PHONE FIVE HOURS!
HUH? NOT SO! IT WAS ONLY *THREE* HOURS!

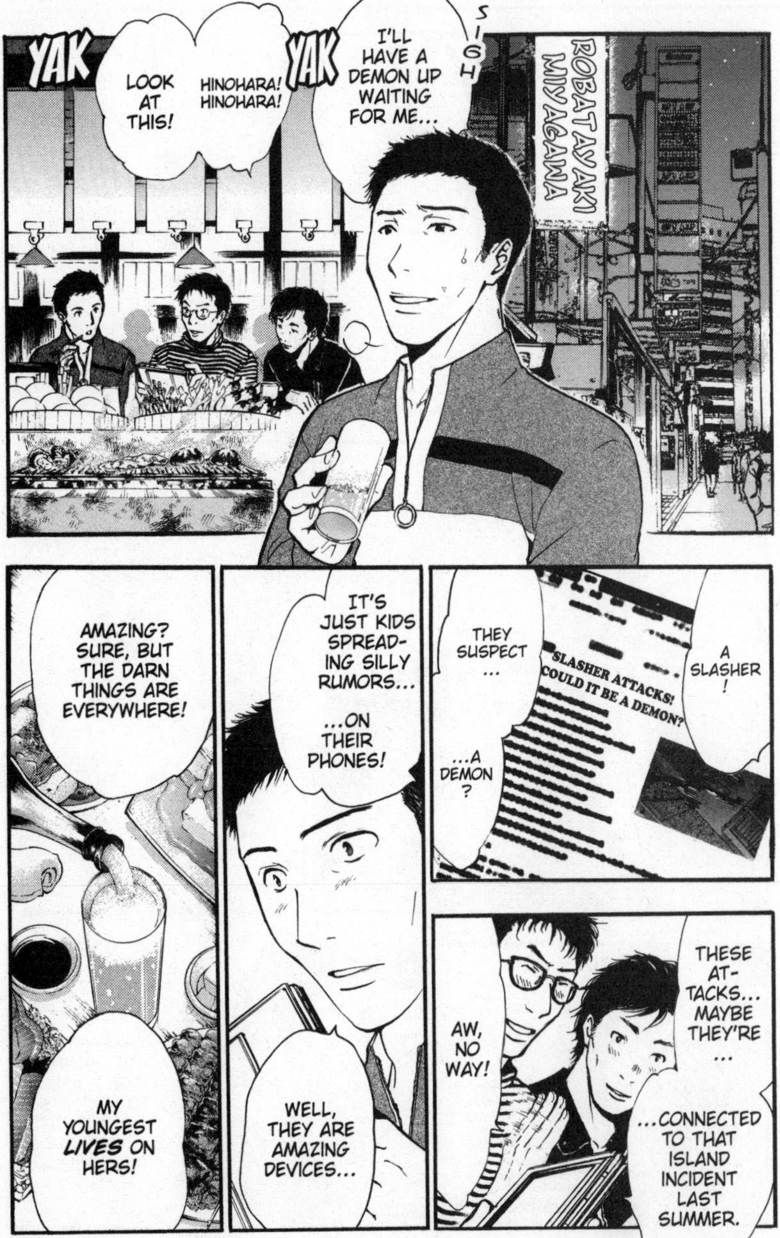
ROBATAYAKI MIYAGAWA
SIGH
I'LL HAVE A DEMON UP WAITING FOR ME...
YAK
HINOHARA! HINOHARA!
LOOK AT THIS!
YAK
A SLASHER!
SLASHER ATTACKS! COULD IT BE A DEMON?
THEY SUSPECT...
...A DEMON?
THESE AT-TACKS... MAYBE THEY'RE...
...CONNECTED TO THAT ISLAND INCIDENT LAST SUMMER.
AW, NO WAY!
IT'S JUST KIDS SPREAD-ING SILLY RUMORS...
...ON THEIR PHONES!
WELL, THEY ARE AMAZING DEVICES...
AMAZING? SURE, BUT THE DARN THINGS ARE EVERYWHERE!
MY YOUNGEST *LIVES* ON HERS!

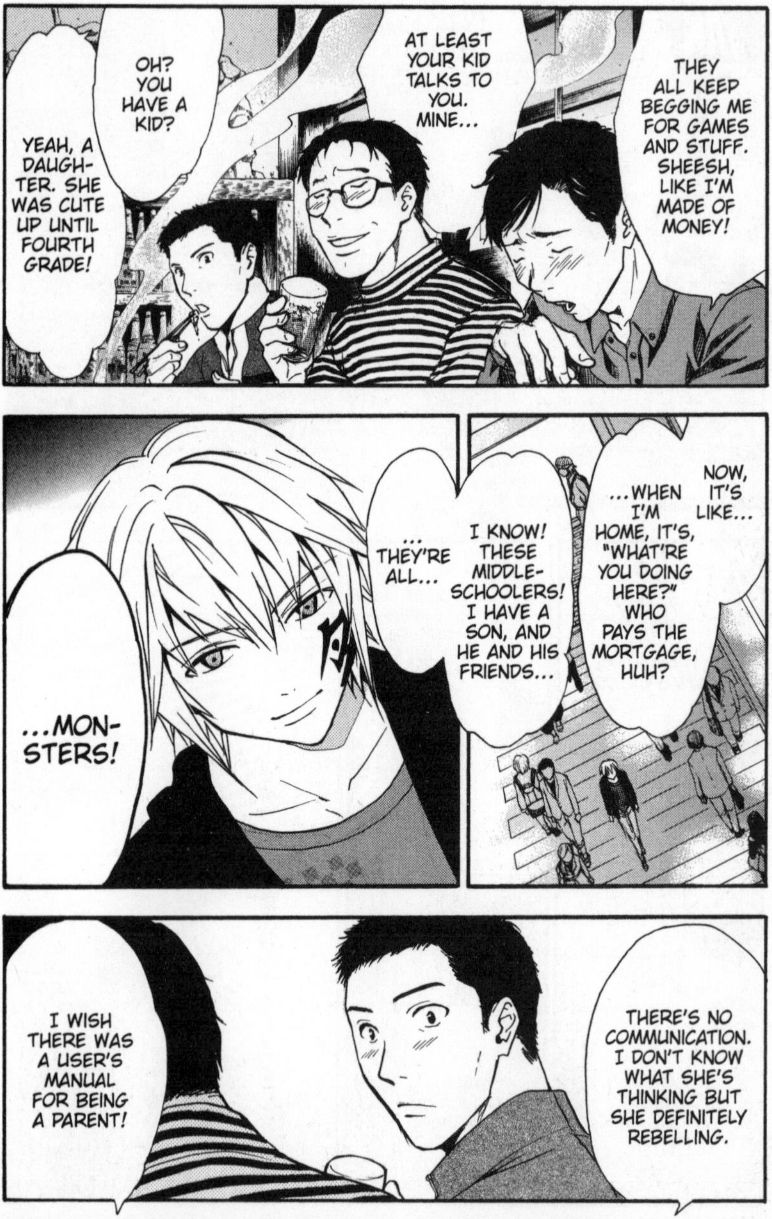
THEY ALL KEEP BEGGING ME FOR GAMES AND STUFF. SHEESH, LIKE I'M MADE OF MONEY!
AT LEAST YOUR KID TALKS TO YOU. MINE...
OH? YOU HAVE A KID?
YEAH, A DAUGHTER. SHE WAS CUTE UP UNTIL FOURTH GRADE!
NOW, IT'S LIKE...
...WHEN I'M HOME, IT'S, "WHAT'RE YOU DOING HERE?" WHO PAYS THE MORTGAGE, HUH?
I KNOW! THESE MIDDLE-SCHOOLERS! I HAVE A SON, AND HE AND HIS FRIENDS...
...THEY'RE ALL...
...MONSTERS!
THERE'S NO COMMUNICATION. I DON'T KNOW WHAT SHE'S THINKING BUT SHE DEFINITELY REBELLING.
I WISH THERE WAS A USER'S MANUAL FOR BEING A PARENT!

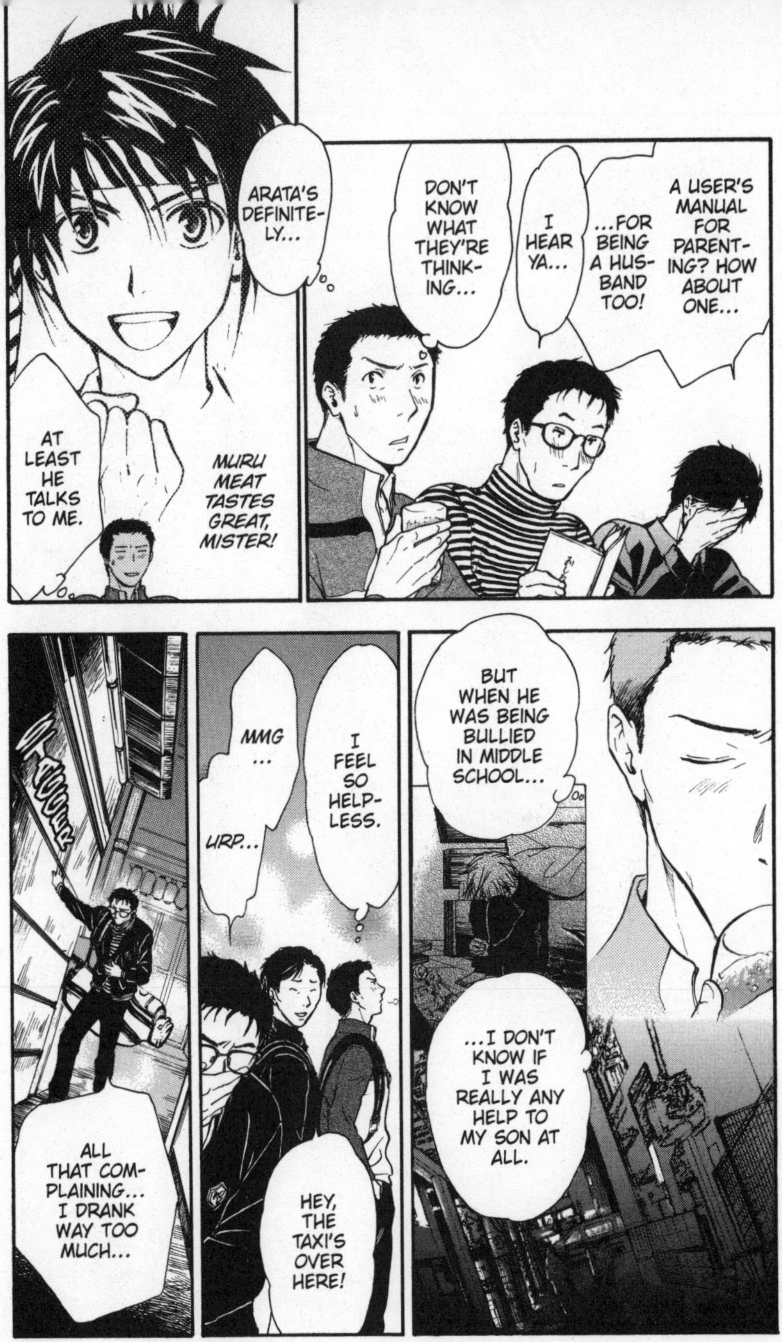
A USER'S MANUAL FOR PARENTING? HOW ABOUT ONE...
...FOR BEING A HUSBAND TOO!
I HEAR YA...
DON'T KNOW WHAT THEY'RE THINKING...
ARATA'S DEFINITELY...
MURU MEAT TASTES GREAT, MISTER!
AT LEAST HE TALKS TO ME.
BUT WHEN HE WAS BEING BULLIED IN MIDDLE SCHOOL...
...I DON'T KNOW IF I WAS REALLY ANY HELP TO MY SON AT ALL.
I FEEL SO HELPLESS.
MMG...
URP...
HEY, THE TAXI'S OVER HERE!
ALL THAT COMPLAINING... I DRANK WAY TOO MUCH...

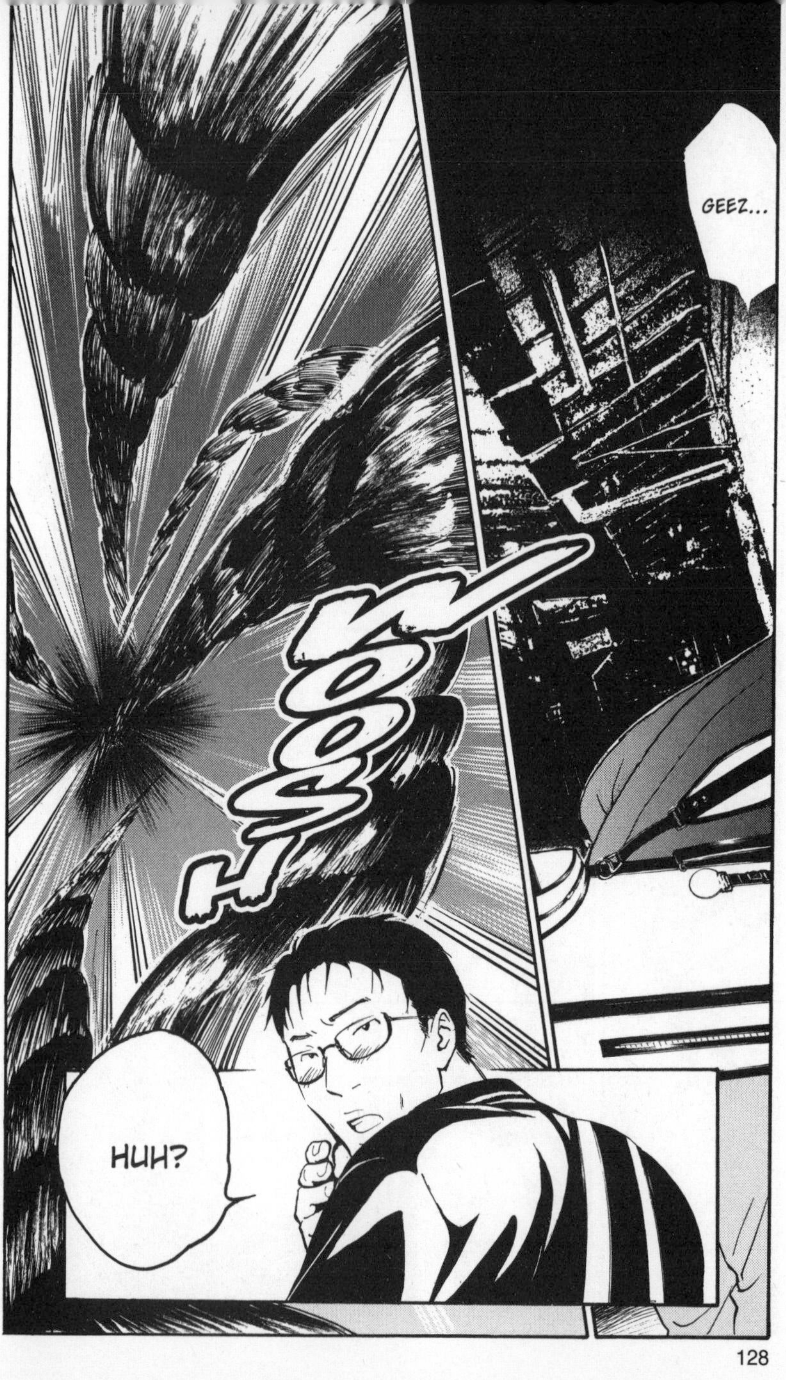
GEEZ...
WOOSH!
HUH?

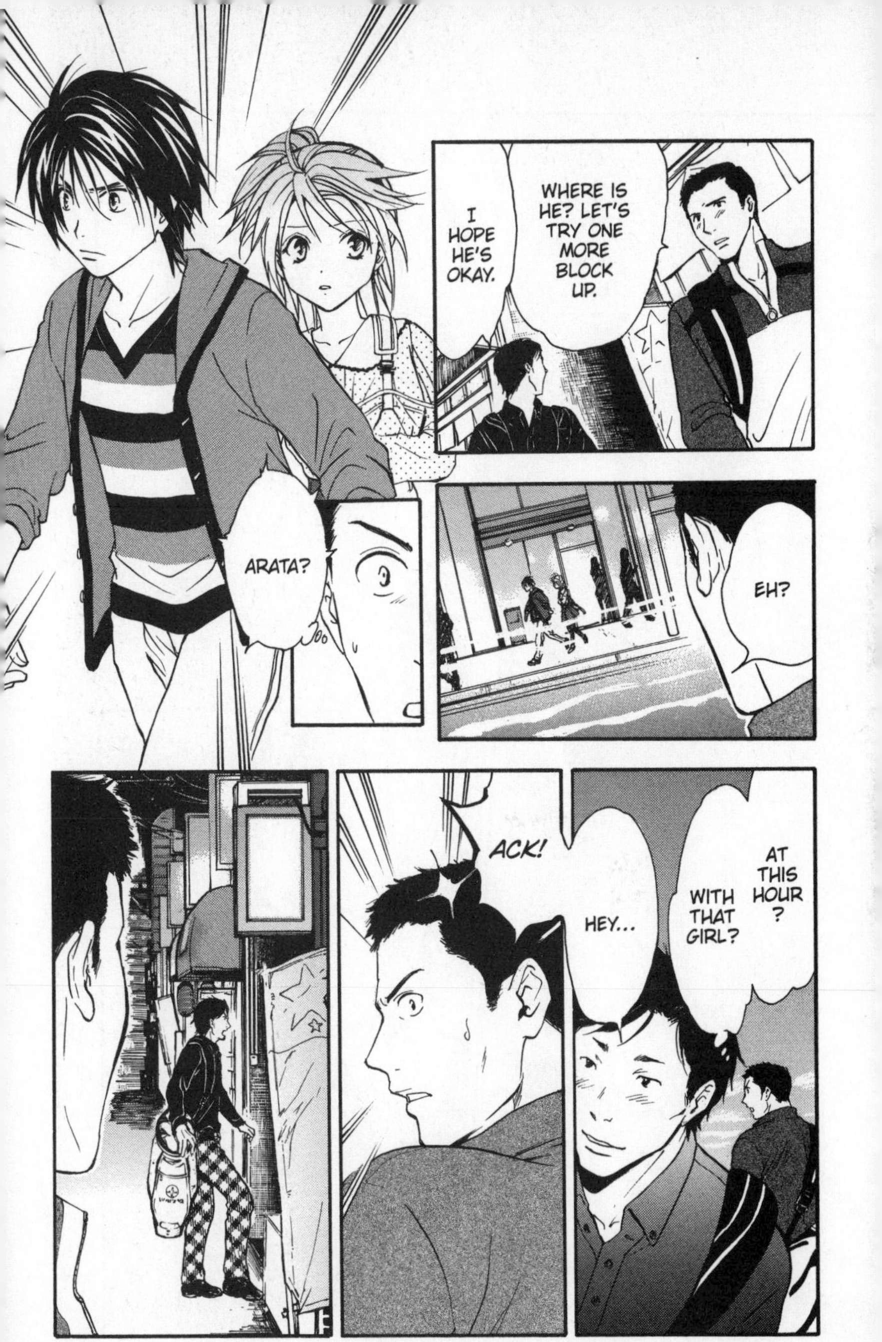
WHERE IS HE? LET'S TRY ONE MORE BLOCK UP.
I HOPE HE'S OKAY.
EH?
ARATA?
AT THIS HOUR?
WITH THAT GIRL?
HEY...
ACK!

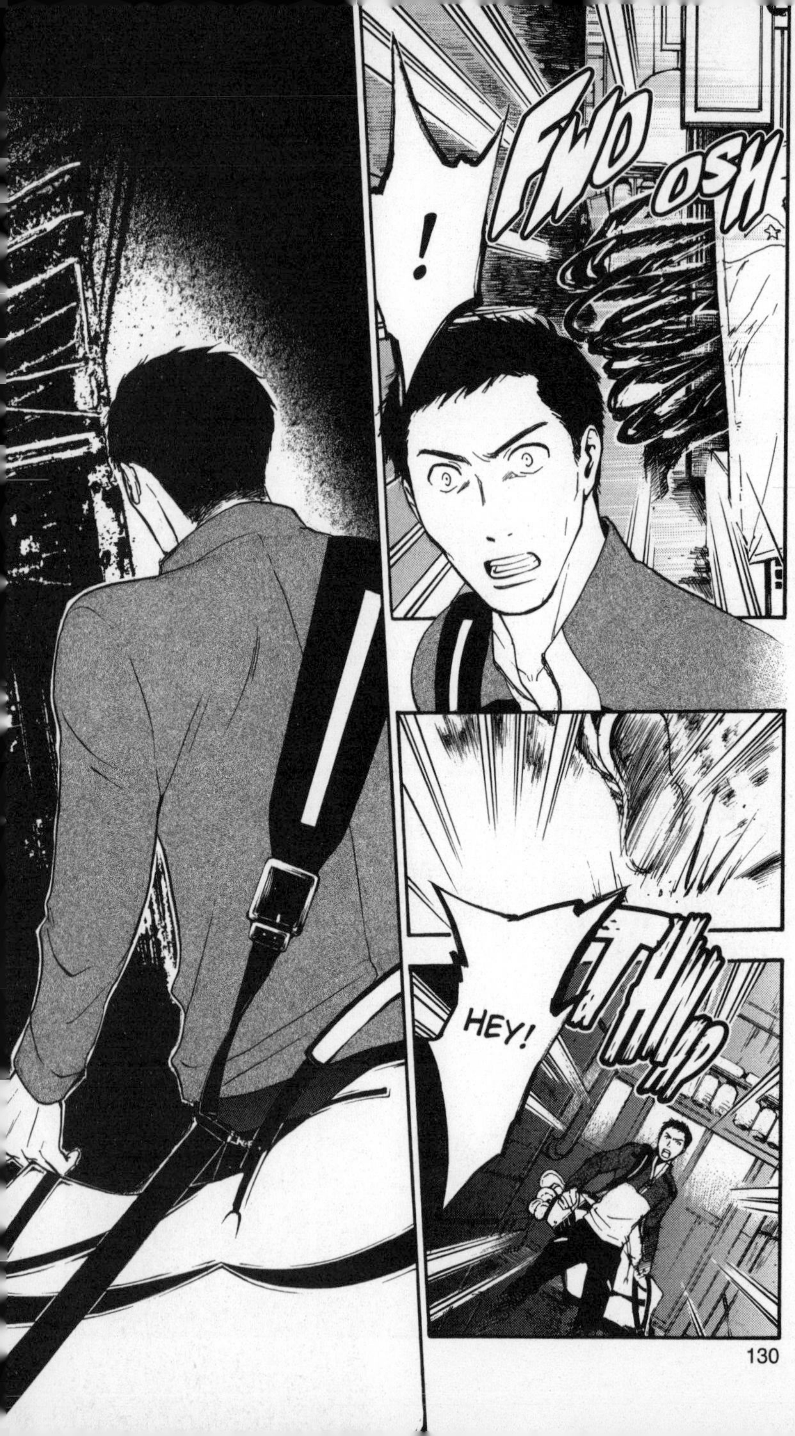
!
FWOOSH
HEY!
THUP

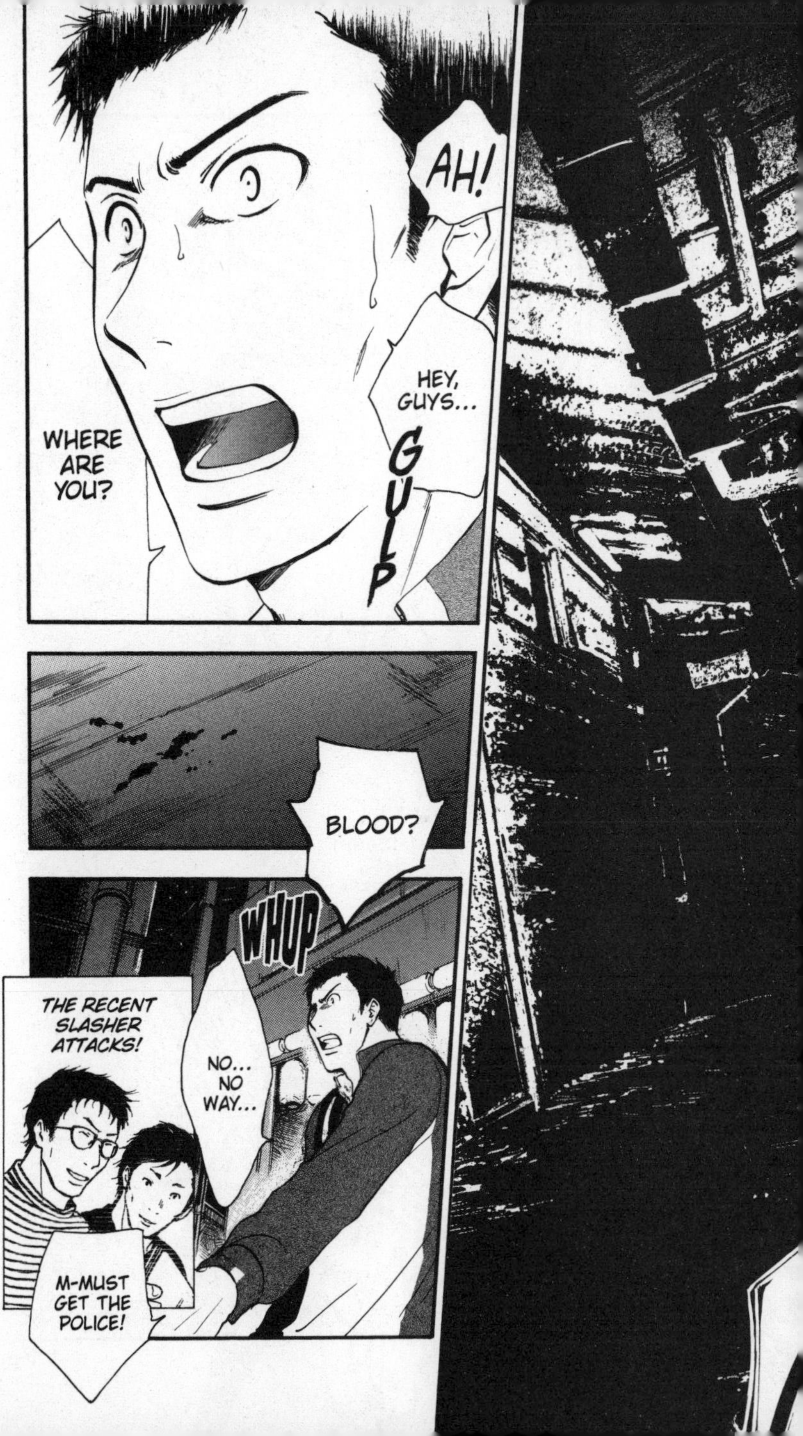
AH!
HEY, GUYS...
GULP
WHERE ARE YOU?
BLOOD?
WHUP
NO... NO WAY...
THE RECENT SLASHER ATTACKS!
M-MUST GET THE POLICE!

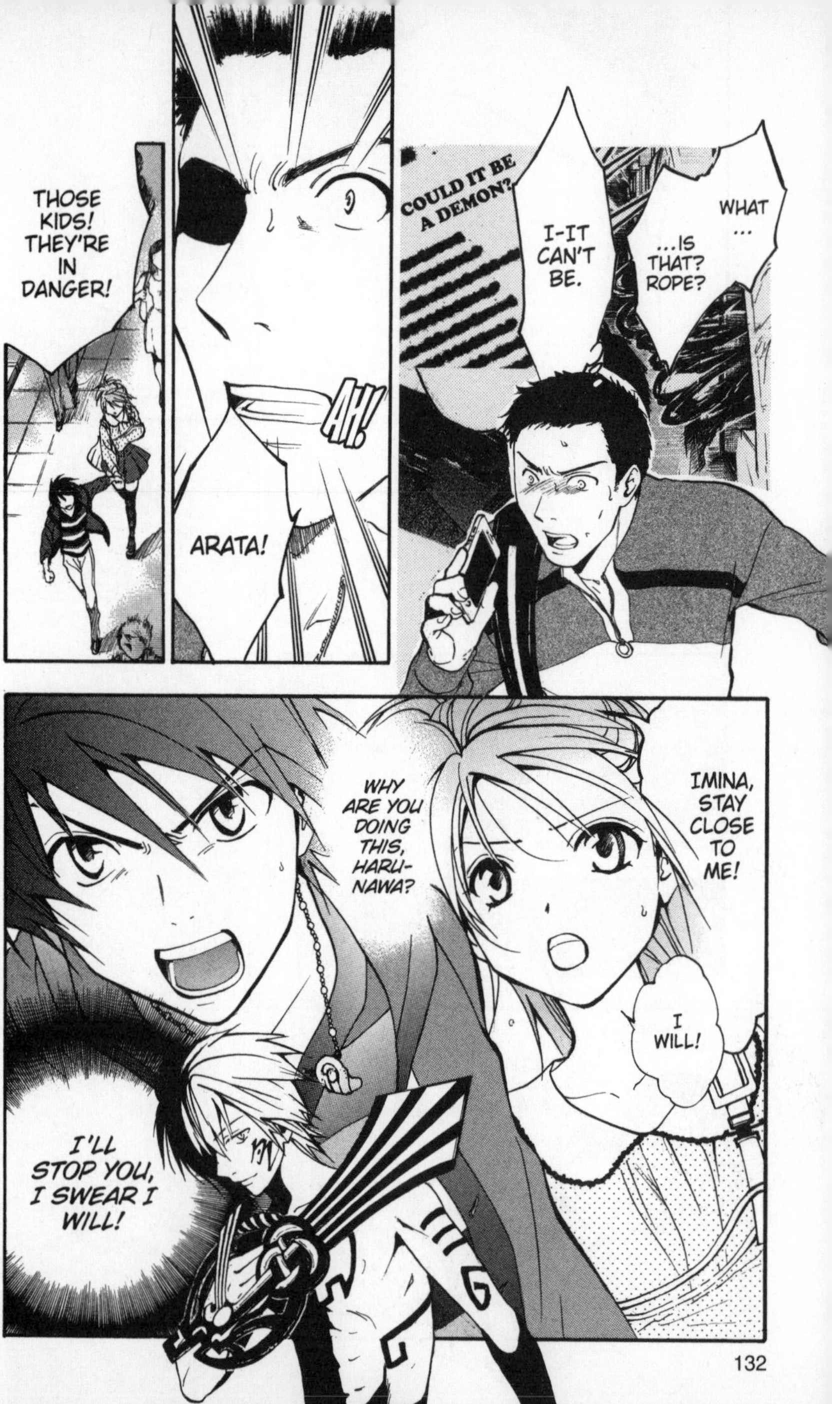
WHAT ...
...IS THAT? ROPE?
I-IT CAN'T BE.
COULD IT BE A DEMON?
AH!
ARATA!
THOSE KIDS! THEY'RE IN DANGER!
IMINA, STAY CLOSE TO ME!
WHY ARE YOU DOING THIS, HARU-NAWA?
I WILL!
I'LL STOP YOU, I SWEAR I WILL!

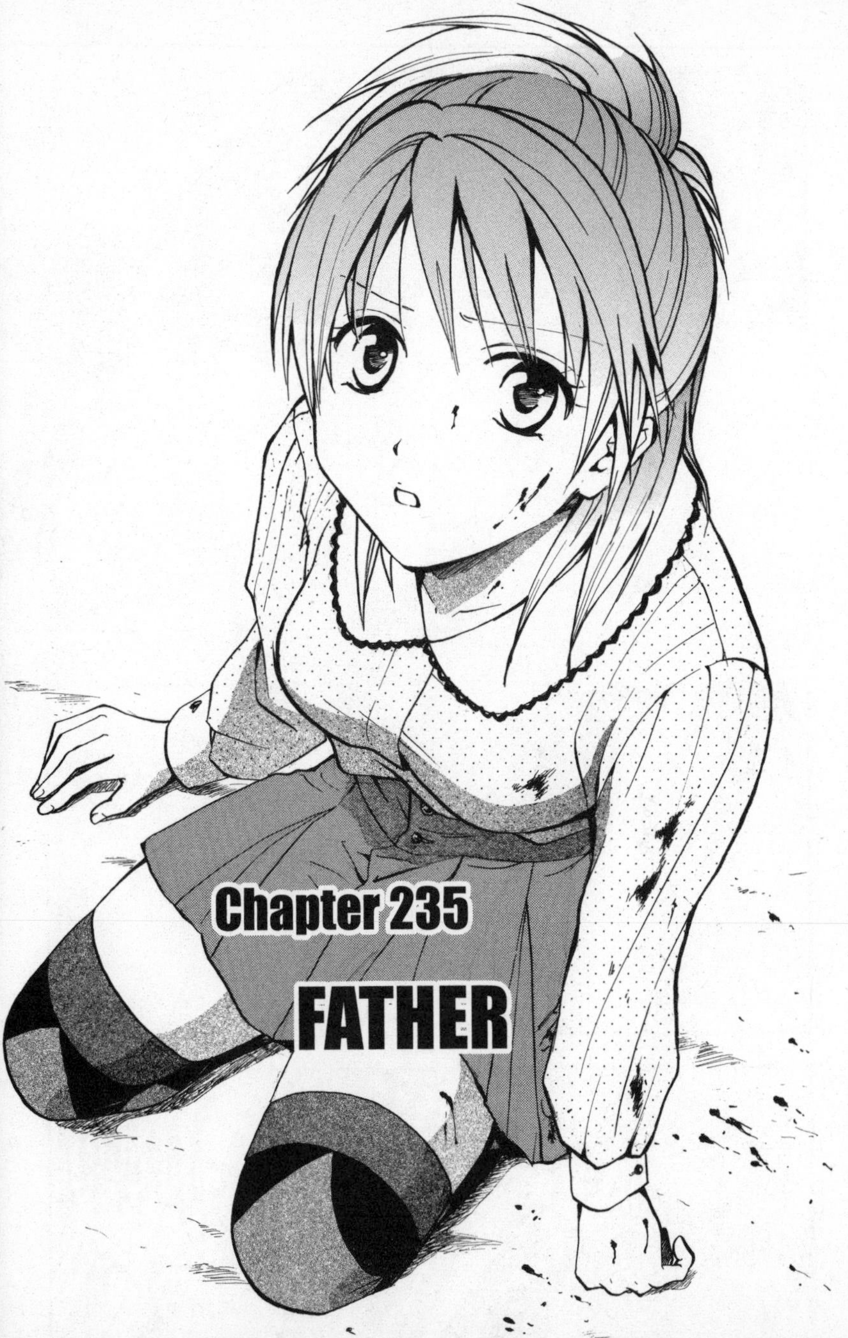
Chapter 235
FATHER

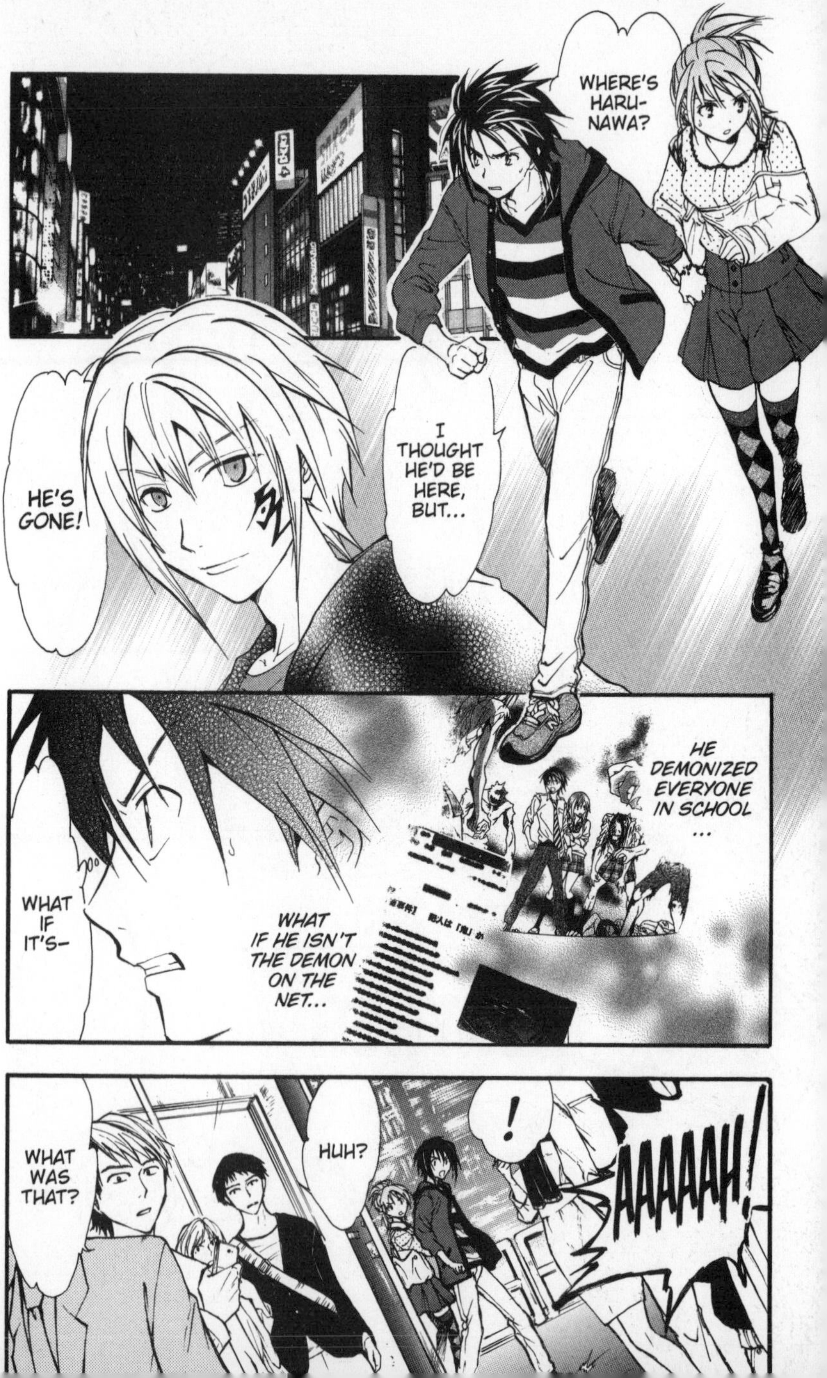
WHERE'S HARU-NAWA?
I THOUGHT HE'D BE HERE, BUT...
HE'S GONE!
HE DEMONIZED EVERYONE IN SCHOOL ...
WHAT IF HE ISN'T THE DEMON ON THE NET...
WHAT IF IT'S-
AAAAAH!
!
HUH?
WHAT WAS THAT?

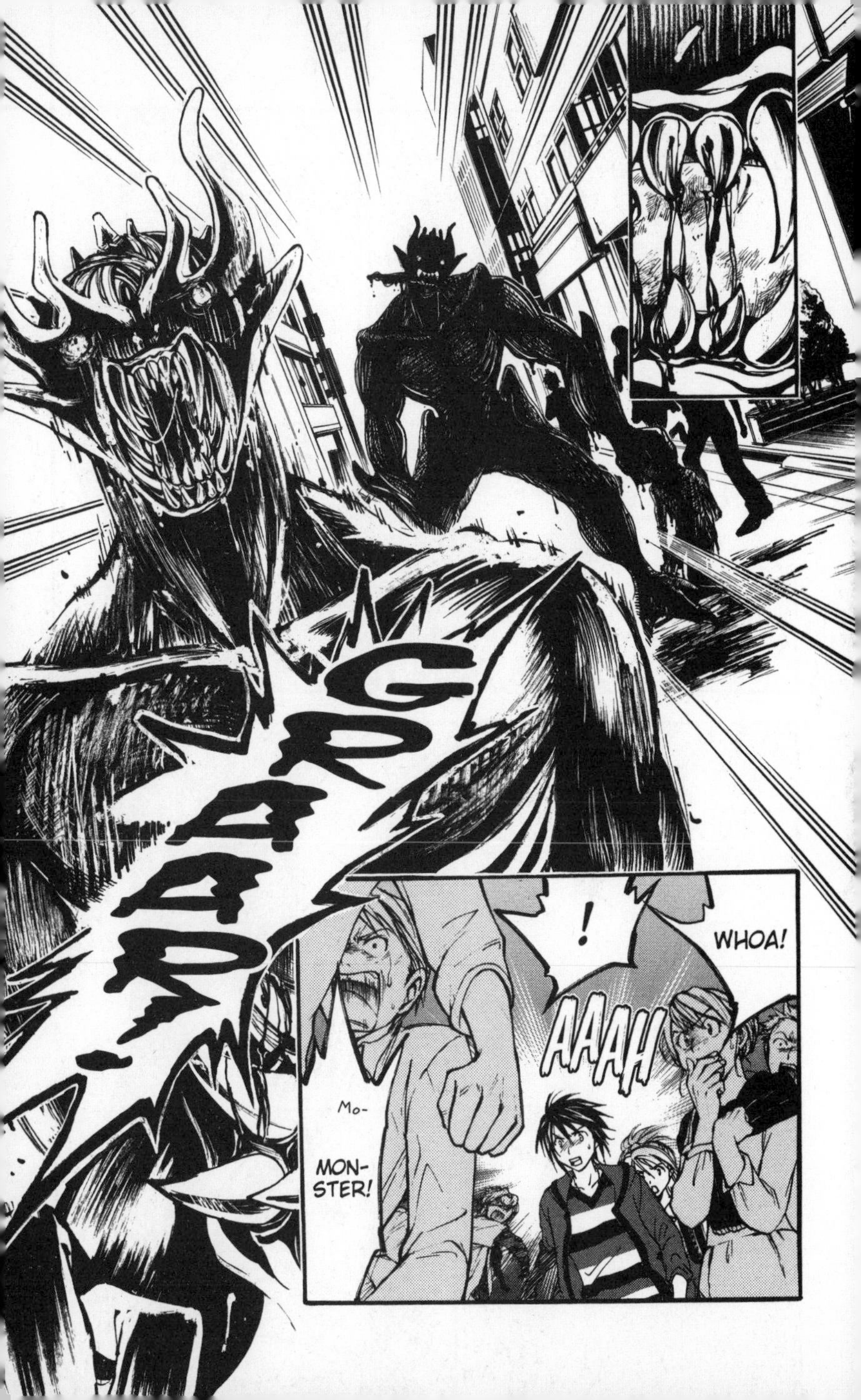
GRAAAR
!
WHOA!
AAAH
Mo-
MON-
STER!

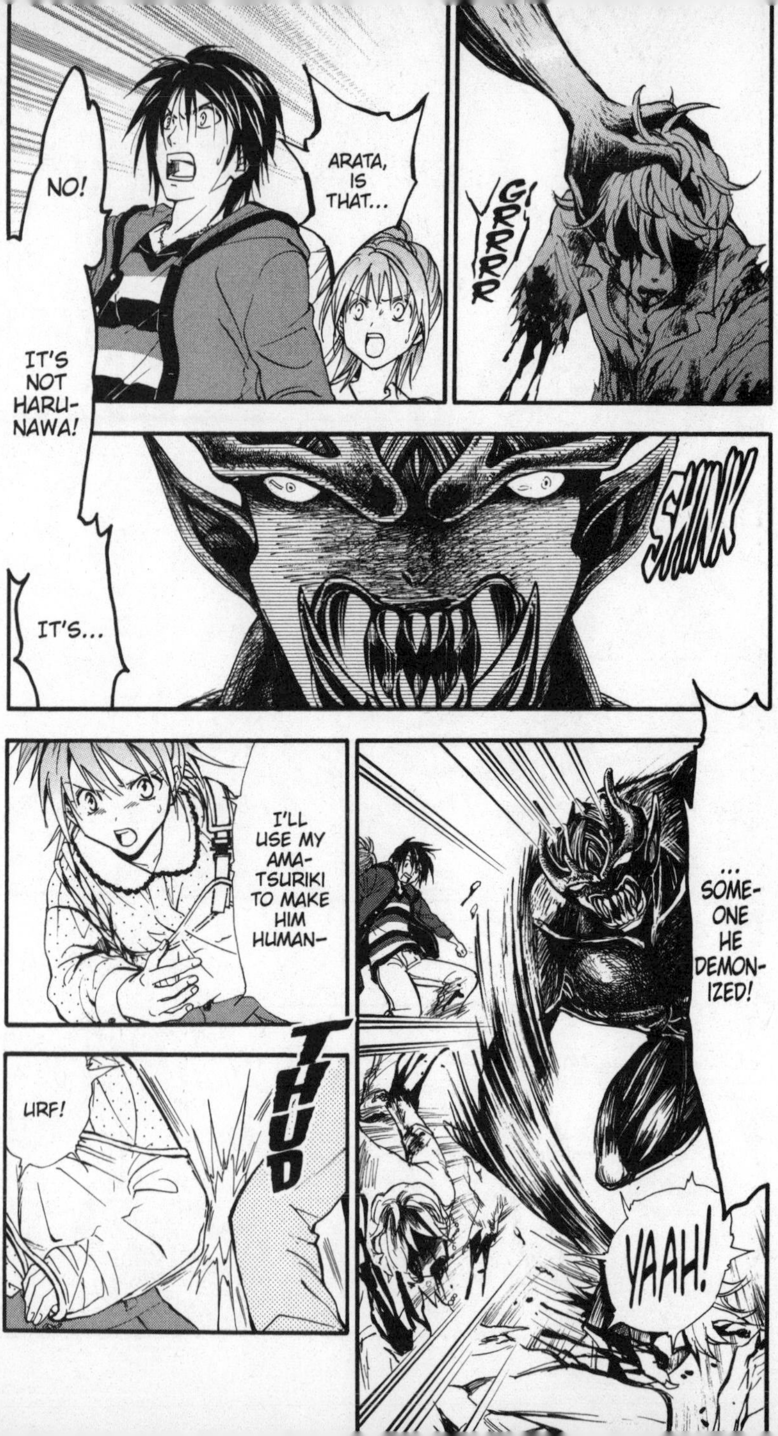
GRRRR
ARATA, IS THAT...
NO!
IT'S NOT HARU-NAWA!
SHINK
IT'S...
...SOME-ONE HE DEMON-IZED!
YAAH!
I'LL USE MY AMA-TSURIKI TO MAKE HIM HUMAN-
THUD
URF!

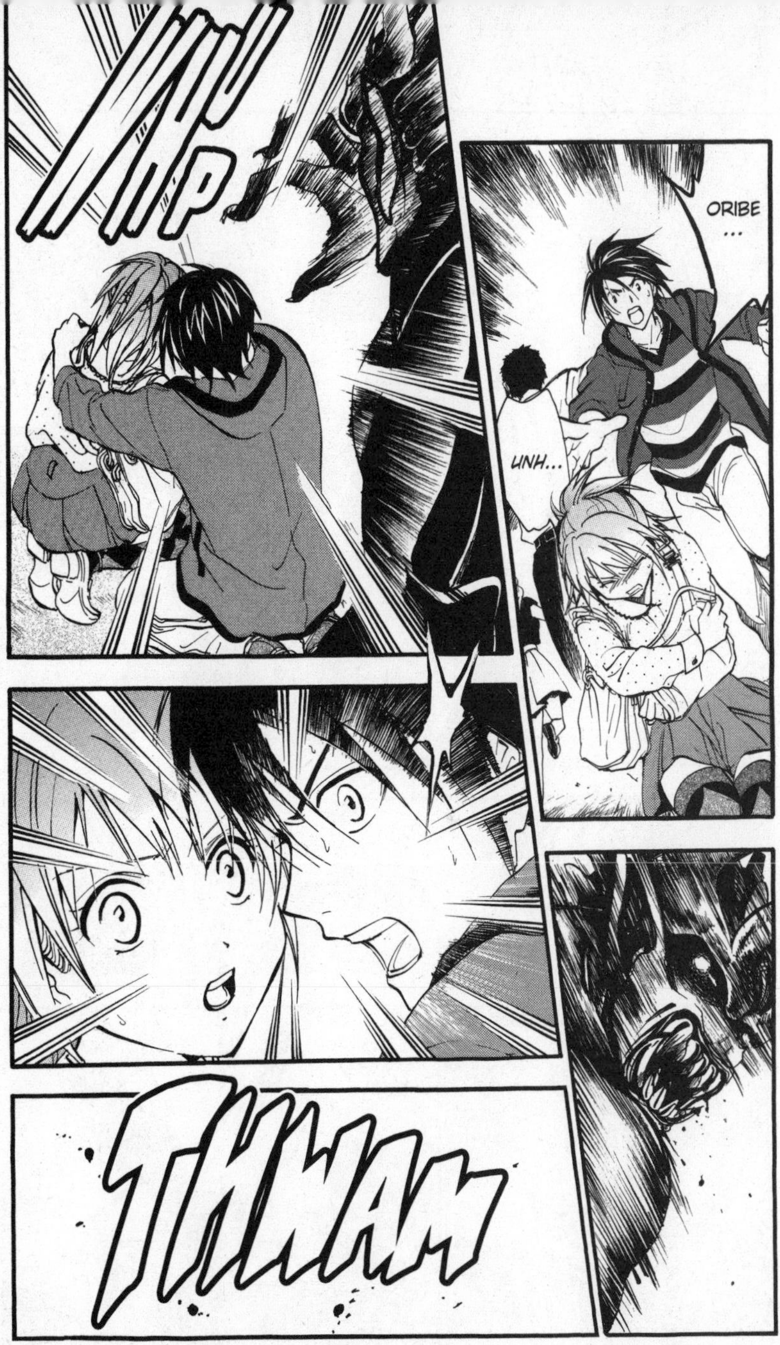
ORIBE ...
UNH...
WHUP
THWAM

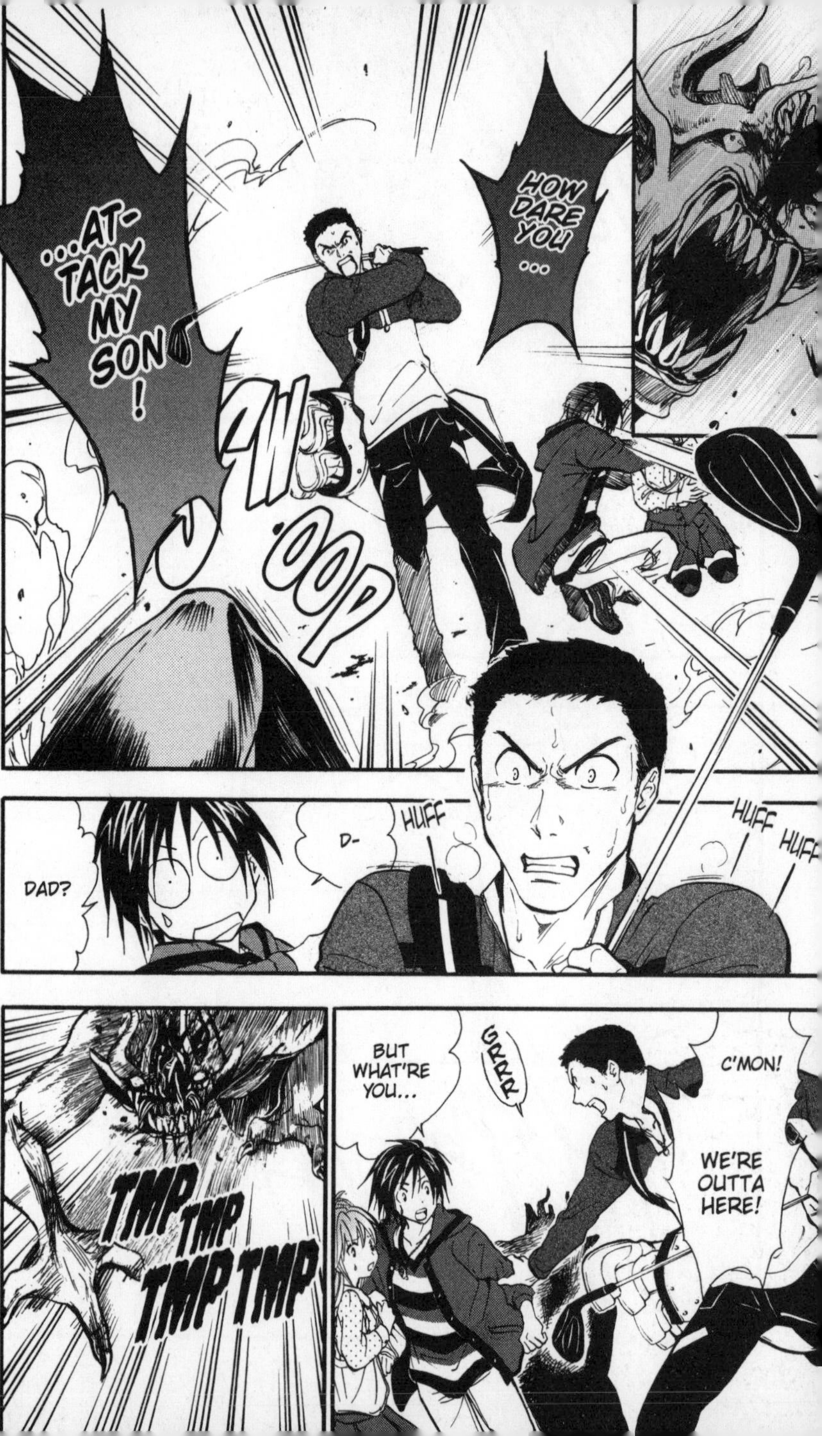
HOW DARE YOU...
...AT-TACK MY SON!
ZWOOP
HUFF HUFF
HUFF
D-
DAD?
C'MON!
WE'RE OUTTA HERE!
GRRR
BUT WHAT'RE YOU...
TMP TMP TMP TMP

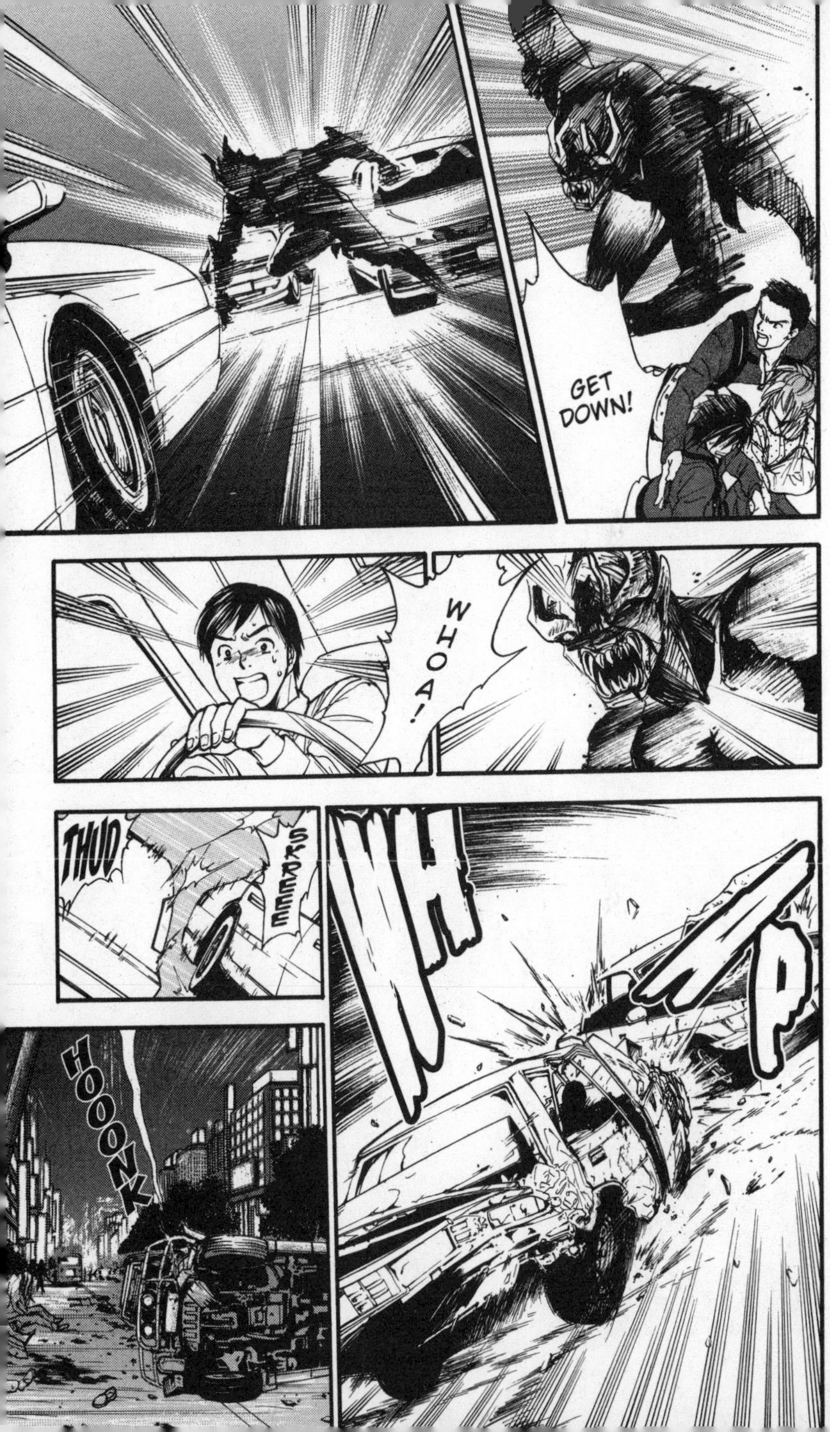
GET DOWN!
WHOA!
WHAP
SKREEE
THUD
HOOONK

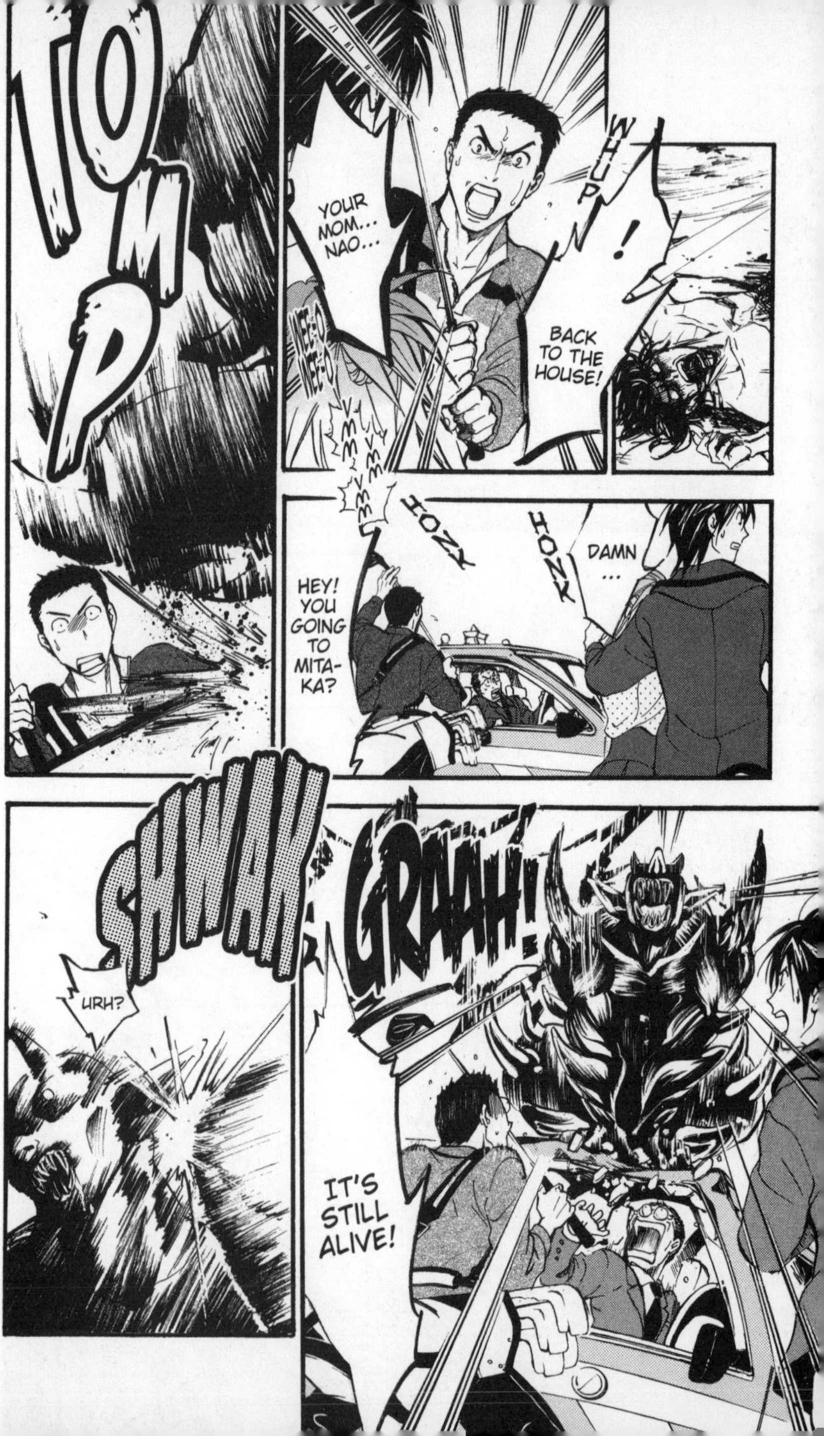
WHUP
!
BACK TO THE HOUSE!
YOUR MOM... NAO...
WEE-O WEE-O
VMM VMM VMM
HONK
HONK
DAMN ...
HEY! YOU GOING TO MITAKA?
TOMP
GRAAH!
IT'S STILL ALIVE!
SHWAK
URH?

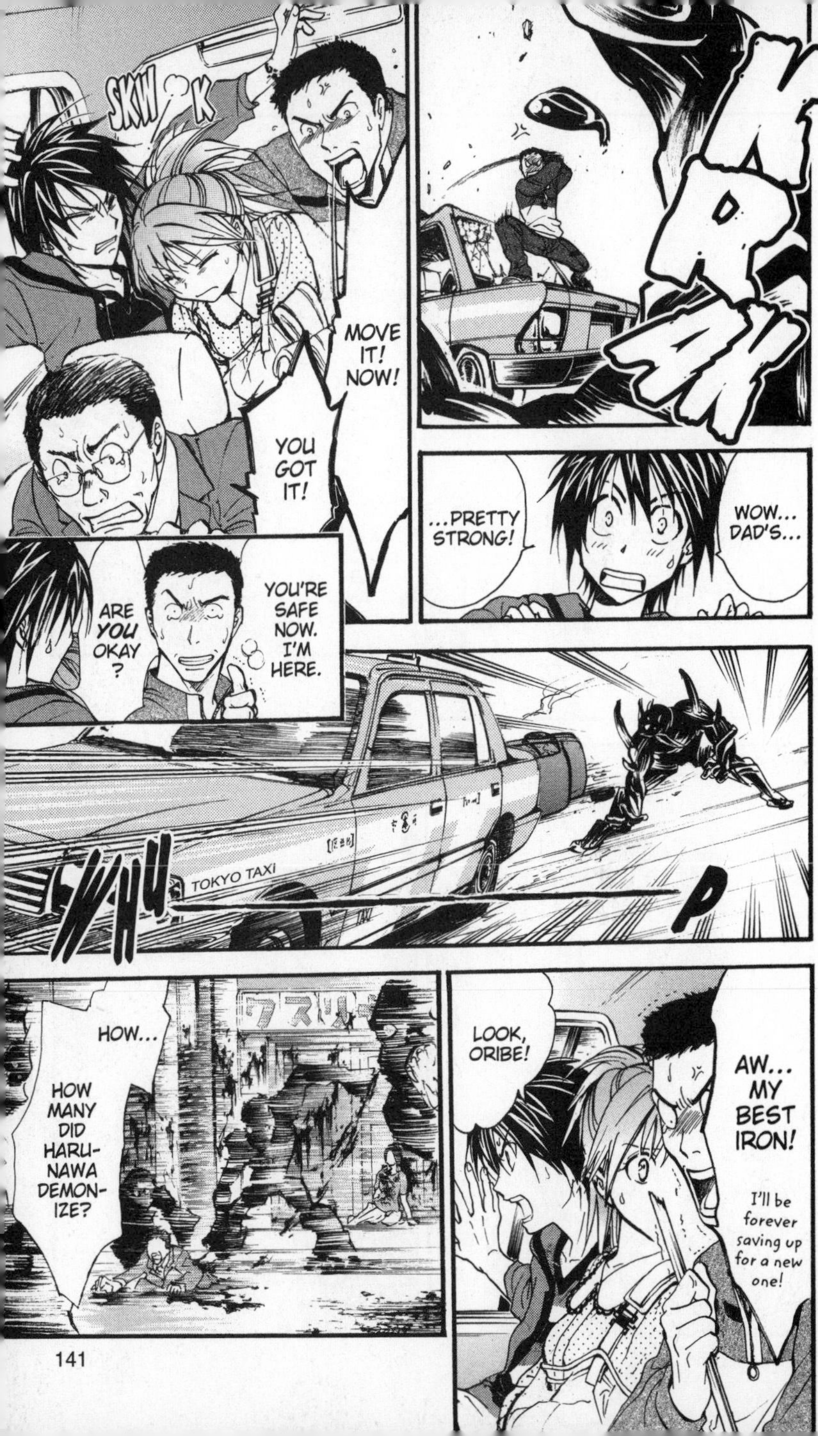
WOW... DAD'S...
...PRETTY STRONG!
SKW K
MOVE IT! NOW!
YOU GOT IT!
YOU'RE SAFE NOW. I'M HERE.
ARE YOU OKAY?
TOKYO TAXI
WHU
P
AW... MY BEST IRON!
LOOK, ORIBE!
I'll be forever saving up for a new one!
HOW...
HOW MANY DID HARUNAWA DEMONIZE?

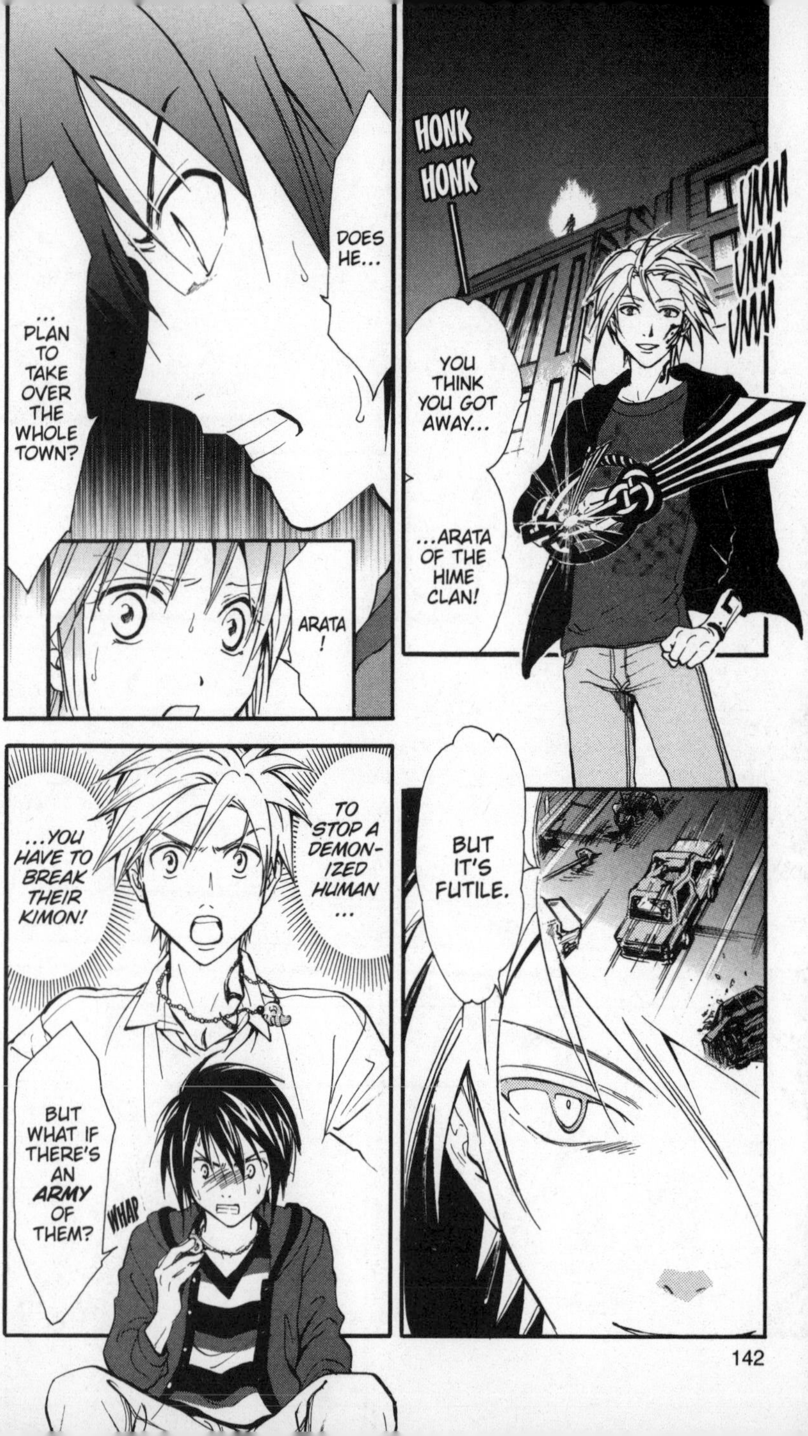
HONK HONK
UMM UMM UMM UMM
YOU THINK YOU GOT AWAY...
...ARATA OF THE HIME CLAN!
DOES HE...
...PLAN TO TAKE OVER THE WHOLE TOWN?
ARATA!
BUT IT'S FUTILE.
TO STOP A DEMONIZED HUMAN...
...YOU HAVE TO BREAK THEIR KIMON!
BUT WHAT IF THERE'S AN ARMY OF THEM?
WHAP

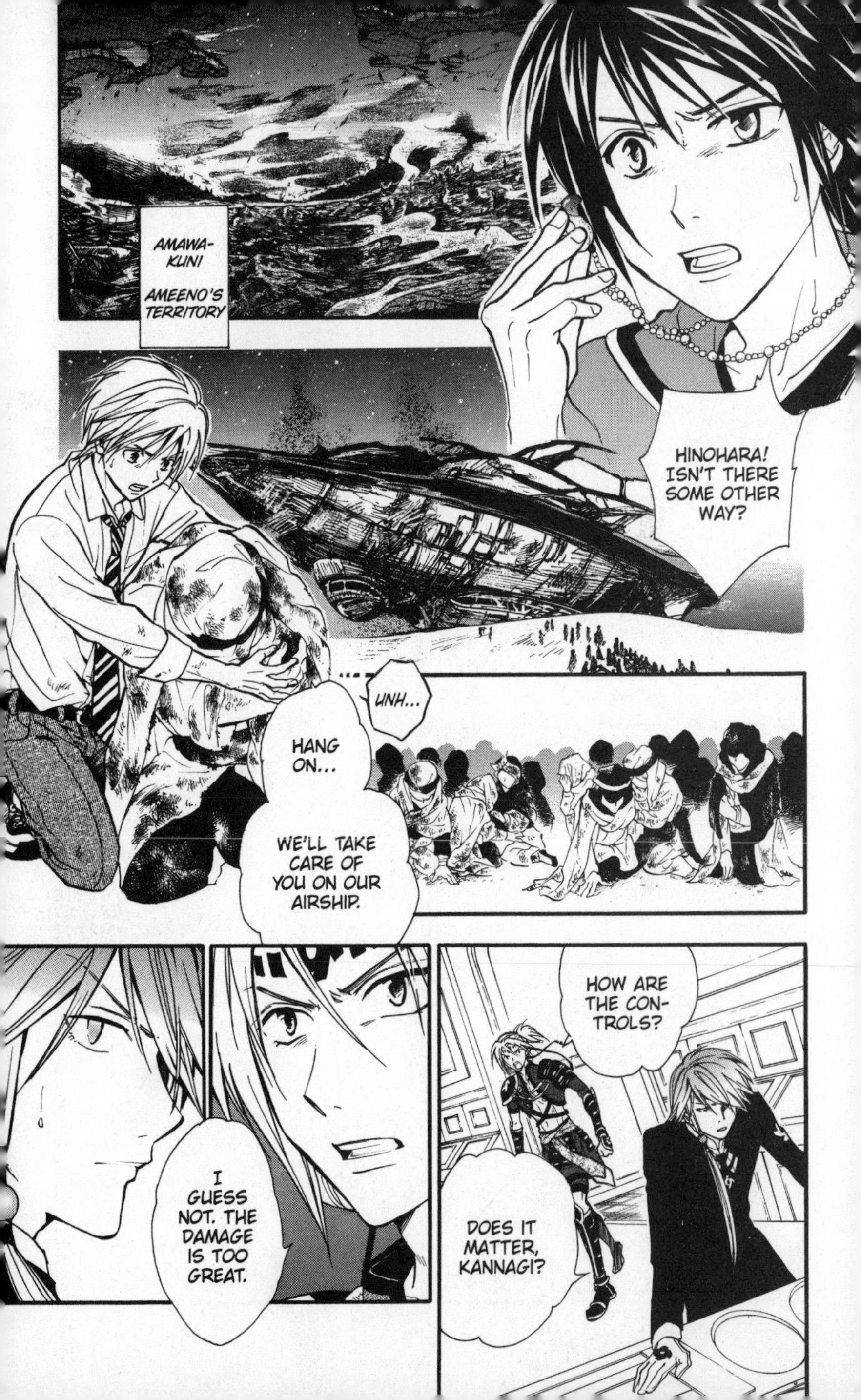
HINOHARA! ISN'T THERE SOME OTHER WAY?
AMAWA-KUNI
AMEENO'S TERRITORY
UNH...
HANG ON...
WE'LL TAKE CARE OF YOU ON OUR AIRSHIP.
HOW ARE THE CON-TROLS?
DOES IT MATTER, KANNAGI?
I GUESS NOT. THE DAMAGE IS TOO GREAT.

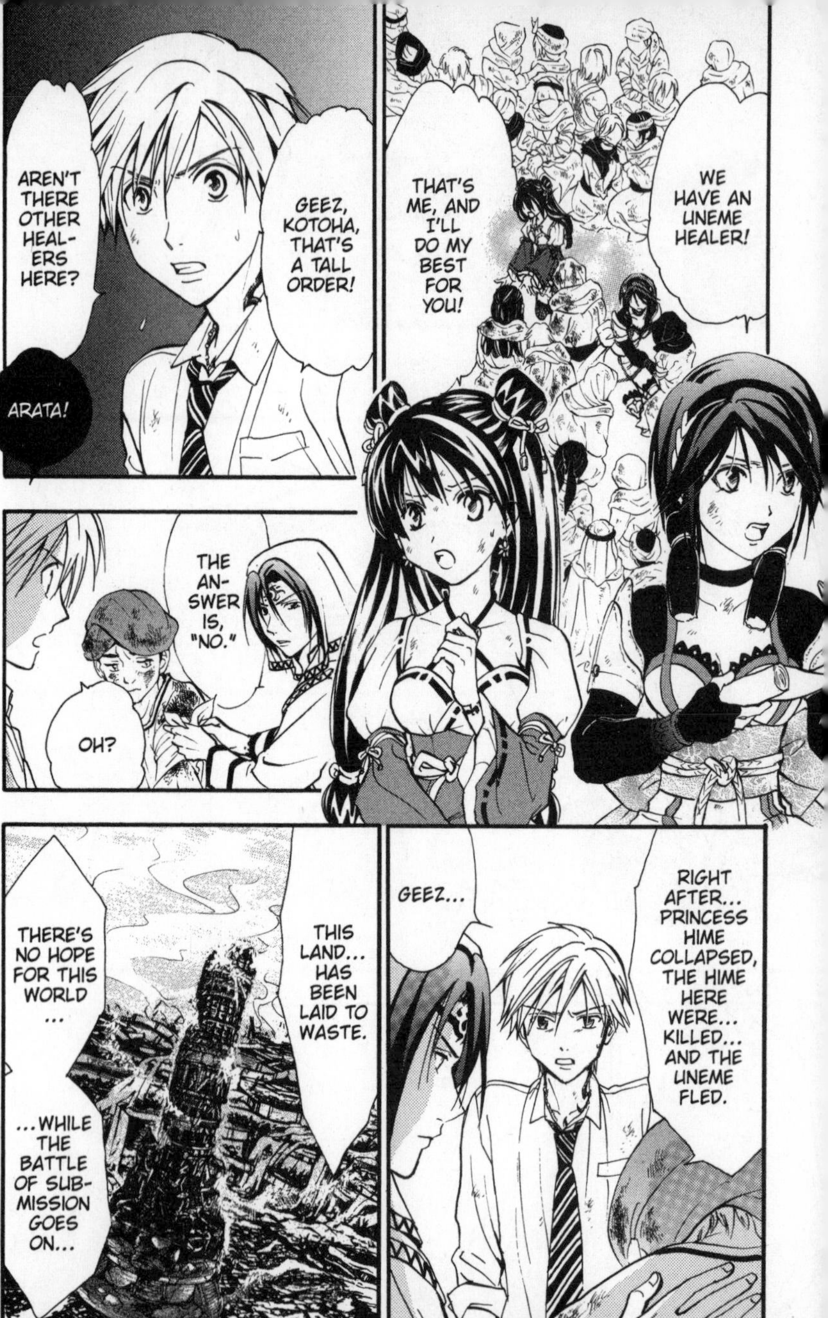
WE HAVE AN UNEME HEALER!
THAT'S ME, AND I'LL DO MY BEST FOR YOU!
GEEZ, KOTOHA, THAT'S A TALL ORDER!
AREN'T THERE OTHER HEALERS HERE?
ARATA!
THE ANSWER IS, "NO."
OH?
RIGHT AFTER... PRINCESS HIME COLLAPSED, THE HIME HERE WERE... KILLED... AND THE UNEME FLED.
GEEZ...
THIS LAND... HAS BEEN LAID TO WASTE.
THERE'S NO HOPE FOR THIS WORLD ...
...WHILE THE BATTLE OF SUBMISSION GOES ON...

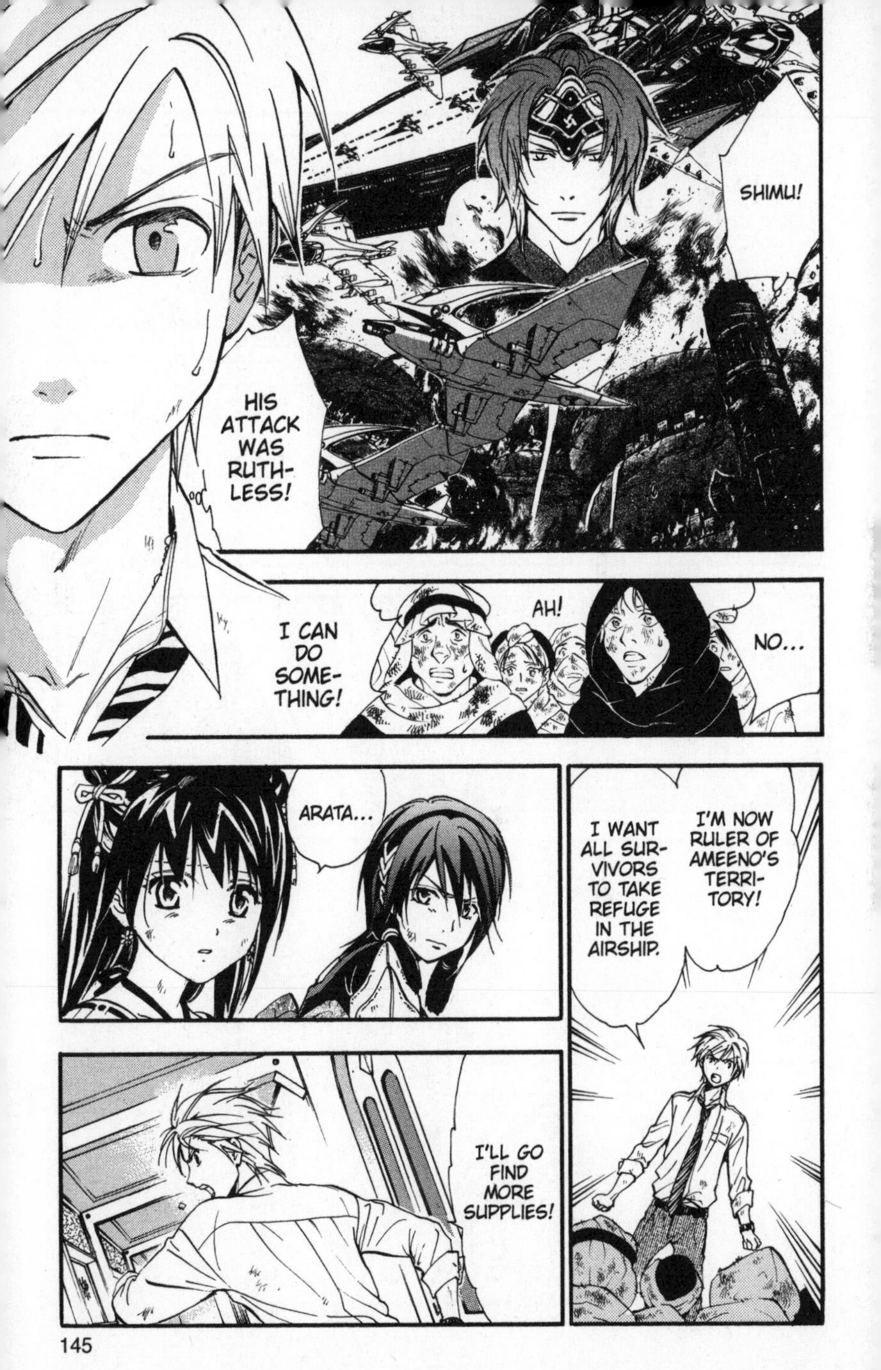
SHIMU!
HIS ATTACK WAS RUTH-LESS!
NO...
AH!
I CAN DO SOME-THING!
I'M NOW RULER OF AMEENO'S TERRI-TORY!
I WANT ALL SUR-VIVORS TO TAKE REFUGE IN THE AIRSHIP.
ARATA...
I'LL GO FIND MORE SUPPLIES!

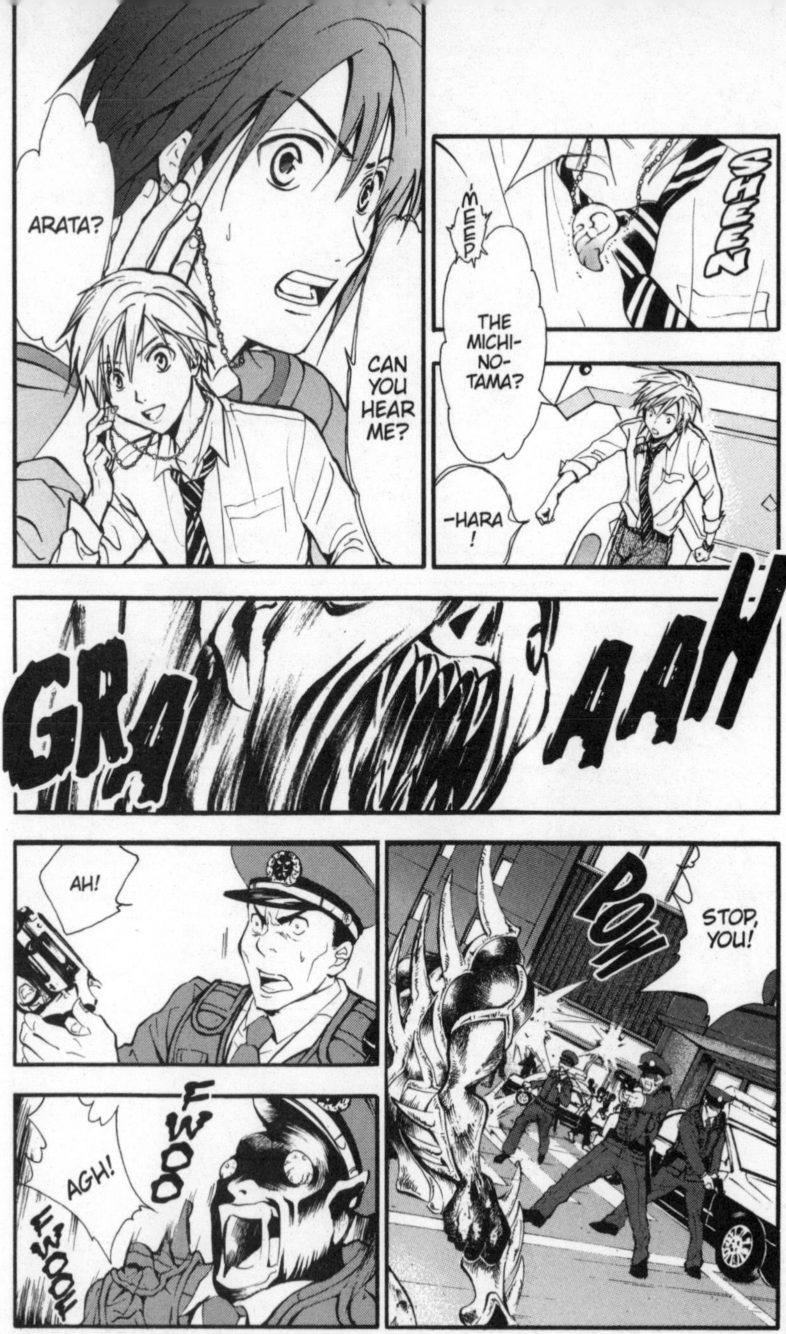
SHEEN
MEEP
THE MICHI-NO-TAMA?
-HARA!
ARATA?
CAN YOU HEAR ME?
GRAAAH
POW
STOP, YOU!
AH!
FWOO
AGH!
FWOOH

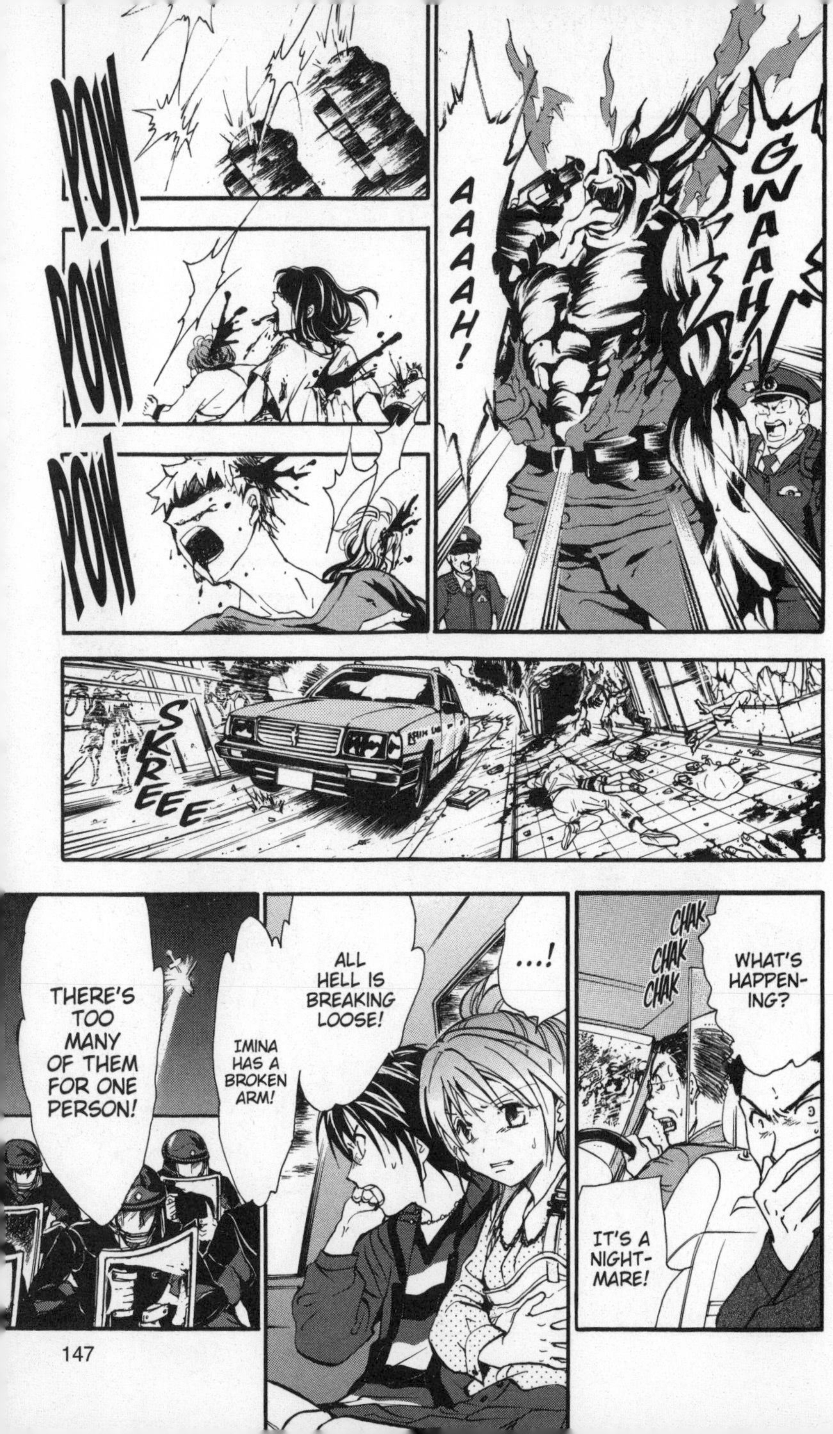
GWAAAH!
AAAAAH!
POW
POW
POW
SKREEEE
CHAK CHAK CHAK
WHAT'S HAPPEN-ING?
IT'S A NIGHT-MARE!
...!
ALL HELL IS BREAKING LOOSE!
IMINA HAS A BROKEN ARM!
THERE'S TOO MANY OF THEM FOR ONE PERSON!

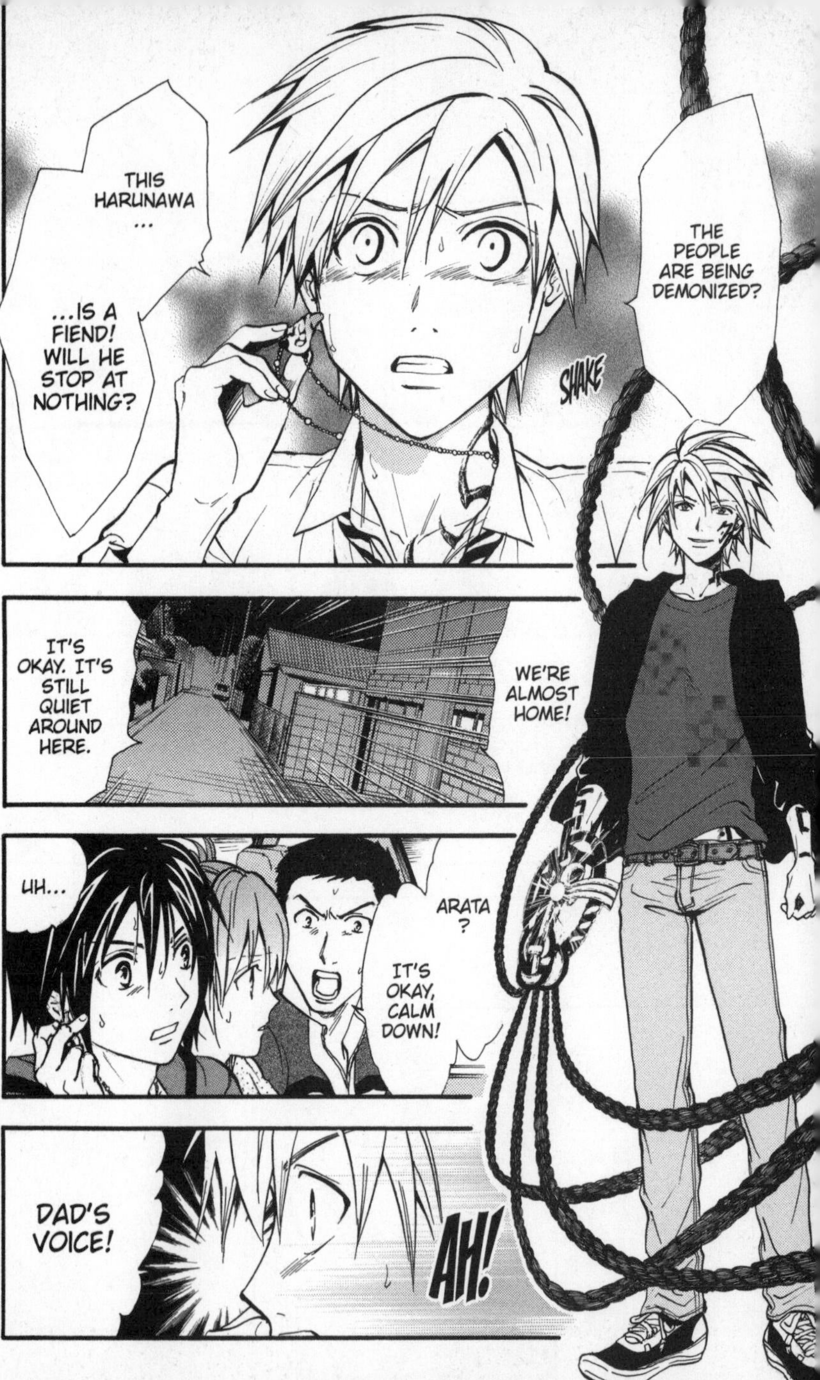
THE PEOPLE ARE BEING DEMONIZED?
SHAKE
THIS HARUNAWA ...
...IS A FIEND! WILL HE STOP AT NOTHING?
WE'RE ALMOST HOME!
IT'S OKAY. IT'S STILL QUIET AROUND HERE.
ARATA ?
IT'S OKAY, CALM DOWN!
UH...
AH!
DAD'S VOICE!

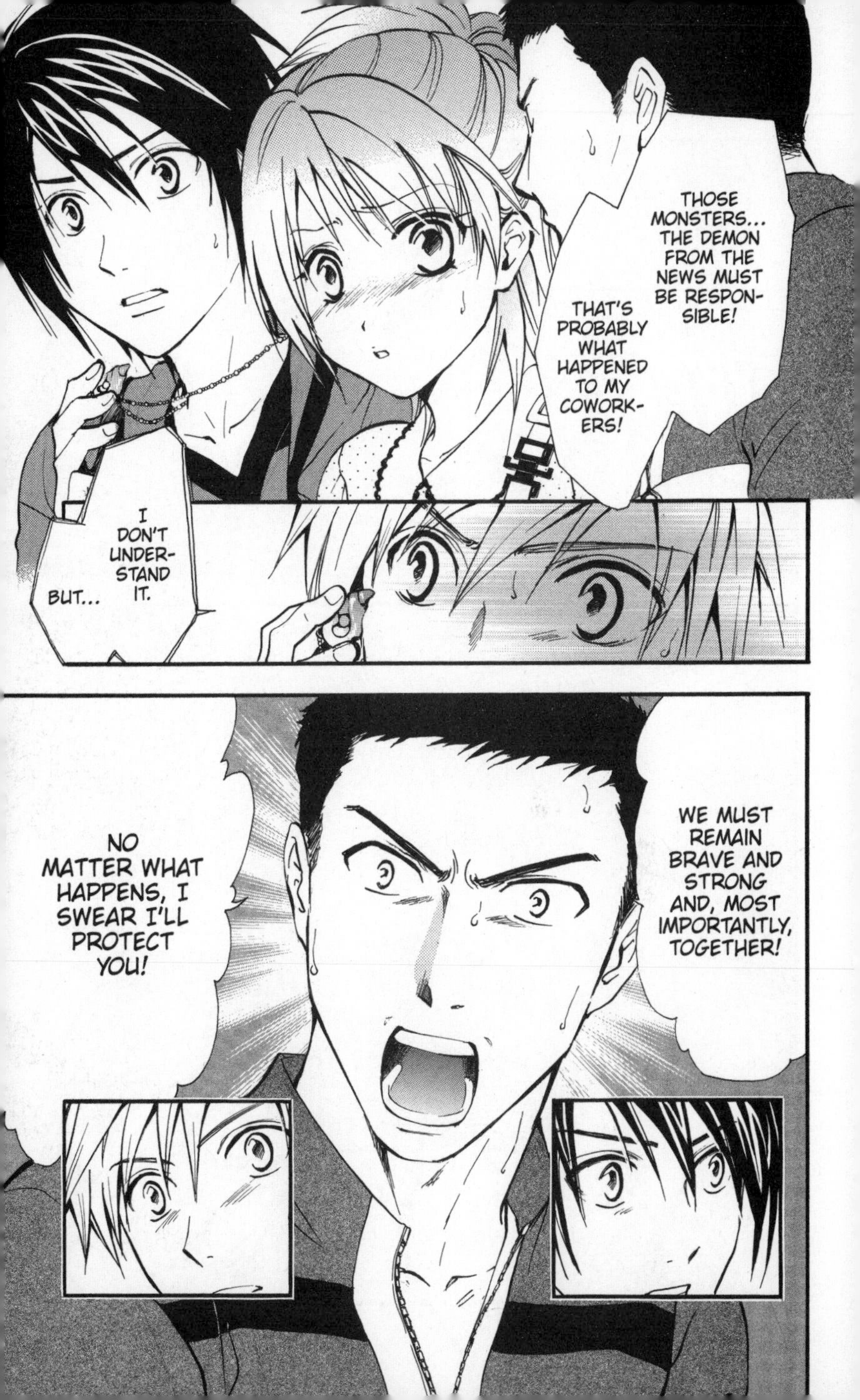
THOSE MONSTERS... THE DEMON FROM THE NEWS MUST BE RESPONSIBLE!
THAT'S PROBABLY WHAT HAPPENED TO MY COWORKERS!
I DON'T UNDERSTAND IT.
BUT...
WE MUST REMAIN BRAVE AND STRONG AND, MOST IMPORTANTLY, TOGETHER!
NO MATTER WHAT HAPPENS, I SWEAR I'LL PROTECT YOU!

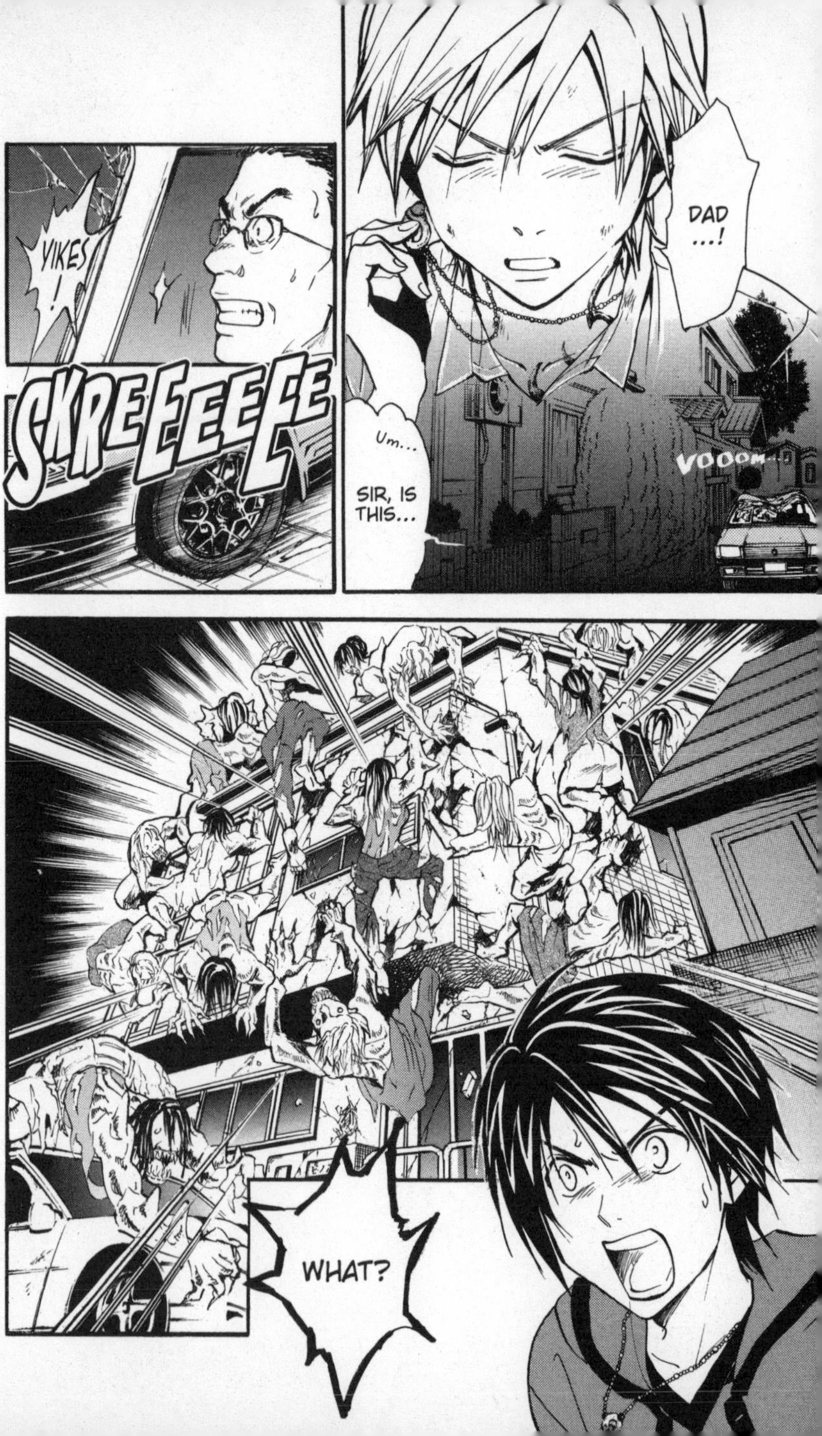
DAD ...!
Um...
VOOOM...
SIR, IS THIS...
YIKES!
SKREEEEEE
WHAT?

Chapter 236
CALAMITY EXPANDS

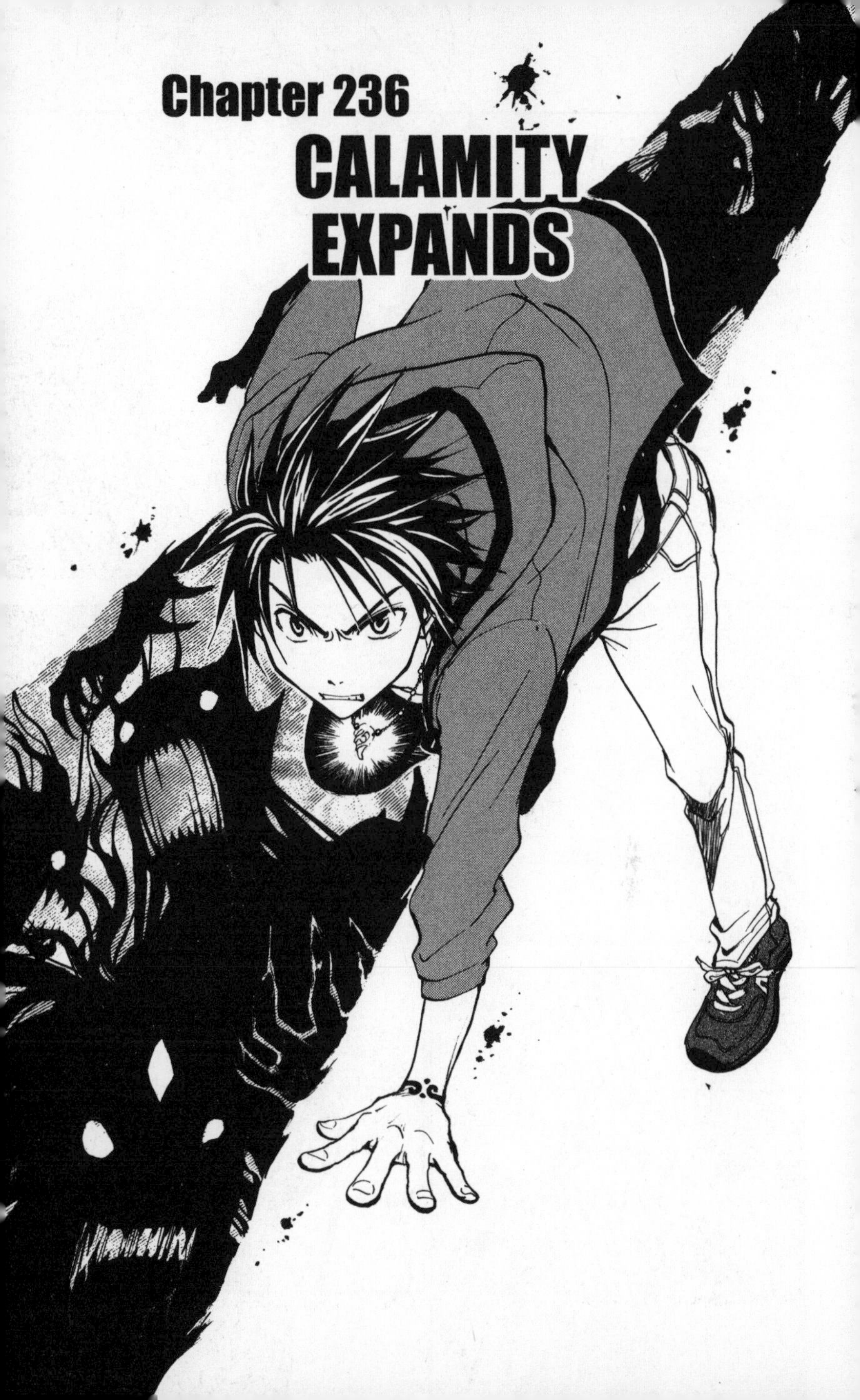

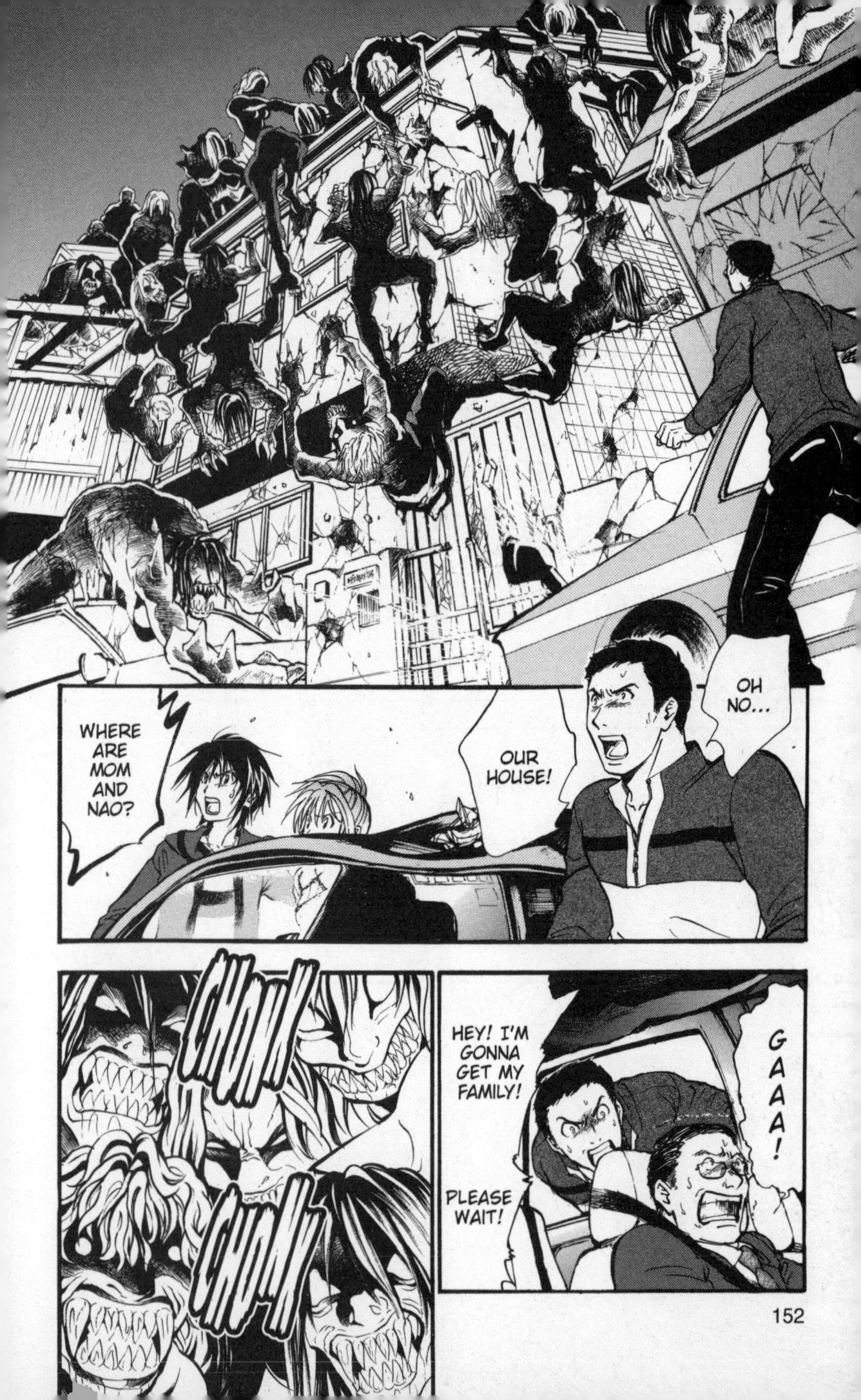
OH NO...
OUR HOUSE!
WHERE ARE MOM AND NAO?
GAAAA!
HEY! I'M GONNA GET MY FAMILY!
PLEASE WAIT!

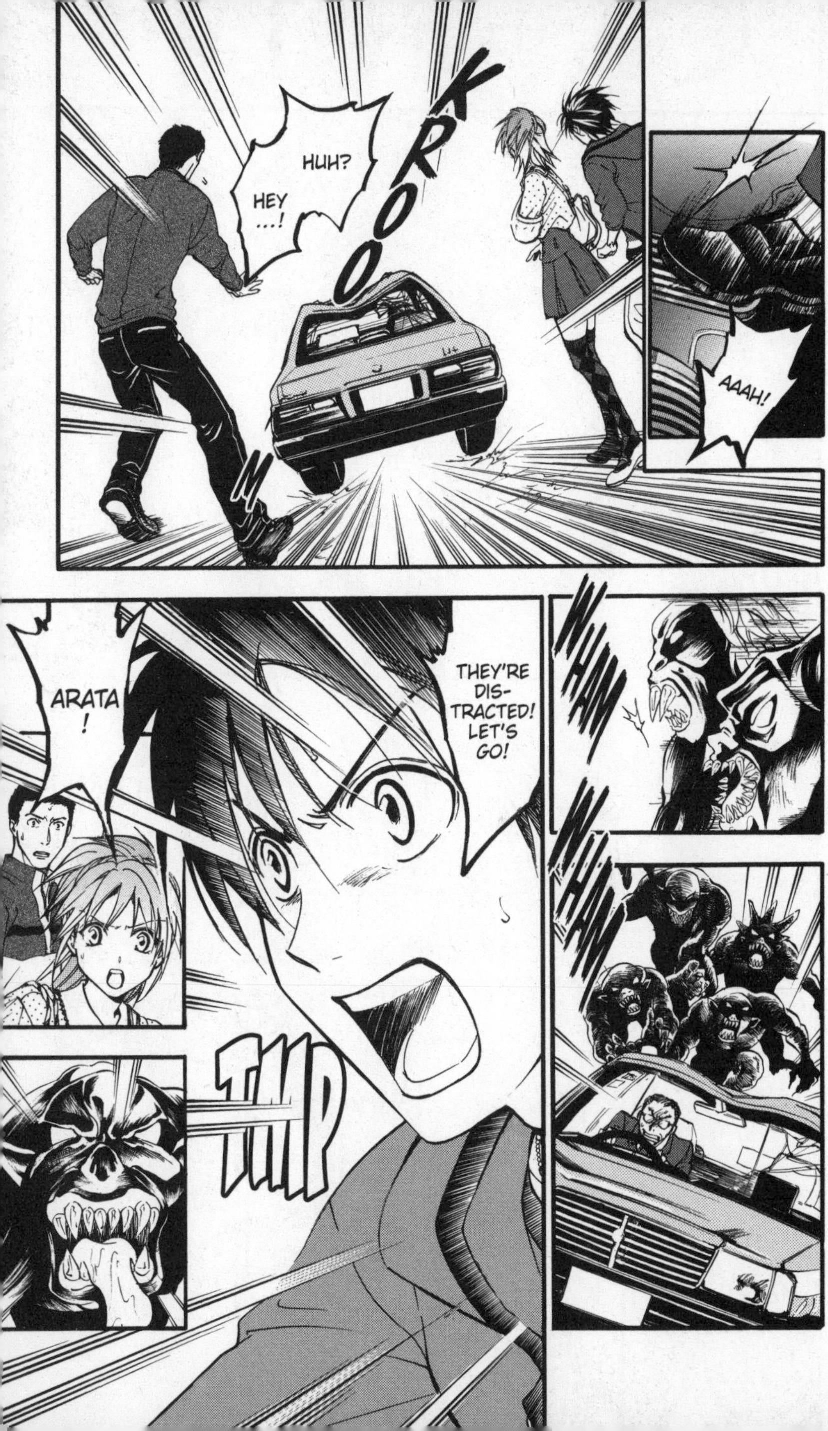
AAAH!
KROOOM
HUH?
HEY ...!
WHAM
WHAM
WHAM
THEY'RE DIS-TRACTED! LET'S GO!
ARATA!
THP

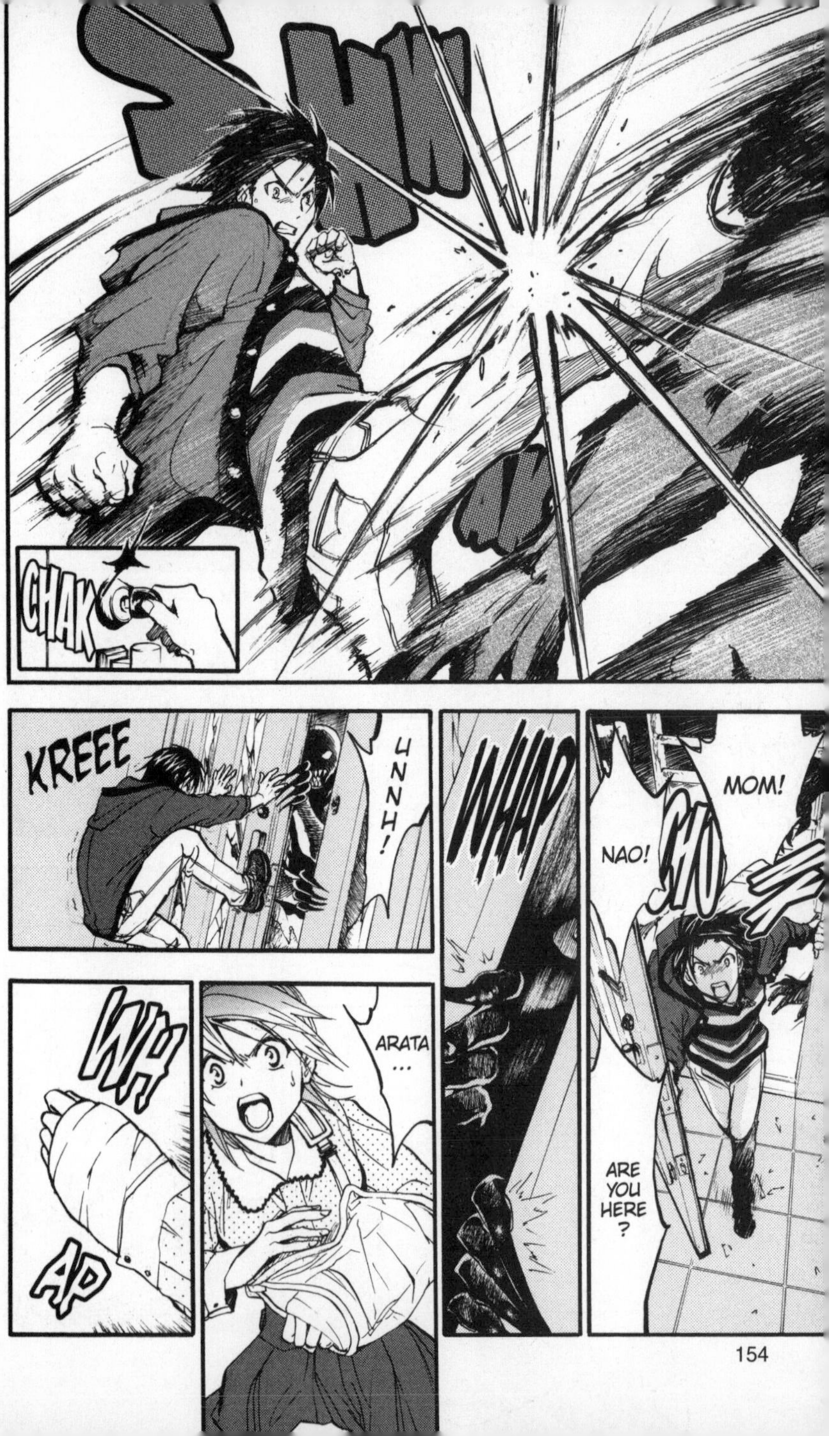
CHAK
MOM!
NAO!
CHO
ARE YOU HERE?
WHAP
UNNH!
KREEE
ARATA...
WH
AP

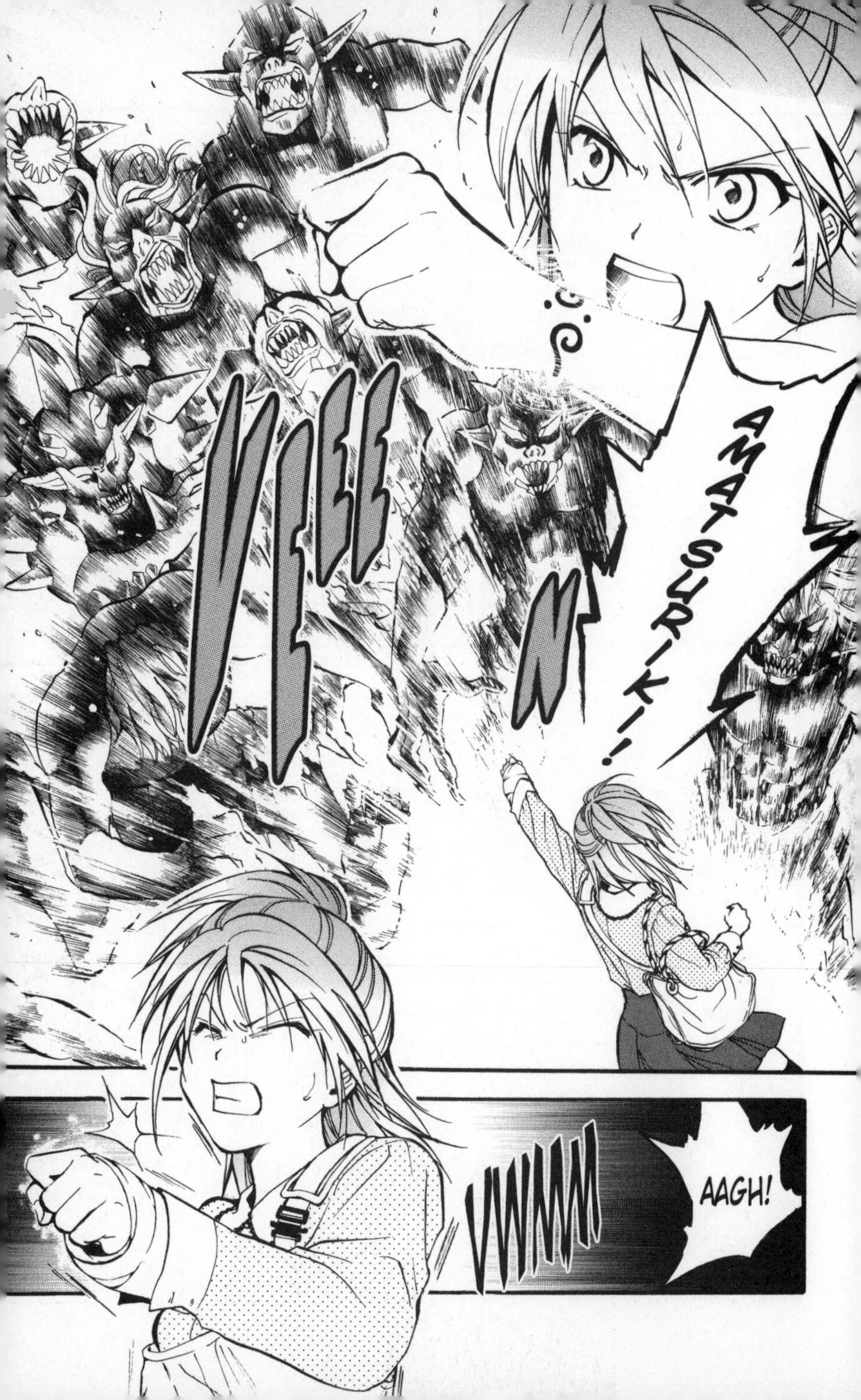
AMATSURIKI!!
VEEE
N
VWMM
AAGH!

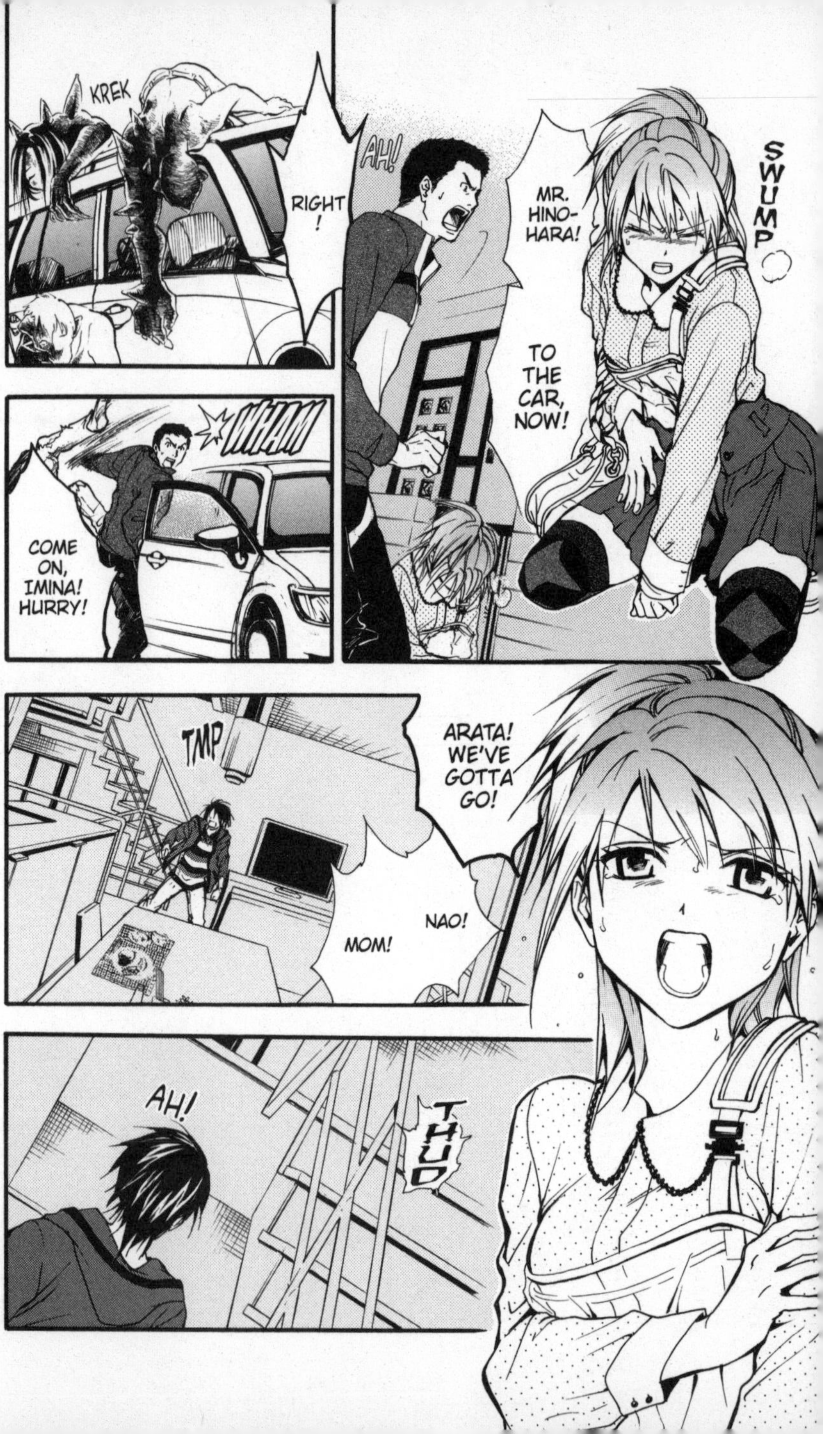
SWUMP
MR. HINOHARA!
TO THE CAR, NOW!
AH!
RIGHT!
KREK
WHAM
COME ON, IMINA! HURRY!
ARATA! WE'VE GOTTA GO!
TMP
NAO!
MOM!
AH!
THUD

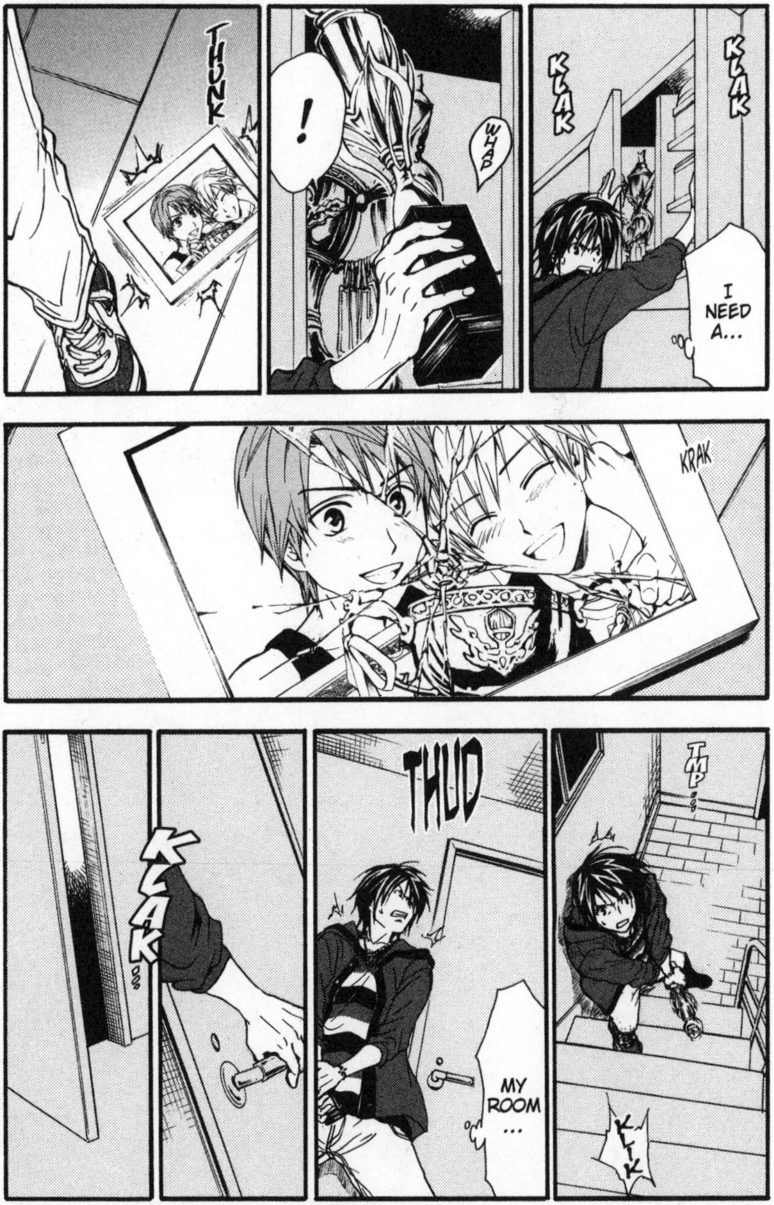
KLAK
KLAK
I NEED A...
!
WHAP
THUNK
KRAK
TMP..
KLIK
THUD
MY ROOM ...
KLAK..

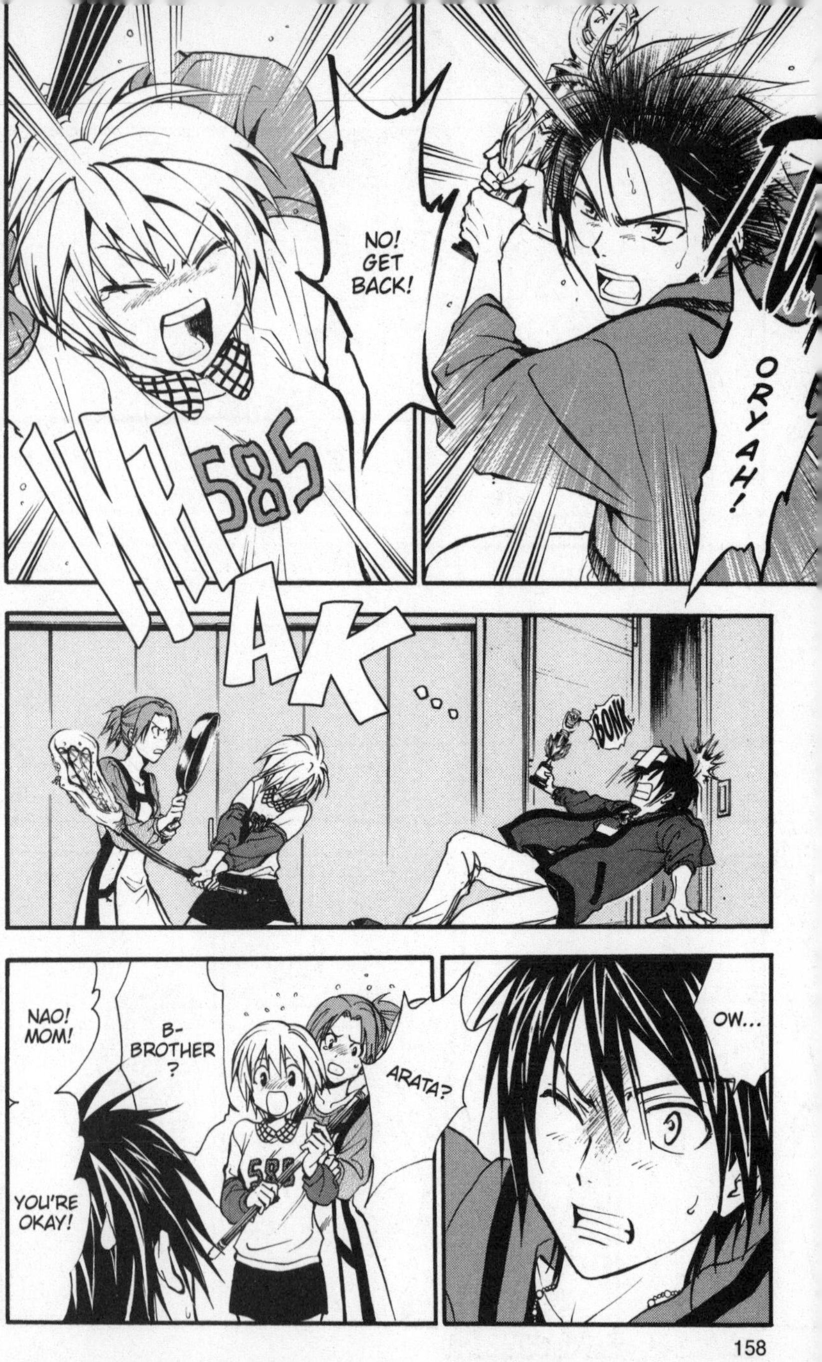
ORYAH!
NO! GET BACK!
WHAK
...
BONK
OW...
ARATA?
B-BROTHER?
NAO! MOM!
YOU'RE OKAY!

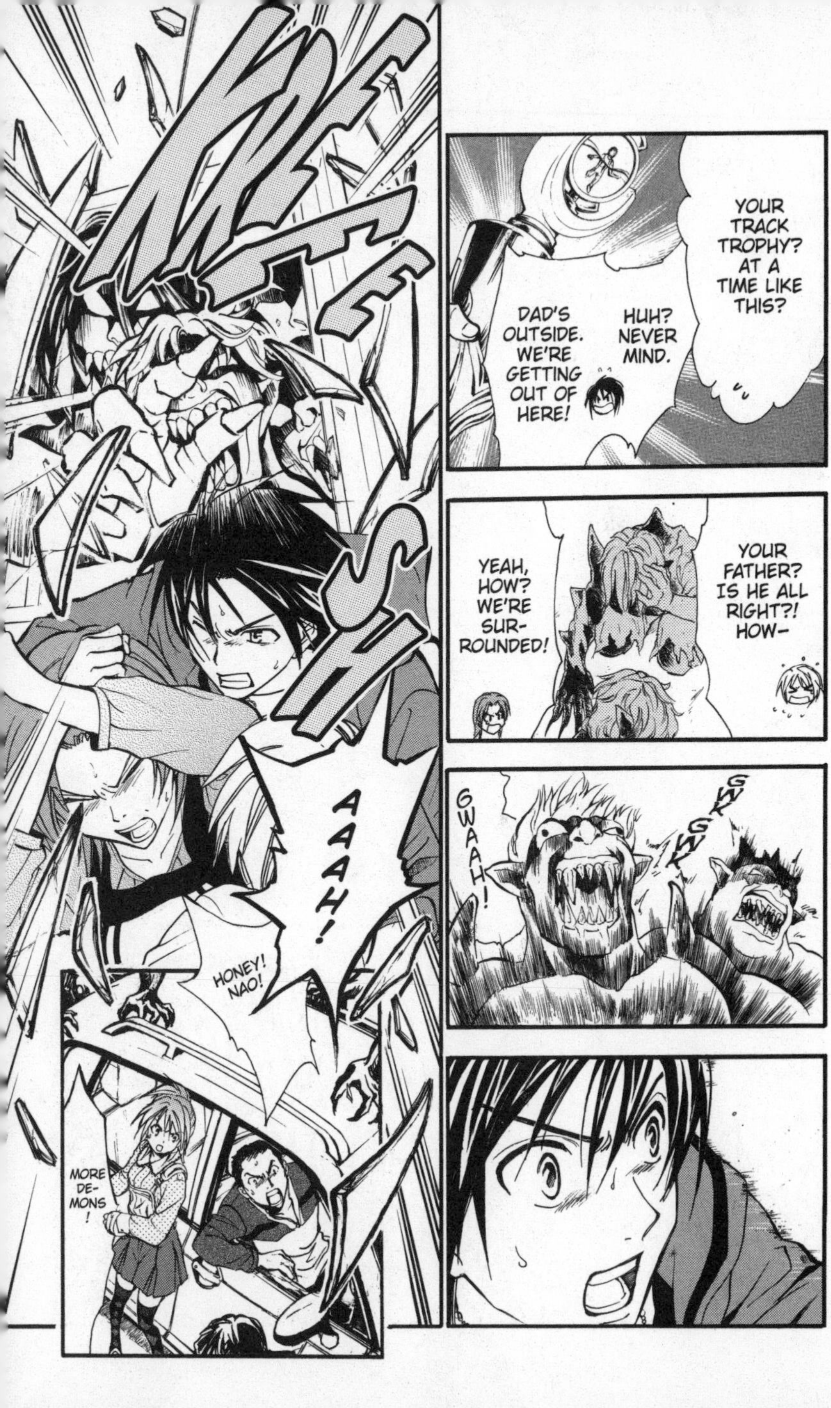
YOUR TRACK TROPHY? AT A TIME LIKE THIS?
HUH? NEVER MIND.
DAD'S OUTSIDE. WE'RE GETTING OUT OF HERE!
YOUR FATHER? IS HE ALL RIGHT?! HOW-
YEAH, HOW? WE'RE SUR-ROUNDED!
GWK GWK
GWAAAH!
AAAAH!
HONEY! NAO!
MORE DE-MONS!

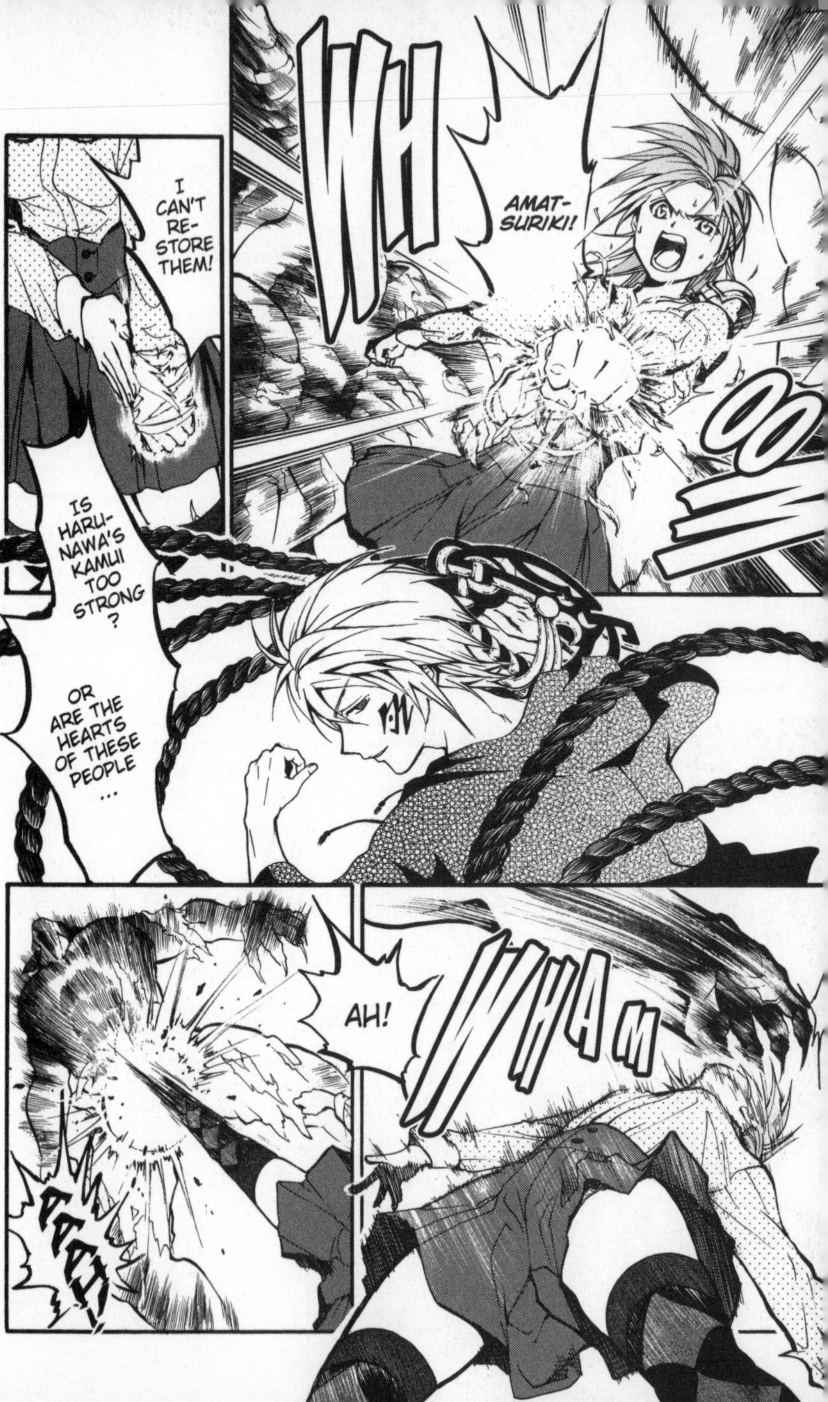
WH
OOM
AMAT-
SURIKI!
I
CAN'T
RE-
STORE
THEM!
IS
HARU-
NAWA'S
KAMUI
TOO
STRONG
?
OR
ARE THE
HEARTS
OF THESE
PEOPLE
...
WHAM
AH!
AAAH!

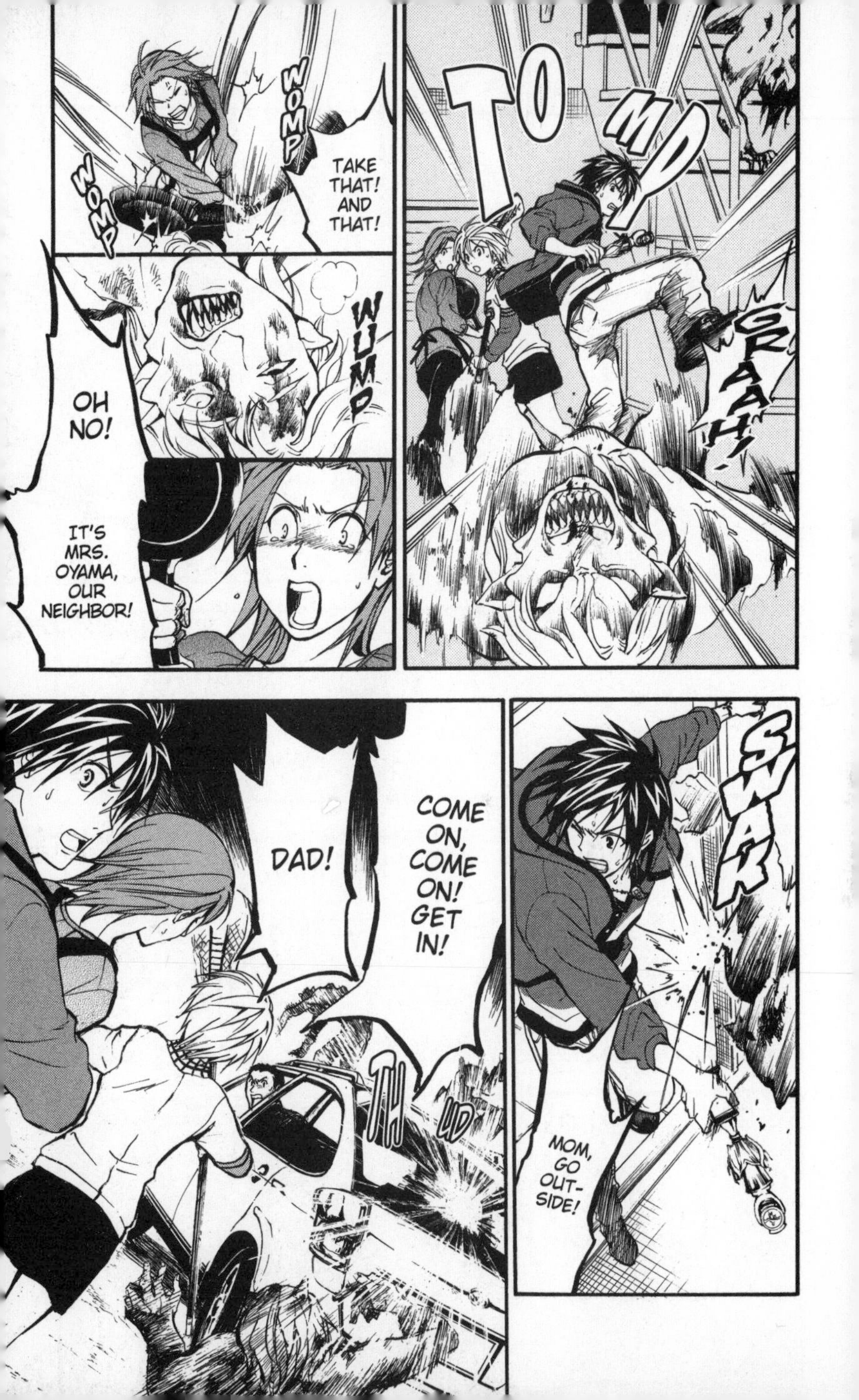
TOMP
GRAAAH!
WOMP
WOMP
TAKE THAT! AND THAT!
WUMP
OH NO!
IT'S MRS. OYAMA, OUR NEIGHBOR!
SWAK
MOM, GO OUT-SIDE!
COME ON, COME ON! GET IN!
DAD!
THUD

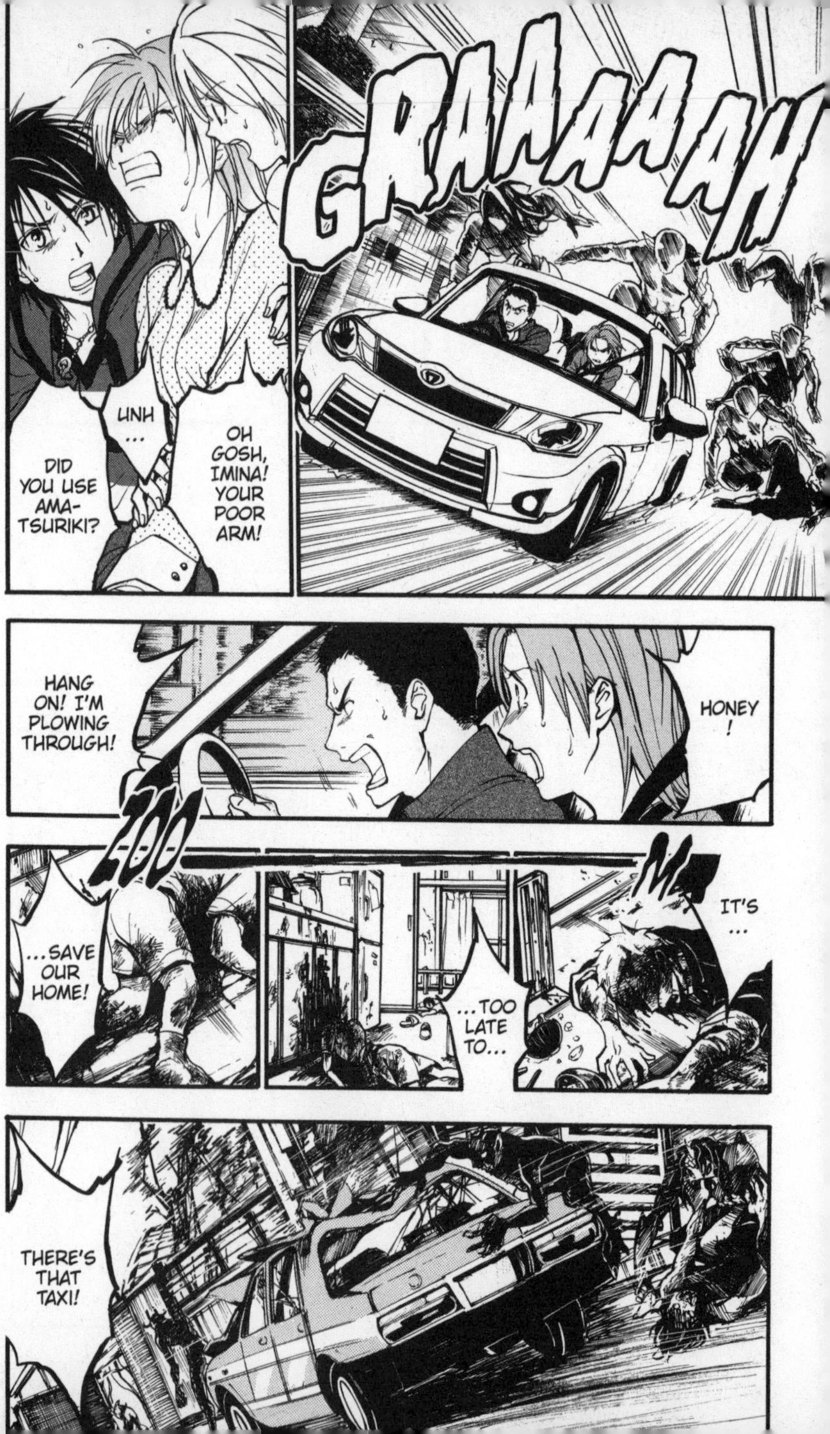
GRAAAAAH
OH GOSH, IMINA! YOUR POOR ARM!
UNH ...
DID YOU USE AMA-TSURIKI?
HONEY!
HANG ON! I'M PLOWING THROUGH!
ZOOM
IT'S ...
...TOO LATE TO...
...SAVE OUR HOME!
THERE'S THAT TAXI!

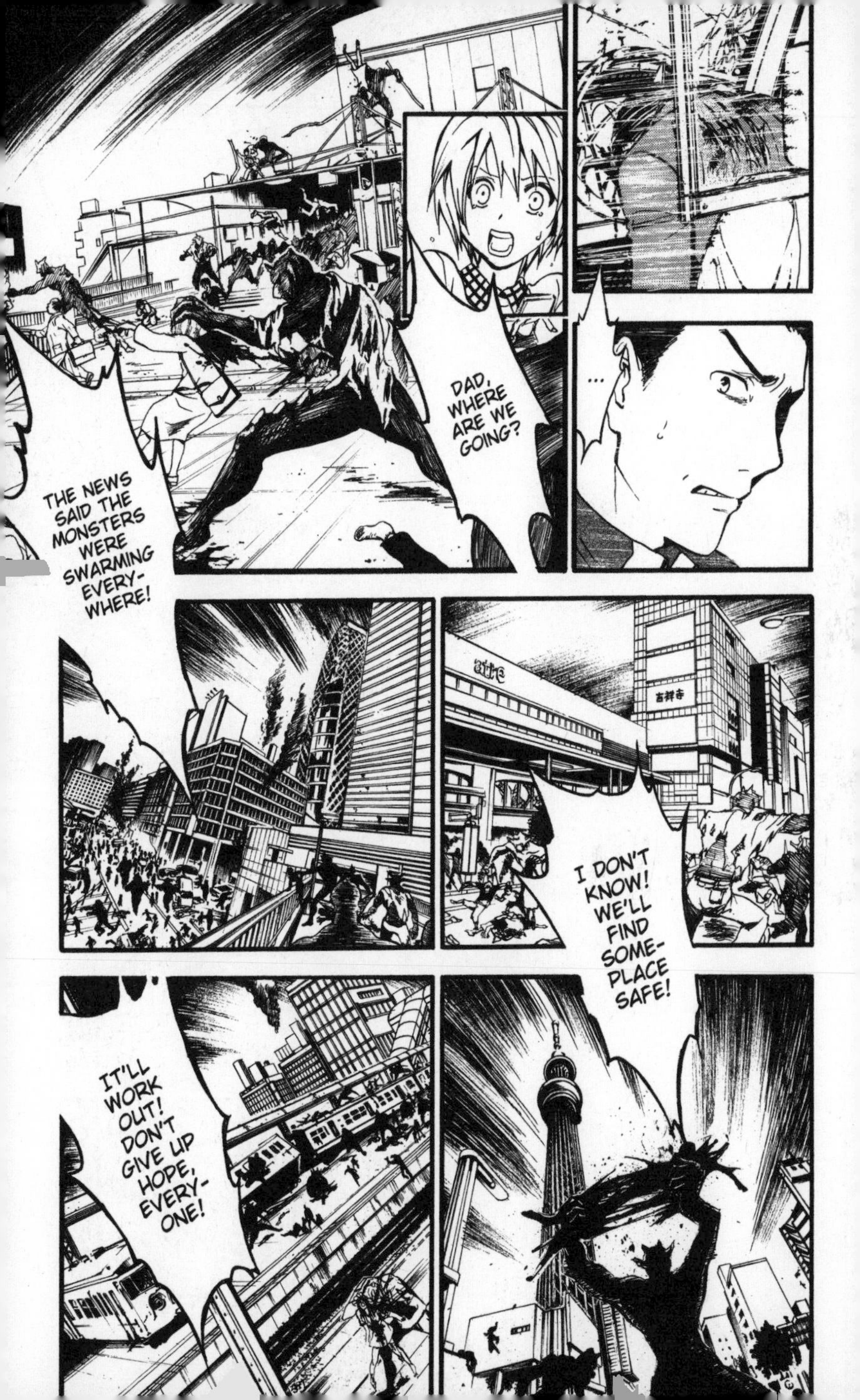
DAD, WHERE ARE WE GOING?
...
THE NEWS SAID THE MONSTERS WERE SWARMING EVERY-WHERE!
atre
吉祥寺
I DON'T KNOW! WE'LL FIND SOME-PLACE SAFE!
IT'LL WORK OUT! DON'T GIVE UP HOPE, EVERY-ONE!

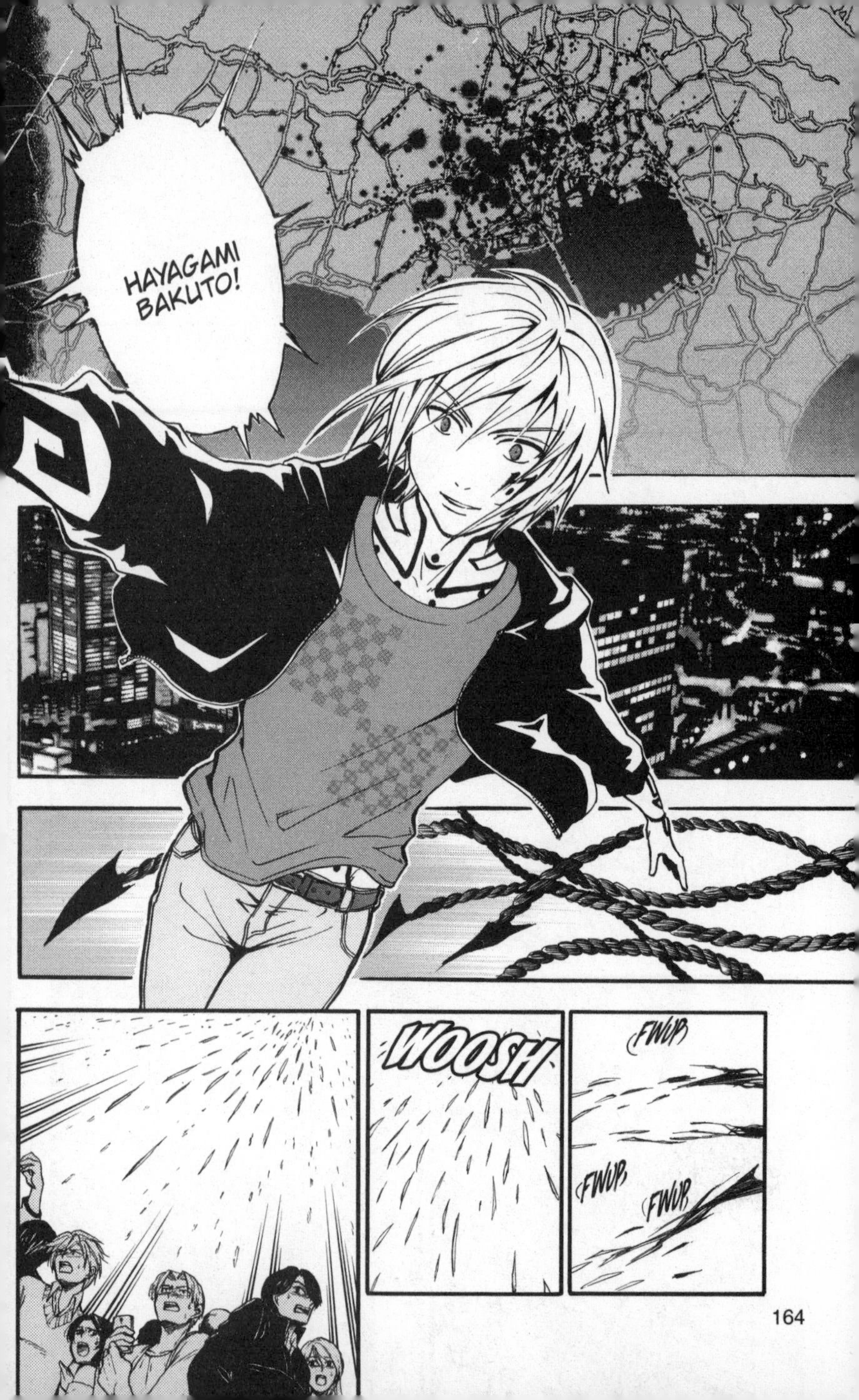
HAYAGAMI BAKUTO!
FWUP
FWUP
FWUP
WOOSH

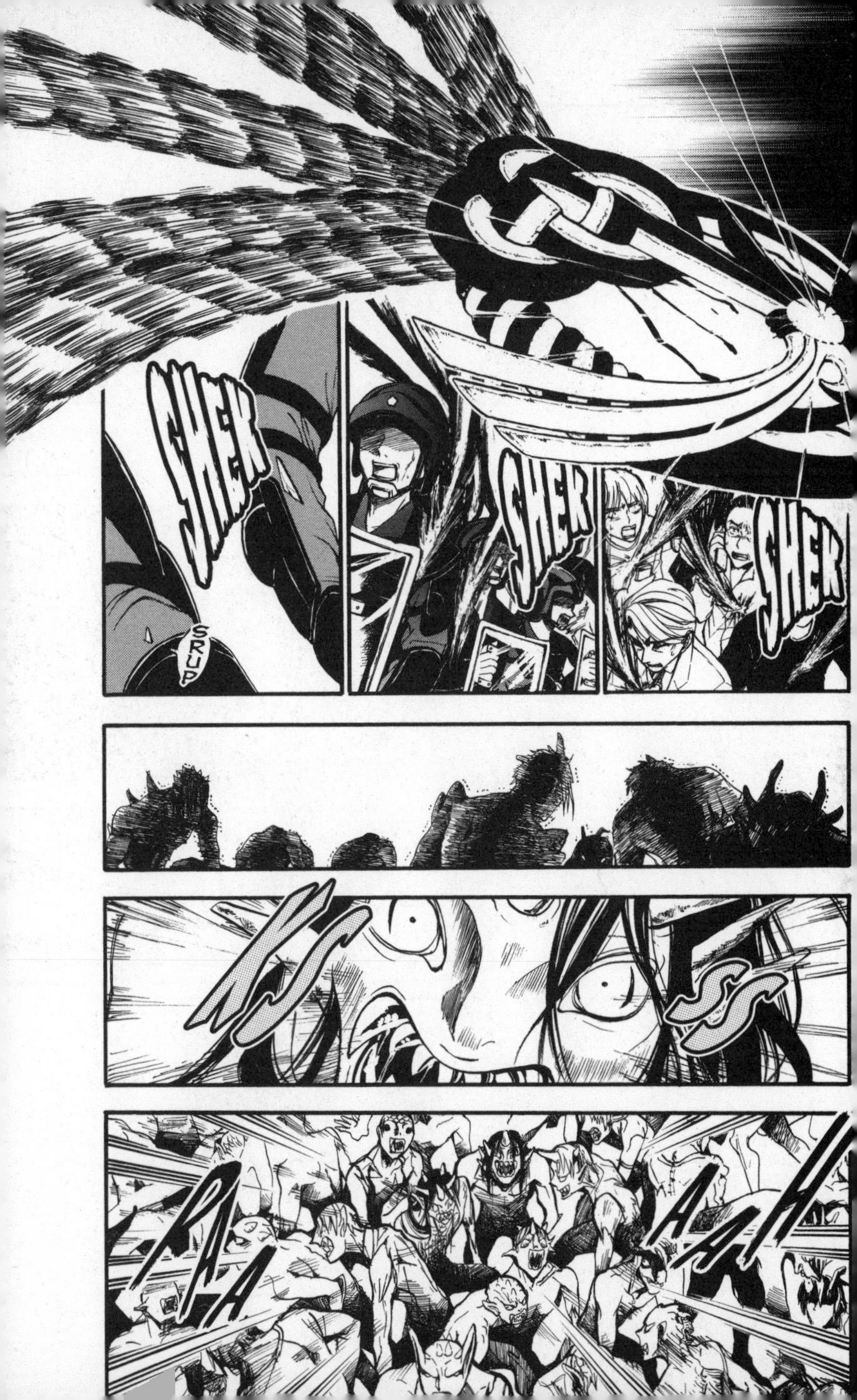
SHEK
SHEK
SHEK
SRUP
RAA AAH

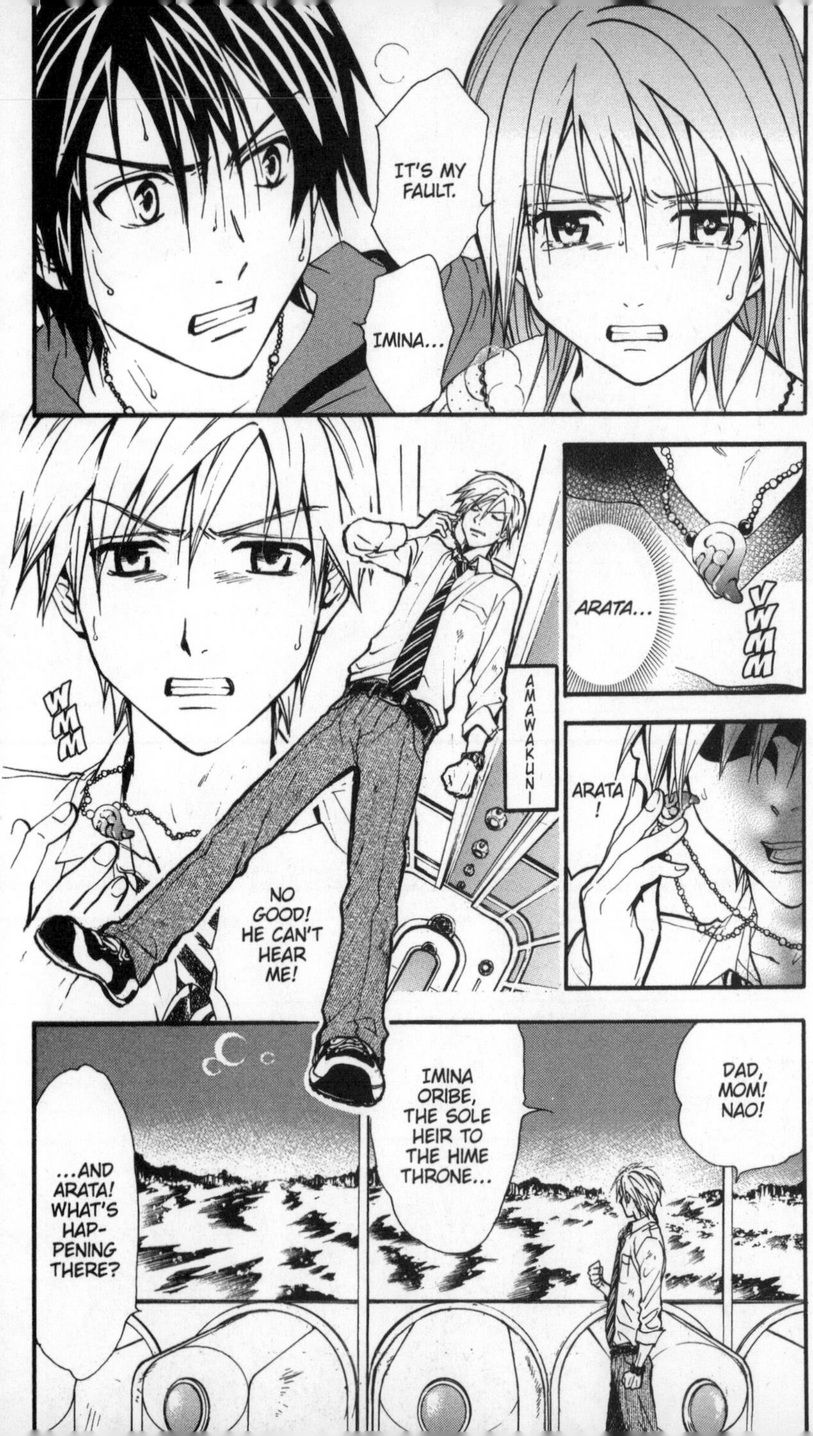
IT'S MY FAULT.
IMINA...
ARATA...
VWMM
ARATA!
AMAWAKUNI
NO GOOD! HE CAN'T HEAR ME!
WMM
DAD, MOM! NAO!
IMINA ORIBE, THE SOLE HEIR TO THE HIME THRONE...
...AND ARATA! WHAT'S HAP-PENING THERE?

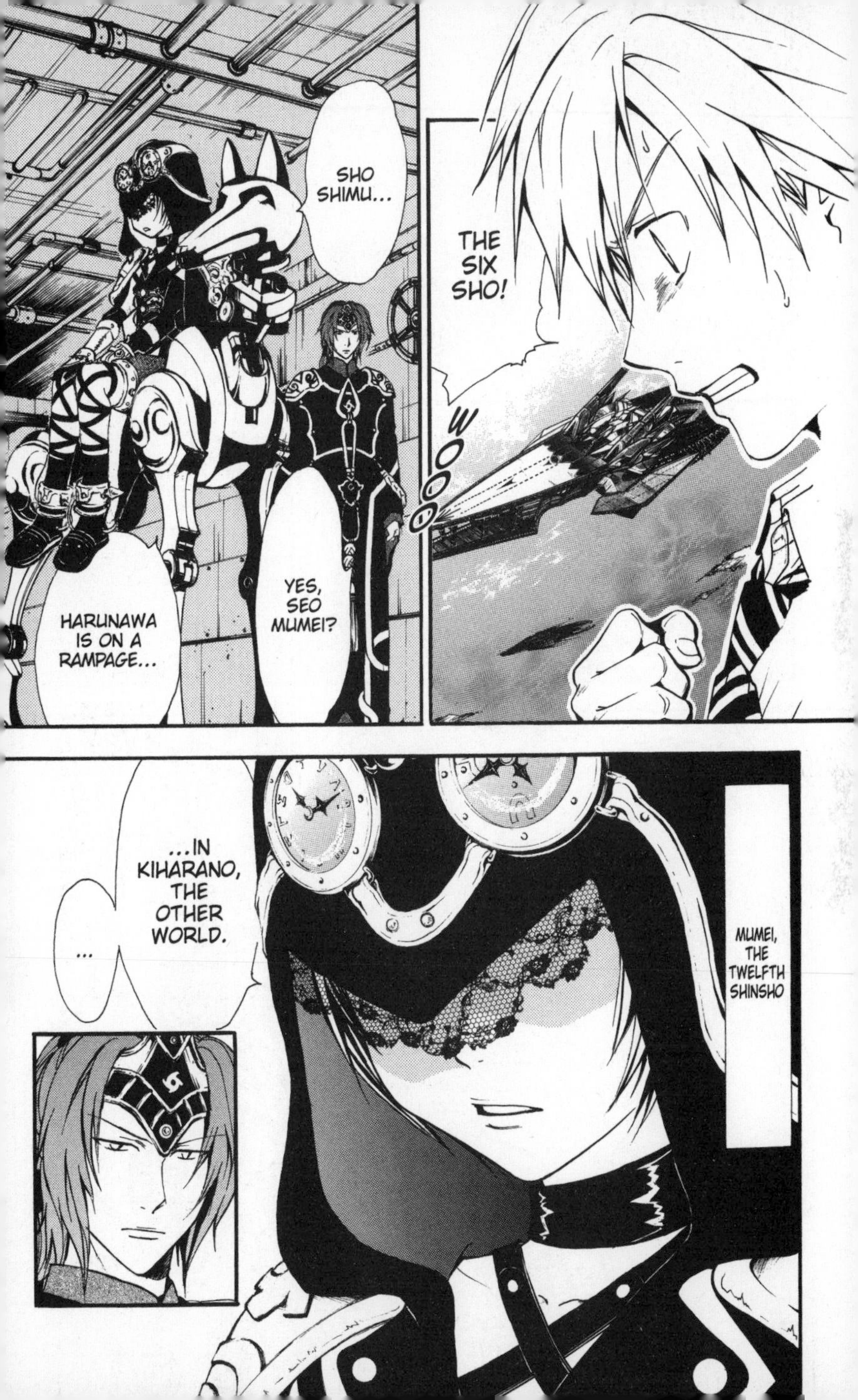
THE SIX SHO!
WOOOO
SHO SHIMU...
YES, SEO MUMEI?
HARUNAWA IS ON A RAMPAGE...
MUMEI, THE TWELFTH SHINSHO
...IN KIHARANO, THE OTHER WORLD.
...

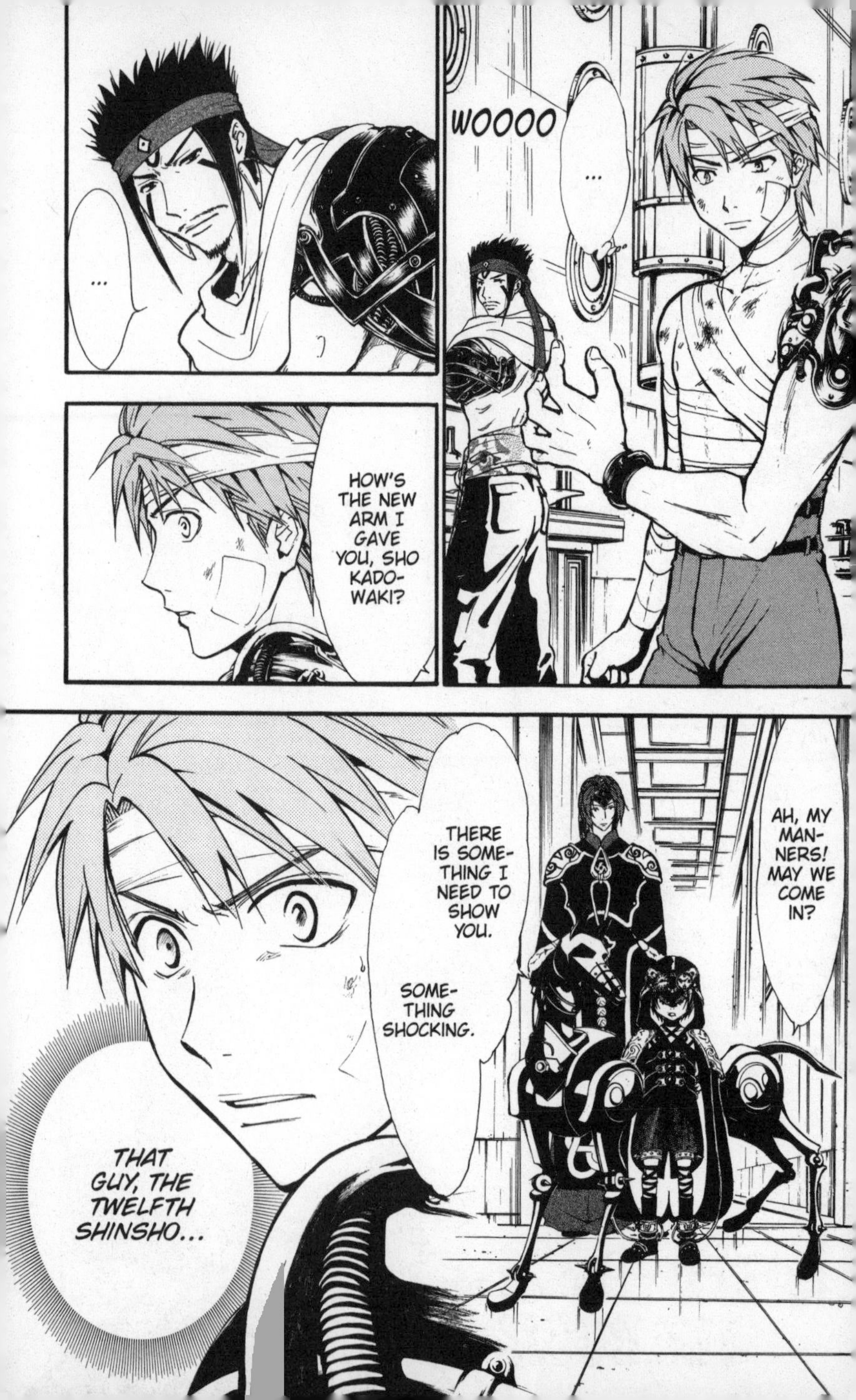
WOOOO
...
...
HOW'S THE NEW ARM I GAVE YOU, SHO KADOWAKI?
AH, MY MANNERS! MAY WE COME IN?
THERE IS SOMETHING I NEED TO SHOW YOU.
SOMETHING SHOCKING.
THAT GUY, THE TWELFTH SHINSHO...

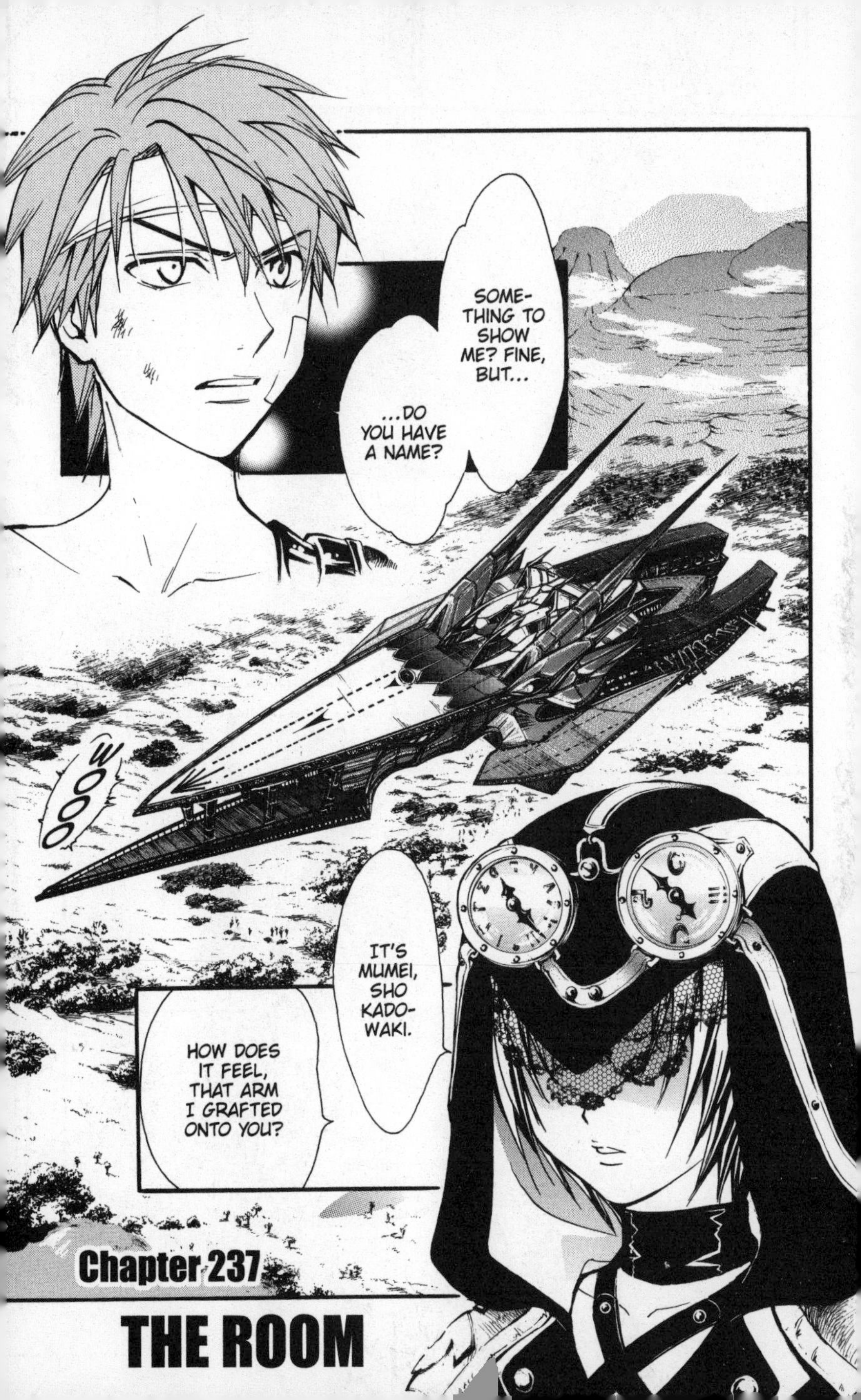
SOME-THING TO SHOW ME? FINE, BUT...
...DO YOU HAVE A NAME?
WOOO
IT'S MUMEI, SHO KADO-WAKI.
HOW DOES IT FEEL, THAT ARM I GRAFTED ONTO YOU?
Chapter 237
THE ROOM

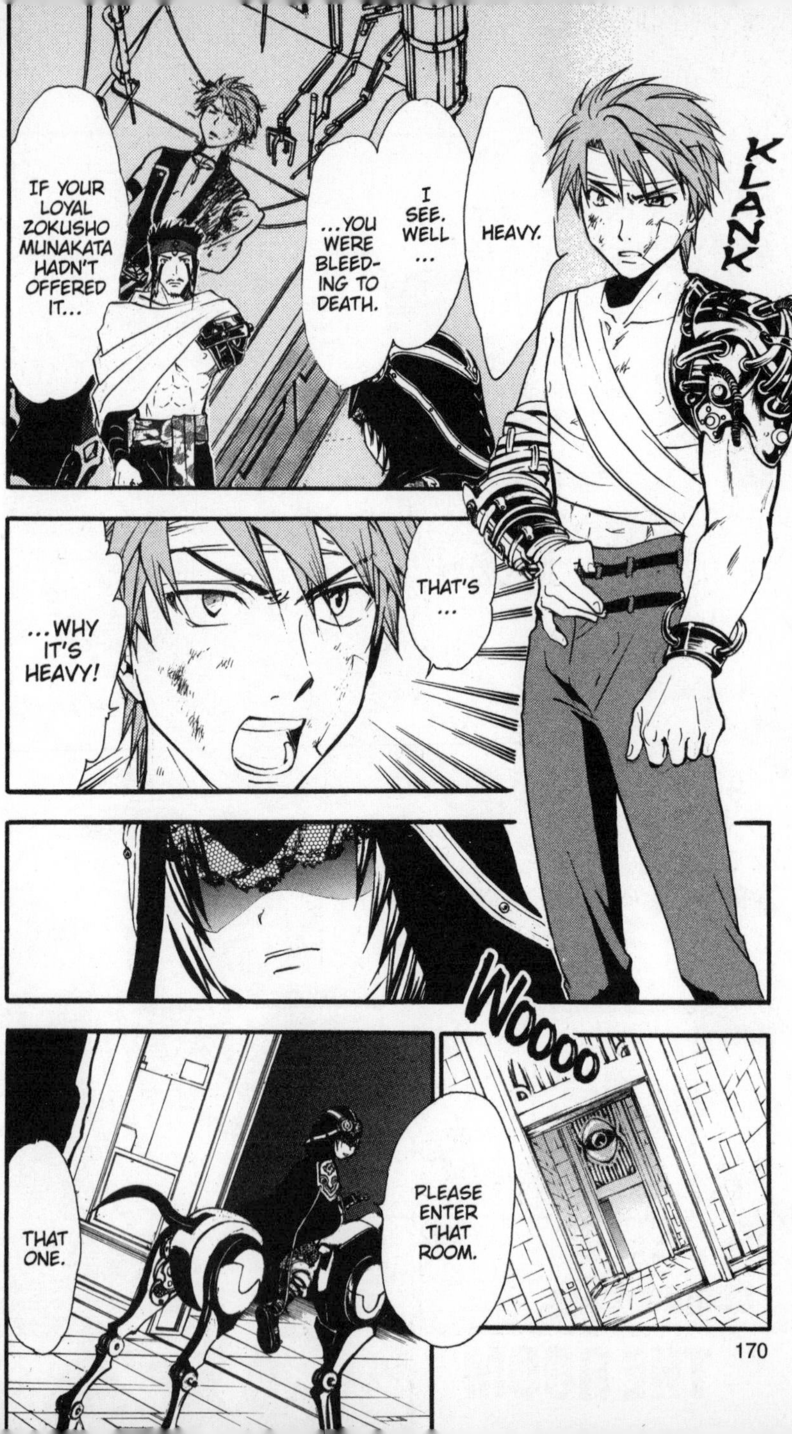
KLANK
HEAVY.
I SEE. WELL ...
...YOU WERE BLEED-ING TO DEATH.
IF YOUR LOYAL ZOKUSHO MUNAKATA HADN'T OFFERED IT...
THAT'S ...
...WHY IT'S HEAVY!
WOOOO
PLEASE ENTER THAT ROOM.
THAT ONE.

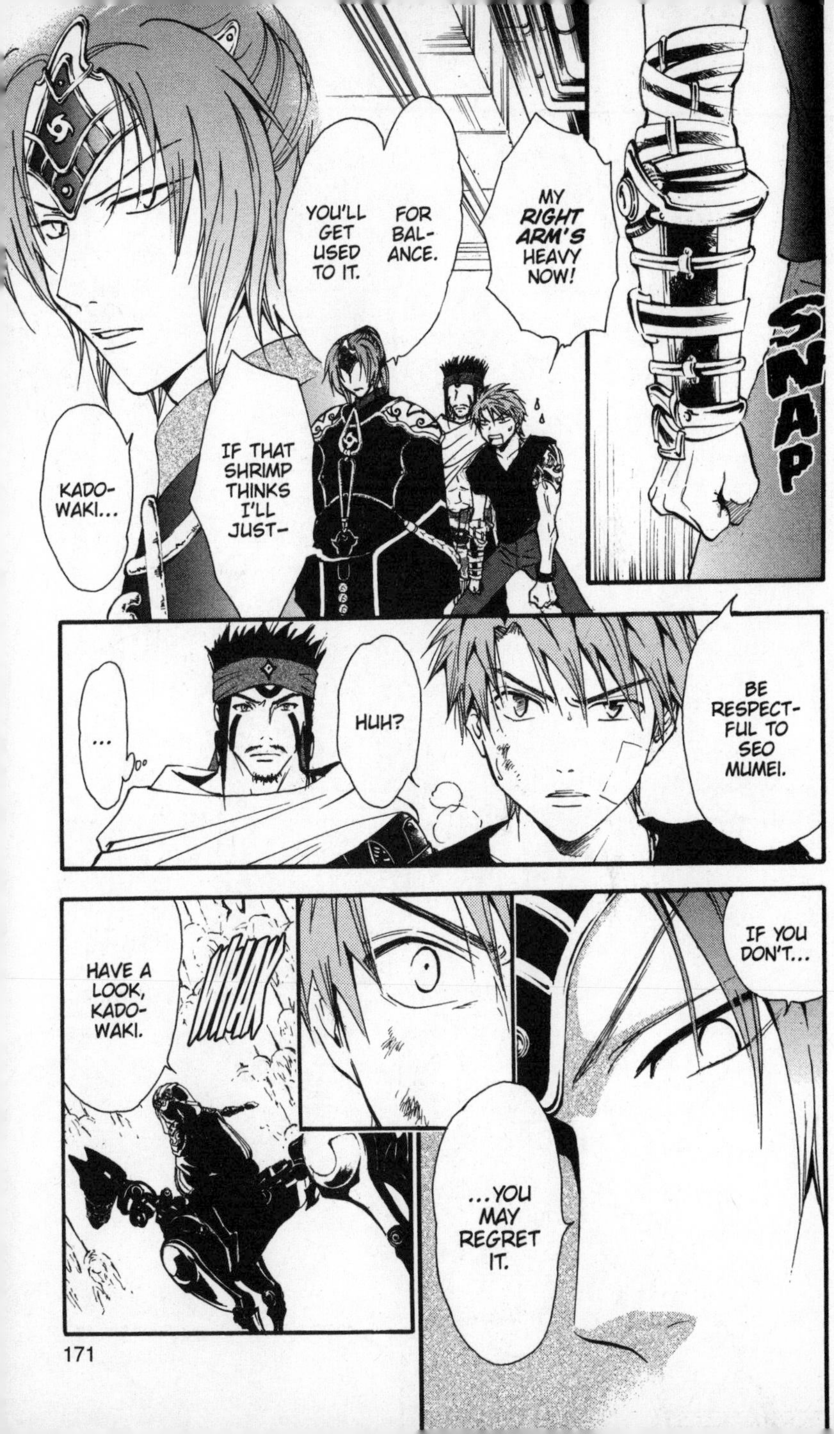
SNAP
MY RIGHT ARM'S HEAVY NOW!
FOR BALANCE.
YOU'LL GET USED TO IT.
IF THAT SHRIMP THINKS I'LL JUST-
KADOWAKI...
BE RESPECTFUL TO SEO MUMEI.
HUH?
...
IF YOU DON'T...
...YOU MAY REGRET IT.
HAVE A LOOK, KADOWAKI.

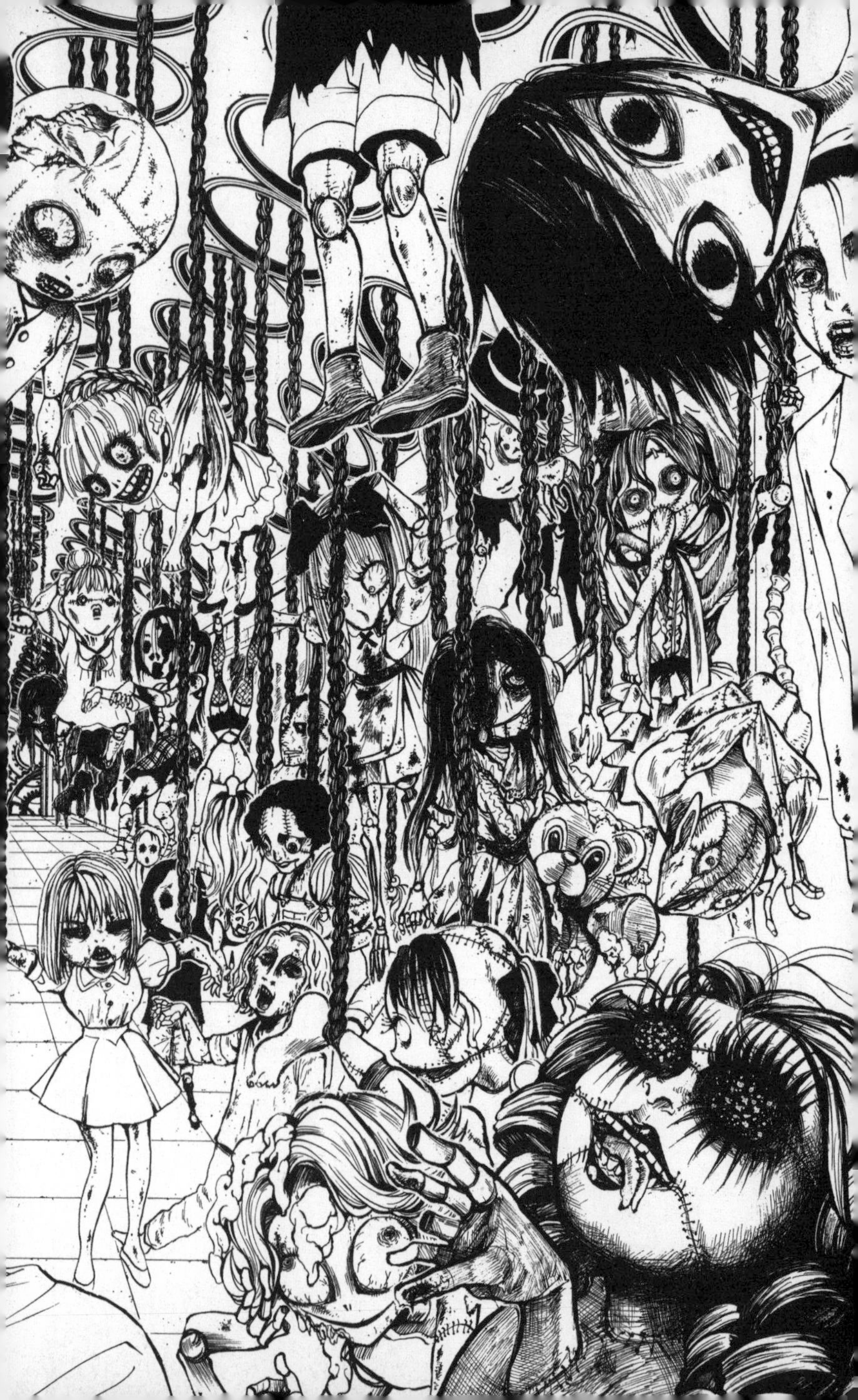

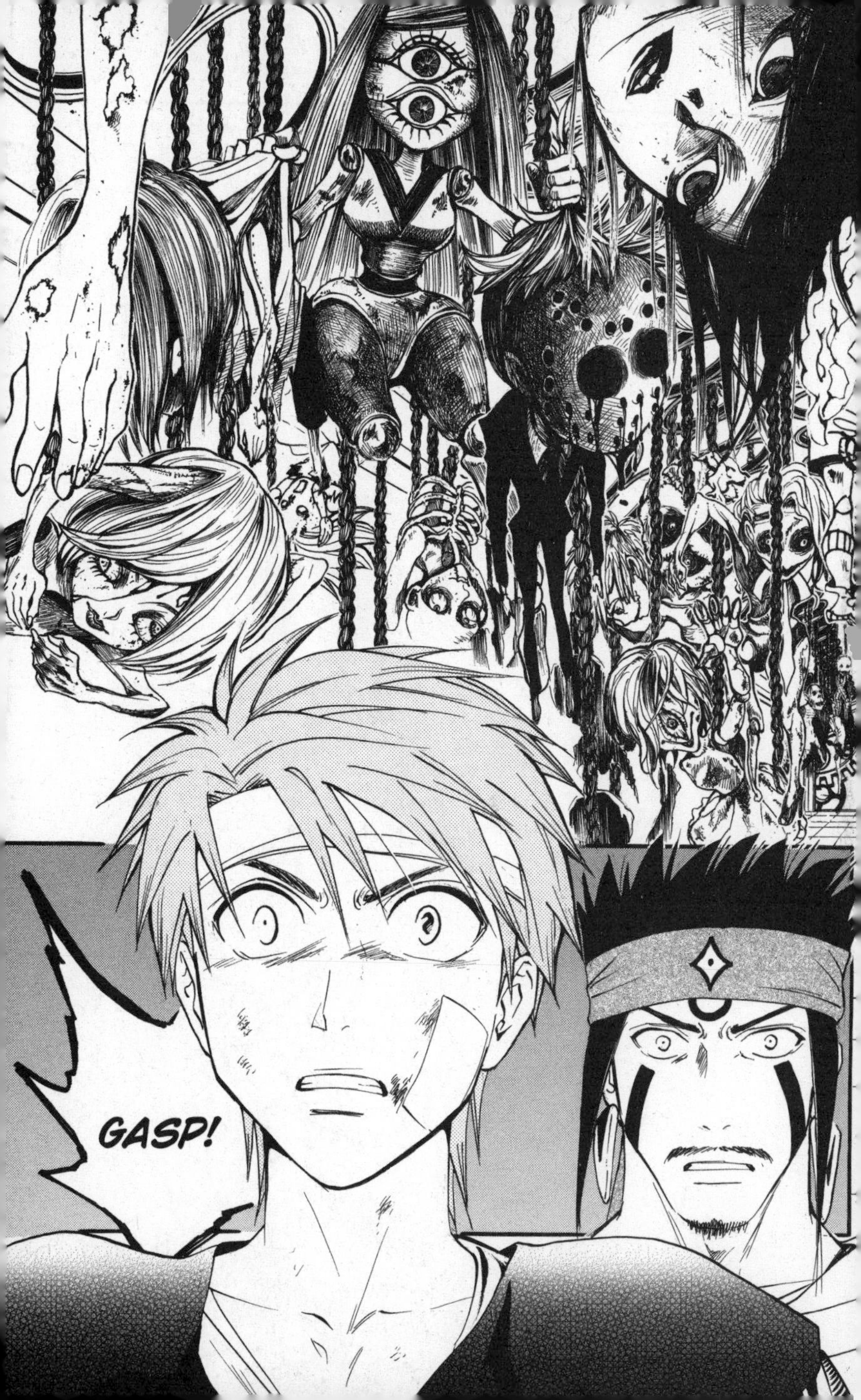
GASP!

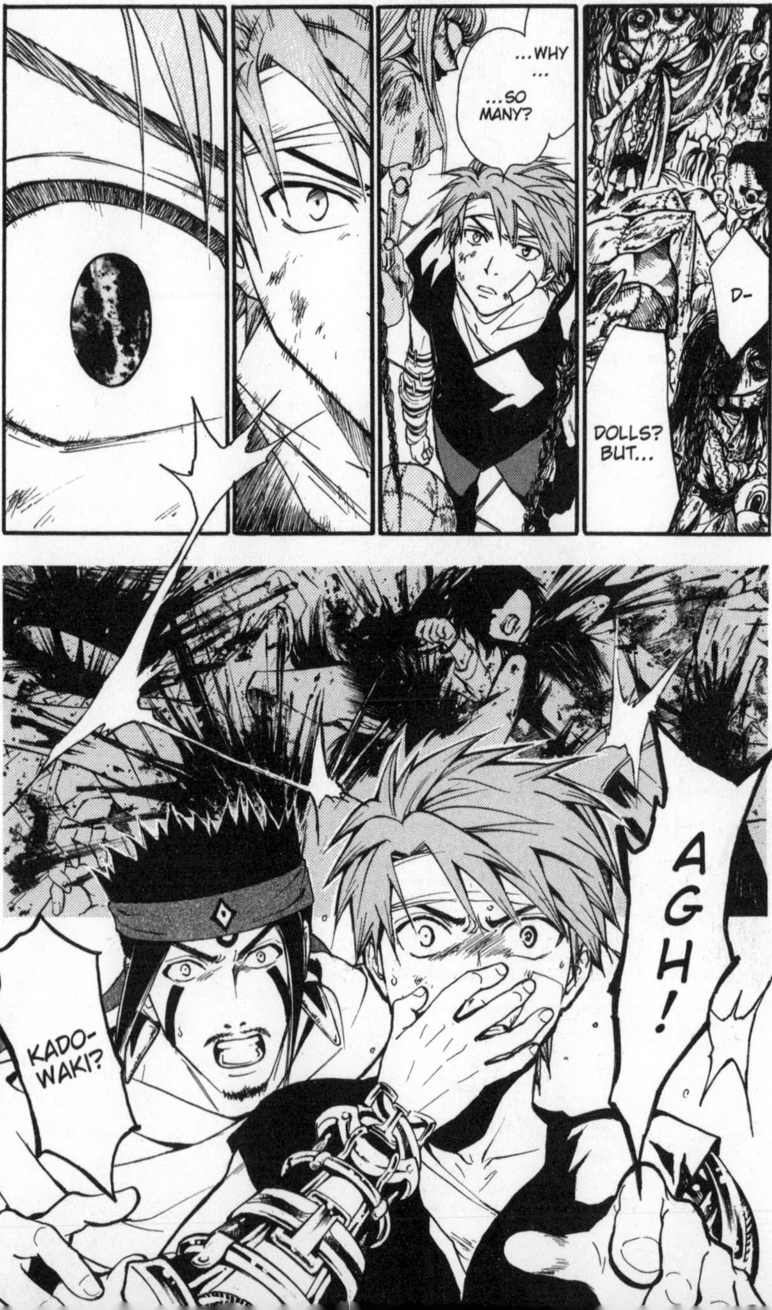
D-
DOLLS? BUT...
...WHY ...
...SO MANY?
AGH!
KADO-WAKI?

TH- THOSE ARE...

YOU FIGURED IT OUT, EH?

OH, RIGHT, YOU HAVE THE EYE OF SHO AKACHI.

AND WITH THAT EYE I SEE...

...THEY'RE THE FLESH AND BONES OF DEAD PEOPLE!

BITS AND PIECES... SEWN TOGETHER!

A CRUDE WAY TO PUT IT.

GLUP

GLUP

BLINK

I PITY THE DEAD. I TRY TO RESURRECT THEM.

I ATTACH THEM TO A BRAIN...

...SO THEY CAN MOVE AS IF ALIVE.

TIP

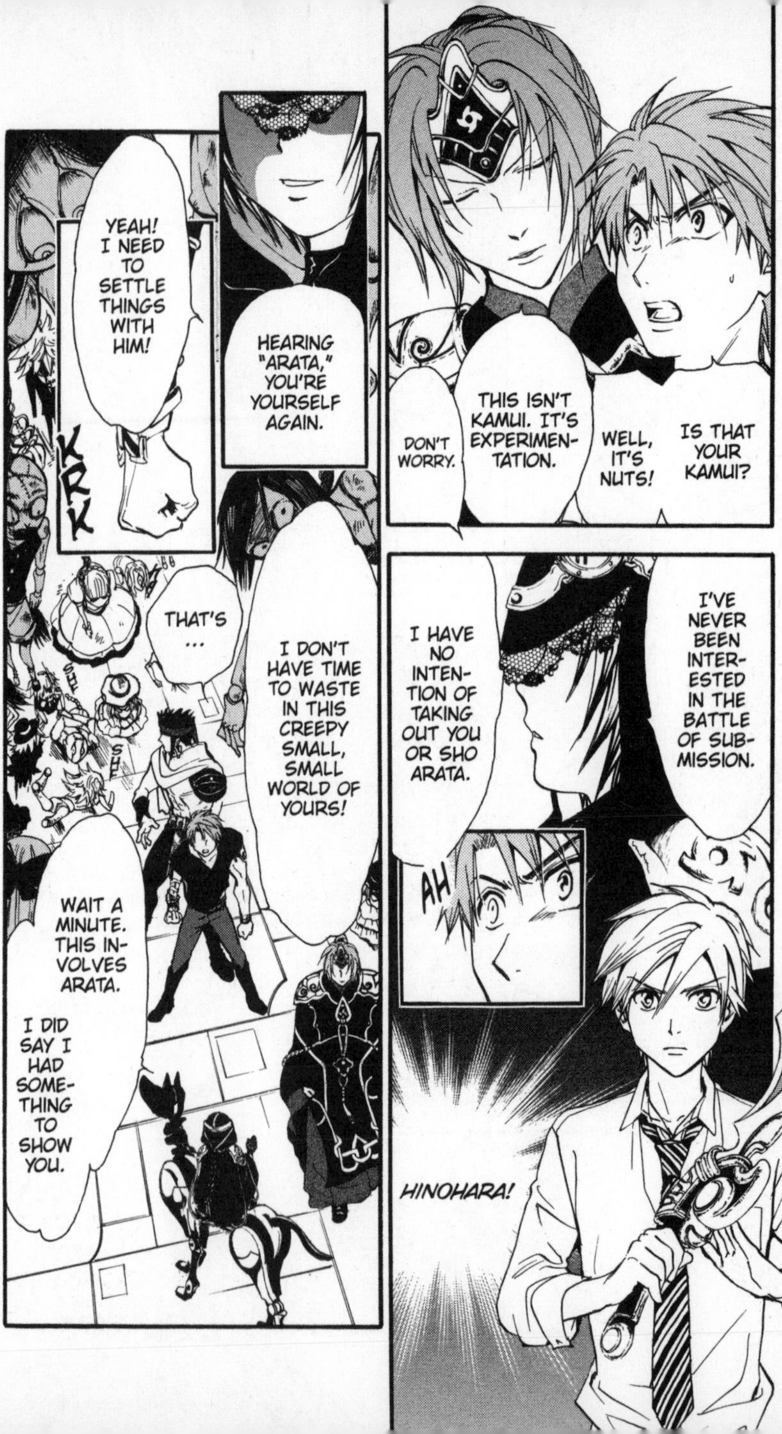

IS THAT YOUR KAMUI?
WELL, IT'S NUTS!
THIS ISN'T KAMUI. IT'S EXPERIMENTATION.
DON'T WORRY.
I'VE NEVER BEEN INTERESTED IN THE BATTLE OF SUBMISSION.
I HAVE NO INTENTION OF TAKING OUT YOU OR SHO ARATA.
AH
HINOHARA!
HEARING "ARATA," YOU'RE YOURSELF AGAIN.
YEAH! I NEED TO SETTLE THINGS WITH HIM!
KRK
I DON'T HAVE TIME TO WASTE IN THIS CREEPY SMALL, SMALL WORLD OF YOURS!
THAT'S...
WAIT A MINUTE. THIS INVOLVES ARATA.
I DID SAY I HAD SOMETHING TO SHOW YOU.

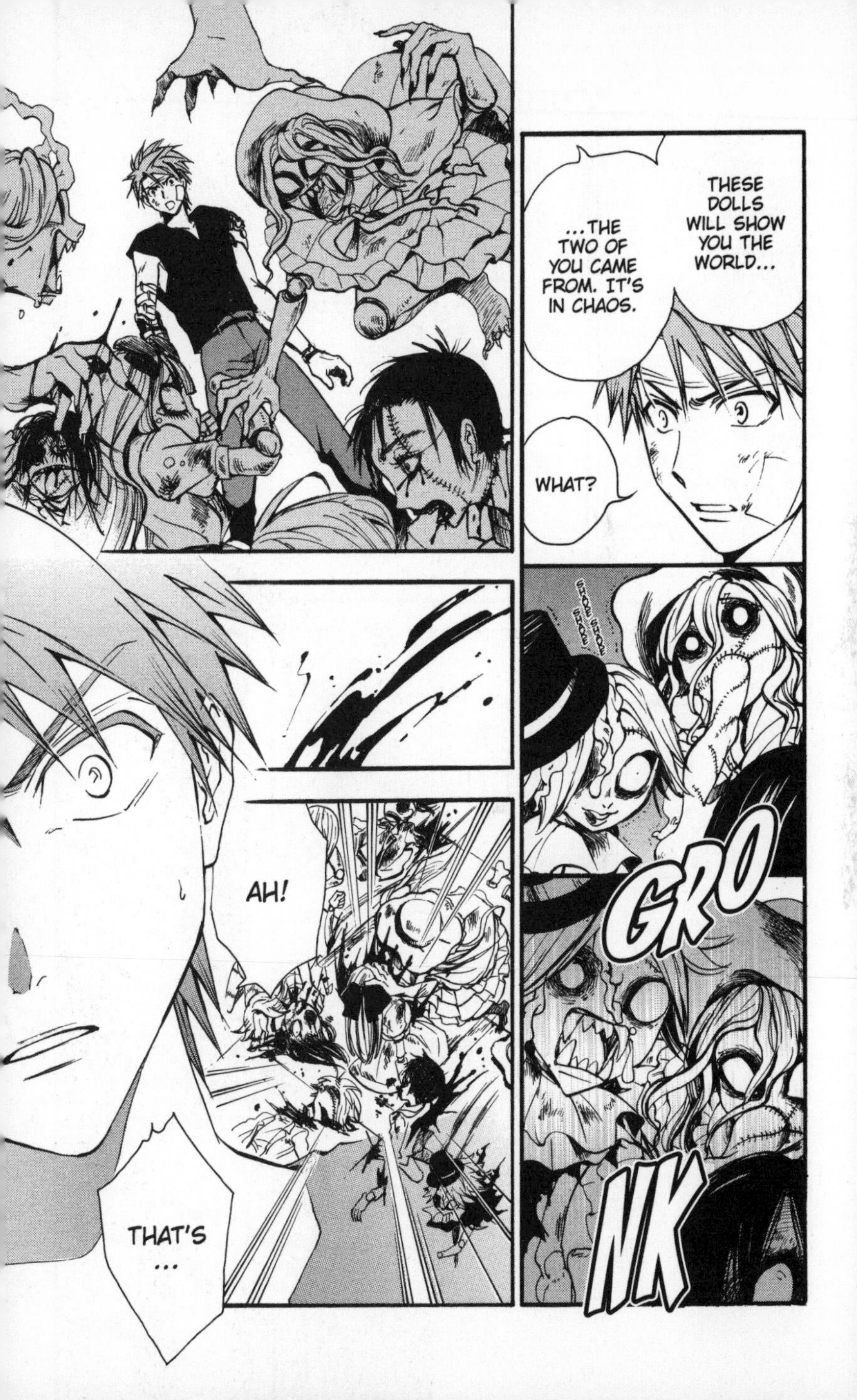
THESE DOLLS WILL SHOW YOU THE WORLD...
...THE TWO OF YOU CAME FROM. IT'S IN CHAOS.
WHAT?
SHAKE SHAKE
SHAKE
GRO
NK
AH!
THAT'S ...

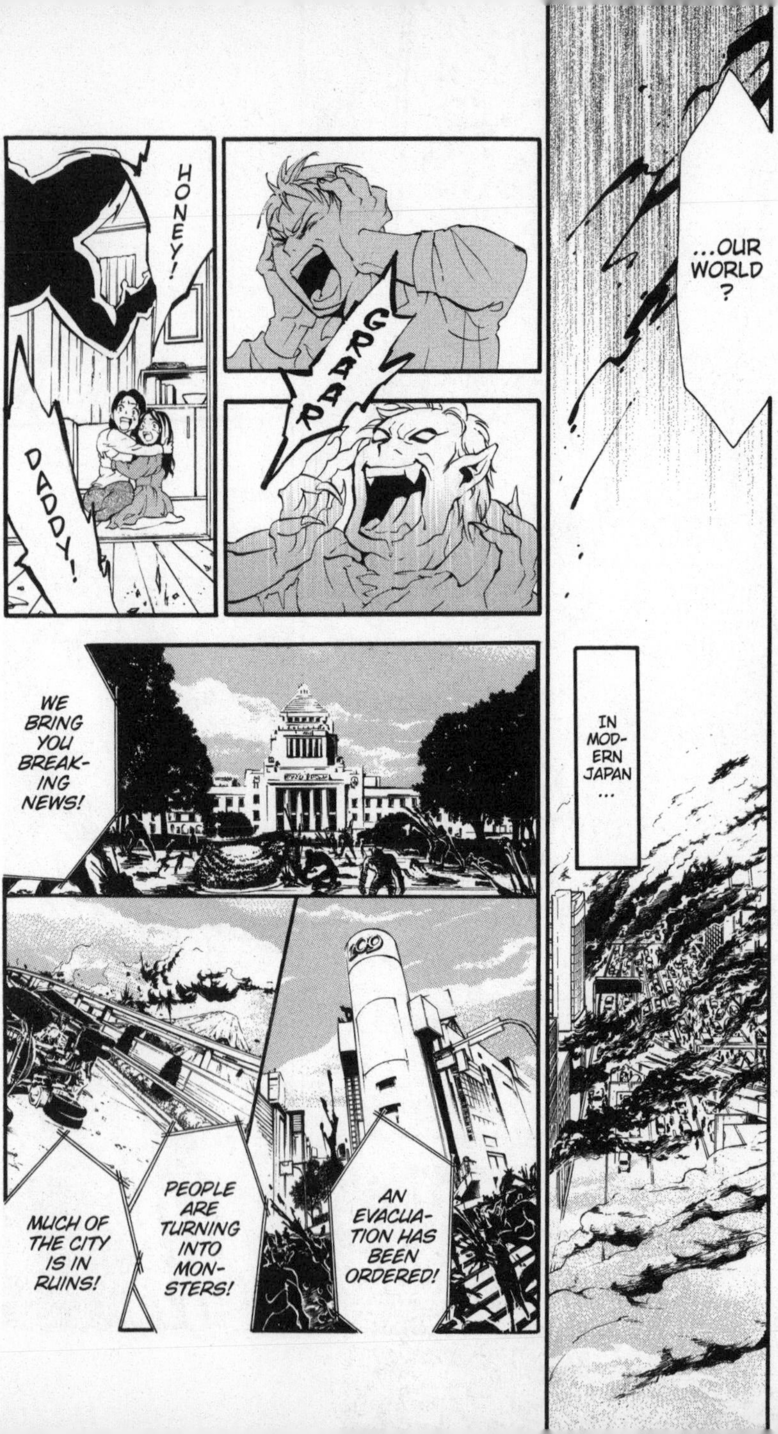
...OUR WORLD?
IN MODERN JAPAN...
GRAAR
HONEY!
DADDY!
WE BRING YOU BREAKING NEWS!
AN EVACUATION HAS BEEN ORDERED!
PEOPLE ARE TURNING INTO MONSTERS!
MUCH OF THE CITY IS IN RUINS!

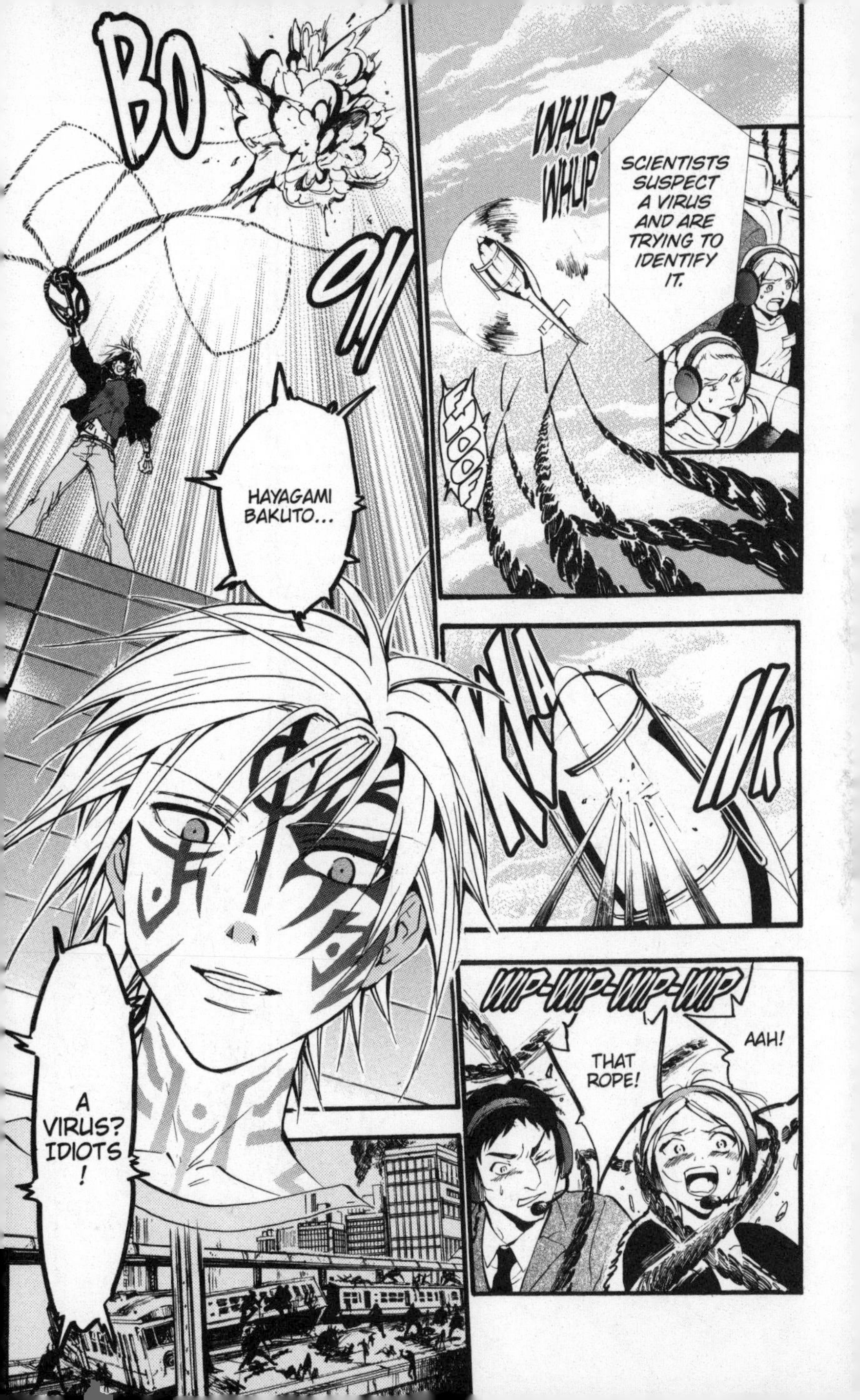
WHUP WHUP
SCIENTISTS SUSPECT A VIRUS AND ARE TRYING TO IDENTIFY IT.
WHANK
WIP-WIP-WIP-WIP
AAH!
THAT ROPE!
BOOM
HAYAGAMI BAKUTO...
A VIRUS? IDIOTS!

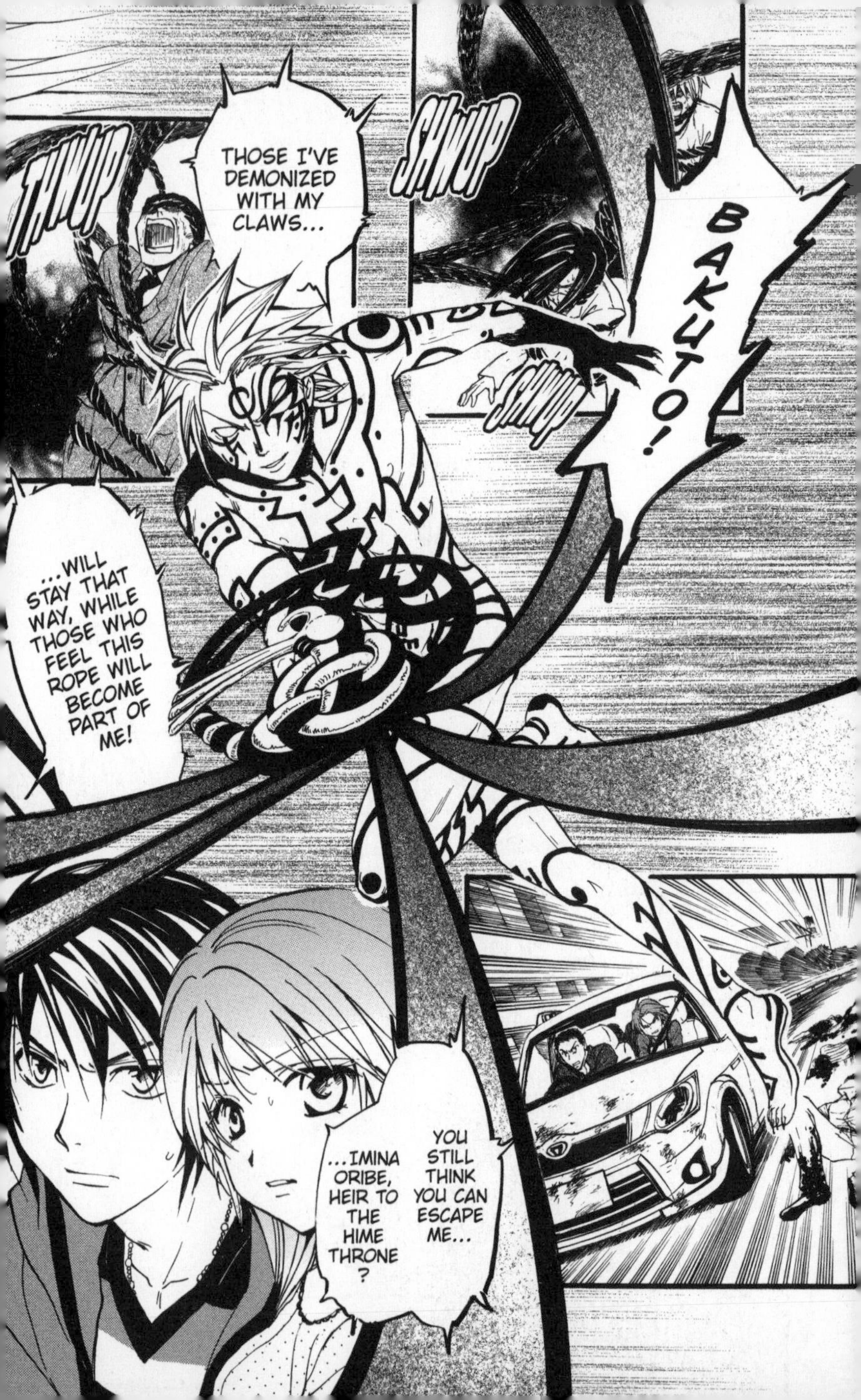
BAKUTO!
SHWUP
THOSE I'VE DEMONIZED WITH MY CLAWS...
THWUP
SHWUP
...WILL STAY THAT WAY, WHILE THOSE WHO FEEL THIS ROPE WILL BECOME PART OF ME!
YOU STILL THINK YOU CAN ESCAPE ME...
...IMINA ORIBE, HEIR TO THE HIME THRONE?

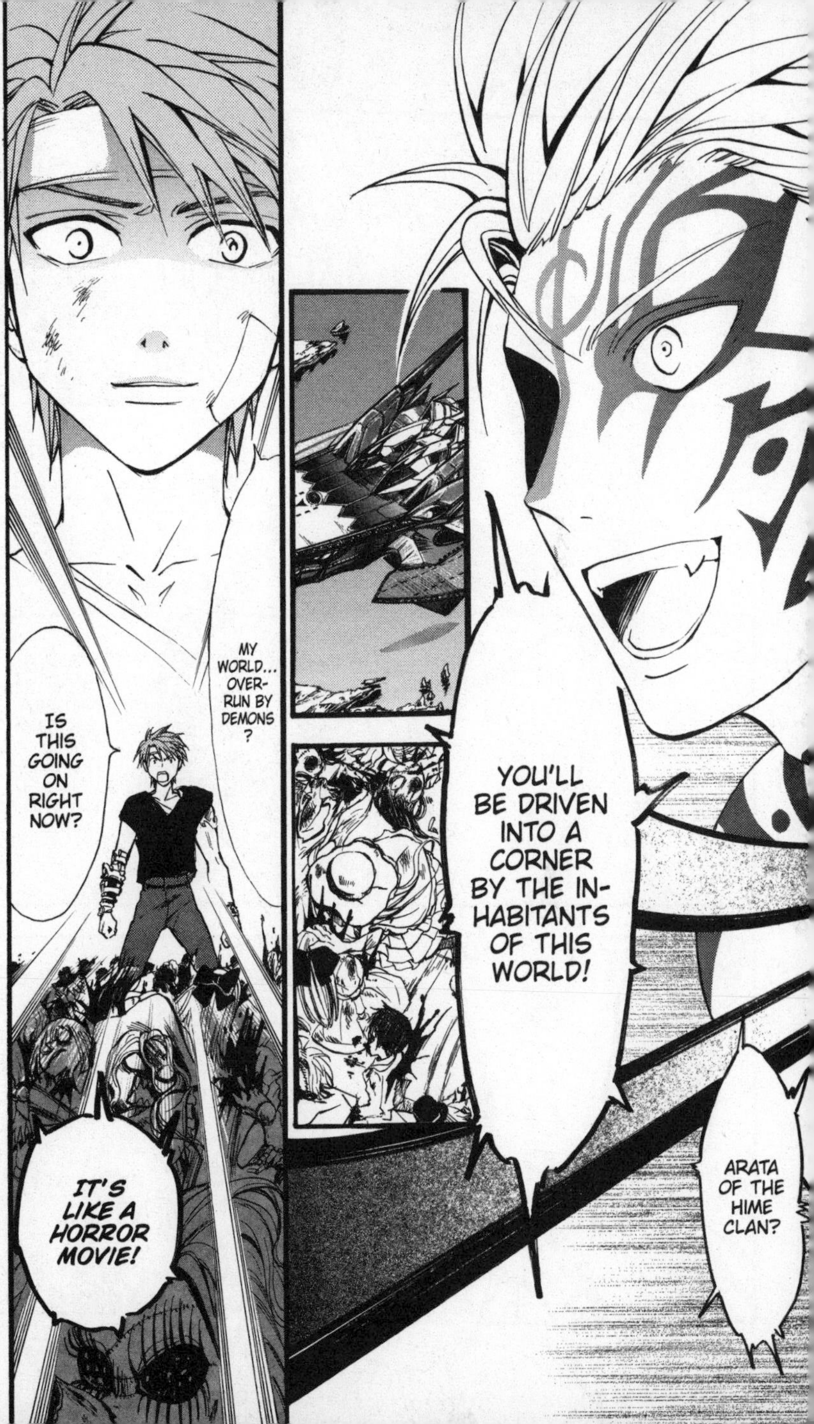
YOU'LL BE DRIVEN INTO A CORNER BY THE IN-HABITANTS OF THIS WORLD!
ARATA OF THE HIME CLAN?
MY WORLD... OVER-RUN BY DEMONS?
IS THIS GOING ON RIGHT NOW?
IT'S LIKE A HORROR MOVIE!

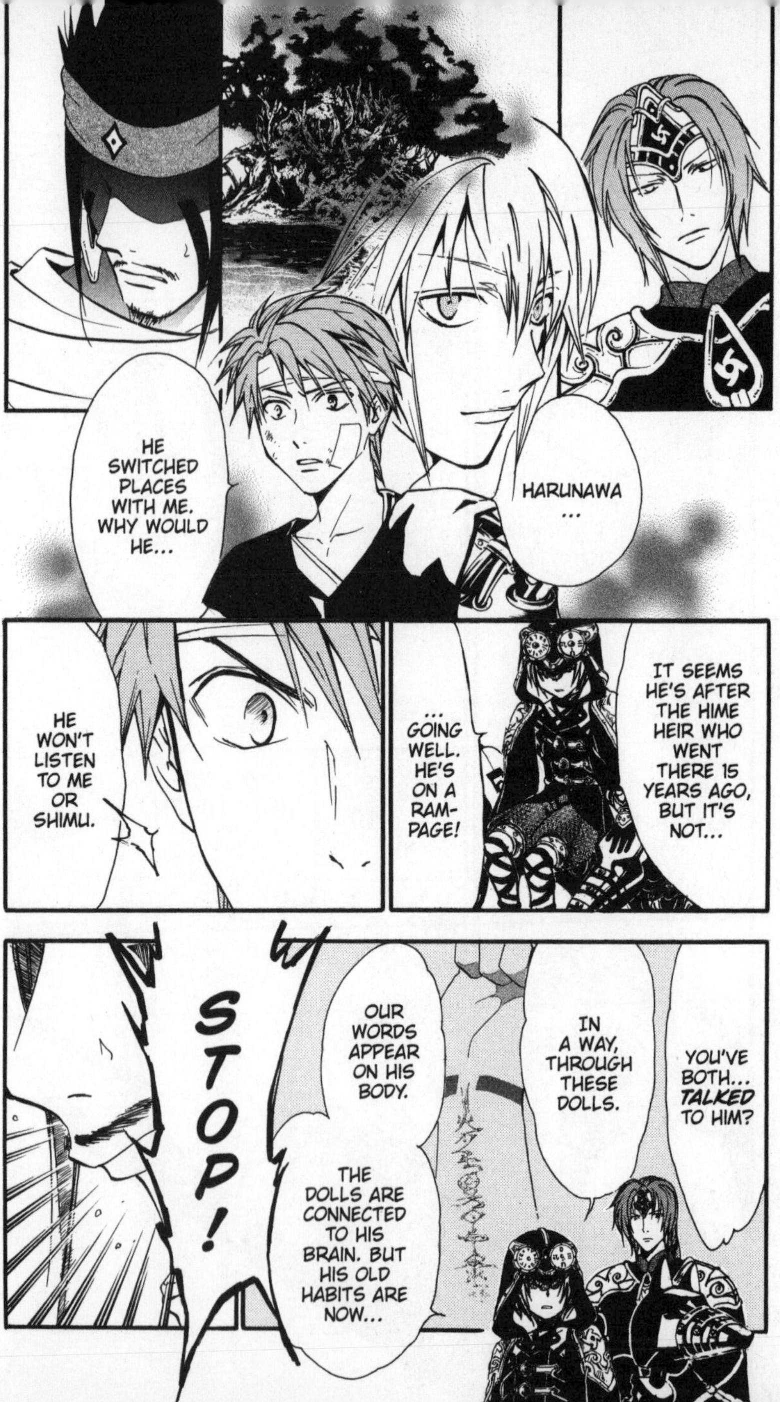
HARUNAWA...
HE SWITCHED PLACES WITH ME. WHY WOULD HE...
IT SEEMS HE'S AFTER THE HIME HEIR WHO WENT THERE 15 YEARS AGO, BUT IT'S NOT...
... GOING WELL. HE'S ON A RAMPAGE!
HE WON'T LISTEN TO ME OR SHIMU.
YOU'VE BOTH... *TALKED* TO HIM?
IN A WAY, THROUGH THESE DOLLS.
OUR WORDS APPEAR ON HIS BODY.
THE DOLLS ARE CONNECTED TO HIS BRAIN. BUT HIS OLD HABITS ARE NOW...
STOP!

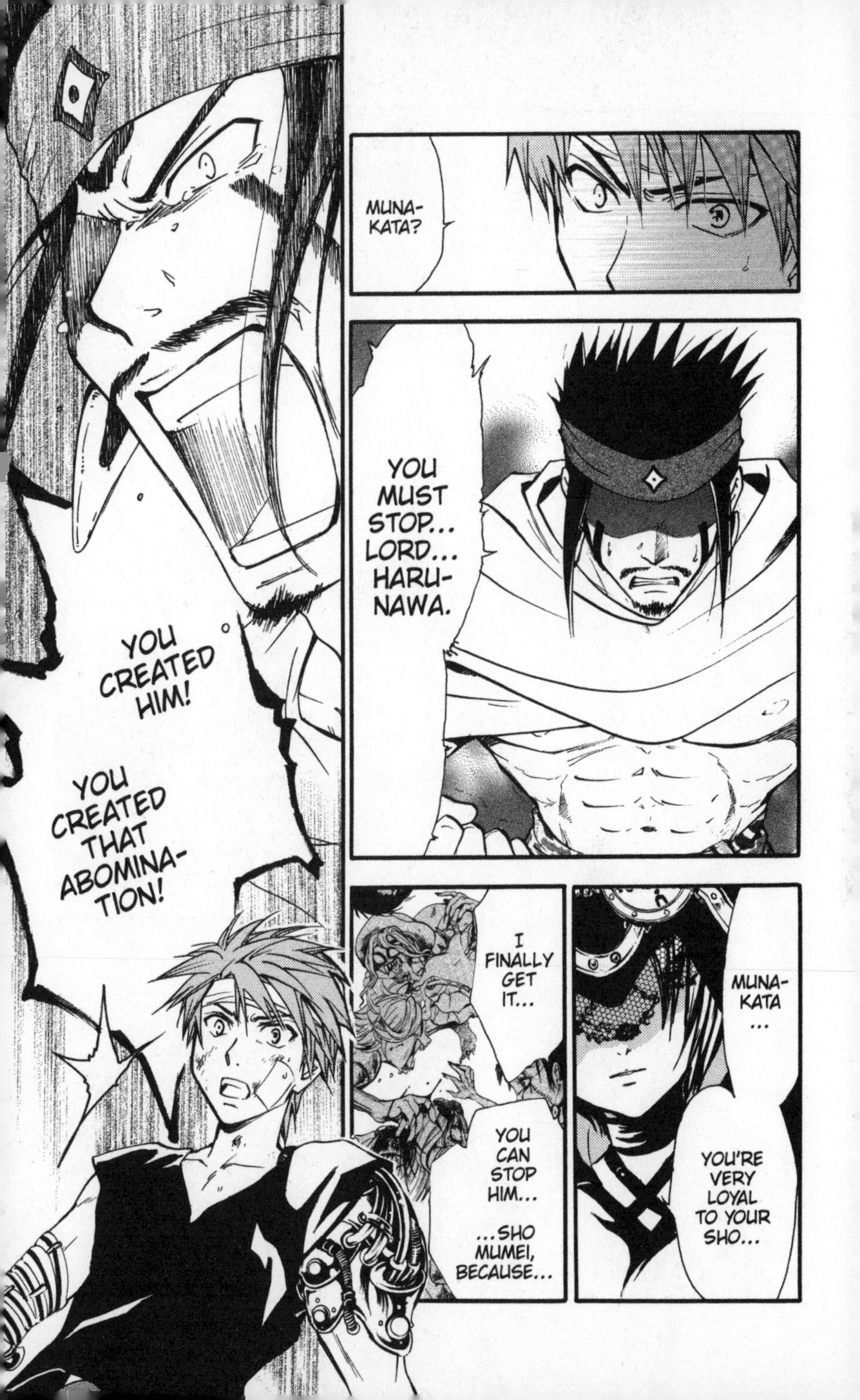
MUNA-KATA?
YOU MUST STOP... LORD... HARU-NAWA.
MUNA-KATA ...
YOU'RE VERY LOYAL TO YOUR SHO...
I FINALLY GET IT...
YOU CAN STOP HIM...
...SHO MUMEI, BECAUSE...
YOU CREATED HIM!
YOU CREATED THAT ABOMINA-TION!

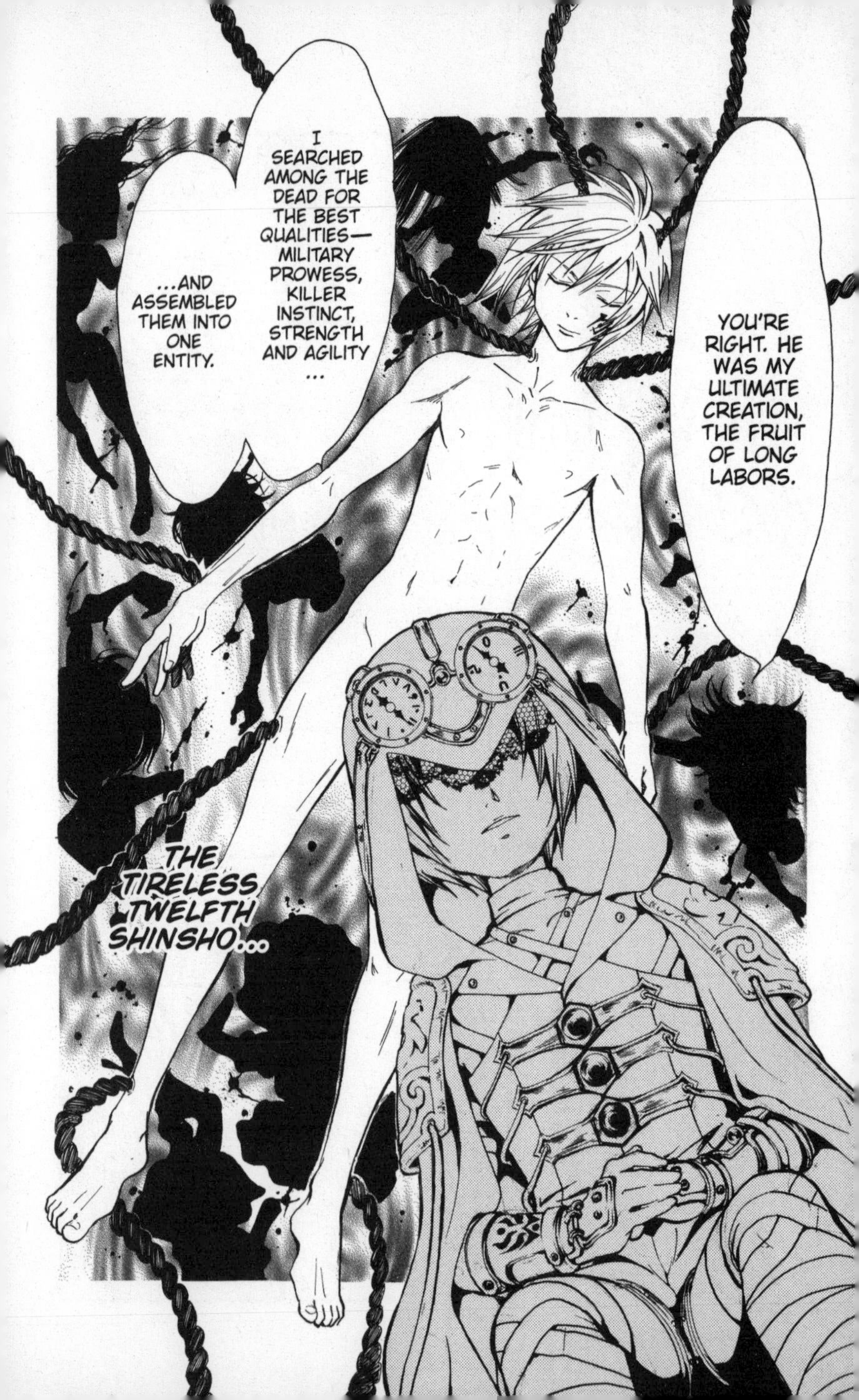
YOU'RE RIGHT. HE WAS MY ULTIMATE CREATION, THE FRUIT OF LONG LABORS.
I SEARCHED AMONG THE DEAD FOR THE BEST QUALITIES—MILITARY PROWESS, KILLER INSTINCT, STRENGTH AND AGILITY ...
...AND ASSEMBLED THEM INTO ONE ENTITY.
THE TIRELESS TWELFTH SHINSHO...

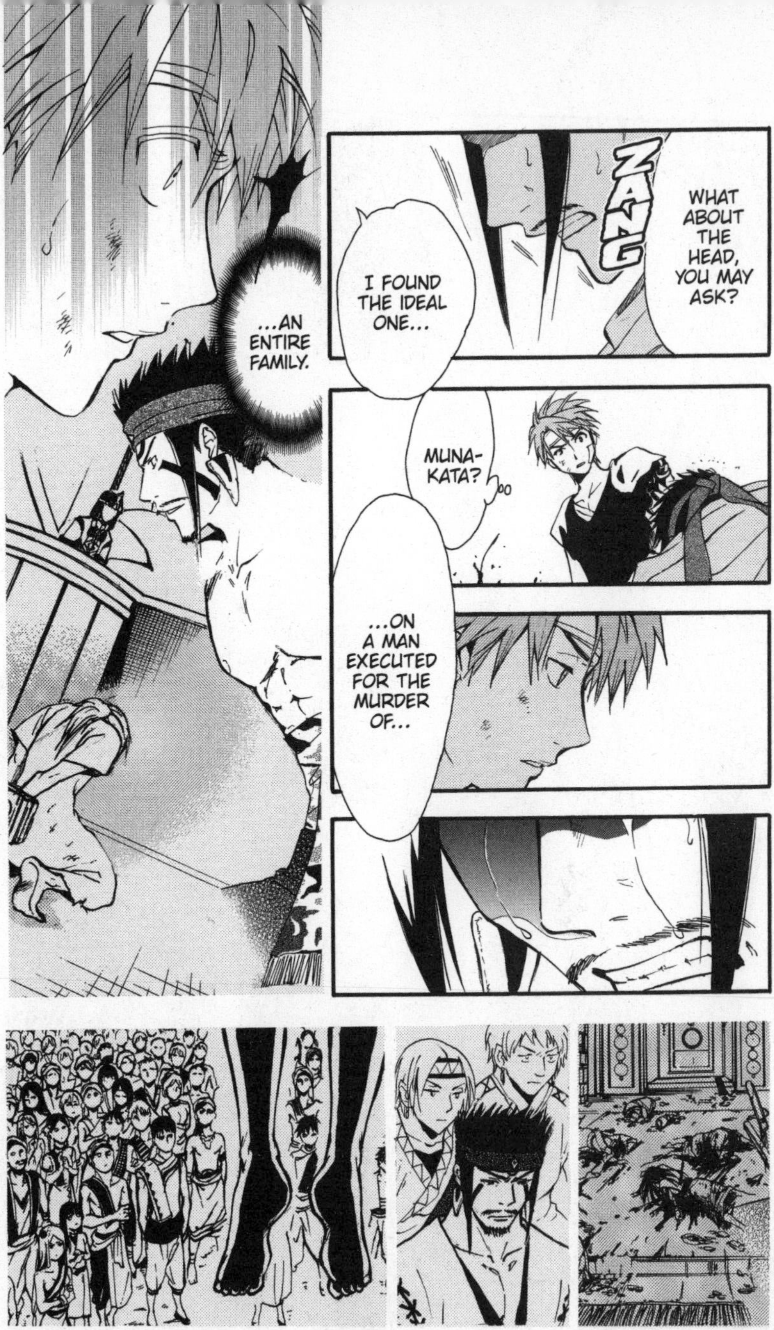
WHAT ABOUT THE HEAD, YOU MAY ASK?
ZANG
I FOUND THE IDEAL ONE...
MUNA-KATA?
...ON A MAN EXECUTED FOR THE MURDER OF...
...AN ENTIRE FAMILY.

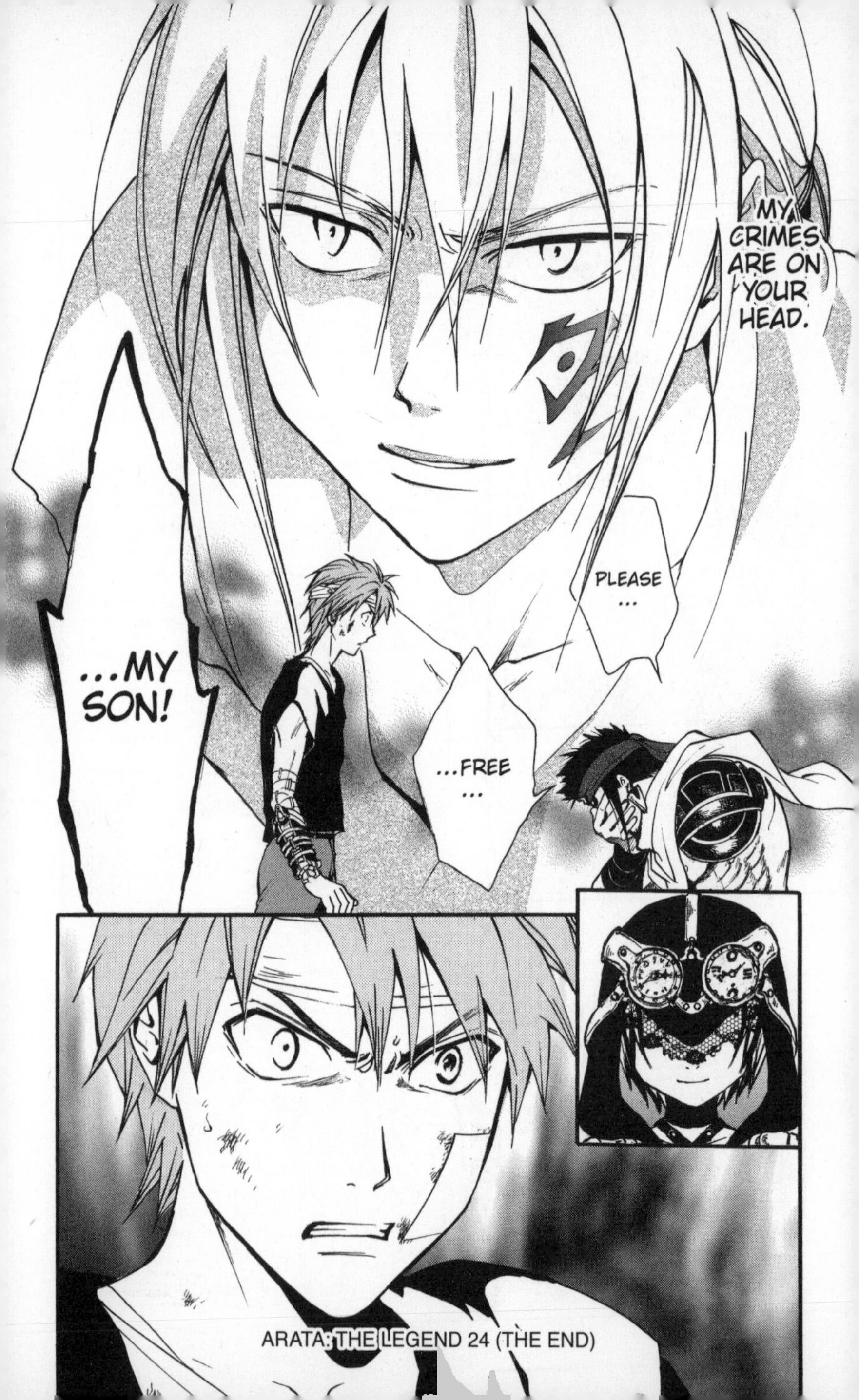
MY CRIMES ARE ON YOUR HEAD.
PLEASE ...
...FREE ...
...MY SON!
ARATA: THE LEGEND 24 (THE END)

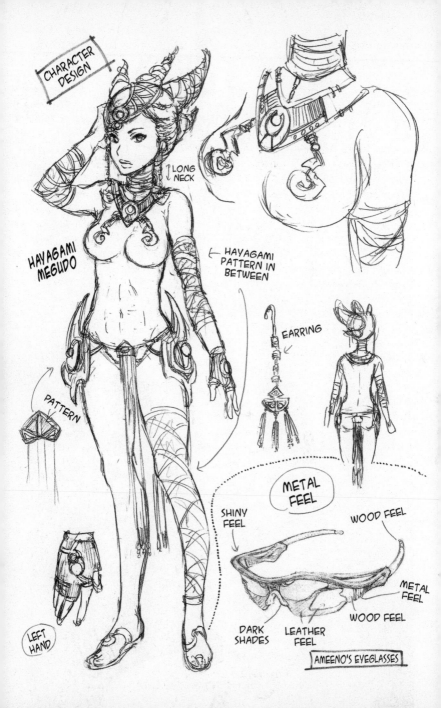

CHARACTER DESIGN

↑ LONG NECK

HAVAGAMI MEGUDO

← HAVAGAMI PATTERN IN BETWEEN

PATTERN

EARRING

METAL FEEL

SHINY FEEL

WOOD FEEL

METAL FEEL

WOOD FEEL

DARK SHADES

LEATHER FEEL

LEFT HAND

AMEENO'S EYEGLASSES

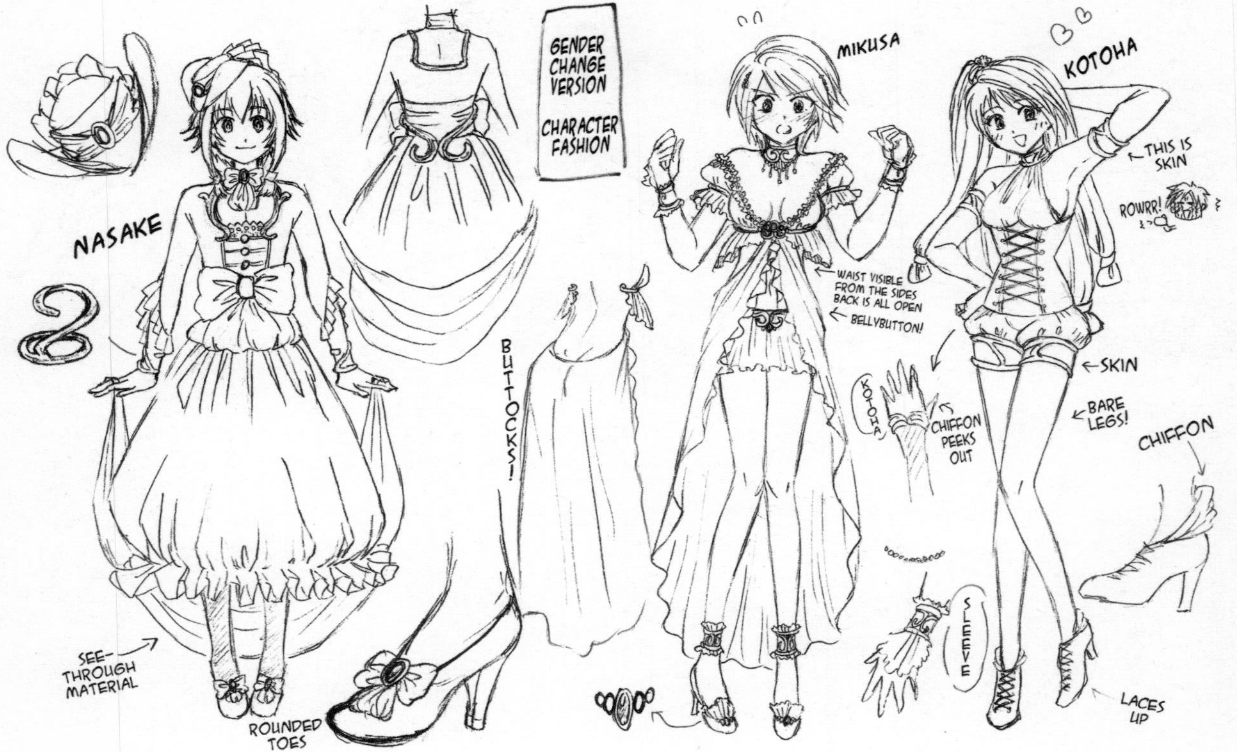
GENDER CHANGE VERSION
CHARACTER FASHION
KOTOHA
THIS IS SKIN
ROWRR!
SKIN
BARE LEGS!
CHIFFON
LACES UP
KOTOHA
CHIFFON PEEKS OUT
SLEEVE
MIKUSA
WAIST VISIBLE FROM THE SIDES
BACK IS ALL OPEN
BELLYBUTTON!
BUTTOCKS!
NASAKE
SEE-THROUGH MATERIAL
ROUNDED TOES

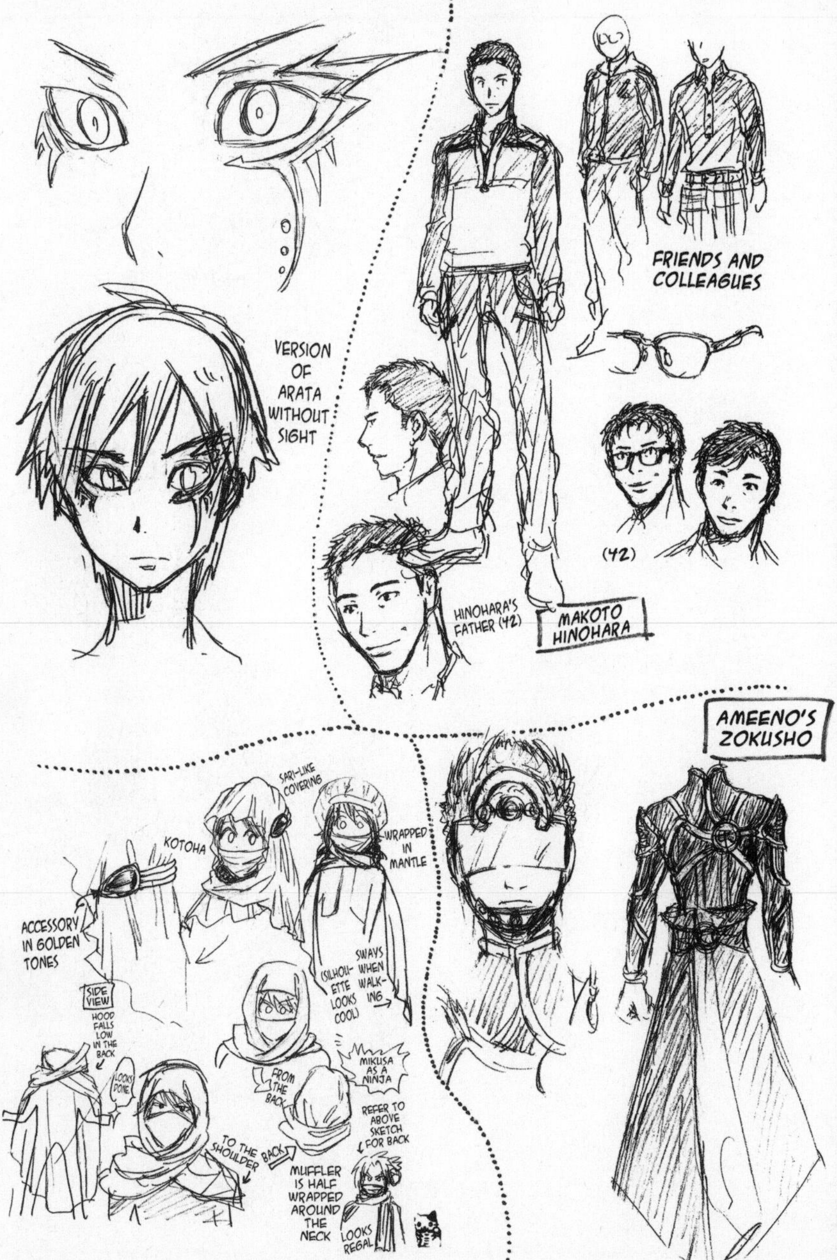
FRIENDS AND COLLEAGUES
(42)
MAKOTO HINOHARA
HINOHARA'S FATHER (42)
VERSION OF ARATA WITHOUT SIGHT
AMEENO'S ZOKUSHO
SARI-LIKE COVERING
WRAPPED IN MANTLE
KOTOHA
ACCESSORY IN GOLDEN TONES
SWAYS WHEN WALKING
(SILHOUETTE LOOKS COOL)
SIDE VIEW
HOOD FALLS LOW IN THE BACK
LOOKS DONE
MIKUSA AS A NINJA
FROM THE BACK
REFER TO ABOVE SKETCH FOR BACK
TO THE SHOULDER
BACK
MUFFLER IS HALF WRAPPED AROUND THE NECK
LOOKS REGAL

Hello, it's been a while! m(_ _)m. [symbol for bow]

I'd taken a break from the magazine series due to poor health, and naturally, this meant that production of these volumes came to a halt as well...

I'm sorry I made you wait for so long...

Thank you very much for your patience!

Quite some time has passed, and I hope there aren't folks who had forgotten, or who hadn't even noticed. For those of you who purchased and read the story and reminisced with each other about how "warm" the story was...please continue to talk about it, like "The next chapters are coming out!" or "It's getting exciting!" and go to the bookstore's magazine section with each other. That would be so cool, and you'll have lots to talk about, and the bookstore owner will be all smiles... that would be a really great way to spend the day with your friends!

Well, I'm not really sure about that, but...

This story is getting more and more exciting, that's for sure! So please stick with me until the climax. m(_ _)m Bow!

–Yuu Watase

AUTHOR BIO

Born March 5 in Osaka, Yuu Watase debuted in the *Shôjo Comic* manga anthology in 1989. She won the 43rd Shogakukan Manga Award with *Ceres: Celestial Legend*. One of her most famous works is *Fushigi Yûgi*, a series that has inspired the prequel *Fushigi Yûgi: Genbu Kaiden*. In 2008, *Arata: The Legend* started serialization in *Shonen Sunday*.

ARATA: THE LEGEND

Volume 24

Shonen Sunday Edition

Story and Art by YUU WATASE

ARATA KANGATARI Vol. 24
by Yuu WATASE
© 2009 Yuu WATASE
All rights reserved.
Original Japanese edition published by SHOGAKUKAN.
English translation rights in the United States of America, Canada, the United Kingdom and Ireland arranged with SHOGAKUKAN.

English Adaptation: Lance Caselman
Translation: JN Productions
Touch-up Art & Lettering: Rina Mapa
Design: Veronica Casson
Editor: Gary Leach

Printed in the U.S.A.

Published by VIZ Media, LLC
P.O. Box 77010
San Francisco, CA 94107

10 9 8 7 6 5 4 3 2 1
First printing, August 2016

www.viz.com

WWW.SHONENSUNDAY.COM

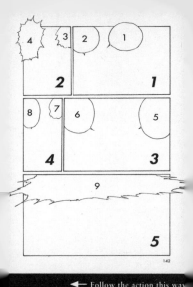

← Follow the action this way

HIS IS THE LAST PAG

ta: The Legend has been printed in
inal Japanese format in order to pres
orientation of the original artwork.

se turn it around and begin reading
t to left. Unlike English, Japanese is read
eft, so Japanese comics are read in revers
from the way English comics are typi
. Have fun with it!